EFFECTIVE VIDEO CODING FOR MULTIMEDIA APPLICATIONS

Edited by **Sudhakar Radhakrishnan**

Effective Video Coding for Multimedia Applications
Edited by Sudhakar Radhakrishnan

Published by InTech

Janeza Trdine 9, 51000 Rijeka, Croatia

Publishing Process Manager Ivana Lorkovic

Technical Editor Teodora Smiljanic

Cover Designer InTech Design Team

Additional hard copies can be obtained from orders@intechopen.com

Effective Video Coding for Multimedia Applications, Edited by Sudhakar Radhakrishnan
p. cm.
ISBN 978-953-307-177-0

For EU product safety concerns:
IN TECH d.o.o., Prolaz Marije Krucifikse Kozulić 3, 51000 Rijeka, Croatia,
info@intechopen.com or visit our website at intechopen.com.

Meet the editor

Dr. Sudhakar Radhakrishnan is currently the Professor and Head of Electronics and Communication Engineering Department., Dr.Mahalingam College of Engineering and Technology, Pollachi, Tamilnadu, India. He wrote a book chapter titled "Wavelet based image compression" in the book titled "Computational Intelligence Techniques in Handling Image Processing and Pattern Recognition" and another 2 books titled "Research issues in Image compression using Wavelet variants", "Practicing Signals and Systems Laboratory using MATLAB" all published by Lambert Academic Publishing (LAP), Germany.(2010). He has published 31 papers in international, national journals and conference proceedings. His areas of research include Digital Image processing, Video coding, Wavelet transforms, Wavelet variants.

Contents

Preface

Information has become one of the most valuable assets in the modern era. Recent technology has introduced the paradigm of digital information and its associated benefits and drawbacks. Within the last 5-10 years, the demand for multimedia applications has increased enormously. Like many other recent developments, the materialization of image and video encoding is due to the contribution from major areas like good network access, good amount of fast processors e.t.c. Many standardization procedures were carrried out for the development of image and video coding. The advancement of computer storage technology continues at a rapid pace as a means of reducing storage requirements of an image and video as most situation warrants. Thus, the science of digital image and video compression has emerged. For example, one of the formats defined for High Definition Television (HDTV) broadcasting is 1920 pixels horizontally by 1080 lines vertically, at 30 frames per second. If these numbers are multiplied together with 8 bits for each of the three primary colors, the total data rate required would be 1.5 GB/sec approximately. Hence compression is highly necessary. This storage capacity seems to be more impressive when it is realized that the intent is to deliver very high quality video to the end user with as few visible artifacts as possible. Current methods of video compression such as Moving Pictures Experts Group (MPEG) standard provide good performance in terms of retaining video quality while reducing the storage requirements. Even the popular standards like MPEG do have limitations. Video coding for telecommunication applications has evolved through the development of the ISO/IEC MPEG-1, MPEG-2 and ITU-T H.261, H.262 and H.263 video coding standards (and later enhancements of H.263 known as H.263+ and H.263++) and has diversified from ISDN and T1/E1 service to embrace PSTN, mobile wireless networks, and LAN/Internet network delivery.

SCOPE OF THE BOOK:

Many books are available for video coding fundamentals.This book is the research outcome of various Researchers and Professors who have contributed a might in this field. This book suits researchers doing their research in the area of video coding.The book revolves around three different challenges namely (i) Coding strategies (coding efficiency and computational complexity), (ii) Video compression and (iii) Error resilience The complete efficient video system depends upon source coding, proper inter and intra frame coding, emerging newer transform, quantization techniques and proper error concealment.The book gives the solution of all the challenges and is available in different sections.

STRUCTURE OF THE BOOK:

The book contains 12 chapters, divided into 5 sections. The user of this book is expected to know the fundamentals of video coding, which is available in all the standard video coding books.

Part 1 gives the introduction to scalable video coding containing two chapters.Chapter 1 deals with scalable video coding, which gives some fundamental ideas about scalable funtionallity of H.264/AVC, comparison of scalable extensions of different video codecs and adaptive scan algorithms for enhancement layers of subband/wavelet based architecture. Chapter 2 deals with the modelling of wireless satellite channel and scalable video coding components in the context of terrestrial broadcasting/Multicasting systems.

Part 2 describes the Intraframe coding (Motion estimation and compensation) organized into three chapters. Chapter 3 deals with the intra prediction scheme in H.264/AVC, which is done in spatial domain by refering to the neighbouring samples of the previously coded blocks which are to the left and/or above the block to be predicted. Chapter 4 describes the efficient scalable video coding based on matching pursuits, in which the scalability is supported by a two layer video scheme. The coding efficiency available is found to be better than the scalabilty.Chapter 5 deals with motion estimation at the decoder, where the compression efficiency is increased to a larger extent because of the omission of the motion vectors from the transmitter.

Part 3 deals with Video compression and Wavelet based coding consisting of 4 chapters. Chapter 6 deals with the introduction to Asymmetrical Principal Component analysis and its role in facial video coding.Chapter 7 deals with the introduction to distributed video coding along with the role of Wavelet based schemes in video coding. Chapter 8 focuses on the accurate correlation modelling in distributed video coding.Chapter 9 presents video coding scheme that utilizes Multistage Lattice Vector Quantization(MLVQ) algorithm to exploit the spatial-temporal video redundancy in an effective way.

Part 4 concentrates on error resilience categorized into 2 chapters. Chapter 10 deals with error concealment using cross layer optimization approach, where the trade-off is made between rate and reliability for a given information bit energy per noise power spectral density with proper error resilient video coding scheme.Chapter 11 describes a low redundancy error resilient scheme for H.264 video transmission in packet-swithched environment.

Part 5 discusses the hardware/software implementation of the video coder organized into a single chapter. Chapter 12 deals with the FPGA Implementation of HW/SW Codesign architecture for H.263 video Coding.The H.263 standard includes several blocks such as Motion Estimation (ME), Discrete Cosine Transform (DCT), quantization (Q) and variable length coding (VLC). It was shown that some of these parts can be optimized with parallel structures and efficiently implemented in hardware/software (HW/SW) partitioned system. Various factors such as flexibility, development cost, power consumption and processing speed requirement should be taken into account for the design. Hardware implementation is generally better than software implementation in processing speed and power consumption. In contrast, software implementation can give a more flexible design solution.It can also be made more suitable for various video applications.

Sudhakar Radhakrishnan
Department of Electronics and Communication Engineering
Dr. Mahalingam College of Engineering and Technology
India

Part 1

Scalable Video Coding

1

Scalable Video Coding

Z. Shahid, M. Chaumont and W. Puech
LIRMM / UMR 5506 CNRS / Universite´ Montpellier II
France

1. Introduction

With the evolution of Internet to heterogeneous networks both in terms of processing power and network bandwidth, different users demand the different versions of the same content. This has given birth to the scalable era of video content where a single bitstream contains multiple versions of the same video content which can be different in terms of resolutions, frame rates or quality. Several early standards, like MPEG2 video, H.263, and MPEG4 part II already include tools to provide different modalities of scalability. However, the scalable profiles of these standards are seldom used. This is because the scalability comes with significant loss in coding efficiency and the Internet was at its early stage. Scalable extension of H.264/AVC is named scalable video coding and is published in July 2007. It has several new coding techniques developed and it reduces the gap of coding efficiency with state-of-the-art non-scalable codec while keeping a reasonable complexity increase.
After an introduction to scalable video coding, we present a proposition regarding the scalable functionality of H.264/AVC, which is the improvement of the compression ratio in enhancement layers (ELs) of subband/wavelet based scalable bitstream. A new adaptive scanning methodology for *intra* frame scalable coding framework based on subband/wavelet coding approach is presented for H.264/AVC scalable video coding. It takes advantage of the prior knowledge of the frequencies which are present in different higher frequency subbands. Thus, by just modification of the scan order of the *intra* frame scalable coding framework of H.264/AVC, we can get better compression, without any compromise on PSNR.
This chapter is arranged as follows. We have presented introduction to scalable video in Section 2, while Section 3 contains a discussion on scalable extension of H.264/AVC. Comparison of scalable extension of different video codecs is presented in Section 4. It is followed by adaptive scan algorithm for enhancement layers (ELs) of subband/wavelet based scalable architecture in Section 5. At the end, concluding remarks regarding the whole chapter are presented in Section 6.

2. Basics of scalability

Historically simulcast coding has been used to achieve scalability. In simulcast coding, each layer of video is coded and transmitted independently. In recent times, it has been replaced by scalable video coding (SVC). In SVC, the video bitstream contains a base layer and number of enhancement layers. Enhancement layers are added to the base layer to further enhance the quality of coded video. The improvement can be made by increasing

the spatial resolution, video frame-rate or video quality, corresponding to spatial, temporal and quality/SNR scalability.
In spatial scalability, the inter-layer prediction of the enhancement-layer is utilized to remove redundancy across video layers as shown in Fig. 1.a. The resolution of the enhancement layer is either equal or greater than the lower layer. Enhancement layer predicted (P) frames can be predicted either from lower layer or from the previous frame in the same layer. In temporal scalability, the frame rate of enhancement layer is better as compared to the lower layer. This is implemented using I, P and B frame types. In Fig. 1.b, I and P frames constitute the base layer. B frames are predicted from I and P frames and constitute the second layer. In quality/SNR scalability, the temporal and spatial resolution of the video remains same and only the quality of the coded video is enhanced as shown in Fig. 2.
Individual scalabilities can be combined to form mixed scalability for a specific application. Video streaming over heterogeneous networks, which request same video content but with different resolutions, qualities and frame rates is one such example. The video content is encoded just once for the highest requested resolution, frame rate and bitrate, forming a scalable bitstream from which representations of lower resolution, lower frame rate and lower quality can be obtained by partial decoding. Combined scalability is a desirable feature for video transmission in networks with unpredictable throughput variations and can be used for bandwidth adaptation Wu et al. (2000). It is also useful for unequal error adaptation Wang et al. (2000), wherein the base layer can be sent over a more reliable channel, while the enhancement layers can be sent over comparatively less reliable channels. In this case, the connection will not be completely interrupted in the presence of transmission error and a base-layer quality can still be received.

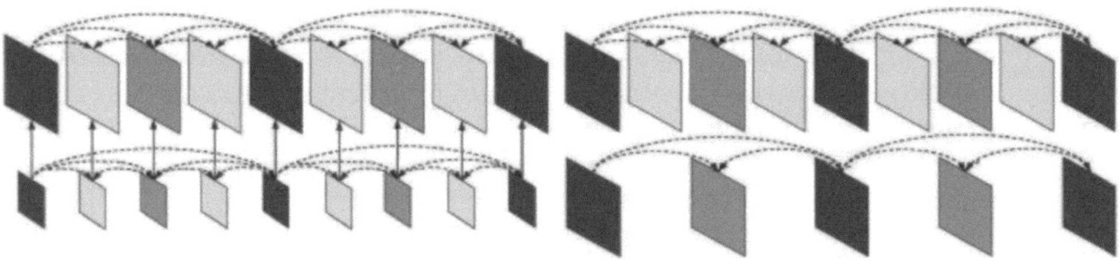

(a) (b)

Fig. 1. Spatial and temporal scalability offered by SVC: (a) Spatial scalability in which, resolution of enhancement layer can be either equal to or greater than resolution of base layer, (b) Temporal scalability in which, first layer containing only I and P frames while second layer contains B frames also. Frame rate of second layer is twice the frame rate of first layer.

3. Scalable extension of H.264/AVC

Previous video standards such as MPEG2 MPEG2 (2000), MPEG4 MPEG4 (2004) and H.263+ H263 (1998) also contain the scalable profiles but they were not much appreciated because the quality and scalability came at the cost of coding efficiency. Scalable video coding (SVC) based on H.264/AVC ISO/IEC-JTC1 (2007) has achieved significant improvements both in terms of coding efficiency and scalability as compared to scalable extensions of prior video coding standards.
The call for proposals for efficient scalable video coding technology was made in October 2003. 12 of the 14 submitted proposals represented scalable video codecs based on a 3-D wavelet

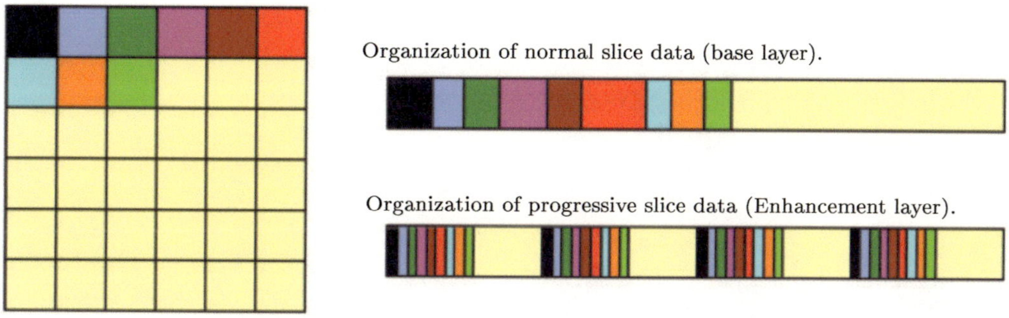

Fig. 2. SNR scalable architecture of SVC.

transform, while the remaining two proposals were extension of H.264/AVC. The scalable extension of H.264/AVC as proposed by Heinrich Hertz Institute (HHI) was chosen as the starting point of Scalable Video Coding (SVC) project in October 2004. In January 2005, ISO and ITU-T agreed to jointly finalize the SVC project as an Amendment of their H.264/AVC standard, named as scalable extension of H.264/AVC standard. The standardization activity of this scalable extension was completed and the standard was published in July 2007, which completed the milestone for scalable extension of H.264/AVC to become the state-of-the-art scalable video codec in the world. Similar to the previous scalable video coding propositions, Scalable extension of H.264/AVC is also built upon a predictive and layered approach to scalable video coding. It offers spatial, temporal and SNR scalabilities, which are presented in Section 3.1, Section 3.2 and Section 3.3 respectively.

3.1 Spatial scalability in scalable extension of H.264/AVC

Spatial scalability is achieved by pyramid approach. The pictures of different spatial layers are independently coded with layer specific motion parameters as illustrated in Fig. 3. In order to improve the coding efficiency of the enhancement layers in comparison to simulcast, additional inter-layer prediction mechanisms have been introduced to remove the redundancies among layers. These prediction mechanisms are switchable so that an encoder can freely choose a reference layer for an enhancement layer to remove the redundancy between them. Since the incorporated inter-layer prediction concepts include techniques for motion parameter and residual prediction, the temporal prediction structures of the spatial layers should be temporally aligned for an efficient use of the inter-layer prediction. Three inter-layer prediction techniques, included in the scalable extension of H.264/AVC, are:

- *Inter-layer motion prediction*: In order to remove the redundancy among layers, additional MB modes have been introduced in spatial enhancement layers. The MB partitioning is obtained by up-sampling the partitioning of the co-located 8x8 block in the lower resolution layer. The reference picture indices are copied from the co-located base layer blocks, and the associated motion vectors are scaled by a factor of 2. These scaled motion vectors are either directly used or refined by an additional quarter-sample motion vector refinement. Additionally, a scaled motion vector of the lower resolution can be used as motion vector predictor for the conventional MB modes.
- *Inter-layer residual prediction*:The usage of inter-layer residual prediction is signaled by a flag that is transmitted for all inter-coded MBs. When this flag is true, the base layer signal

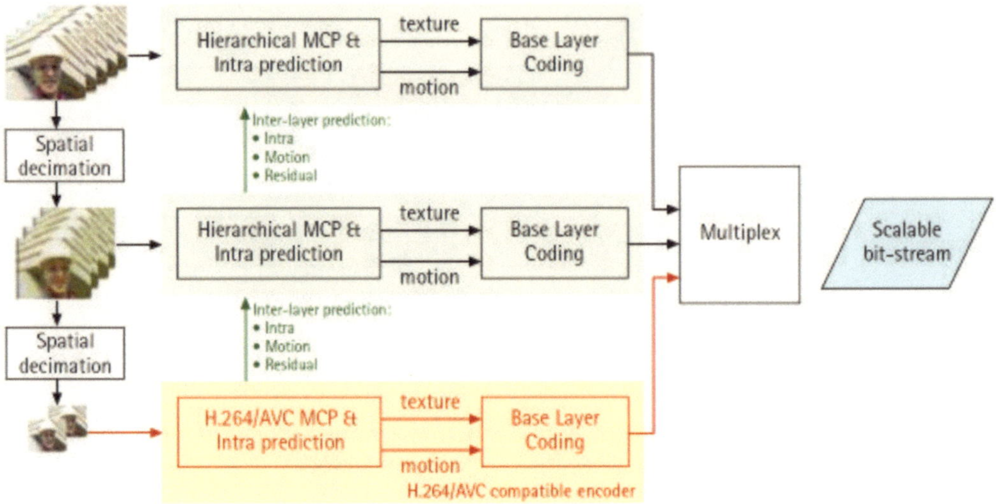

Fig. 3. Spatial scalable architecture of scalable extension of H.264/AVC.

of the co-located block is block-wise up-sampled and used as prediction for the residual signal of the current MB, so that only the corresponding difference signal is coded.

- *Inter-layer intra prediction*:Furthermore, an additional intra MB mode is introduced, in which the prediction signal is generated by up-sampling the co-located reconstruction signal of the lower layer. For this prediction it is generally required that the lower layer is completely decoded including the computationally complex operations of motion-compensated prediction and deblocking. However, this problem can be circumvented when the inter-layer intra prediction is restricted to those parts of the lower layer picture that are intra-coded. With this restriction, each supported target layer can be decoded with a single motion compensation loop.

3.2 Temporal scalability in scalable extension of H.264/AVC

Temporal scalable bitstream can be generated by using hierarchical prediction structure without any changes to H.264/AVC. A typical hierarchical prediction with four dyadic hierarchy stages is depicted in Fig. 4. Four temporal scalability levels are provided by this structure. The first picture of a video sequence is intra-coded as IDR picture that are coded in regular (or even irregular) intervals. A picture is called a key picture when all previously coded pictures precede this picture in display order. A key picture and all pictures that are temporally located between the key picture and the previous key picture consist of a group of pictures (GOP). The key pictures are either intra-coded or inter-coded using previous (key) pictures as reference for motion compensated prediction, while the remaining pictures of a GOP are hierarchically predicted. . For example, layer 0, 1, 2 and 3 contains 3, 5, 9 and 18 frames respectively in Fig. 4.

3.3 SNR scalability in scalable extension of H.264/AVC

For SNR scalability, scalable extension of H.264/AVC provides coarse-grain SNR scalability (CGS) and medium-grain SNR scalability (MGS). CGS scalable coding is achieved using the same inter-layer prediction mechanisms as in spatial scalability. MGS is aimed at increasing

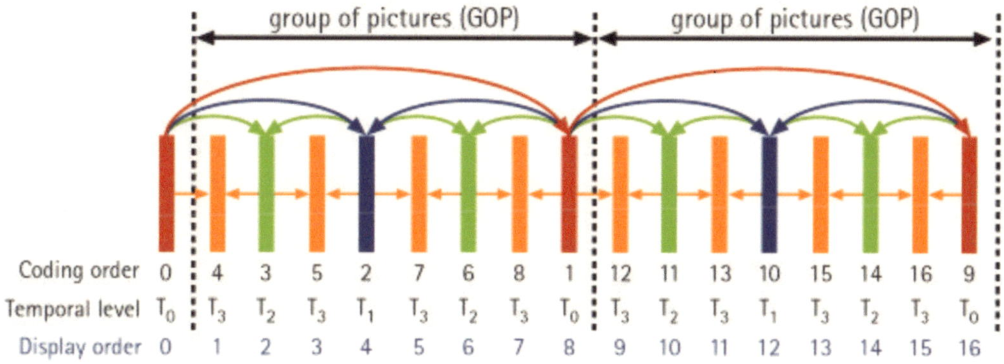

Fig. 4. Temporal scalable architecture of Scalable extension of H.264/AVC.

the granularity for SNR scalability and allows the adaptation of bitstream adaptation at network adaptation layer (NAL) unit basis. CGS and MGS are presented in details in Section 3.3.1 and Section 3.3.2 respectively.

3.3.1 Coarse-grain SNR scalability

Coarse-grain SNR scalable coding is achieved using the concepts for spatial scalability. The same inter-layer prediction mechanisms are employed. The only difference is that base and enhancement layers have the same resolution. The CGS only allows a few selected bitrates to be supported in a scalable bitstream. In general, the number of supported rate points is identical to the number of layers. Switching between different CGS layers can only be done at defined points in the bitstream. Furthermore, the CGS concept becomes less efficient when the relative rate difference between successive CGS layers gets smaller.

3.3.2 Medium-grain SNR scalability

In order to increase the granularity for SNR scalability, scalable extension of H.264/AVC provides a variation of CGS approach, which uses the quality identifier Q for quality refinements. This method is referred to as MGS and allows the adaptation of bitstream adaptation at a NAL unit basis. With the concept of MGS, any enhancement layer NAL unit can be discarded from a quality scalable bitstream and thus packet based SNR scalable coding is obtained. However, it requires a good controlling of the associated drift. MGS in scalable extension of H.264/AVC has evolved from SNR scalable extensions of MPEG2/4. So it is pertinent to start our discussion from there and extend it to MGS of H.264/AVV.
The prediction structure of FGS in MPEG4 Visual was chosen in a way that drift is completely omitted. Motion compensation prediction in MPEG4 FGS is usually performed using the base layer reconstruction for reference as illustrated in Fig. 5.a. Hence loss of any enhancement packet does not result in any drift on the motion compensated prediction loops between encoder and decoder. The drawback of this approach, however, is the significant decrease of enhancement layer coding efficiency in comparison to single layer coding, because the temporal redundancies in enhancement layer cannot be properly removed.
For SNR scalability coding in MPEG2, the other extreme case was specified. The highest enhancement layer reconstruction is used in motion compensated prediction as shown in

Fig. 5.b. This ensures a high coding efficiency as well as low complexity for the enhancement layer. However, any loss or modification of a refinement packet results in a drift that can only be stopped by intra frames.

For the MGS in scalable extension of H.264/AVC, an alternative approach, which allows certain amount of drift by adjusting the trade off between drift and enhancement layer coding efficiency is used. The approach is designed for SNR scalable coding in connection with hierarchical prediction structures. For each picture, a flag is transmitted to signal whether the base representations or the enhancement representations are employed for motion compensated prediction. Picture that only uses the base representations (Q=0) for prediction is also referred as key pictures. Fig. 6 illustrates how the key picture can be combined with hierarchical prediction structures.

All pictures of the coarsest temporal level are transmitted as key pictures, and thus no drift is introduced in the motion compensated loop of temporal level 0. In contrast to that, all temporal refinement pictures are using the highest available quality pictures as reference in motion compensated prediction, which results in high coding efficiency for these pictures. Since key pictures serve as the resynchronization point between encoder and decoder reconstruction, drift propagation can be efficiently contained inside a group of pictures. The trade off between drift and enhancement layer coding efficiency can be adjusted by the choice of GOP size or the number of hierarchy stages.

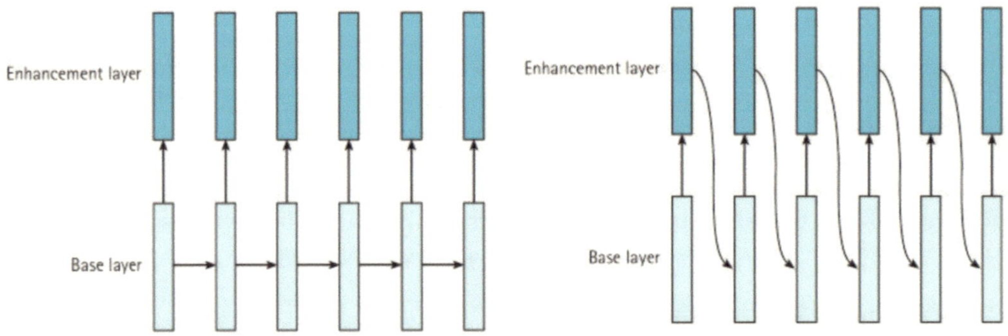

Fig. 5. SNR scalable architecture for (a) MPRG4, (b) MPRG2.

4. Performance comparison of different scalable architectures

In comparison to early scalable standards, scalable extension of H.264/AVC provides various tools for improving efficiency relative to single-layer coding. The key features that make the scalable extension of H.264/AVC superior than all scalable profiles are:

- The employed hierarchical prediction structure that provides temporal scalability with several levels improves the coding efficiency and effectiveness of SNR and spatial scalable coding.
- The concept of key pictures controls the trade off between drift and enhancement layer coding efficiency. It provides a basis for efficient SNR scalability, which could not be achieved in all previous standards.
- New modes for inter-layer prediction of motion and residual information improves coding efficiency of spatial and SNR scalability. In all previous standards, only residual information can be refined at enhancement layers.

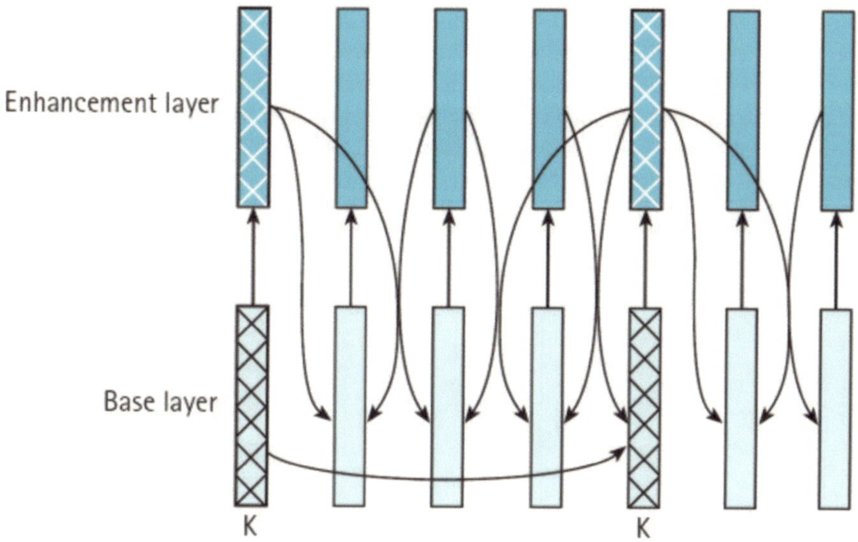

Fig. 6. SNR scalable architecture of Scalable extension of H.264/AVC.

- The coder structure is designed in a more flexible way such that any layer can be configured to be the optimization point in SNR scalability. MPEG2 is designed in the sense that enhancement layer is always optimized but the base layer may suffer from a serious drift problem that causes significant quality drop. MPEG4 FGS, on the other way round, usually coded in a way to optimize base layer and the coding efficiency of enhancement layer is much lower than single layer coding. In scalable extension of H.264/AVC, the optimum layer can be set to any layer with a proper configuration Li et al. (2006).
- Single motion compensated loop decoding provides a decoder complexity close to single layer decoding.

To conclude, with the advances mentioned above, scalable extension of H.264/AVC, has enabled profound performance improvements for both scalable and single layer coding. Results of the rate-distortion comparison show that scalable extension of H.264/AVC clearly outperforms early video coding standards, such as MPEG4 ASP Wien et al. (2007). Although scalable extension of H.264/AVC still comes at some costs in terms of bitrate or quality, the gap between the state-of-the-art single layer coding and scalable extension of H.264/AVC can be remarkably small.

5. Adaptive scan for high frequency (HF) subbands in SVC

Scalable video coding (SVC) standard Schwarz & Wiegand (2007) is based on pyramid coding architecture. In this kind of architecture, the total spatial resolution of the video processed is the sum of all the spatial layers. Consequently, quality of subsequent layers is dependent on quality of base layer as shown in Fig. 7.a. Thus, the process applied to the base layer must be the best possible in order to improve the quality.
Hsiang Hsiang (2008) has presented a scalable dyadic intra frame coding method based on subband/wavelet coding (DWTSB). In this method, LL subband is encoded as the base layer

while the high frequency subbands are encoded as subsequent layers as shown in Fig. 7.b. With this method, if the LL residual is encoded, then higher layer can be encoded at a better quality than base layer, as illustrated in Fig. 7.c. The results presented by Hsiang have proved to be better than H.264 scalable video coding Wiegand et al. (April 2007) for intra frame. In dyadic scalable intra frame coding, the image is transformed to wavelet subbands and then the subbands are encoded by base-layer H.264/AVC. Since each wavelet subband possesses a certain range of frequencies, zigzag scan is not equally efficient for scanning the transform coefficients in all the subbands.

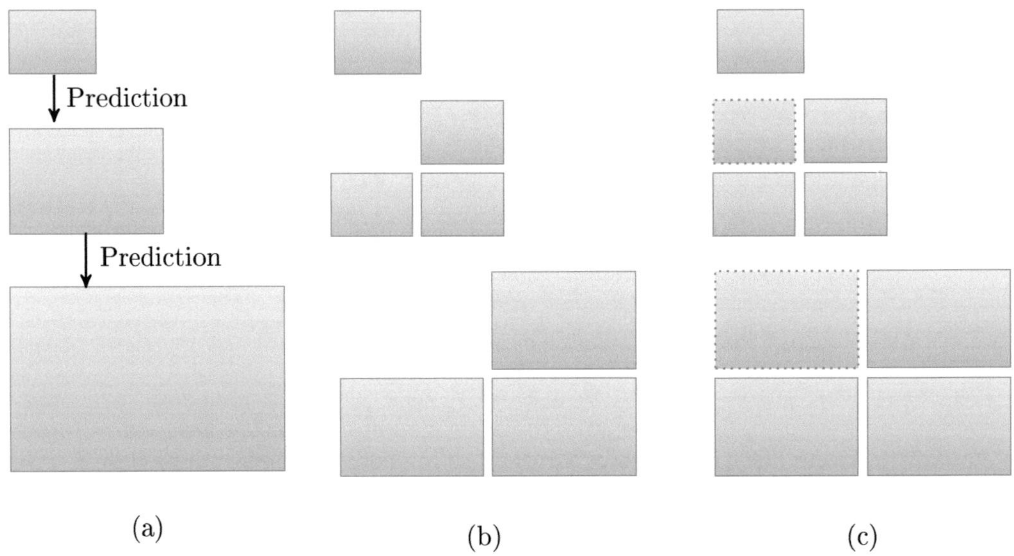

Fig. 7. Different scalable video coding approaches: (a) Pyramid coding used in JSVM, (b) Wavelet subband coding used in JPEG2000, (c) Wavelet subband coding for dyadic scalable intra frame.

This section presents a new scanning methodology for intra frame scalable coding framework based on a subband/wavelet (DWTSB) scalable architecture. It takes advantage of the prior knowledge of the frequencies which are present in different higher frequency (HF) subbands. An adaptive scan (DWTSB-AS) is proposed for HF subbands as traditional zigzag scan is designed for video content containing most of its energy in low frequencies. Hence, we can get better compression by just modification of the scan order of DCT coefficients. The proposed algorithm has been theoretically justified and is thoroughly evaluated against the current SVC test model JSVM and DWTSB through extensive coding experiments. The simulation results show the proposed scanning algorithm consistently outperforms JSVM and DWTSB in terms of PSNR.

5.1 Scan methodology

Let the QTCs be 2-dimensional array given as:

$$P_{m \times n} = \{p(i,j) : 1 \le i \le m, i \le j \le n\}. \tag{1}$$

After scanning the 2-dimensional array, we get a 1-dimensional array $Q_{mn} = \{1, ..., mn\}$, using a bijective function from $P_{m\times n}$ to Q_{mn}. Indeed, scanning of a 2D array is a permutation in which each element of the array is accessed exactly once.
Natural images generally consist of slow varying areas and contain lower frequencies both horizontally and vertically. After a transformation in the frequency domain, there are lot of non-zero transform coefficients (NZ) in the top left corner. Consequently, zigzag scan is more appropriate to put QTCs with higher magnitude at the start of the array.
Entropy coding engine is designed to perform better when:

1. It gets most of the non-zero QTCs in the beginning of scanned and long trail of zeros at its end.
2. Magnitude of non-zero coefficients is higher at the start of the scanned array.

This is the case for slowly changing video data when quantized coefficients are scanned by traditional zigzag scan.
Substituting the image by its wavelet subbands, each subband contains a certain range of frequencies. Zigzag scan is thus no more efficient for all the subbands as the energy is not concentrated in top left corner of 4x4 transform block. Each subband should be scanned in a manner that entropy coding module do maximum possible compression. In other words, most of the non-zero QTCs should be in the beginning and a long trail of zeros at the end of the scanned array.

5.2 Analysis of each subband in transform domain

In DWTSB scalable video architecture, an image is transformed to wavelet subbands and the LL subband is encoded as base layer by traditional H.264/AVC. In the enhancement layer, LL subband is predicted from the reconstructed base layer. Each high-frequency subband is encoded independently using base-layer H.264/AVC as shown in Fig. 8.

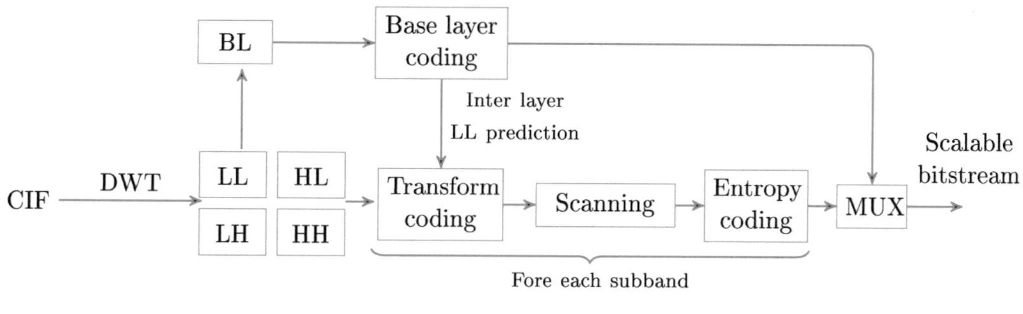

Fig. 8. DWTSB scalable architecture based on H.264/AVC.

For this work, we have used wavelet critical sampling setting. Daubechies 9/7 wavelet filter set has been used to transform the video frame to four wavelet subbands. The work has been performed on 'JVT-W097' Hsiang (2007) which is referenced H.264 JSVM 8.9 with wavelet framework integrated.
In order to analyze each subband in transform domain, we propose to divide the 2D transform space into 4 areas, *e.g.* as shown in Fig. 9.a for LL subband. The area-1 contains most of the energy and has most of NZs. The area-2 and area-3 contain comparatively less number of NZs and only one frequency is dominant in these areas: either horizontal or vertical. The area-4 contains the least number of NZs. Fig. 9.a shows the frequency distribution in LL

subband. It contains the lower frequencies in both horizontal and vertical directions and transform coefficients in this subband are scanned by traditional zigzag scan as illustrated in Fig. 9.b.

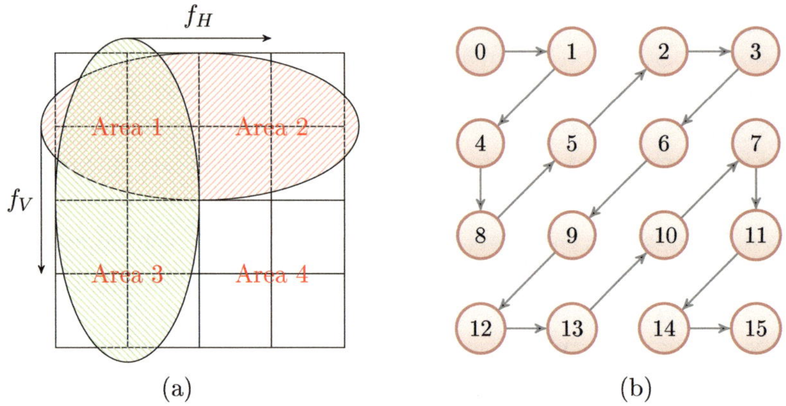

Fig. 9. Analysis of LL subband: (a) Dominant frequencies in transformed coefficients of LL subband, (b) Zigzag scan is suitable for such type of frequency distribution.

5.3 Adaptive scan for HF subbands

In this section we present our proposition which is to use DWTSB scalable architecture along-with adaptive scan (DWTSB-AS) for HF subbands. We analyze the frequencies present in HL, LH and HH subbands in order to adapt the scanning processes.

HL and LH subbands do not contain horizontal and vertical frequencies in equal proportion. HL subband contains most of the high frequencies in horizontal direction while LH contains most of high frequencies in vertical direction. Because of non-symmetric nature of frequencies the scan pattern in not symmetric for HL and LH subbands except in the area-1 which contains both of the frequencies.

In HL subband, there are high horizontal frequencies and low frequencies in vertical direction. Area which contains many NZs should be then in top right corner, as illustrated in Fig. 10.a. Based on this, it should be scanned from top right corner to bottom left corner in a natural zigzag, as shown in Fig. 10.b. But separation of frequencies in subbands is not ideal and depends on the type of wavelet/subband filter used. It is also affected by rounding errors. So this simple zigzag scan is modified to get better results. Experimental results show that DC coefficient still contains higher energy than other coefficients and should be scanned first. It is followed by a scan from the top left corner in a horizontal fashion till element 11, as illustrated in Fig. 10.c. At this position, we have two candidates to be scanned next: element 5 and element 15. We have already scanned the area-1 and zigzag scan is no more feasible. So, element 15 is then selected to be scanned first as it contains higher horizontal frequencies which are dominant in this subband. The same principle is true for the rest of scan lines and unidirectional scan from bottom to top gives better results, thus giving priority to the coefficients which contain higher horizontal frequencies.

Similarly for LH subband, there are low horizontal frequencies and high frequencies in vertical direction. This subband contains most of the NZs in bottom left corner, as illustrated in Fig. 11.a. Based on this, LH subband should be scanned in a zigzag fashion from bottom left corner to top right corner as shown in Fig. 11.b. But due to reasons similar to HL subband,

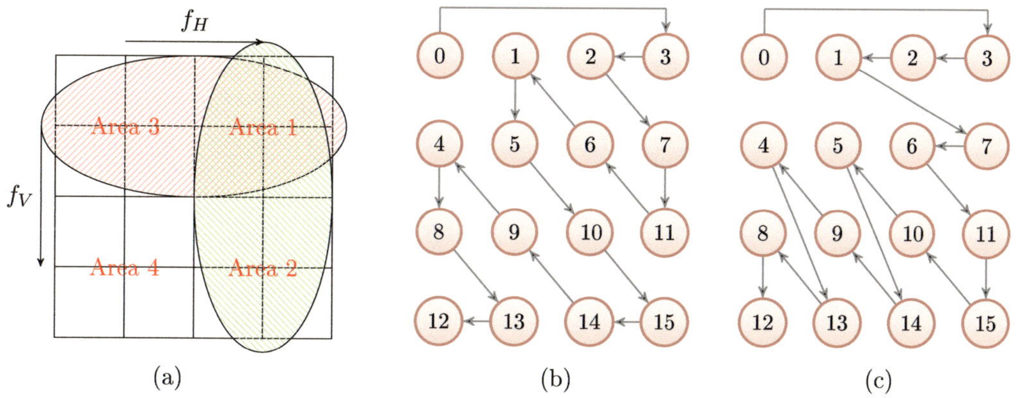

Fig. 10. Analysis of HL subband: (a) Dominant frequencies in QTCs of this subband, (b) Simple zigzag scan proposed for such type of frequency distribution, (c) Proposed scan for HL subband.

this simple scan is modified to a more efficient scan, illustrated Fig. 11.c. DC coefficient is scanned first. It is followed by a scan from the bottom left corner in a zigzag fashion till element 5. Thereafter, unidirectional scan which gives priority to the coefficients containing higher vertical frequencies, is performed.

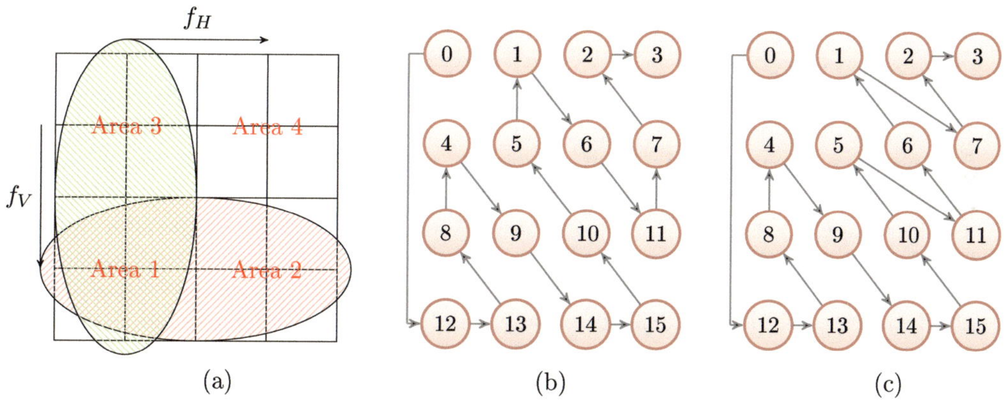

Fig. 11. Analysis of LH subband: (a) Dominant frequencies in QTCs of this subband, (b) Simple zigzag scan proposed for such type of frequency distribution, (c) Proposed scan for LH subband.

HH subband contains higher frequencies both in horizontal and vertical directions as shown in 12.a. Frequencies which contain NZs should then be in bottom right. In this subband, DC coefficient contains the least energy and is scanned at the end. So it should be scanned from bottom right corner to top left corner in a zigzag fashion as shown in Fig. 12.b.

5.4 Experimental results

For the experimental results, nine standard video sequences have been used for the analysis in CIF and QCIF format. To apply our approach we have compressed 150 frames of each sequence at 30 fps.

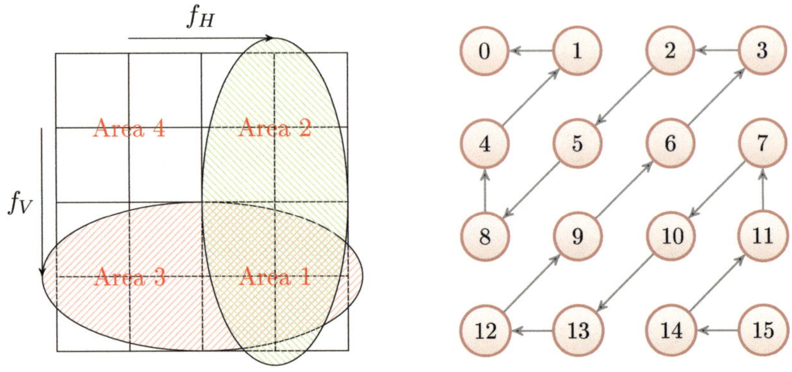

(a) (b)

Fig. 12. Analysis of HH subband: (a) Dominant frequencies in QTCs of this subband, (b) Inverse zigzag scan proposed for such type of frequency distribution.

For the experimental results, nine benchmark video sequences have been used for the analysis in QCIF format. Each of them represents different combinations of motion (fast/slow, pan/zoom/rotation), color (bright/dull), contrast (high/low) and objects (vehicle, buildings, people). The video sequences 'bus', 'city' and 'foreman' contain camera motion while 'football' and 'soccer' contain camera panning and zooming along with object motion and texture in background. The video sequences 'harbour' and 'ice' contain high luminance images with smooth motion. 'Mobile' sequence contains a complex still background and foreground motion.

DWTSB dyadic intra frame coding has already been demonstrated to perform better results than JSVM. Results illustrated in Fig. 13 for QP value 18 show that DWTSB-AS coding improves results comparing to DWTSB coding. In particular, adaptive scanning helps the entropy coder to perform a better coding and then gives a better compression without any compromise on quality. HH subband offers the best results since the appropriate scan for this subband is exactly opposite to simple zigzag scan. For example, for 'bus' video sequence, DWTSB-AS has reduced the overall bitstream size for the three high frequency subbands (HL, LH and HH) from **2049 kB to 1863 kB** as shown in Fig. 13.a. File size of base layer and its residual remains the same since no modification has been made in their scan pattern. The improvements for the overall 2-layer video have been shown in Fig. 13.a for all the video sequences. Fig. 13.b-d show the file size reduction for HL, LH and HH subbands respectively. To see the performance as a function of the QP value over the whole rate distortion (R-D) curve, we have tested the proposed scans over 150 frames of the same benchmark video sequences with QP values of 18, 24, 30 and 36. The results show that the performance of adaptive scan is consistent over the whole curve for all the benchmark sequences. Rather adaptive scans perform at high QP values times. Hence our scan performs better for all high frequency subbands over the whole R-D curve. Fig. 14.a gives the performance analysis overall 2-layer video *mobile* at different QP values since Fig. 14.b-d give the performance analysis for the video *mobile* at different QP values for the three subbands HL, LH and HH respectively.

To summarize, we have presented a new adaptive scanning methodology for DWTSB scalable architecture of dyadic intra frames in Section 5.4. We have described in detail the DWTSB-AS scheme. DWTSB-AS has done a significant file size reduction without any computation load

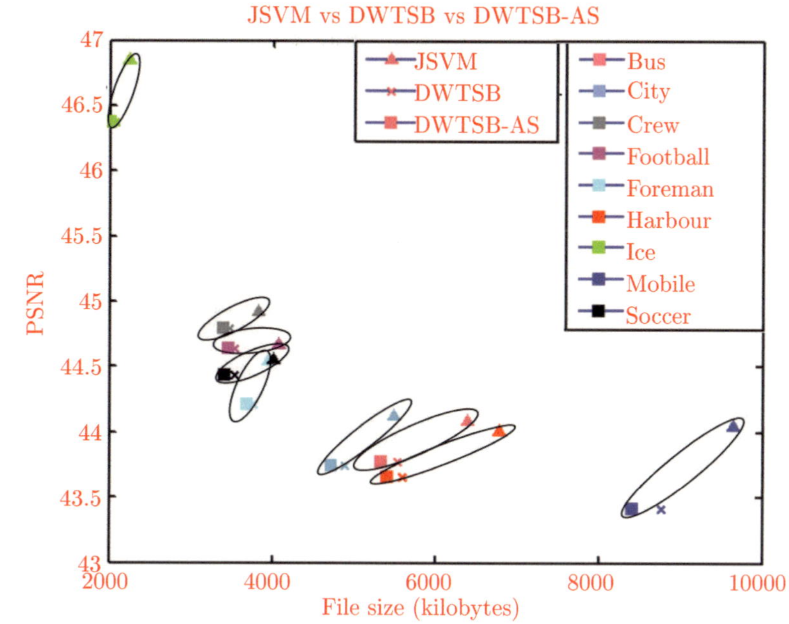
JSVM vs DWTSB vs DWTSB-AS
JSVM
DWTSB
DWTSB-AS
Bus
City
Crew
Football
Foreman
Harbour
Ice
Mobile
Soccer
PSNR
47
46.5
46
45.5
45
44.5
44
43.5
43
2000
4000
6000
8000
10000
File size (kilobytes)

(a)

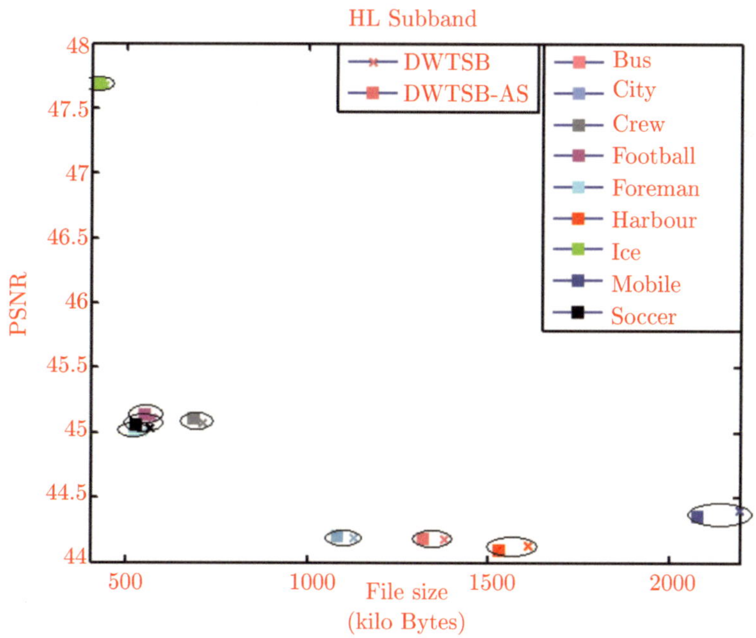
HL Subband
DWTSB
DWTSB-AS
Bus
City
Crew
Football
Foreman
Harbour
Ice
Mobile
Soccer
PSNR
48
47.5
47
46.5
46
45.5
45
44.5
44
500
1000
1500
2000
File size
(kilo Bytes)

(b)

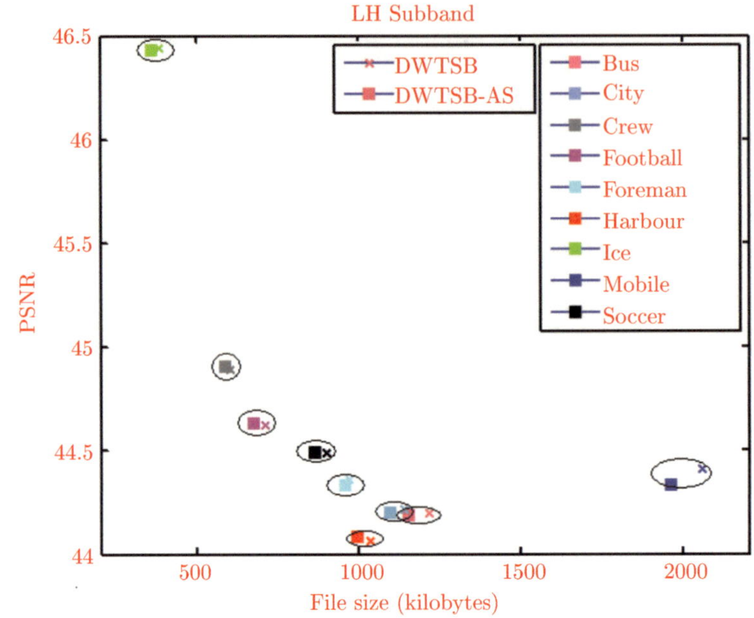

(c)

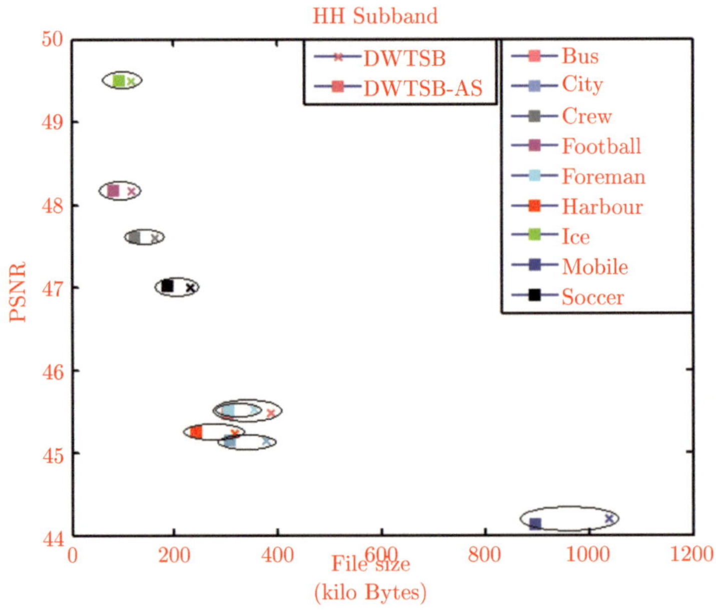

(d)

Fig. 13. Comparison of JSVM, DWTSB and DWTSB-AS: (a) Global comparison for two layer scalable bitstreams, (b) HL subband comparison, (c) LH subband comparison, (d) HH subband comparison.

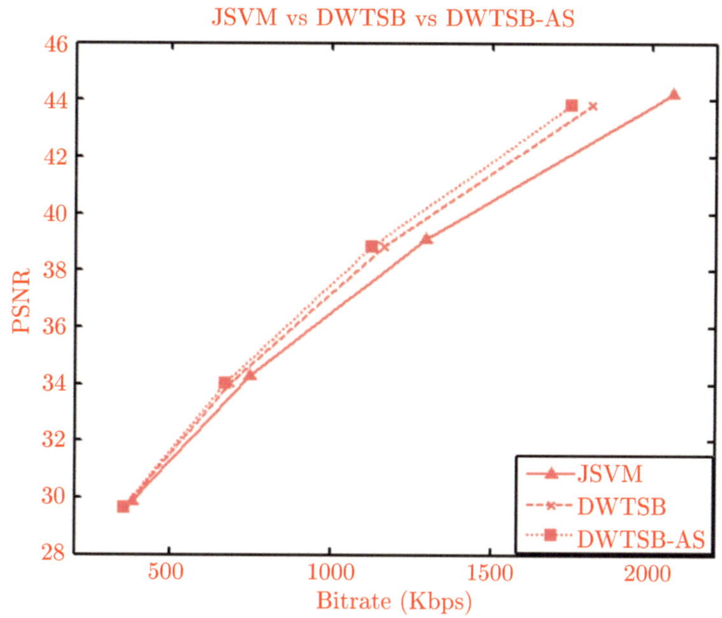
JSVM vs DWTSB vs DWTSB-AS
PSNR
Bitrate (Kbps)
JSVM
DWTSB
DWTSB-AS
46
44
42
40
38
36
34
32
30
28
500
1000
1500
2000

(a)

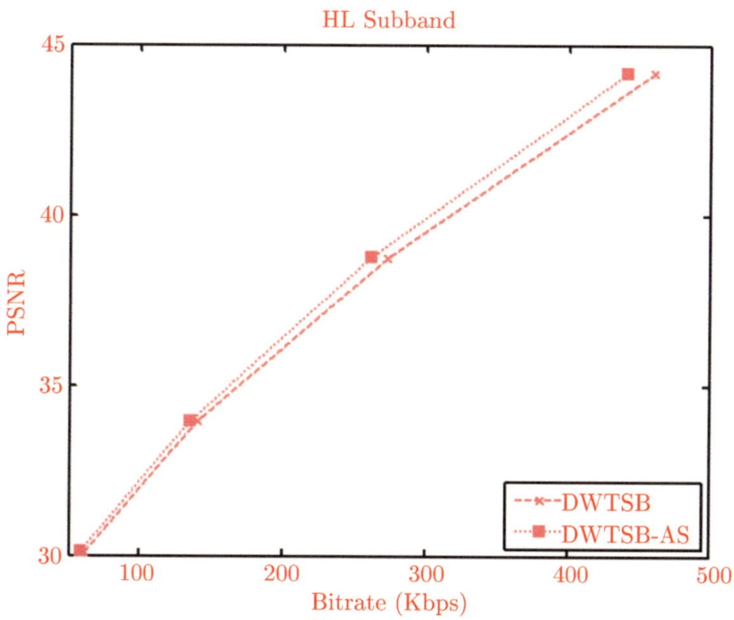
HL Subband
PSNR
Bitrate (Kbps)
DWTSB
DWTSB-AS
45
40
35
30
100
200
300
400
500

(b)

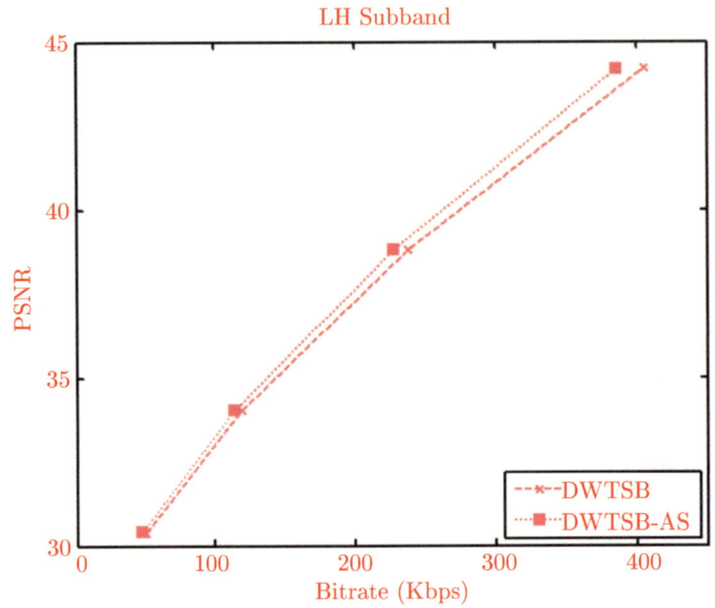

(c)

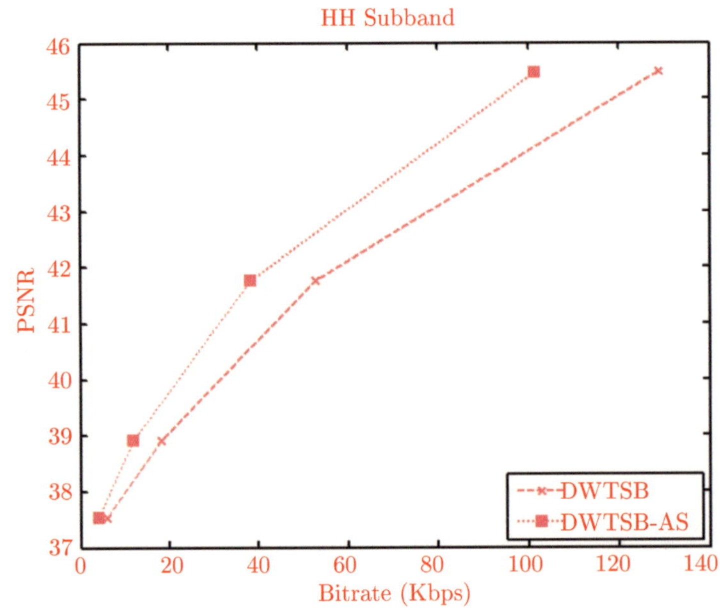

(d)

Fig. 14. Performance comparison of JSVM, DWTSB and DWTSB-AS for *mobile* video sequence over whole QP range: (a) Global comparison for two layer scalable bitstreams, (b) HL subband, (c) LH subband, (d) HH subband.

for the same quality as compared to DWTSB coding. Effectiveness of subband-specific scan for DWTSB scalable video has been elaborated by showing experimental results on several benchmark video sequences containing diverse content.

6. Summary

In this chapter, we have presented the scalable extension of H.264/AVC and its comparison with previous scalable video architectures. Extra prediction modes in spatial scalability and SNR scalability have resulted in extra performance of this architecture. It is followed by our contribution related to spatially scalable video. First of all, we have presented the DWT based spatial scalable architecture. It is followed by proposed adaptive scanning methodology for DWTSB scalable coding framework. We have described in detail the DWTSB-AS coding and we have shown that DWTSB-AS coding has done a significant file size reduction without any computation load for the same quality as compared to DWTSB coding Shahid et al. (2009). We have then elaborated the effectiveness of subband-specific scan for two layers by showing experimental results applied on several standard video sequences.

7. References

H263 (1998). ITU Telecommunication Standardization Sector of ITU, Video Coding for Low Bitrate Communication, *ITU-T Recommendation H.263 Version 2*.

Hsiang, S. (2007). CE3: Intra-frame Dyadic Spatial Scalable Coding Based on a Subband/Wavelet Filter Banks Framework, Joint Video Team, Doc. JVT-W097.

Hsiang, S. (2008). A New Subband/Wavelet Framework for AVC/H.264 Intra-Frame Coding and Performance Comparison with Motion-JPEG2000, *SPIE, Visual Communications and Image Processing*, Vol. 6822, pp. 1–12.

ISO/IEC-JTC1 (2007). Advanced Video Coding for Generic Audio-Visual Services, *ITU-T Recommendation H.264 Amendment 3, ISO/IEC 14496-10/2005:Amd 3 - Scalable extension of H.264 (SVC)* .

Li, Z., Rahardja, S. & Sun, H. (2006). Implicit Bit Allocation for Combined Coarse Granular Scalability and Spatial Scalability, *IEEE Transactions on Circuits and Systems for Video Technology* 16(12): 1449 –1459.

MPEG2 (2000). ISO/IEC 13818-2:2000 Information Technology – Generic Coding of Moving Pictures and Associated Audio Information: Video, 2nd Edition.

MPEG4 (2004). ISO/IEC 14496-2:2004 Information Technology – Coding of Audio-Visual Objects: Visual, 3rd Edition.

Schwarz, H. & Wiegand, T. (2007). Overview of the Scalable Video Coding Extension of the H.264/AVC Standard, *IEEE Transactions on Circuits and Systems for Video Technology* 17(9): 1103–1120.

Shahid, Z., Chaumont, M. & Puech, W. (2009). An Adaptive Scan of High Frequency Subbands of Dyadic Intra Frame in MPEG4-AVC/H.264 Scalable Video Coding, *Proc. SPIE, Electronic Imaging, Visual Communications and Image Processing*, Vol. 7257, San Jose, CA, USA, p. 9.

Wang, Y., Wenger, S., Wen, J. & Katsaggelos, A. (2000). Error Resilient Video Coding Techniques, *IEEE Signal Processing Magazine* 17(4): 61 –82.

Wiegand, T., Sullivan, G., Richel, J., Schwartz, H., Wien, M. & eds. (April 2007). Joint Scalable Video Model (JSVM) 10, *JVT-W202*.

Wien, M., Schwarz, H. & Oelbaum, T. (2007). Performance Analysis of SVC, *IEEE Transactions on Circuits and Systems for Video Technology* 17(9): 1194 –1203.

Wu, M., Joyce, R. & Kung, S. (2000). Dynamic Resource Allocation via Video Content and Short-Term Traffic Statistics, *Proc. IEEE International Conference on Image Processing*, Vol. 3, pp. 58–61.

2

Scalable Video Coding in Fading Hybrid Satellite-Terrestrial Networks

Dr. Georgios Avdikos
National Technical University of Athens (NTUA)
Greece

1. Introduction

Broadband satellite multimedia (BSM) systems will be an integral part of the global information infrastructure as one of the major technologies providing both broadband access and broadcast services (Skinnemoen & Tork, 2002). Recent commercial deployments show that users not only would like to have access to value-added services (e.g., mobile internet, multimedia streaming, etc.) but are also willing to pay more for them and in particular for video services (Sattler). The introduction of video coding technology in the satellite application space opens up new and challenging topics; digital video applications have to face potentially harsher transmission environments than ones they were originally designed to work with (e.g., HDTV, Mobile TV), especially as regards traversing packet networks with the presence of satellite links. Towards approaching the satellite multimedia application delivery needs, H.264/MPEG4 Advanced Video Coding (AVC) (Ostermann et al, 2004), as the latest entry of international video coding standards, has demonstrated significantly improved coding efficiency, substantially enhanced error robustness, and increased flexibility and scope of applicability relative to its predecessors (Marpe et al, 2002). In the last decade, there is a growing research interest for the transmission and study of multimedia content over IP networks (Chou & van der Schaar, 2007) and wireless networks (Rupp, 2009). In an increasing number of applications, video is transmitted to and from satellite networks or portable wireless devices such as cellular phones, laptop computers connected to wireless local area networks (WLANs), and cameras in surveillance and environmental tracking systems. Wireless networks are heterogeneous in bandwidth, reliability, and receiver device characteristics. In (satellite) wireless channels, packets can be delayed (due to queuing, propagation, transmission, and processing delays), lost, or even discarded due to complexity/power limitations or display capabilities of the receiver (Katsaggelos et al, 2005). Hence, the experienced packet losses can be up to 10% or more, and the time allocated to the various users and the resulting goodput1 for multimedia bit stream transmission can also vary significantly in time (Zhai et al, 2005). This variability of wireless resources has considerable consequences for multimedia applications and often leads to unsatisfactory user experience due to the high bandwidths and to very stringent delay constraints. Fortunately, *multimedia applications* can cope with a certain amount of packet losses depending on the used sequence characteristics, compression schemes, and error concealment strategies available at the receiver (e.g., packet losses up to 5% or more can be tolerated at times). Consequently, unlike file transfers, real time multimedia applications do not require a complete insulation from packet losses, but rather require the application layer *to cooperate* with the lower layers to select the optimal wireless transmission strategy that maximizes the multimedia performance. Thus, to achieve a high level of acceptability and proliferation of wireless multimedia, in particular wireless video (Winkler, 2005), several key requirements need to be satisfied by multimedia streaming solutions (Wenger, 2003) over such channels: (i) easy adaptability to wireless bandwidth fluctuations due to cochannel interference, multipath fading (Pätzold, 2002), mobility, handoff, competing traffic, and so on; (ii) robustness to partial data losses caused by the packetization of video frames and high packet error rates. This chapter tackles in a unified framework both the (satellite) wireless channel modeling and scalable video coding components in the context of satellite-terrestrial broadcasting/multicasting systems (Kiang et al, 2008). It should be mentioned that the literature is poor in the analysis of the effects produced by corrupted bits in compressed video streams (Celandroni et al, 2004), and an attempt is done here to contribute some results to this open field of research. Some technical aspects both in terms of the video coding system and the satellite channel are provided in Section II. Section III deals with the joint source and channel simulation, and Section IV presents the simulation results. The last Section V contains the conclusions and future improvements on the proposed work.

2. Technical background

2.1 Video coding scheme (AVC, SVC)

H.264, or MPEG-4 AVC (advanced video coding) (ITU-T, 2003) is the state-of-the-art video coding standard (Richardson, 2005). It provides improved compression efficiency, a comprehensive set of tools and profile/level specifications catering for different applications. H.264/AVC (Ostermann et al, 2004) has attracted a lot of attention from industry and has been adopted by various application standards and is increasingly used in a broad variety of applications. It is expected that in the near-term future H.264/AVC will be commonly used in most video applications. Given this high degree of adoption and deployment of the new standard and taking into account the large investments that have already been taken place for preparing and developing H.264/AVC-based products, it is quite natural to now build a SVC scheme as an extension of H.264/AVC and to reuse its key features. Furthermore, its specification of network abstraction layer (NAL) separate from the video coding layer (VCL) makes the standard much more network-friendly as compared with all its predecessors. The standard is first established in 2003 jointly by ITU-T VCEG (video Coding Experts Group) and ISO/IEC MPEG (Moving Picture Experts Group). The partnership, known as JVT (Joint Video Team), has been constantly revising and extending the standards ever since. SVC Considering the needs of today's and future video applications as well as the experiences with scalable profiles in the past (Cycon et al, 2010), the success of any future SVC standard critically depends on the following essential requirements. Similar coding efficiency compared to single-layer coding—for each subset of the scalable bit stream.

- Little increase in decoding complexity compared to single layer decoding that scales with the decoded spatio-temporal resolution and bit rate.
- Support of temporal, spatial, and quality scalability.

- Support of a backward compatible base layer (H.264/AVC in this case).
- Support of simple bit stream adaptations after encoding.

SVC (Scalable Video Coding) (Schwarz et al, 2003) is the newest extension established in late 2007. Formally known as Annex G extension to H.264, SVC allows video contents to be split into a base layer and several enhancement layers, which allows users with different devices and traffic bearers with different capacities to share the video without provided multiple copies of different qualities.

2.2 SVC in our approach

Although scalability in video is not a new concept, the recent standardization acts as a catalyst to its acceptance into different market segments. In our approach, a layered approach to video coding similar to SVC is used to split video payload into 2 streams (Kiang et al, 2008). The base layer provides near-guaranteed, low resolution video whereas the enhancement layer provides the additional information required to improve the base-layer to a the low- and high-fidelity videos, it should be transmitted with a higher protection against corruption due to channel errors. Video coding in this work involves both AVC and a layered approached similar to SVC (based on AVC). For completeness, some crucial factors that make AVC a superior video coding standard are listed below:

- INTRA pictures and INTRA- regions within INTER pictures are coded with prediction from neighboring blocks. The prediction can be done in different directions, depending on the way the regions are textured (e.g. horizontal or vertical striped, checked boxed patterns etc.)
- Variable block-sizes are allowed in both INTRA- (16x16 and 4x4) and INTER-modes (16x16, 16x8, 8x16, 8x8 and other sub-8x8 blocks in multiple of 4).
- Motion estimation with possible resolution down to ¼- pixels.
- New integer-based 4x4 transform and options 8x8 transform.
- 6-tap filters for ½-pixel and bilinear filter for ¼-pixel luma-sample resolutions.
- Quantization based on logarithmic-scale.
- In-loop loop filter for removing blocking effects.

The SVC extension enables the AVC encoder to produce and base layer and incrementally improve the quality by providing differential information. Three types of scalability can be

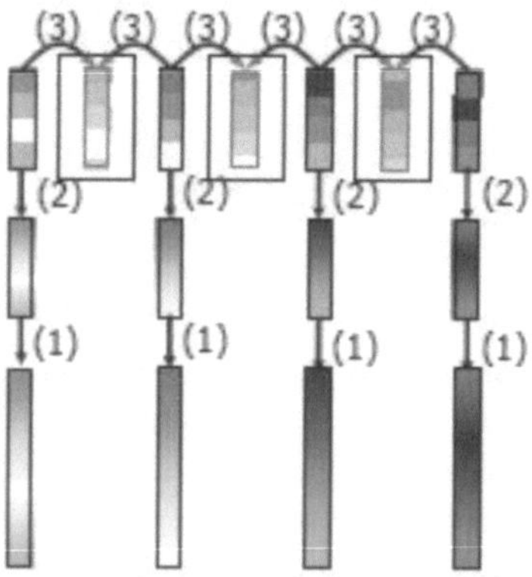

Fig. 1. Different scalabilities: (1) Spatial; (2) SNR (quality); (3) temporal (Kiang et al, 2008).

identified based on how the incremental information is used to improve quality. They are (1) spatial scalability (variation of picture resolution), (2) SNR scalability (variation of quality) and (3) temporal scalability (variation of frame rate). The 3 forms of scalability are illustrated in the figure 1. Different combinations of scalability can be used to adapt to the channel conditions.
In this approach, spatial scalability is issued to produce the enhanced video layer.

2.3 Fading hybrid satellite terrestrial networks

In mobile radio communications, the emitted electromagnetic waves often do not reach the receiving antenna directly due to obstacles blocking the line-of-sight path. In fact, the received waves are a superposition of waves coming from all directions due to reflection, diffraction, and scattering caused by buildings, trees, and other obstacles. This effect is known as *multipath propagation* (Pätzold, 2002). A typical scenario for the terrestrial mobile radio channel is shown in Figure 2. Due to the multipath propagation, the received signal consists of an infinite sum of attenuated, delayed, and phase-shifted replicas of the transmitted signal, each influencing each other. Depending on the phase of each partial wave, the superposition can be constructive or destructive. Apart from that, when transmitting digital signals, the form of the transmitted impulse can be distorted during transmission and often several individually distinguishable impulses occur at the receiver due to multipath propagation. This effect is called the *impulse dispersion*. The value of the impulse dispersion depends on the propagation delay differences and the amplitude relations of the partial waves. Multipath propagation in a frequency domain expresses itself in the non-ideal frequency response of the transfer function of the mobile radio channel. As a consequence, the channel distorts the frequency response characteristic of the transmitted signal. The distortions caused by multipath propagation are linear and have to be compensated for on the receiver side, for example, by an equalizer.

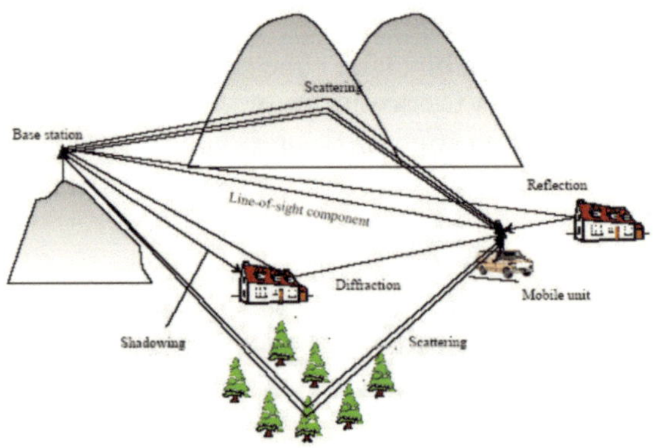

Fig. 2. Fading phenomena in a multipath wireless network (Pätzold, 2002).

Besides the multipath propagation, also the *Doppler effect* has a negative influence on the transmission characteristics of the mobile radio channel. Due to the movement of the mobile unit, the Doppler effect causes a frequency shift of each of the partial waves. Our analysis in this work considers the propagation environment in which a mobile-satellite system operates. The space between the transmitter and receiver is termed the channel. In a mobile satellite network, there are two types of channel to be considered: the mobile channel, between the mobile terminal and the satellite; and the fixed channel, between the fixed Earth station or gateway and the satellite. These two channels have very different characteristics, which need to be taken into account during the system design phase. The more critical of the two links is the mobile channel, since transmitter power, receiver gain and satellite visibility are restricted in comparison to the fixed-link.

By definition, the mobile terminal operates in a dynamic, often hostile environment in which propagation conditions are constantly changing. In a mobile's case, the local operational environment has a significant impact on the achievable quality of service (QoS). The different categories of mobile terminal, be it land, aeronautical or maritime, also each have their own distinctive channel characteristics that need to be considered. On the contrary, the fixed Earth station or gateway can be optimally located to guarantee visibility to the satellite at all times, reducing the effect of the local environment to a minimum. In this case, for frequencies above 10 GHz, natural phenomena, in particular rain, govern propagation impairments. Here, it is the local climatic variations that need to be taken into account. These very different environments translate into how the respective target link availabilities are specified for each channel. In the mobile-link, a service availability of 80–99% is usually targeted, whereas for the fixed-link, availabilities of 99.9–99.99% for the worst-month case can be specified.

Mobile satellite systems (Ibnkahla, 2005) are an essential part of the global communication infrastructure, providing a variety of services to several market segments, such as aeronautical, maritime, vehicular, and pedestrian. In particular, the two last cases are jointly referred to as the *land mobile satellite (LMS)* segment and constitute a very important field of application, development, and research, which has attracted the interest of numerous scientists in the last few decades. One fundamental characteristic of an LMS system is the necessity to be designed for integration with a terrestrial mobile network counterpart, in order to optimize the overall benefits from the point of view of the users and network operators. In essence, satellite and terrestrial mobile systems share the market segment along with many technical challenges and solutions, although they also have their own peculiar characteristics. A classic and central problem in any mobile communication system is that of modeling electromagnetic propagation characteristics. In LMS communications, as for terrestrial networks, multipath fading and shadowing are extremely important in determining the distribution of the received power level. In addition, it is common to also have a strong direct or specular component from the satellite to the user terminal, which is essential to close the link budget, and which modifies significantly the statistics with respect to terrestrial outdoor propagation In terms of *modeling the LMS propagation channel* (Lehner & Steingass, 2005), there are three basic alternatives: geometric analytic, statistical, and empirical. Generally speaking, the statistical modeling approach is less computationally intensive than a geometric analytic characterization, and is more phenomenological than an empirical regression model. The most remarkable advantage of statistical models is that they allow flexible and efficient performance predictions and system comparisons under different modulation, coding, and access schemes. For these reasons, in the first part of this chapter we focus our attention on a thorough review of statistical LMS propagation models, considering large- and small-scale fading, single-state and multistate models, first- and second-order characterization, and narrowband and wideband propagation.

2.4 Land mobile satellite channel

Both vehicular and pedestrian satellite radio communications are more commonly referred to as the Land Mobile Satellite (LMS) channel. LMS constitutes a very important field of application, development, and research, which has attracted the interest of numerous scientists in the last few decades (Ibnkahla, 2005). In the LMS channel, received signals are characterized by both coherent and incoherent components including direct signals, ground reflections, and other multipath components. The relative quality and intensity of each component varies dynamically in time (Mineweaver et al, 2001), based on various parameters. Shadowing of the satellite signal is caused by obstacles in the propagation path, such as buildings, bridges, and trees. Shadowed signals will suffer deep fading with substantial signal attenuation. The percentage of shadowed areas on the ground, as well as their geometric structure, strongly depend on the type of environment. For low satellite elevation the shadowed areas are larger than for high elevation. Especially for streets in urban and suburban areas, the percentage of signal shadowing also depends on the azimuth angle of the satellite (Lutz et al, 2000). Due to the movement of non-geostationary satellites, the geometric pattern of shadowed areas is changing with time. Similarly, the movement a mobile user translates the geometric pattern of shadowed areas into a time series of good and bad states. The mean duration of the good and bad state, respectively, depends on the type of environment, satellite elevation, and mobile user speed (Lutz et al, 2000). A popular and relatively robust two-state model for the description of the land-mobile satellite channel was introduced by (Lutz et al, 1991). The fading process is switched between Rician fading, representing unshadowed areas with high received signal power (good channel state) and Rayleigh/lognormal fading, representing areas with low received signal power (bad channel state) (Lutz, 1998). An important parameter of the model is the time-share of shadowing, *A*, representing the percentage of time when the channel is in the bad state, ranging from less that 1% on certain highways to 89% in some urban environments.

3. Joint source and channel estimation

The basic simulation involves video application encoding, channel simulation, video decoding and finally video quality analysis. Figure 3. below depicts the overall simulation system. For the SVC simulation, the base layer and enhancement layer are passed through separate channel simulators and are corrupted independently. For the AVC case, only channel is used as there is no enhancement layer. This model is used to simulate different channel conditions and a fixed set of iterations are used to collect statistical data. The following sections provide a detailed description of each functional block.

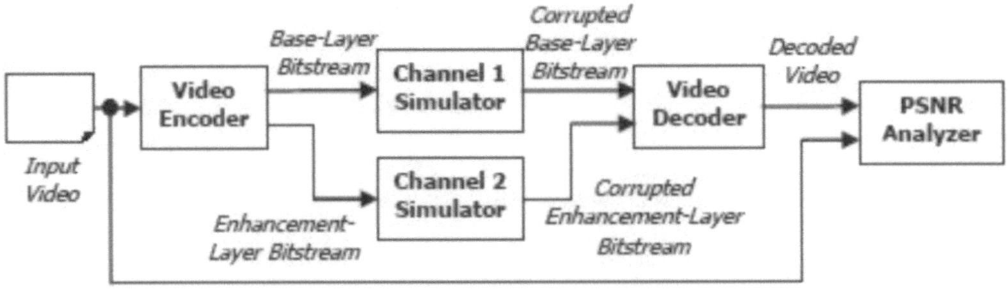

Fig. 3. Overall simulation system architecture (Kiang et al, 2008).

3.1 Video encoder

The 2-layer encoder system is illustrated in Figure 4. below:

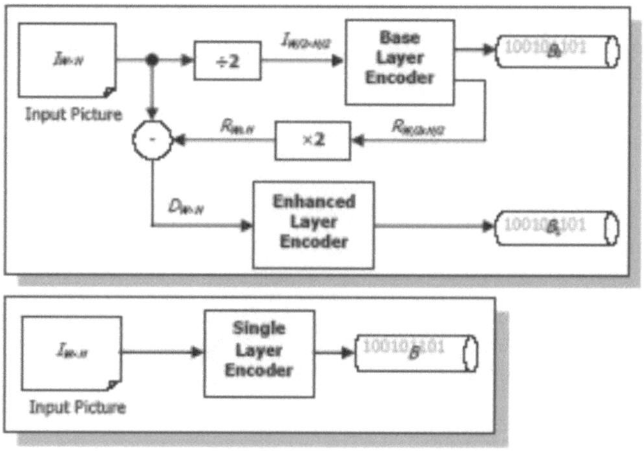

Fig. 4. Encoder architectures (top: 2-layer, bottom: single-layer) (Kiang et al, 2008).

Every input picture $IW\times H$, is decimated by 2 via a simple decimation filter. The resulting decimated picture $IW/2\times H/2$ serves as an input to the Base Layer AVC encoder to obtain the base layer bit-stream, $B0$. The reconstructed picture from the base layer encoder ($RW/2\times H/2$) is up-sampled by 2, and the resulting picture $RW\times H$. is subtracted pixel-by-pixel from the input picture $IW\times H$. The 'difference' picture ($DW\times H$)is the input to the enhancement layer encoder which produces enhancement layer bit-stream, $B1$. $B0$ and $B1$ is output to their respective channel simulators. For the case of a single layer encoder, only $B0$ is output. However, it should be noted that as a reference, we ensure that the bit-rate of the single layer encoder, R, is similar in value of the total bit rates of the base-layer $R0$ and enhancement-layer $R1$. That is:

$$R \approx R_0 + R_i \tag{1}$$

3.2 Channel simulator

The error model in the channel simulator is based on a Gilbert-Elliot 2-state Markov model. Based on field measurements, the Gilbert-Elliot model has been shown to approximate the land mobile satellite channel quite well (Schodorf, 2003).

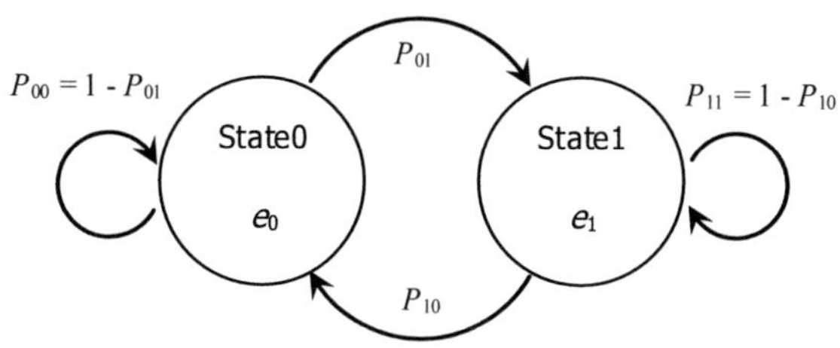

Fig. 5. Gilbert-Elliot channel model.

It assumes that a channel has a good and bad state, *S*0 and *S*1. Each state has a bit-error rate (BER), *e*0 and *e*1. The BERs in general depend on the frequency and coding scheme and on environmental conditions (e.g., number of paths between source and destination). The good state has a lower BER. The state transition probability *P*01 is the probability of the channel changing from *S*0 to *S*1. The four transition probabilities form the transition probability matrix:

$$\begin{bmatrix} P_{00} & P_{10} \\ P_{01} & P_{11} \end{bmatrix} = \begin{bmatrix} 1-P_{01} & P_{10} \\ P_{01} & 1-P_{10} \end{bmatrix} \quad (2)$$

Continually multiplying (2) will achieve a steady condition in which any 2-valued column vector, when premultiplied with the resulting matrix will achieve an invariant column vector; the value of this column vector denotes the long-term probability the *S*0 and *S*1 will occur respectively. This is the probability at which the states are likely to occur and is given by:

$$P_0 = \frac{P_{10}}{P_{01}+P_{10}} \quad ; \quad P_1 = \frac{P_{01}}{P_{01}+P_{10}} \quad (3)$$

This probability distribution { *P*0, *P*1 } is used to initialize the state at the beginning of each transmission packet. The transition probabilities (only two of which are independent) determine the mean duration and frequency of the error bursts. Thus the mean duration of periods of time spent in the bad state (i.e., the mean burst length) is given by (Carey, 1992):

$$D_b = \sum_{j=0}^{\infty} P_{11}^{j} = \frac{1}{1-P_{11}} = \frac{1}{P_{10}} \quad (4)$$

Similarly the mean duration of periods between bursts is (Carey, 1992):

$$D_g = \frac{1}{P_{01}} \quad (5)$$

Simulation of each packet is carried out independently. If an encoded video frame is smaller than the fixed packet size, the whole frame is transmitted within one packet. Else the frame is fragmented into fixed size packets (with the exception of the last packet) and transmitted independent of each other. Every bit within a packet is checked via a random number generated between 0 and 1.0. If the number is less than the BER value of the current state, the bit is deemed to be corrupted and the whole packet is discarded. A frame with one or more discarded fragment is also deemed to be lost and will not be decoded by the decoder. At every bit, the state is checked for transition based on the current transition probability. This description assumes transmission of data one bit at a time, so that the model's decision, in terms of state transition, occurs for each bit. In systems (e.g., using QAM) where a single transmitted symbol carries more than one bit, the decision occurs once per symbol (Carey, 1992). The following figure contains the flow chart of the process:

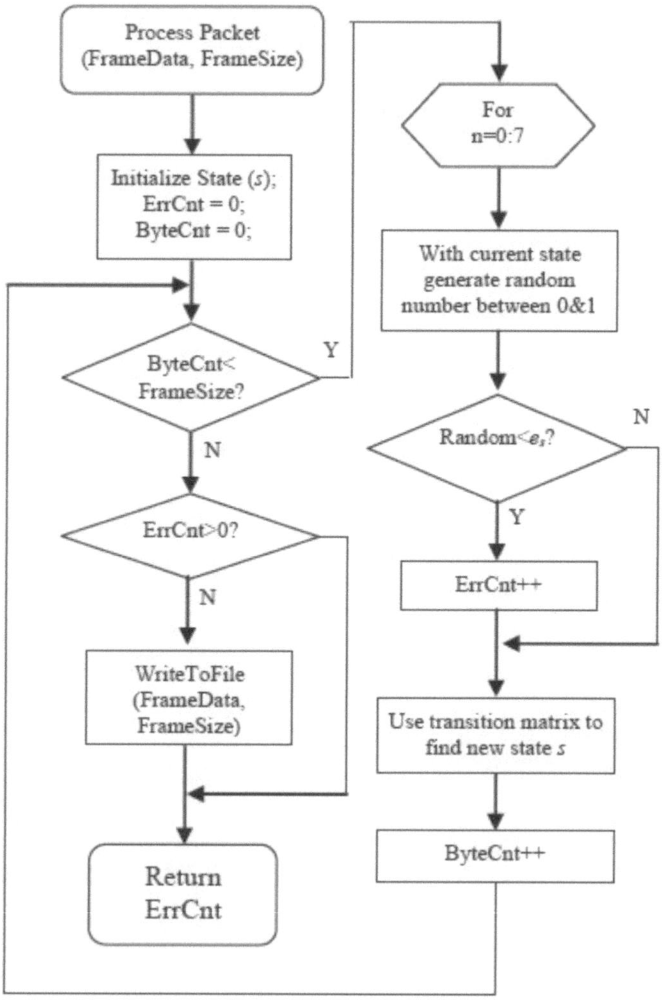

Fig. 6. Bit-based corruption and state-transition flow chart in channel simulator (Kiang et al, 2008).

3.3 Video decoder

The single-layer and 2-layer decoder architectures are shown in Figure 7. below:

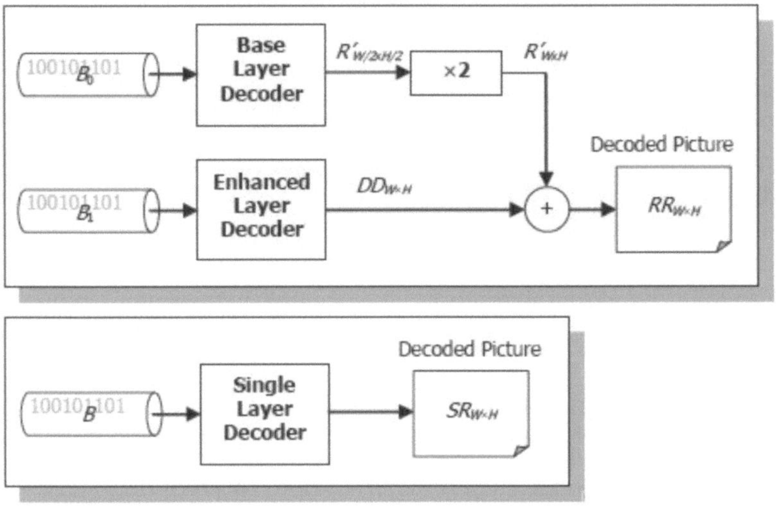

Fig. 7. Decoder architectures (top: 2-layer, bottom: single-layer) (Kiang et al, 2008).

It should be noted that in absence of errors in channel 1, $R'W{\times}H$ in Figure 4. and $R'W{\times}H$ in Figure 7. are identical. When channel 2 is corrupted, $RRW{\times}H = R'W{\times}H$. Hence, in the case of corruption in Channel 2, the 2-layer decoder can still output a relatively good quality video from channel 1. Similar case cannot be said of the single-layer system. Of course, the above claim is only true provided $B0$ in channel 1 is not corrupted. When the latter happens, the overall quality of the 2-layer system may be lower than that in the single layer system. However, chances of that happening are relatively small when $B0$ is more protected from errors than B. Furthermore, due to the fact that $R0 > R$, packet errors are much lower in $B0$ even if both are protected equally and the channel conditions are identical.

In the presence of packet errors, some decoded pictures may have been corrupted. Intra pictures (I) encoded separately whilst Predictive pictures (P) and bidirectional-predictive pictures (B) are predicted from previously decoded pictures and hence they bear dependencies with other pictures. Same can be said of the relationship between pictures from the base- and enhancement-layers. In spite of the numerous error concealment techniques available, this paper applies the simple method of repeating previously decoded picture.

In Figure 8., I*n* pictures are Intra pictures and P*nm* is the *m*th Predictive picture since *n*th Intra picture, which is reference from P*n*,*m*-1. E frames are enhancement picture based on the corresponding base-layer picture. The figure depicts which picture is displayed in the presence of packet losses.

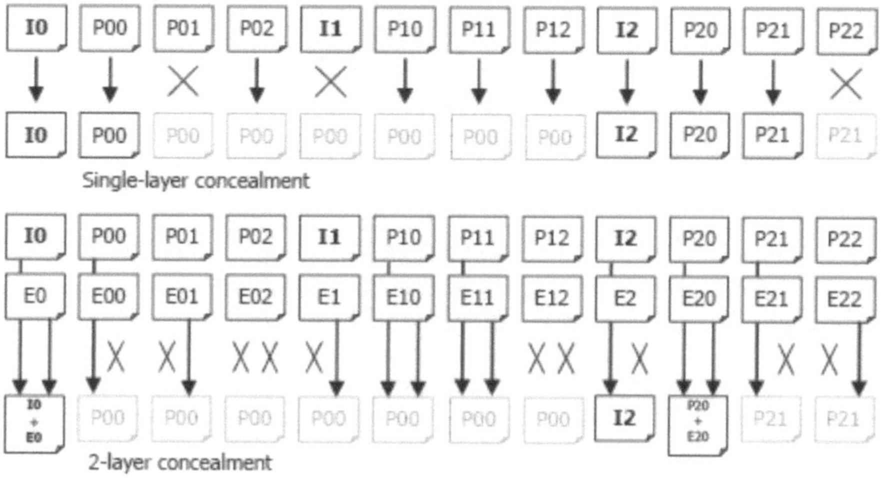

Fig. 8. Simple concealment based on "previous good picture" method (Kiang et al, 2008).

3.4 PSNR quality analyzer

We have decided to use the Peak Signal-to-Noise Ratio (PSNR) as a measurement of received video quality in the presence of losses. PSNR is traditionally used by video coding community to measure the fidelity of the compressed video with respect to its original input. Assuming a picture $I(x,y)$ of dimension $W\times H$ is compressed and the reconstructed picture after decompression is $R(x,y)$. The fidelity measure of PSNR between I and R is given as:

$$PSNR(I|R) = 10 \cdot \log_{10}\left(\frac{255^2 \times W \times H}{\sum_{x=0}^{W-1}\sum_{y=0}^{H-1} \left(I(x,y) - R(x,y)\right)^2} \right) \quad (6)$$

In our case, the PSNR value used in (6) of the current reconstructed picture is reference with the original input picture used by the encoder. Since the encoded bit-streams are corrupted by error channel some frames may have been lost. This results in the loss of synchronization between the input and the reconstructed pictures. This problem is circumvented by tagging each encoded picture with a sequence number. This number is traced within the decoder and the PSNR analyzer. Lost pictures will be substituted with a previous good picture. This is a typical scenario found in practical systems.

3.5 Simulation conditions - assumptions

The primary objective of the simulation phase is to evaluate the performance of the video coding techniques (i.e., single layered and two-layered), in different satellite channel quality conditions. Two experiments have been carried out in connection to the aforementioned objective:

1) A 2 Mbps single-layered video coded stream is transmitted over a satellite link. Different channel quality conditions are simulated by configuring the input parameters of the Gilbert-Elliot model, namely *P01, P10, e0,* and *e1*. The coded video sequence is then injected with errors and the performance of the coding scheme is recorded in terms of the PSNR objective quality metric.
2) In this experiment, the two-state Markov channel model characterizing the shadowing process (i.e., switching between good and bad channel states) was extended to two separate channels (Lutz et al, 1998). More specifically, two layered video coded streams, namely the base and enhancement layers (each one at 1Mbps), are transmitted over two separate satellite links. Enhancement layers encode additional information that, using the base layer as a starting point, can be used to reconstruct higher quality, resolution, or temporal versions of the video during the decode process. Without the base layer, no video reconstruction is possible. Simulated channel combinations are divided into two categories: the first one considers both channels under the same conditions in terms of BER, and the second one applies more protection to the base layer (lower BER) and less protection to the enhancement layer (higher BER). In our simulations, the following conditions and assumptions are made:

- Simulations have been carried out using the channel simulator fed with the well known Foreman video sequence.
- Packets affected by at least one (1) bit in error are discarded, and the decoder loses the entire payload they contain.
- Each video packet is small enough to fit into one communication frame. Each video coded stream has 250 4CIF (704x576) picture frames at 25 fps. Hence duration of 10 seconds is assumed.

The first frame of the coded video sequence always passes uncorrupted through the channel simulator – this is a valid assumption as in the long run, channels unable to transmit any frames at all are practically useless.

- For each channel, the video stream is broadcasted to 500 stationary users. This means that all users of a specific broadcasting session experience the same channel conditions.

Channels are emulated by configuring the input parameters of the Gilbert-Elliot channel simulator. In the simulated scenarios the value of P10 is set to a specific value, and the value of P01 varies so as to represent a range of channel conditions with different values of the average error probability (Masala et al, 2004) (BER in the "bad" state). The idea is to distinguish between various classes of users that lie within the satellite spot-beam coverage area.

4. Simulation results

To illustrate the multilayer video, we down-sample the 4CIF (704x576) sequence by 1/2 and encode the base layer with AVC. We then employ the spatial scalability to produce the enhancement layer. The simulation results concerning the objective quality vs. channel BER of both single- and two-layered coding schemes have been plotted in Figure 9. The three lines correspond to different channel quality conditions for: 1) single-layered video coding, 2) two-layered video coding with equal BER conditions for base and enhancement layers, and 3) two layered video coding with more protection applied to the base and less to the enhancement layers (BERbase< BERenhancement).

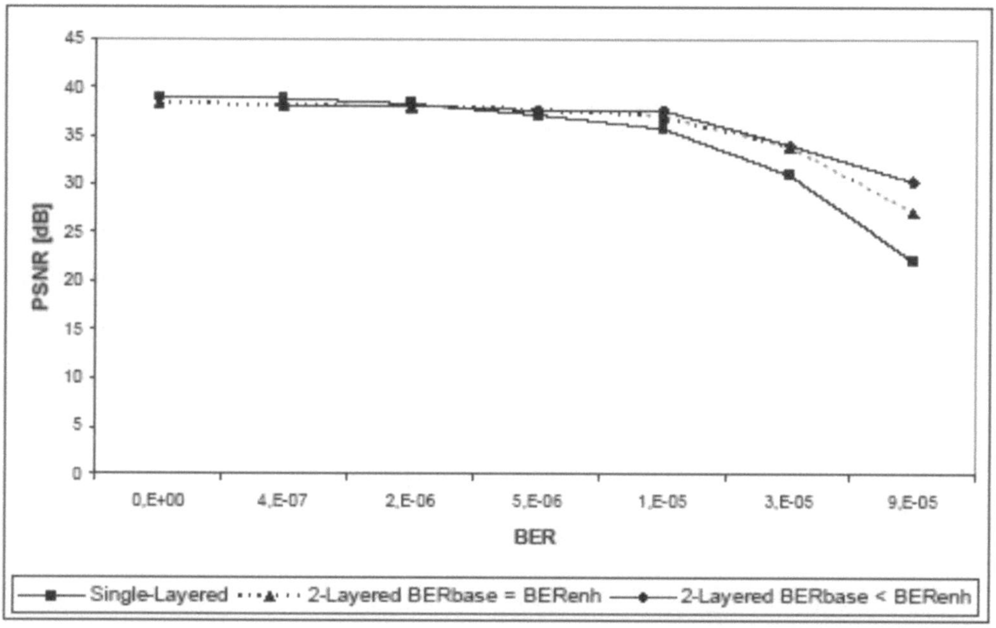

Fig. 9. PSNR (left axis) versus BER for transmission of a H.264 coded sequence. Three cases are reported: the first one refers to singe layered H.264 AVC encoded video, the second refers to a two-layered scalable video based on H.264 assuming that both channels fall under the same conditions in terms of BER. The third refers to a two-layered scalable where more protection is applied to the base layer and less protection to the enhancement layer, resulting in lower BER in the base layer.

The quality measure PSNR reflected in the plot is the 'aggregate' value, or the average value of all the simulations performed with the same channel conditions. The first point in the graph is derived from ideal (i.e., lossless) channel conditions (i.e., eb = 0), where the PSNR indicates maximum quality of the decoded video stream. As we move towards the right side of the graph, channel conditions tend to deteriorate, and the same happens to the quality of the received video stream. For low BERs and up to a specific transition point (situated around a value of 5x10-6), the single-layered scheme shows better performance than the two-layered case. This is mainly attributed to the fact that more overhead is introduced to the scalable scheme for error resilience purposes. The cross-point in general depends on the channel coding scheme, packetization, and also error concealment techniques. The superiority of the two-layered case is evident as harsher channel conditions start to dominate. The maximum observed difference in objective quality is about 5 dB (22.18 dB for single-layer and 27.15 dB for two-layered at 9x10-5). In the case of the unequal error protection, where the base layer has higher protection (e.g., channel block coding) than the enhancement layer, the quality of the decoded sequence is further enhanced as we move towards more unfavorable channel conditions. This shows that under severly bad channel conditions, higher protection should be given to the base layer in order for the 2-layer decoder to consistently produce a relatively good-quality video.

5. Conclusion and future directions

In this chapter, we tackled the multimedia (video) application over a fading satellite-terrestrial network by applying the scalable video coding over a land mobile system assuming a 2-state Markov model. By splitting video into 2-layers (Base/Enhanced) and transmitting them in 2 separate satellite channels, the overall quality measured in terms of aggregate PSNR value is improved over the single-layered scenario. Results from our 2-state Markov channel model support this claim. Moreover, applying higher protection to base layer at the expense of the enhancement layer further improves the aggregate viewer experience. However, the current system has the following room for improvements and will be covered in future work:

- More layers of SVC (including temporal scalability should be used.
- Research into optimal packetization and layering strategies should be looked into.
- Error concealment strategies in connection with the video coding scheme shall be investigated.
- Current channel model should be augmented by a good physical and MAC layer simulator.
- Interleaving and channel error protection schemes (e.g., parity bits, FEC codes) should be examined towards and end-to-end simulation.
- Simulations should include mobile users.

6. Acknowledgments

The author would like to express his sincere thanks to Mr. George Papadakis (now at Intracom Defense Electronics) and Dr. Chiew Tuan Kiang (Institute for Infocomm Research, A*STAR), for their major contribution to the relative research work.

7. References

Advanced Video Coding for Generic Audiovisual Services, ITU-T Rec. H.264 and ISO/IEC 14496-10 (MPEG-4 AVC) (2003). ITU-T and ISO/IEC JTC 1, Version 1.

Advanced Video Coding for Generic Audiovisual Services, ITU-T Rec. H.264 and ISO/IEC 14496-10 (MPEG-4 AVC) (2008). ITU-T and ISO/IEC JTC 1, Version 8 (including SVC extension).

Carey J. M. (1992). "Error Burst Detection", United States Patent 5416788, March 1992.

Celandroni N., Davoli F., Ferro E., Vingola S., Zappatore S., & Zinicola A. (2004). An Experimental Study on the Quality-of-Service of Video Encoded Sequences Over an Emulated Rain-Faded Satellite Channel, IEEE Journal on Selected Applications in Communications, Vol. 22, No. 2, pp. 229-237.

Chou P. A. & van der Schaar M. (2007). *Multimedia over IP and wireless networks: Networks, compression, networking, and systems*, Elsevier, ISBN-10: 0-12-088480-1.

Cycon H. L., Schmidt T. C., Wählisch M., Winken M., Marpe D., Hege G., & Palkow M. (2010). Optimized Temporal Scalability for H.264-based Codecs and its Application to Video Conferencing, *Proc. 14th IEEE International Symposium on Consumer Electronics (ISCE 2010)*, Braunschweig, Germany.

Ibnkahla M. (2005). *Signal Procesing for Mobile Communications Handbook*, CRC Presss.

Katsaggelos A. K., Zhai F., Eisenberg Y. & Berry R. (2005). Energy-efficient wireless video coding and delivery, *IEEE Wireless Communications,* pp. 24-30.

Kiang C.-T., Papadakis G. & Avdikos G. (2008). Satellite-Terrestrial Broadcasting/Multicasting Systems: Channel Modelling and Scalable Video Coding Approach, *Proc. of Signal Processing for Space Communications,* IEEE Xplore. pp. 1-6.

Lehner A. & Steingass A. (2005). The land mobile satellite navigation multipath channel -A statistical analysis *Proc. of the 2nd Workshop on Positioning, Navigation and Communication (WPNC'05) & 1st Ultra-Wideband Expert Talk (UET'05),* pp. 119-126.

Lutz E. (1998). Issues in satellite personal communication systems, *Wireless Networks Journal,* Vol. 4, No. 2, pp. 109-124.

Lutz E., Werner M. & Jahn A. (2000). *Satellite Systems for Personal and Broadband Communications,* Springer.

Lutz E., Cygan D., Dippold M., Dolainsky F., & Papke W. (1991). The land mobile satellite communication channel - recording, statistics, and channel model, *IEEE Transactions on Vehicular Technology,* Vol. 40, No. 2, pp. 375-386.

Mineweaver J. L., Stadler J. S., Tsao S. & Flanagan M. (2001). Improving TCP/IP performance for the land mobile satellite channel, *Proc. MILCOM 2001,* Vol. 1, pp. 711-718.

Marpe D., Wiegand T., & Sullivan G. J. (2006). The H.264/MPEG4 Advanced Video Coding Standard and its Applications, *IEEE Communications Magazine,* Vol. 44, No. 8, pp. 134-143.

Masala E., Chiasserini C. F., Meo M., & De Martin J. C. (2004). Real-Time Transmission of H.264 Video Over 802.11B-Based Wireless Ad Hoc Networks", In: H. Abut, J.H.L Hansen, and K. Takeda, "DSP for In-Vehicle and Mobile Systems", 1st Edition, Springer, pp. 193-208.

Ostermann J., Bormans J., List P., Marpe D., Narroschke M., Pereira F., Stockhammer T., & Wedi T. (2004), Video Coding with H.264 / AVC: Tools, Performance, and Complexity, *IEEE Circuits and Systems Magazine,* Vol. 4, No. 1, pp. 7-28.

Pätzold M, (2002). *Mobile Fading channels,* John Wiley and Sons, ISBN 0471 49549 2.

Radha H., van der Schaar M., & Karande S. (2004). Scalable Video TranScaling for the Wireless Internet, *EURASIP Journal of Applied Signal Processing* (JASP)—Special issue on Multimedia over IP and Wireless Networks, No. 2, pp. 265–279.

Richardson I.E.G. (2005). *H.264 and MPREG-4 Video Compression, Video Coding for the Next-Generation Multimedia,* John Wiley & Sons, Ltd.

Rupp M. (2009). *Video and Multimedia Transmissions over Cellular Networks: Analysis, Modelling and Optimization in Live 3G Mobile Communications,* John Wiley & Sons Ltd, ISBN 9780470699331.

Sattler C. Broadcast Mobile Convergence Forum: Prof. Dr C. Sattler: "Mobile broadcast business models - A state-of-the-art study", available at http://www.bmcoforum.org

Schwarz H., Marpe D. & Weigand T. (2007). Overview of the Scalable Video Coding Extension of H.264/AVC Standard, *IEEE Transcations on Circuits and Systems for Video Technology,* Vol. 17, No. 9. pp 1103-1120.

Schodorf J. (2003). EHF satellite communications on the move: Experimental results, *Technical Report 1087,* MIT Lincoln Laboratory.

Sheriff E. R. & Hu Y. F. (2001). *Mobile Satellite communication networks,* John Wiley and Sons, 2001, ISBN 0471 72047 X.

Simon M. K. & Alouini MS. (2005). *Digital Communications over fading channels,* Wiley-Interscience, Seond Edition, ISBN 0-471-64953-8.

Skinnemoen H. & Tork H. (2002). Standardization Activities within Broadband Multimedia, *IEEE International Communications Conference,* Vol. 5, pp. 3010-3014.

Wegner, S. (2003). H.264/AVC over IP, *IEEE Trans. On Circuits and Systems for Video Technology,* 13(7), pp. 645-657.

Winkler S. (2005). *Digital Video Quality,* John Wiley Sons, Ltd.

Zhai F., Eisenberg Y., Pappas T., Berry R. & Katsaggelos A. K. (2005). Joint source-channel coding and power adaptation for energy efficient wireless video communications, *Signal Processing: Image Communication,* pp. 371-387.

Part 2

Coding Strategy

3

Improved Intra Prediction of H.264/AVC

Mohammed Golam Sarwer and Q. M. Jonathan Wu
University of Windsor
Canada

1. Introduction

H.264/AVC is the latest international video coding standard developed by ITU-T Video Coding Expert Group and the ISO/IEC Moving Picture Expert Group, which provides gains in compression efficiency of about 40% compared to previous standards (ISO/IEC 14496-10, 2004, Weigand et al., 2003). New and advanced techniques are introduced in this new standard, such as intra prediction for I-frame encoding, multi-frame inter prediction, small block-size transform coding, context-adaptive binary arithmetic coding (CABAC), de-blocking filtering, etc. These advanced techniques offer approximately 40% bit rate saving for comparable perceptual quality relative to the performance of prior standards (Weigand ct al., 2003). H.264 intra prediction offers nine prediction modes for 4x4 luma blocks, nine prediction modes for 8x8 luma blocks and four prediction modes for 16 x 16 luma blocks. However, the rate-distortion (RD) performance of the intra frame coding is still lower than that of inter frame coding. Hence intra frame coding usually requires much larger bits than inter frame coding which results in buffer control difficulties and/or dropping of several frames after the intra frames in real-time video. Thus the development of an efficient intra coding technique is an important task for overall bit rate reduction and efficient streaming.
H.264/AVC uses rate-distortion optimization (RDO) technique to get the best coding mode out of nine prediction modes in terms of maximizing coding quality and minimizing bit rates. This means that the encoder has to code the video by exhaustively trying all of the nine mode combinations. The best mode is the one having the minimum rate-distortion (RD) cost. In order to compute RD cost for each mode, the same operation of forward and inverse transform/quantization and entropy coding is repetitively performed. All of these processing explains the high complexity of RD cost calculation. Therefore, computational complexity of encoder is increased drastically. Using nine prediction modes in intra 4x4 and 8x8 block unit for a 16x16 macroblock (MB) can reduce spatial redundancies, but it may needs a lot of overhead bits to represent the prediction mode of each 4x4 and 8x8 block. Fast intra mode decision algorithms were proposed to reduce the number of modes that needed calculation according to some criteria (Sarwer et al.,2008, Tsai et al., 2008, Kim, 2008, Pan et al., 2005, Yang et al., 2004). An intra mode bits skip (IBS) method based on adaptive single-multiple prediction is proposed in order to reduce not only the overhead mode bits but also computational cost of the encoder (Kim et al., 2010). If the neighbouring pixels of upper and left blocks are similar, only DC prediction is used and it does not need prediction mode bits or else nine prediction modes are computed. But the IBS method suffers with some drawbacks a) the reference pixels in up-right block are not considered for similarity

measure. If variance of reference pixels of upper and left blocks is very low, diagonal-down-left and vertical-left-modes are not similar to all other modes. But IBS considered all modes produce similar values. In this case, only DC prediction mode is not enough to maintain good PSNR and compression ratio. b) In IBS, each block is divided into two categories, either DC modes or all 9 modes. That's why; the performance improvement is not significant for very complex sequences such as Stefan because only small amount of blocks are predicted by DC mode for these types of sequences. c) also computational expensive square operations are used in variance and threshold calculation which is hardware inconvenient in both encoder and decoder side. In order to reduce the intra mode bits, methods for estimating the most probable mode (MPM) are presented in (Kim et al., 2008, Lee et al., 2009). But the performance improvements are not significant.

The rest of this chapter is organized as follows. Section 2 provides the review of intra-prediction method of H.264/AVC. In Section 3, we describe the proposed method. The experimental results are presented in Section 4. Finally, section 5 concludes the paper.

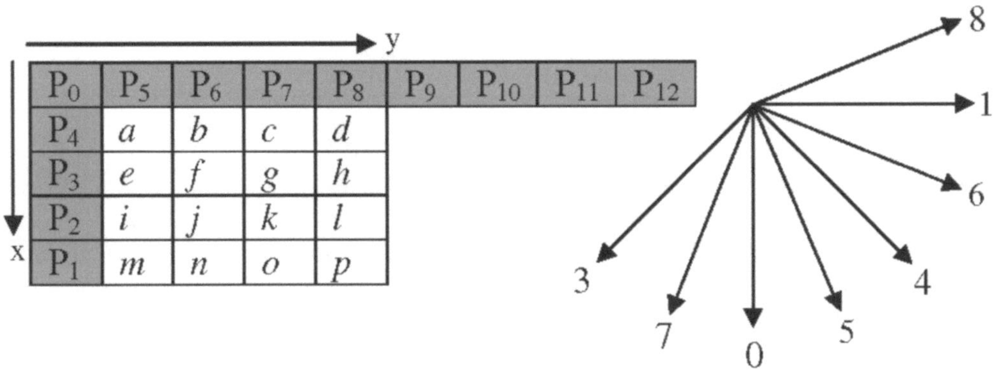

Fig. 1. Labelling and direction of intra prediction (4x4)

2. Intra prediction of H.264/AVC

In contrast to some previous standards (namely H.263+ and MPEG-4 Visual), where intra prediction has been conducted in the transform domain, intra prediction in H.264/AVC is always conducted in spatial domain, by referring to neighbouring samples of previously coded blocks which are to the left and/or above the block to be predicted. For the luma samples, intra prediction may be formed for each 4x4 block or for each 8x8 block or for a 16x16 macroblock. There are a total of 9 optional prediction modes for each 4x4 and 8x8 luma block; 4 optional modes for a 16x16 luma block. Similarly for chroma 8x8 block, another 4 prediction directions are used. The prediction block is defined using neighbouring pixels of reconstructed blocks. The prediction of a 4x4 block is computed based on the reconstructed samples labelled P_0-P_{12} as shown in Fig. 1 (a). The grey pixels (P_0-P_{12}) are reconstructed previously and considered as reference pixels of the current block. For correctness, 13 reference pixels of a 4x4 block are denoted by P_0 to P_{12} and pixels to be predicted are denoted by a to p. Mode 2 is called DC prediction in which all pixels (labelled a to p) are predicted by $(P_1+P_2+P_3+P_4+P_5+P_6+P_7+P_8)/8$. The remaining modes are defined according to the different directions as shown in Fig. 1 (b). To take the full advantages of all modes, the H.264/AVC encoder can determine the mode that meets the best RD tradeoff using RD optimization mode decision scheme. The best mode is the one having minimum rate-distortion cost and this cost is expressed as

$$J_{RD} = SSD + \lambda \cdot R \tag{1}$$

Where the SSD is the sum of squared difference between the original blocks **S** and the reconstructed block **C**, and it is expressed by

$$SSD = \sum_{i=1}^{4}\sum_{j=1}^{4}(s_{ij} - c_{ij})^2 \tag{2}$$

where s_{ij} and c_{ij} are the (i, j)th elements of the current original block **S** and the reconstructed block **C**. In equation (1), the R is the true bits needed to encode the block and λ is an exponential function of the quantization parameter (QP). A strong connection between the local Lagrangian multiplier and the QP was found experimentally as (Sullivan & Weigand, 1998)

$$\lambda = 0.85 \times 2^{(QP-12)/3} \tag{3}$$

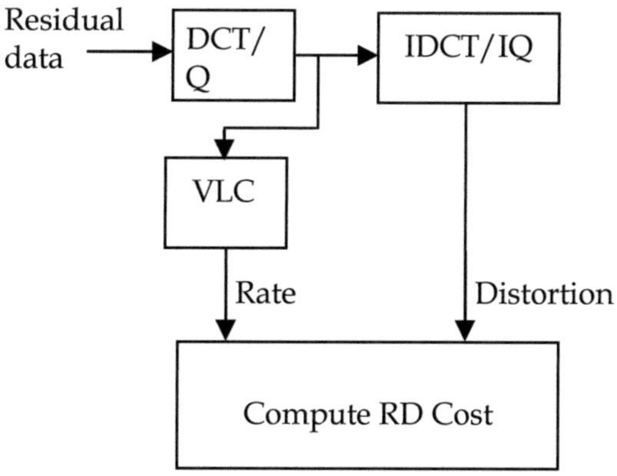

Fig. 2. Computation of RD cost

Fig. 2 shows the computational process of RD cost for 4x4 intra modes. As indicated in Fig. 2, in order to compute RD cost for each mode, same operation of forward and inverse transform/quantization and variable length coding is repetitively performed. All of these processing explains the high complexity of RD cost calculation.

After the best mode is acquired, it will be encoded into the compressed bit stream. The choice of intra prediction mode for each block must be signalled to the decoder and this could potentially require a large number of bits especially for 4x4 blocks due to the large number of modes. Hence the best mode is not directly encoded into the compressed bit stream. Intra modes for neighbouring blocks are highly correlated and for example if a previously-encoded block was predicted using mode 2, it is likely that the best mode for current block is also mode 2. To take advantage of this correlation, predictive coding is used to signal 4x4 intra modes.

For current 4x4 block, a mode is predicted based on the modes of upper and left blocks and this mode is defined as the most probable mode (MPM). In the standard of H.264/AVC, the

MPM is inferred according to the following rules; if the left neighbouring block or the up neighbouring block is unavailable, the MPM is set to 2(DC) or else the MPM is set to the minimum of the prediction mode of left neighbouring block and the up neighbouring block. For intra prediction according to each prediction mode, the encoder uses the condition of the MPM with a flag to signal the prediction mode. If the MPM is the same as the prediction mode, the flag is set to "1" and only one bit is needed to signal the prediction mode. When the MPM and prediction mode is different, the flag is set to "0" and additional 3 bits are required to signal the intra prediction mode. Encoder has to spend either 1or 4 bits to represent the intra mode.

N	N	N	N	N	N	N	N	N
N	*a*	*b*	*c*	*D*				
N	*e*	*f*	*g*	*H*				
N	*i*	*j*	*k*	*L*				
N	*m*	*n*	*o*	*P*				

Fig. 3. Case 1: All of the reference pixels have same value

3. Proposed improved 4x4 Intra prediction method

3.1 Adaptive number of modes

Although H.264/AVC intra coding method provides good compression ratio, owing to the use of nine prediction modes of 4x4 luma blocks, its computational complexity increases drastically. Using nine prediction modes in intra 4x4 block unit for a 16x16 MB can reduce the spatial redundancies, but it may needs a lot of overhead bits to represent the prediction mode of each 4x4 block. Based on the variation of neighboring pixels, the proposed method classifies a block as one of three different cases.

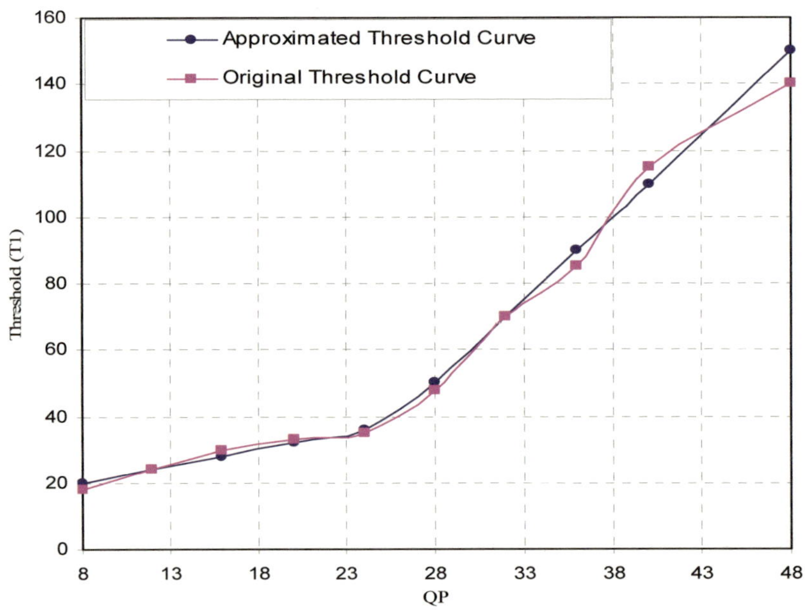

Fig. 4. Variation of threshold T_1 with QP

a. Case 1:

As shown in Fig. 3, if all of the reference pixels are same, the prediction values of nine directional predictions are same. In this case, it does not need to calculate the entire prediction modes. Only DC mode can be used, so that the prediction mode bit can be skipped. If variance σ_1 of all of the neighboring pixels is less than the threshold T_1, only DC prediction mode is used. The variance σ_1 and mean μ_1 is defined as,

$$\sigma_1 = \sum_{i=1}^{12} |P_i - \mu_1| \text{ , and } \mu_1 = \left\lfloor (\sum_{i=1}^{12} P_i) / 12 \right\rfloor \tag{4}$$

where P_i is the i-th reference pixel of Fig. 1(a) and μ_1 is the mean value of block boundary pixels. In order to set the threshold T_1, we have done several experiments for four different types of video sequences (*Mother & Daughter, Foreman, Bus* and *Stefan*) with CIF format at different QP values. *Mother & Daughter* represents simple and low motion video sequence. *Foreman* and *Bus* contain medium detail and represent medium motion video sequences. *Stefan* represents high detail and complex motion video sequence. By changing the threshold, we observed the RD performance and found that threshold T_1 is independent on the type of video sequence but depends on the QP values. Fig. 4 shows the variation of selected threshold T_1 with QP values. The original threshold curve is generated by averaging the threshold values of all four sequences for each QP. By using the polynomial fitting technique, the generalized threshold value T_1 is approximated as follows:

$$T_1 = \begin{cases} QP + 12 & \text{if } QP \le 24 \\ 5QP - 90 & \text{Otherwise} \end{cases} \tag{5}$$

b. Case 2:

As shown in Fig. 5, if all of the reference pixels of up and up-right blocks are same, vertical, diagonal-down-left, vertical-left, vertical-right and horizontal-down modes produce the same prediction value. That's why, in the proposed method we have chosen only vertical prediction mode from this group. If variance σ_2 of the neighboring pixels of up and up-right blocks is less than the threshold T_2, four prediction modes (vertical, horizontal, diagonal-down-right and horizontal-up) are used. Instead of using 3 bits of original encoder, each of four prediction modes is represented by 2 bits that is shown in Table 1. Threshold T_2 is selected as same way of T_1. T_2 also depends on the QP and better results were found at $T_2 = \lfloor (2T_1 / 3) \rfloor$. The variance σ_2 and mean μ_2 are defined as,

$$\sigma_2 = \sum_{i=5}^{12} |P_i - \mu_2| \text{, and } \mu_2 = \left\lfloor (\sum_{i=5}^{12} P_i) / 8 \right\rfloor \tag{6}$$

where μ_2 is the mean value of block boundary pixels of top and top-right blocks.

The flow diagram of the proposed method is presented in Fig. 6. The variance σ_1 and threshold T_1 are calculated at the start of the mode decision process and if the variance is less than the threshold ($\sigma_1 < T_1$) only DC prediction mode is used. In this case computational expensive RDO process is skipped and a lot of computations are saved. In

Mode	Binary representation
Vertical	00
Horizontal	01
Diagonal-down-right	10
Horizontal-up	11

Table 1. Binary representation of modes of case 2

P_0	N	N	N	N	N	N	N	N
P_4	*a*	*b*	*c*	*d*				
P_3	*e*	*f*	*g*	*h*				
P_2	*i*	*j*	*k*	*l*				
P_1	*m*	*n*	*o*	*p*				

Fig. 5. Case 2: The reference pixels of up and up-right blocks have same value

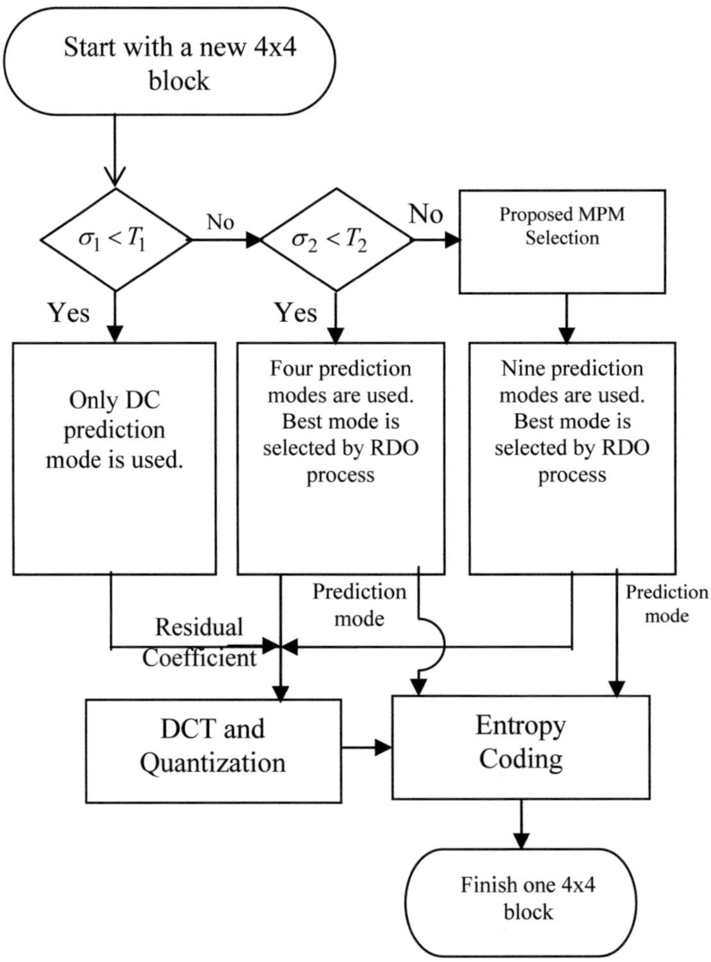

Fig. 6. Flow diagram of proposed method

addition, no bit is necessary to represent intra prediction mode because only one mode is used. In the decoder side, if $\sigma_1 < T_1$, decoder understands that DC prediction mode is the best prediction mode. On the other hand, if $\sigma_1 < T_1$ is not satisfied, encoder calculates the variance σ_2 and threshold T_2. If $\sigma_2 < T_2$, vertical, horizontal, diagonal-down-right and horizontal-up modes are used as candidate modes in RDO process. A substantial saving in computations is achieved using 4 prediction modes instead of 9 modes of the original RDO process. The best mode is the mode which has the smallest rate-distortion cost. In order to represent the best mode, 2 bits are sent to the decoder and Table 1 shows the four prediction modes with corresponding binary representations. As shown in Table 1, if the diagonal-down-right mode is selected as the best mode, the encoder sends "10" to the decoder. In this category, only 2 bits are used to represent the intra prediction mode whereas 3 bits are used in the original encoder. Consequently a large number of intra prediction mode bits are saved.

If $\sigma_2 < T_2$ is not satisfied, nine prediction modes are used as the candidate mode and one of them is selected through the RDO process, as in H.264/AVC. In this case, based on the MPM either 1 or 4 bits are allocated to represent the intra prediction mode. The new prediction mode numbers are recorded and compared against H.264/AVC in Table 2. Since diagonal-down-left, vertical-right, horizontal-down and vertical-left predictions modes are not utilized in the previous cases, the probability of these modes are high in this case and thus these modes are defined as small numbers. Similarly mode numbers for other modes are higher value.

From some simulations, we have found that a significant number of blocks still calculate 9 prediction modes. If the MPM is the best mode, only 1 bit is used; otherwise 4 bits are required to represent the prediction mode. Therefore, if we can develop a more accurate method to estimate the MPM, a significant percentage of blocks will use only 1 bit for mode information.

Mode	Mode number H.264/AVC	Mode number Proposed
Diagonal-down-left	3	0
Vertical-right	5	1
Horizontal-down	6	2
Vertical-left	7	3
Vertical	0	4
Horizontal	1	5
DC	2	6
Diagonal-down-right	4	7
Horizontal-up	8	8

Table 2. Prediction modes recording of the proposed method

3.2 Selection of Most Probable Mode (MPM)

Natural video sequences contain a lot of edges and these edges are usually continuous thus indicating that the prediction direction of neighboring blocks and that of current block is also continuous. Let us consider that X is the current block as shown in Fig. 7 and four neighboring blocks are denoted as A, B, C and D. So if the upper block (B) is encoded with vertical mode, the mode of current block is more likely to be vertical mode. Similarly, if mode of up-left block (C) is diagonal-down-left mode (mode 4 in Fig. 1(b)), then the mode of the current block is more likely to be diagonal-down-left mode. If the direction from the neighboring block to the current block is identical to the prediction mode direction of the neighboring block, there is a high possibility that the best prediction mode of the current block is also identical to the prediction mode direction. Based on this idea, the weight of the proposed MPM method is proportional to the absolute difference between block direction and mode directions. The mode direction (θ_m) is calculated based on the direction of Fig. 1 (b) and tabulated in Table 3.

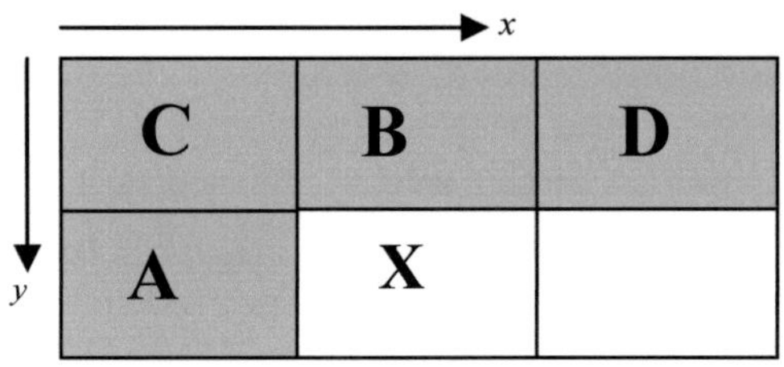

Fig. 7. Current and neighbouring blocks

Mode	Direction
Vertical	$\pi / 2$
Horizontal	0
Diagonal-down-left	$3\pi / 4$
Diagonal-down-right	$\pi / 4$
Vertical- right	$3\pi / 8$
Horizontal-down	$\pi / 8$
Vertical-left	$5\pi / 8$
Horizontal-up	$-\pi / 8$

Table 3. Mode directions (θ_m)

The block direction (θ_B) and block distance (D_B) are calculated by the following set of equations.

$$\theta_B = \tan^{-1} \frac{y_c - y_n}{x_c - x_n} \tag{7}$$

$$D_B = |y_c - y_n| + |x_c - x_n| \tag{8}$$

Where, (x_c, y_c) and (x_n, y_n) are the position of current and neighboring block, respectively. The mode of the neighboring block is denoted as M_n . Weight is also dependent on the distance between the current block and neighboring block. If the distance between the current and neighboring block is higher, the correlation between the blocks is lower and weight is also low. Based on these observations weight of neighboring mode M_n is calculated as

$$W(M_n) = \min[0, \frac{\alpha}{D_B} - \beta|\theta_B - \theta_m|] \quad (9)$$

where α and β are the proportionally constant and min(P,Q) means minimum value between P and Q. Based on simulation, α and β are selected as 6 and $\frac{8}{\pi}$.
Instead of using two neighboring blocks A and B in the original H.264/AVC encoder, the proposed method utilizes the prediction mode used in the four neighboring blocks (A, B, C and D). The weight of the prediction mode of each neighboring block is calculated and updated by adding the weight of same mode. Since, DC has no unified direction, if the neighboring mode is DC, the weight corresponding to this block is set to 0. The weight of each prediction mode is counted up and find out the mode with highest weight $W_{\max}$. If the maximum weight $W_{\max}$ is very low, it seems that there is no continuation of edges. In this case, possibility of DC prediction mode to be the best mode is higher. If maximum weight $W_{\max}$ is less than a threshold T_{MPM}, the MPM is the DC mode; otherwise the MPM is the mode with maximum weight $W_{\max}$. Following is the step by step algorithm of the proposed method.

Step 1: Initialize weight (W) of each mode to zero.

Step 2:

For each of the four neighboring blocks (A, B, C and D),

If neighboring mode $M_n = DC$, $W(M_n) \mathrel{+}= 0$.

Otherwise

a. Calculate block direction, θ_B and D_B

b. Find mode direction of the neighboring mode M_n from Table 3.

c. Calculate weight of neighboring mode:

$$W(M_n) \mathrel{+}= \min[0, \frac{\alpha}{D_B} - \beta|\theta_B - \theta_m|]$$

End of block

Step 3: Find the maximum weight $W_{\max}$ and the mode that has maximum weight.

Step 4: If maximum weight $W_{\max}$ is less than T_{MPM}, the most probable mode is the DC mode; otherwise MPM is the mode with maximum weight $W_{\max}$.

In order to find the threshold T_{MPM}, we have done some simulations. Four different types of video sequences (*Mother & Daughter, Foreman, Bus* and *Stefan*) were encoded by changing the value of T_{MPM} from 1 to 10 and RD performances were observed. Better results were found at $T_{MPM} = 5$. In order to reduce the computation of (9), α / D_B and θ_B of neighboring blocks A, B, C and D are pre-calculated and stored in a Table. For example, α / D_B is 6 for block A and B, and equal to 3 for block C and D. θ_B is equal to 0, $\pi/2$, $\pi/4$, and $-\pi/4$ for block A, B, C and D, respectively.

4. Simulation results

To evaluate the performance of the proposed method, JM 12.4 (JM reference software) reference software is used in simulation. Different types of video sequences with different resolutions are used as test materials. A group of experiments were carried out on the test sequences with different quantization parameters (QPs). All simulations are conducted under Windows Vista operating system, with Pentium 4 2.2 G CPU and 1 G RAM. Simulation conditions are (a) QPs are 28, 36, 40, 44 (b) entropy coding: CABAC (c) RDO on (d) frame rate: 30 fps, (e) only 4x4 mode is used and (f) number of frames: 100. The comparison results are produced and tabulated based on the average difference in the total encoding (ΔT_1 %), the average PSNR differences ($\Delta PSNR$), and the average bit rate difference ($\Delta R\%$). PSNR and bit rate differences are calculated according to the numerical averages between RD curves derived from original and proposed algorithm, respectively. The detail procedure to calculate these differences can be found in (Bjontegaard, 2001). The encoding (ΔT %) complexity is measured as follows

$$\Delta T\% = \frac{T_{original} - T_{proposed}}{T_{original}} \times 100 \tag{10}$$

where, $T_{original}$ denotes the total encoding time of the JM 12.4 encoder and $T_{proposed}$ is total encoding time of the encoder with proposed method.

Sequence	IBS (Kim et al., 2010)		Proposed	
	Δ PSNR	Δ Rate%	Δ PSNR	Δ Rate%
Grand Mother (QCIF)	0.37	-15.4	0.42	-17.0
Salesman (QCIF)	0.32	-12.9	0.40	-14.6
Stefan (QCIF)	0.10	-2.7	0.20	-6.0
Container (QCIF)	0.09	-3.1	0.18	-6.7
Car phone (QCIF)	0.66	-18.4	0.83	-23.8
Silent (CIF)	0.35	-15.4	0.42	-18.0
Bus (CIF)	0.11	-3.8	0.15	-4.1
Hall (CIF)	0.32	-8.6	0.42	-11.3
Mobile Calendar (HD-1280x720)	0.19	-6.8	0.27	-9.8
Average	0.28	-9.7	0.37	-12.4

Table 4. PSNR and bit rate comparison

	IBS (Kim et al., 2010) ΔT %	Proposed ΔT %
Grand Mother (QCIF)	39.7	49.1
Salesman (QCIF)	31.2	35.7
Stefan (QCIF)	17.9	22.6
Container (QCIF)	31.3	37.9
Car phone (QCIF)	33.8	42.0
Silent (CIF)	35.8	43.0
Bus (CIF)	16.4	28.8
Hall (CIF)	38.8	45.0
Mobile Calendar (HD-1280x720)	27.6	33.0
Average	30.3	37.5

Table 5. Complexity comparison of proposed method

The RD performance comparisons are presented in Table 4. In case of the IBS method, the average PSNR improvement is about 0.28 dB and average bit rate reduction is about 9.7%. Whereas in our proposed method, the average PSNR improvement is about 0.37 db and average bit rate reduction is about 12.4%. Out of all video sequences listed in Table 4, the best performance improvement was accomplished for *Car Phone* video sequence; bit rate reduction is about 23.8% and PSNR improvement is 0.83 dB. This is understandable because most of the blocks of this sequence are classified as either case 1 or case 2. The PSNR improvement and bit rate reduction of worst case (*Bus*) is 0.15 dB and 4.14%, respectively.

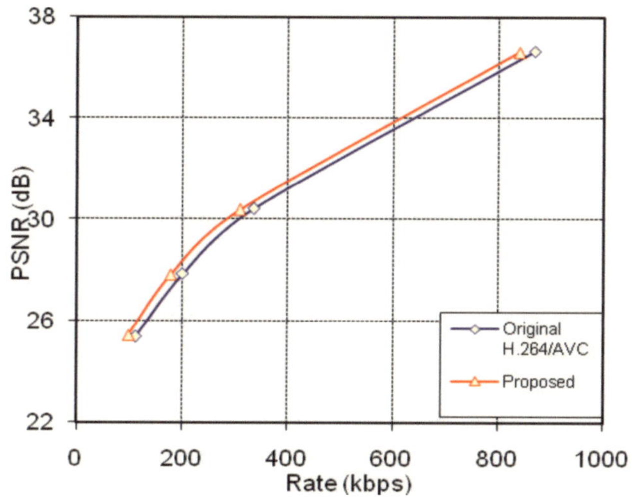

Fig. 8 (a). RD curves of original and proposed method (Salesman QCIF)

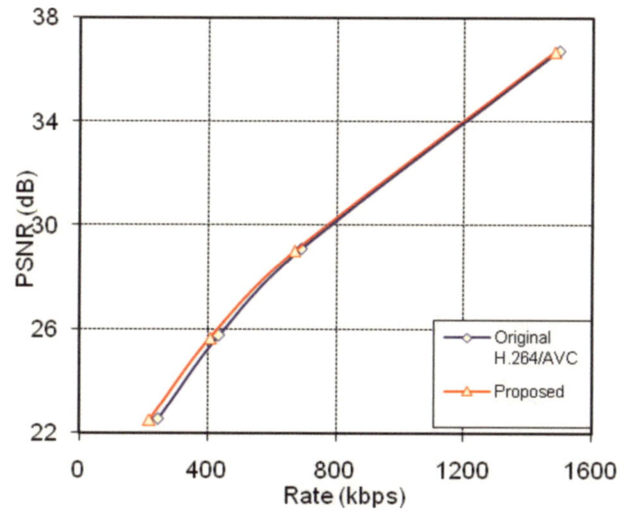

Fig. 8 (b). RD curves of original and proposed method (Stefan QCIF)

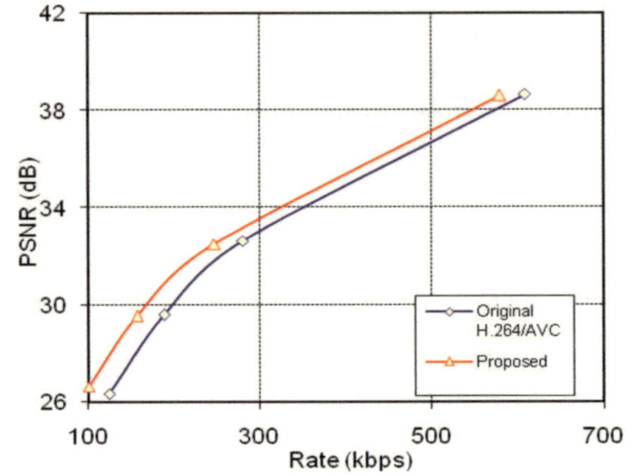

Fig. 8 (c). RD curves of original and proposed method (Car phone QCIF)

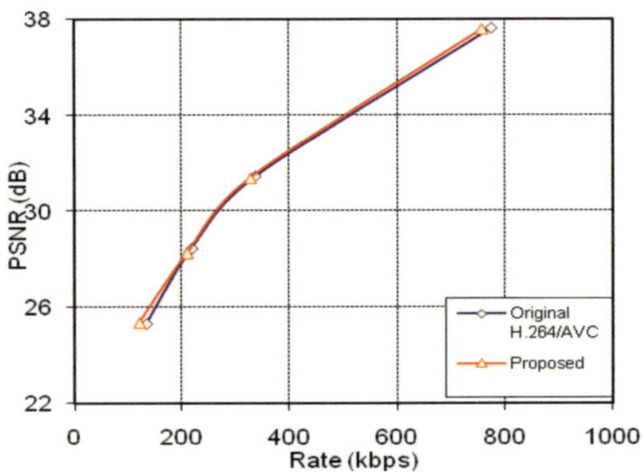

Fig. 8 (d). RD curves of original and proposed method (Container QCIF)

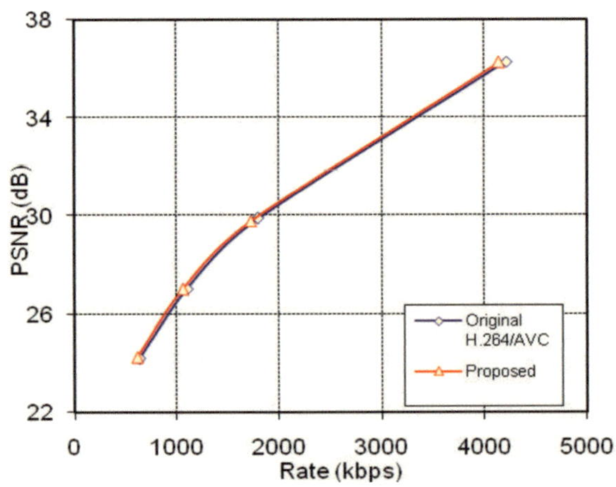

Fig. 8 (e). RD curves of original and proposed method (Bus CIF)

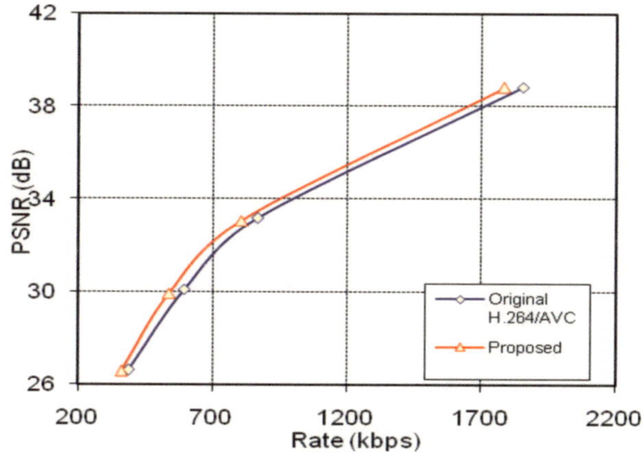

Fig. 8 (f). RD curves of original and proposed method (Hall CIF)

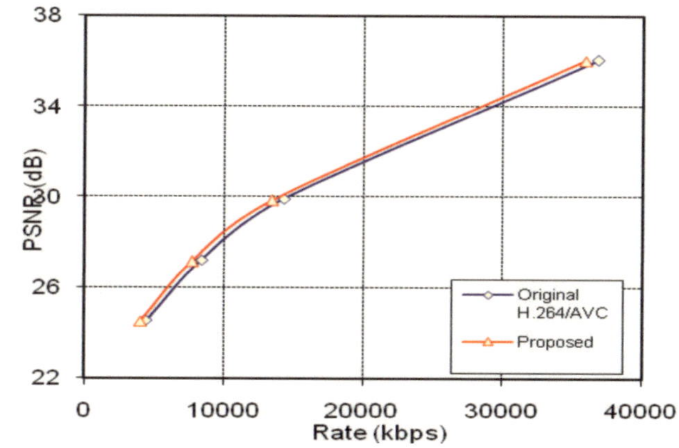

Fig. 8 (g). RD curves of original and proposed method (Mobile Calendar HD)

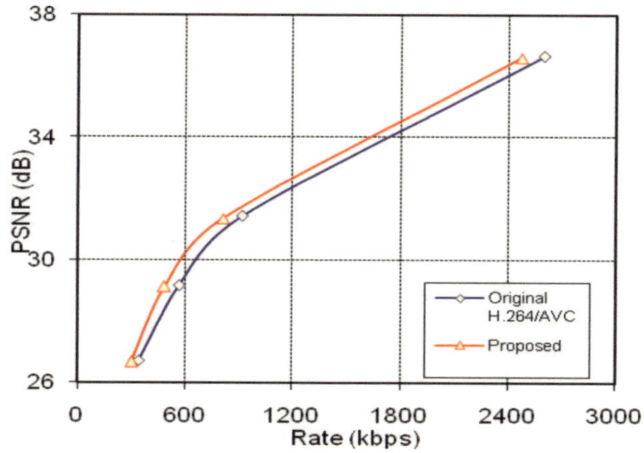

Fig. 8 (h). RD curves of original and proposed method (Silent CIF)

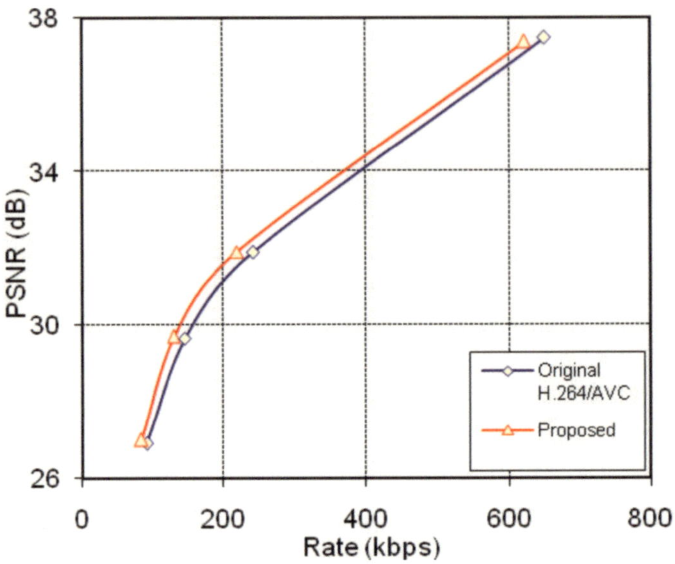

Fig. 8 (i). RD curves of original and proposed method (Grand Mother QCIF)

The computational reduction realized with our proposed method is tabulated in Table 5. Although the proposed method introduces some overhead calculation to select the MPM, the overall computation reductions is still significant and about 7% faster than the method in [6]. The proposed method saves about 37.5% computation of original H.264/AVC intra coder. . The rate-distortion (RD) curves of six different types of video sequences are plotted in Fig. 8. It is shown that RD curve of our proposed method is always superior to that of the original H.264/AVC encoder.

5. Conclusion

In this paper, an intra mode bit rate reduction scheme for representing the intra prediction mode is described. H.264/AVC intra encoder uses nine prediction modes in 4x4 block unit to reduce the spatial redundancies. Too many intra modes not only increase the encoder complexity but also increase the number of overhead bits. In the proposed method, the numbers of prediction modes for each 4x4 block are selected adaptively. Based on the similarities of the reference pixels, each block is classified as one of three categories. This paper also estimates the most probable mode (MPM) from the prediction mode direction of neighbouring blocks which have different weights according to their positions. Experimental results confirm that the proposed method saves 12.4% bit rate, improves the video quality by 0.37 dB on average, and requires 37% less computations than H.264/AVC intra coder. The proposed method not only improves the RD performance but also reduces the computational complexity of H.264/AVC intra coder.

6. References

Bjontegaard G. (2001) Calculation of average PSNR differences between RD-curves, presented at the *13th VCEG-M33 Meeting*, Austin, TX, April 2001.

ISO/IEC 14496-10 (2004), Information Technology-Coding of audio-visual objects-Part: 10: *Advanced Video Coding. ISO/IEC JTC1/SC29/WG11*

JM reference software 12.4,
http://iphome.hhi.de/suehring/tml/download/old_jm/jm12.4.zip

Kim B. G. (2008) Fast selective intra mode search algorithm based on adaptive thresholding scheme for H.264/AVC encoding. *IEEE Transaction on Circuits and Systems for Video Technology*, vol. 18, no. 1, pp. 127-133, ISSN: 1051-8215.

Kim D. Y., Kim D. K., and Lee Y. L., (2008) A New Method for Estimating Intra Prediction Mode in H.264/AVC, *IEICE Transactions on Fundamentals of Electronics, Communications and Computer Sciences*, vol. E91-A, pp. 1529-1532, ISSN: 1745-1337.

Kim D. Y., Han K. H. , and Lee Y. L. (2010), Adaptive single-multiple prediction of H.264/AVC intra coding. , *IEEE Transaction on Circuits and Systems for Video Technology*, vol. 20, no. 4, pp. 610-615, ISSN: 1051-8215.

Lee J. , Choi J. S. , Hong J. , and Choi H. (2009) Intra-mixture Prediction Mode and Enhanced Most Probable Mode Estimation for Intra Coding in H.264/AVC, *Fifth International Joint Conference on INC, IMS and IDC*, pp. 1619-1622, Seoul Korea, August 2009.

Pan F. , Lin X., Rahardja S. , Lim K. P., Li Z. G., Wu D., and Wu S. (2005). Fast Mode Decision Algorithm for Intra-prediction in H.264/AVC Video Coding. *IEEE Transaction on Circuits and Systems for Video Technology*, vol. 15, no. 7, pp-813-822, July 2005, ISSN: 1051-8215.

Sarwer M. G. , Po. L. M., and Wu. J. (2008) Fast Sum of Absolute Transformed Difference based 4x4 Intra Mode Decision of H.264/AVC Video Coding Standard, *Elsevier Journal of Signal Processing: Image Communications*, vol. 23, No. 8, pp. 571-580, ISSN: 0923-5965.

Sullivan G. J., and Wiegand T. (1998) Rate-distortion optimization for video compression. *IEEE Signal Processing Magazine*, vol. 15, pp. 74-90, ISSN: 1053-5888.

Tsai A. C. , Paul A. , Wang, J. C, and Wang J. F. (2008) Intensity gradient technique for efficient Intra prediction in H.264/AVC, *IEEE Transaction on Circuits and Systems for Video Technology*, vol. 18, no. 5, pp. 694-698, ISSN: 1051-8215.

Weigand T., Sullivan, G. Bjontegaard, and G.,Luthra (2003), A. Overview of H.264/AVC Video Coding Standard. IEEE Transaction on Circuits and Systems for Video Technology. vol. 13, No. 7, pp 560-576, ISSN: 1051-8215.

Wiegand T., Schwarz H. , Joch A., Kossentini F., and Sullivan G. J. (2003) Rate-constrained coder control and comparison of video coding standards. IEEE Transaction on Circuits and Systems for Video Technology . vol 13, no. 7, pp.688-703, ISSN: 1051-8215.

Yang C. L. , Po L. M., and Lam W. H. (2004) A fast H.264 Intra Prediction algorithm using Macroblock Properties," *Proceedings of International Conference on Image Processing* ,pp 461-464, Singapore, October, 2004, IEEE.

4

Efficient Scalable Video Coding Based on Matching Pursuits

Jian-Liang Lin[1] and Wen-Liang Hwang[2]
[1]*MediaTek Inc.*
[2]*Institute of Information Science, Academia Sinica, Taiwan and the Department of Information Management at Kainan University, Taiwan*

1. Introduction

Efficient encoding of motion residuals is essential for low-delay video applications in which videos are encoded by hybrid motion compensation and a residual encoding structure. Current standard video coding systems use hybrid motion compensation and the discrete cosine transform (DCT), where the number of bases needed to encode a residual block is the same as the number of the pixels in the block. An encoded frame is predicted from its previous reconstructed frame, and a residual image is then encoded by a non-redundant transformation, such as the DCT, or an approximation of the DCT using integer coefficients.

As well as nonredundant transformation, a frame-based technique called matching pursuit (MP) has been proposed to encode motion residual images. Mallat and Zhang (Mallat & Zhang, 1993) were the first to propose a matching pursuit algorithm that decomposes a signal into a linear combination of bases within an overcomplete dictionary. Vetterli and Kalker have translated motion compensation and DCT hybrid video coding into a matching pursuit technique, and encoded frames by the matching pursuit algorithm and a dictionary composed of motion blocks and DCT bases (Vetterli & Kalker, 1994). In (Neff & Zakhor, 1997), Neff and Zakhor show that using a matching pursuit algorithm to encode motion residual images achieves a better performance than a DCT-based algorithm in terms of PSNR and perceptual quality at very low bit rates. The results in (Lin et al., 2005) also demonstrate that the matching pursuit FGS coding scheme performs better than MPEG-4 FGS at very low bit rates. Unlike a transform-based decoder, a matching pursuit decoder does not require an inverse transform; therefore, it is less complex. In a transform-based decoder, loop filtering and post processing are usually applied at very low bit rates to remove blocking and ringing artifacts, whereas a matching pursuit decoder can achieve comparable quality without such filtering and processing (Neff et al., 1998). Because the matching pursuit algorithm is a data-dependent frame-based representation, a matching pursuit video coding technique cannot be directly translated from conventional transform-based approaches. We must therefore develop a new matching pursuit video coding technique that can deal with quantization noise in the matching pursuit algorithm (Neff & Zakhor, Sept. 2000; Vleeschouwer & Zakhor, 2002), multiple description coding for reliable transmission (Tang & Zakhor, 2002), scalable bit-stream generation (Al-Shaykh et al., 1999; Vleeschouwer & Macq, 2000; Rose & Regunathan, 2001), and dictionary learning and adaptation (Engan et al., 2000).

In real video communication applications over wire and wireless networks, channel capacity varies constantly, so scalability at the bit-stream level is an important feature of multimedia communications. It is necessary, therefore, to develop a video coding and transmission technique that encodes a video sequence once, and allows different clients to decode the video by receiving only part of the bit-stream, according to their available bandwidth. Depending on the scalability specification, a scalable video coding scheme can support scalability either in the frame rate, video resolution, SNR quality, or a hybrid of these. Based on a hybrid motion compensation and bit-plane DCT coding scheme, MPEG-4 scalable video coding is proposed as a means of achieving fine-grain scalability (Li, 2001). The drawback of this approach is that, to avoid the drifting problem, it only uses the information of the base layer to predict the next frame; therefore, it yields lower coding efficiency than non-scalable video coding schemes at the same bit-rate. Recently, several approaches based on motion-compensated temporal filtering (MCTF) have been proposed to improve coding efficiency and solve the drifting problem encountered in closed-loop hybrid coding systems (Ohm et al., 2004; M10569/S03, 2004). Although, the hybrid motion-compensation and residual encoding scheme may not be the best solution for video scalability, it is simple and only incurs a small delay in performing motion-compensation compared to a scalable video coding scheme based on MCTF. Even so, current approaches based on hybrid motion compensation and residual encoding schemes using the DCT are still inefficient, especially at low bit-rates.

Scalable video coding schemes based on matching pursuit have been proposed as a means of achieving scalability (Al-Shaykh et al., 1999; Vleeschouwer & Macq, 2000). In (Al-Shaykh et al., 1999), scalability is supported by successively en-coding groups of atoms; thus, it is constricted by the number of atoms determined by the encoder. Generally, providing video coding with scalability degrades the coding performance. A two-layer video coding scheme achieves better coding efficiency at the expense of coarser scalability. In a two-layer system, the base layer gives a lower quality of coded video, while the enhancement layer gives a higher quality; moreover, the information of the enhancement layer is used in motion-compensation to achieve better coding efficiency.

2. Atom search

As mentioned in the previous section, matching pursuit (MP) is a greedy algorithm that decomposes a signal into a linear combination of bases within an overcomplete dictionary. The matching pursuit algorithm is usually only approximated due to its massive computational complexity.

An MP-based codec yields a better PSNR and perceptual quality than a transform-based codec, and its decoder is simpler (Neff et al., 1998). However, it cannot be used in applications that require real time bi-directional communications, because the encoder consumes a massive amount of computation time. A matching pursuit encoder does not obtain all the coefficients in one step, but iteratively finds the frame coefficient that has the largest absolute inner product value between a residual and all the bases. The inner product value and the base from which the value is obtained are called an atom. Many approaches have been proposed to simplify the complex encoding stage. One approach approximates the codewords of a dictionary with a linear combination of simpler codewords so that the computation is easier (Redmill et al., 1998; Czerepi´nski et al., 2000; Neff & Zakhor, 2002; Vleeschouwer and Macq, 1999; Jeon & Oh, 2003). This technique can be further developed by combining the inner product calculation and the atom finding components (Lin et al., 2007).

Another method pre-calculates and stores all the inner products between bases so that the encoder can update the inner products with the pre-calculated values of the bases, in-stead of re-calculating the inner products between a residual and the bases at each iteration (Mallat & Zhang, 1993). This is an efficient way to decompose a one-dimensional signal. However, it is totally unsuitable for video coding, because there are too many inner products between the bases. In the popular Gabor dictionary used in matching pursuit video encoding, there are 400 codewords, each of which is at most 35 by 35 pixels. Consequently, the inner products between the bases need at least a 30 giga-byte memory (assuming four bytes for a real value).

This difficulty prevents the matching pursuit algorithm achieving its best performance. The most popular approach for finding an atom is that proposed by Neff and Zakhor (Neff & Zakhor, 1997)], whereby a residual frame is divided into blocks and, at each iteration, an atom is found within the block with the highest energy. This approach is modified in (Al-Shaykh et al., 1999), which gives an energy weight to each block so that the more atoms chosen from a block, the smaller the energy weight of that block will be. Therefore, the block is less likely to be chosen in later iterations. The energy-weight approach reduces the likelihood that the majority of atoms will be selected from a few blocks, and improves the PSNR performance of Neff and Zakhor's algorithm.

2.1 Matching pursuit algorithm and atom extraction

There are many ways to decompose a signal into an overcomplete base set (dictionary). However, obtaining the best linear combination of bases is an NP-hard problem (Davis, 1994). The matching pursuit algorithm is a frame-based approach that represents a signal by a succession of greedy steps (Mallat & Zhang, 1993). At each iteration, the signal is projected onto the base that approximates the signal most efficiently. Let D be a dictionary of over-complete image bases $\{g_\gamma(x)\}$, where γ is the index. The algorithm decomposes an image into a linear expansion of the bases in the dictionary by a succession of greedy steps as follows. The image f(x) is first decomposed into

$$f(x) = < f(x), g_{\gamma_0}(x) > g_{\gamma_0}(x) + Rf(x), \tag{2.1}$$

where $g_{\gamma_0}(x) = \arg_{g_\gamma(x) \in D} \max\{| < f(x), g_\gamma(x) > |\}$ and Rf(x) is the residual image after approximating f(x) in the direction of $g_{\gamma_0}(x)$. The dictionary element $g_{\gamma_0}(x)$ together with the inner product value $< f(x), g_{\gamma_0}(x) >$ is called an *atom*. The matching pursuit algorithm then decomposes the residual image Rf(x) by projecting it onto a basis function of D, which is the same as the process for f(x). After M iterations, an approximation of the image f(x) can be obtained from the M atoms by

$$\tilde{f}_M(x) = \sum_{k=0}^{M-1} < R^k f(x), g_{\gamma_k}(x) > g_{\gamma_k}(x) \tag{2.2}$$

and $\tilde{f}_M(x)$ converges strongly to f(x) as $M \rightarrow \infty$.

The matching pursuit algorithm decomposes the signal structure according to the order of importance; therefore, the most significant structures are likely to be extracted first. As the dictionary is redundant, the reconstruct signal will converge to signal f(x) after sufficient iterations. The rate of convergence is dependent on the statistics of the signal and the choice of dictionary. Neff and Zakhor apply the algorithm to encode the motion residual images in video coding by using a 2-D separable Gabor dictionary to decompose the residual image.

For each iteration, a basis is selected from the dictionary to match the residual image. The corresponding inner product, basis index, and location are defined as an atom.
Instead of recalculating the inner products at each iteration, Mallat and Zhang (Mallat & Zhang, 1993) developed the matching pursuit update algorithm. At the kth iteration, let

$$g_{\gamma_k} = \max_\gamma | < R^k f(x),\ g_\gamma > | \tag{2.3}$$

be the base of the largest absolute inner product value. The new residual signal $R^{k+1}f$ is

$$R^{k+1}f(x) = R^k f(x) - < R^k f(x), g_{\gamma_k} > g_{\gamma_k}. \tag{2.4}$$

The inner products between $R^{k+1}f(x)$ and the bases $\{g_\gamma\}$ are represented by

$$< R^{k+1}f(x), g_\gamma > = < R^k f(x), g_\gamma > - < R^k f(x), g_{\gamma_k} > < g_{\gamma_k}, g_\gamma >. \tag{2.5}$$

Because $< R^k f(x), g_\gamma >$ and $< R^k f(x), g_{\gamma_k} >$ were calculated in the previous iteration, and if $< g_{\gamma_k}, g_\gamma >$ is pre-calculated, this update operation only needs one addition and one multiplication. However, the algorithm needs a huge amount of space to store all non-zero $< g_{\gamma_k}, g_\gamma >$ in an image and it is only practical for one-dimensional signal decomposition. Thus, the matching pursuit update algorithm cannot be used in video encoding. Instead, the proposed approach in (Neff & Zakhor, 1997; Al-Shaykh et al., 1999) divides a residual into blocks and, at each iteration, the matching pursuit algorithm is applied to the block with the highest energy. This approach is both simple and efficient, and has been implemented in many MP-based video codecs.
As the above algorithms find an atom from the largest (weighted) energy block, we call them one-block algorithms. These approaches are simple and efficient, but their coding performance may be unsatisfactory. Although the performance can be improved by finding an atom from more than one block, there is still the issue of the massive number of inner products between a residual and the bases in the blocks. To solve this problem, we approximate a residual in a subspace, spanned by a small number of bases within a few blocks (Lin et al., March 2006). The bases and the blocks are selected according to the content of the residual, while the coding performance and efficiency are determined by the number of bases and the number of blocks. Simulations show that the algorithm achieves better subjective and objective performances and requires less run-time than one-block algorithms for various sequences at low bit-rates.
Since the bases in the dictionary are redundant, as the number of iterations increases, the redundancy in linear combinations also increases. To solve this problem, an orthogonal matching pursuit algorithm has been proposed to reduce the redundancy between bases (Davis, 1994). At each iteration, the projection of bases on the selected orthogonal basis is removed, but it does not normalize the orthogonal basis; therefore, the basis selection unfair. To ensure that all bases have the same norm, instead of selecting the maximum absolute inner product between a signal and the orthogonal basis, we have proposed an orthonormal matching pursuit algorithm that finds the maximum absolute inner product after normalization (Lin et al., May 2006). Using the orthonormal matching pursuit algorithm, a signal can be approximated efficiently with a linear combination of selected bases so that the redundancy between the selected bases can be successfully removed.

2.2 Dictionary design

Since matching pursuit codecs are asymmetrical (as the complexity of the decoder is low, while the complexity of the encoder is extremely high), the dictionary design is a very important issue. It affects the complexity of the encoder, as well as the subjective and objective performance of matching pursuit video codec. The traditional dictionary design for reducing complexity is the 2-D separable dictionary (Neff & Zakhor, 1997). To further reduce the complexity of this dictionary, another approach has been proposed to approximate it with a low cost factorized separable dictionary in which larger basis functions in the 2-D separable dictionary are represented as a successive convolution of short basis functions (Vleeschouwer & Macq, 1999; Czerepi´nski et al., 2000). Although the complexity is drastically reduced, the disadvantage of this approach is that the dictionary is restricted within a 2-D separable set; thus, the design of the dictionary may not be optimal in terms of coding performance.

To overcome the restrictions of the 2-D separable dictionary, another dictionary design has been proposed to generate a non-separable 2-D dictionary by approximating any arbitrary basis function by a linear combination of elementary functions (Redmill et al., 1998; Neff & Zakhor, 2002). In this approach, the elementary dictionary and the order of bases are usually chosen heuristically, which affects the coding performance. Therefore, developing a systematic dictionary design approach to approximate any arbitrary dictionary is essential. In (Lin et al., 2007), we propose a systematic dictionary approximation scheme by using the most important eigenfunctions of the target dictionary to approximate each basis in the dictionary. Since the structures of eigenfunctions may be very complex, we transform these eigenfunctions into a dyadic wavelet domain and approximate each eigenfunction by the most significant dyadic wavelet transform coefficients. This framework allows a trade-off between the approximation quality and the complexity, depending on the number of eigenfunctions and the number of wavelet coefficients used to construct the approximated dictionary. Associated with a treebased search algorithm in atom selection, a combined efficient dictionary design structure and atom extraction scheme is thus proposed.

3. Scalable video coding

As the development of multimedia applications grow, video techniques have been gradually changing from one-to-one (simulcast) to one-to-many (multicast) communications. Due to channel capacity variation and disparate requirements for different receivers, it is necessary to develop video coding and transmission techniques that are efficient and scalable to Internet heterogeneity. Although representing a video with multiple redundancy in different bit rates is a simple solution for multicasting in most commercial systems, this approach cannot efficiently cope with channel capacity variation (McCanne et al., 1997; Li, 2001). In contrast, video scalability is a better solution as it generates a single bit-stream for all intended recipients, and each decoder can reconstruct a varied quality video within a specific bit rate range. Depending on the specification of receivers, a scalable system can support scalability either in frame rate (temporal scalability), frame resolution (spatial scalability), frame quality (SNR scalability) or a hybrid of these (hybrid scalability). Despite the fact that many scalable coding methods have been developed in recent years, they are still inefficient, especially at low bit rates (Girod et al., 2002). Most of the existing systems use hybrid motion-compensated DCT for video coding. Although the hybrid motion-compensation algorithm may not be the best solution for video scalability, the hybrid scheme is simple, efficient, and has a small delay in performing frame prediction. In our study, we focus on developing SNR scalability algorithms at low bit rates in a hybrid motion-compensation video coding system in which the frame residuals are encoded using matching pursuits.

Certain matching pursuit SNR-scalable schemes have been proposed in (Al-Shaykh et al., 1999; Vleeschouwer & Macq, 2000). An FGS produces a continuous bit-stream with increasing PSNR for a wide range of bit rates. A matching pursuit FGS coding algorithm is presented in (Al-Shaykh et al., 1999) in which enhancement layer scalability is achieved by successively encoding groups of atoms in which the number of atoms in a group is the primary parameter controlling scalability. A better coding efficiency than FGS can be obtained at the expense of coarser scalability. A two-layer system is coarse scalable because the bit-stream does not provide a continuous quality improvement over a wide range of bit rates. The lower layer delivers minimal bit rates while the upper layer delivers the highest possible quality. An estimation-theoretic approach to improve the performance of a two-layer system is proposed in (Rose & Regunathan, 2001) in which prediction was made from the previous base layer and enhancement layer.

Both our SNR FGS video codec and our two-layer SNR scalable video codec are based on successive bit-plane quantization coding of the atoms selected from motion residuals using matching pursuits (Lin et al., 2005). The proposed FGS algorithm uses bit-plane coding and uses the spatial and temporal dependence between bit-planes to exploit the redundancy in the bit-planes. The efficiency of our algorithm in encoding atom positions lies in using quadtree to represent a bit-plane and to perform bit-plane prediction. Our experiments indicate that our algorithm can achieve a 1 to 2 bits reduction in encoding atom positions to that of the theoretical lower bound given in (Al-Shaykh et al., 1999). This bound is derived from the assumption that atom positions are uniformly and identically distributed random variables in each frame. The bound can be out-performed if the redundancy of atom positions is exploited. We then combine position coding and progressive refinement of atom modula in our matching pursuit FGS structure.

A two-layer scalable system is able to decide which layer to emphasize without changing bit rates. If available bandwidth is full most of the time, a bit-stream is generated by using more information from the residuals of the high quality (enhancement) layer. Likewise, if it is limited, the residuals of the low quality (base) layer are emphasized. Using a linear combination of base layer and enhancement layer residuals in a two-layer scalable system has attracted much attention since it was published in (Al-Shaykh et al., 1999). Following this combination approach, we propose the use of a combined frame obtained from a linear combination of the reconstructed base layer and enhancement layer images to estimate motion vectors. Since both base and enhancement layer reconstructed images are used in our motion vector estimation, a better performance is attained in the enhancement layer (Lin et al., 2005).

4. Progressive atom coding

4.1 Set partitioning coding of atoms

When motion residual images are encoded using matching pursuits, the coding efficiency lies in economically encoding atoms. An atom includes an inner product value as well as a basis function containing location and index. Following, we will illustrate an algorithm which can efficiently encode atoms progressively.

Following the well-known set partitioning strategy adopted in the EZW (Shapiro, 1993) and SPIHT (Said & Pearlman, 1996) algorithms, we apply the bit-plane based successive-approximation quantization (SAQ) on the inner product values to encode the atoms selected from a motion residual using matching pursuits. This algorithm will successively improve the resolution of a residual frame from many scans of the bit-planes to find new significant atoms and refine the values of existing significant atoms. Initially, all atoms are assumed insignificant. Let the N_{BP}-th bit-plane be the most significant bit-plane of all the atoms. At the i-th step, a threshold whose value is set to $2^{N_{BP}-i}$ is compared to the inner products of insignificant atoms. An insignificant atom becomes significant when its absolute inner product value is larger than the current threshold. The positions and the index of the basis function and the sign of the inner product of the atom are encoded, and then the atom is added to the significant set (also called *AtomList*). The atom will remain in the significant set and the atom's inner product value will be successively refined by the following refinement steps.

When a matching pursuit is used together with a bit-plane based SAQ, the positions of atoms must be carefully handled to ensure coding efficiency. The energy of a transformed-based coding method is usually concentrated in some bases. This occurs in low-low frequency bands for DCT transform, and in coarser scales for a wavelet transform. There are efficient bit-plane scanning orders for both DCT and wavelet transform. The left subfigure of Figure 1 shows one DCT method using a zig-zag order. The middle subfigure shows one wavelet transform method using a tree order. Unlike the transformed-based coding methods, the atoms of a matching pursuit can be randomly positioned in a residual frame, as shown in the rightmost subfigure. The energies of atoms are scattered over the residual frame according to the contents in the frame. Thus, neither DCT zig-zag ordering nor wavelet tree ordering can encode the atom positions efficiently. In consequence, we should develop an efficient scanning order for the atom positions in a bit-plane to attain better coding efficiency.

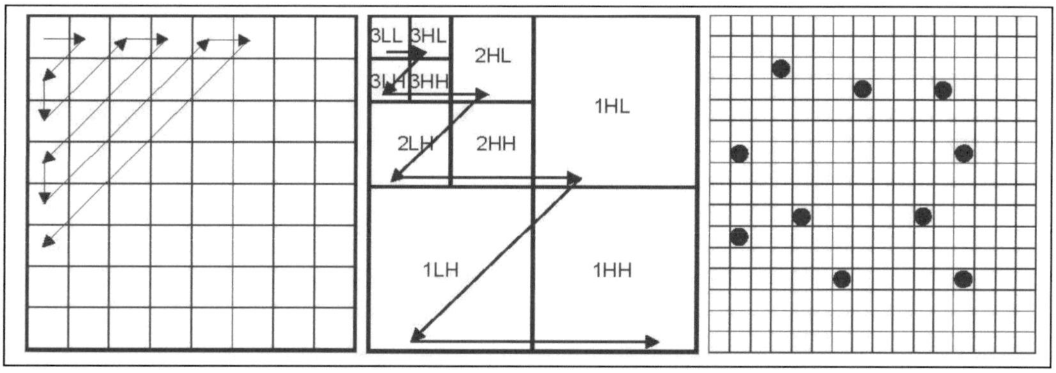

Fig. 1. Left:DCT scan-order. Middle:EZW scan-order. Right:Atom positions.

4.2 Quadtree and quadtree prediction of atom position

Position coding efficiency is dependent on the number of atoms in a bit-plane. To specify this dependency, a theoretical lower bound for atom positions is proposed in (Al-Shaykh et al., 1999) as a comparison reference for atom position encoding algorithms. The lower bound is derived by assuming that atoms are uniformly and independently distributed on an $N_1 \times N_2$ image and that no pixel of the image has more than one atom. The latter assumption is valid at low bit rates since only a few atoms are selected in a residual, and the probability that more than one atom exists at each pixel location is low. Our simulation on sequences Akiyo and Container at low bit rates shows that the probability that more than one atom are selected at the same location is less than 1%. If there are n atoms on the image, the entropy for encoding the positions of an atom will be $\log2 \binom{N_1 \times N_2}{n} / n$. Note that atoms usually distribute non-uniformly in residuals. This bound can be out-performed if an atom position encoding algorithm takes advantage of non-uniformity in atom distribution and removes the redundancy among them.

In (Al-Shaykh et al., 1999), the *NumberSplit* algorithm is presented to encode atom positions built on a multidimensional searching algorithm. In this algorithm, the total number of atoms of a residual frame is decided and given to a decoder. A frame is then separated into two halves, and the number of atoms in the first half is given to the decoder. The number is entropy-coded by an adaptive Huffman table which is built according to the number of atoms to be coded at each frame. The decoder can use the total number of atoms and the number of atoms in the first half to obtain the number of atoms in the other half. Each half is further divided recursively until it reaches either one pixel or a region that contains no atom. In (Al-Shaykh et al., 1999), atoms tend to cluster around regions of high residual error. By taking advantage of non-uniform atom clustering in a residual, the *NumberSplit* method spends an average of 0.25 bit per atom position less than the theoretical lower bound. Nevertheless, the *NumberSplit* algorithm does not explore temporal dependencies between residual frames, and encoding the number of atoms yields a relatively complex entropy coder which requires more computation to achieve efficiency. In contrast to this algorithm, we propose an algorithm based on a quadtree representation of a bit-plane. This algorithm predicts the quadtree for the adjacent bit-plane using the quadtree for the current bit-plane to remove spatial and temporal redundancy. Simulations show that the efficiency of our approach in encoding atom positions is improved to 1 to 2 bits below that of the theoretical low bound for uniform independent atom distribution.

We will explain how we implement quadtree, then give the details of simulation results. Quadtree is a simple image decomposition algorithm and has been used successfully in representing binary images at different resolution levels (Shusterman & Feder, 1994). A bit-plane can be represented by a quadtree. If the entire bit-plane has at least one atom, we label the root node "1". Four children, representing four quadrants of the bit-plane, are added to the root node. If the bit-plane has no atom, we label it "0". This process can be applied recursively to each of the four children until each child node represents a single pixel. Thus, if the image size is $2^{l_{max}} \times 2^{l_{max}}$, the quadtree has at most $l_{max} + 1$levels. Quadtree-based multi-resolution representation is resistant to small variations of bit patterns between bit-planes. An example is given in Figure 2 where the bit patterns at level 0 (the finest resolution of the quadtree) are different in (a) and (b). However, at upper levels of quadtrees of (a) and (b) (which correspond to coarser resolutions of the quadtrees) the same patterns occur. In other words, the small variations of 0 and 1 between the bit-planes do not propagate to upper levels. Hence, if two bit-planes have a lot of bit pattern overlap, the quadtree of one bit-plane can be used to efficiently predict the quadtree of the other bit-plane.

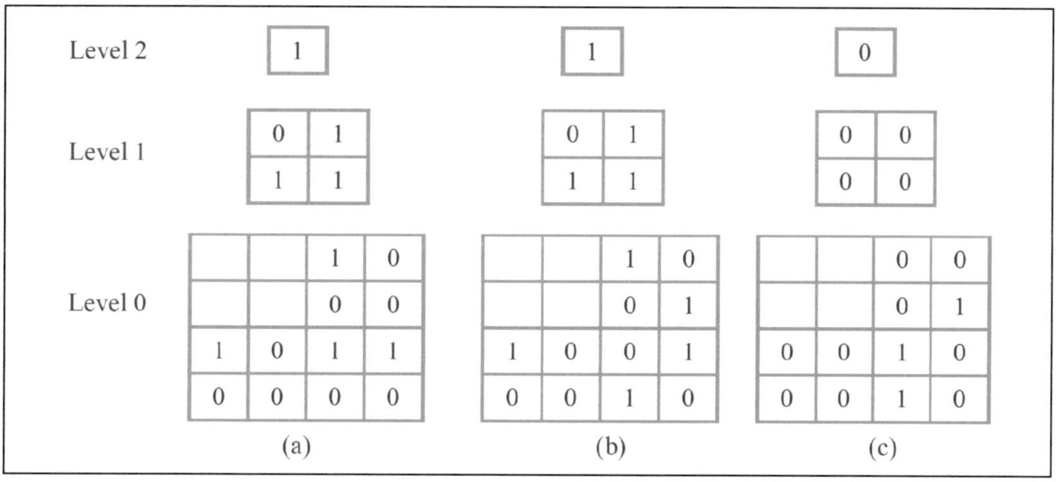

Fig. 2. Quadtree and quadtree prediction. (a) The quadtree to be predicted. (b) The quadtree from which to predict. (c) The EXCLUSIVE OR of (a) and (b). Note that one can obtain (a) by (b) EXCLUSIVE OR (c).

In video encoding at low bit rates, corresponding bit-planes in two consecutive frames and adjacent bit-planes within a frame tend to have many redundant structures. The temporal and spatial dependences of these bit-planes are exploited in the following recursive *Quadtree_Prediction* algorithm. The bit-plane b of the current frame is first represented as a quadtree Q_b^t. The quadtree is then predicted either from the quadtree of the corresponding bit-plane in the previous frame or from the quadtree of the union of all the previous bit-planes at the same frame. We use $Q_b^t(k, i, j)$ to denote the node at the (i, j)-th position in level k of the quadtree corresponding to the b-th bit-plane in the t-th residual frame. For any P-frame in a GOP, starting from the most significant bit-plane (which is the N_{BP}-th bit-plane) toward the least significant bit-plane, our encoder enters this algorithm from the root node of Q_b^t. The nodes in the tree are then traversed from the root in the depth-first order. Note that other multi-dimensional tree search orderings can be used to traverse a quadtree (Le & Lei, 1999). We give our encoder prediction algorithm as follows. We use notation Q'^t_b to denote the differential quadtree which was obtained from predicting Q_b^t from that of its previous bit-planes. Note that our decoder uses the same algorithm described below, except that Q_b^t and Q'^t_b in the algorithm are switched.

$Quadtree\_Prediction(Q_b^t, k, i, j)$

{

IF Q_b^{t-1} is used to predict Q_b^t

(1)Output the bit $(Q_b'^t(k,i,j) = Q_b^t(k,i,j) \oplus Q_b^{t-1}(k,i,j))$;

OTHERWISE

(2)Output the bit $(Q_b'^t(k,i,j) = Q_b^t(k,i,j) \oplus \bigcup_{p=b+1}^{N_{BP}} Q_p^t(k,i,j))$;

IF $Q_b^t(k,i,j) = 0$

The node is a leaf node;

ELSE IF ($Q_b^t(k,i,j) = 1$ and $k = 0$)

(3) The node is a leaf node and associates with one or more atoms;

(4) The index of the basis and sign of the inner product of each atom and

a symbol indicating the last atom at the position are entropy encoded;

ELSE encode its four children

(5) $Quadtree\_Prediction(Q_b^t, k-1, 2i, 2j)$;

(6) $Quadtree\_Prediction(Q_b^t, k-1, 2i, 2j+1)$;

(7) $Quadtree\_Prediction(Q_b^t, k-1, 2i+1, 2j)$;

(8) $Quadtree\_Prediction(Q_b^t, k-1, 2i+1, 2j+1)$;

}.

(1) in the above algorithm uses temporal prediction of the current bit-plane. Differences in quadtrees are obtained from using EXCLUSIVE OR ($\oplus$) on corresponding nodes in Q_b^t and Q_b^{t-1}. (2) uses spatial prediction in which the quadtree corresponding to the bit-plane obtained from the union of the bit-planes from b + 1 to N_{BP} in the current frame is used to predict, again by EXCLUSIVE OR, the quadtree of the current bit-plane. In (3) and (4), a "1" at a terminal node indicates new significant atoms whose basis indexes and signs of their inner products are then entropy-encoded. Since more than one atom can become significant at a location of a bit-plane, we introduce one symbol *last*, with a value of either 1 or 0, which indicates whether an atom is the last atom at a given position of a bit-plane. In our implementation, each atom is associated with a triplet (*index, sign, last*). If two atoms become significant at the same location of a bit-plane, then the *last* in the first atom is 0 and the *last* of the second atom is 1. Two atoms may become significant at the same location but in different bit-planes. In this case, the *last* of both atoms is 1.

If a node is not a leaf, then its four children are visited in a depth-first search order. Figure 2 is a simple example illustrating (a) the quadtree for the current bit-plane (to be predicted) and (b) the previous bit-plane (from which to predict). The differential quadtree (c) is the result of applying EXCLUSIVE OR on the corresponding nodes in (a) and (b). The blanks in the top left corner of all subfigures indicate that nodes located there are not encoded since their parent nodes have value 0. One can recover (a) from using EXCLU-SIVE OR on (b) and (c). The differential quadtree in (c) is traversed in depth-first order and yields the sequence 00000000000101100. Since there are many zeroes, the entropy of the differential quadtree is relatively low. Moreover, the symbols used in the sequence are only zeroes and ones, thus they can be encoded efficiently via the adaptive arithmetic code. When applying our algorithm to encode atoms, the index of the basis function, the sign of inner product value, and the last symbol of each atom are each entropy-encoded by adaptive arithmetic codes.

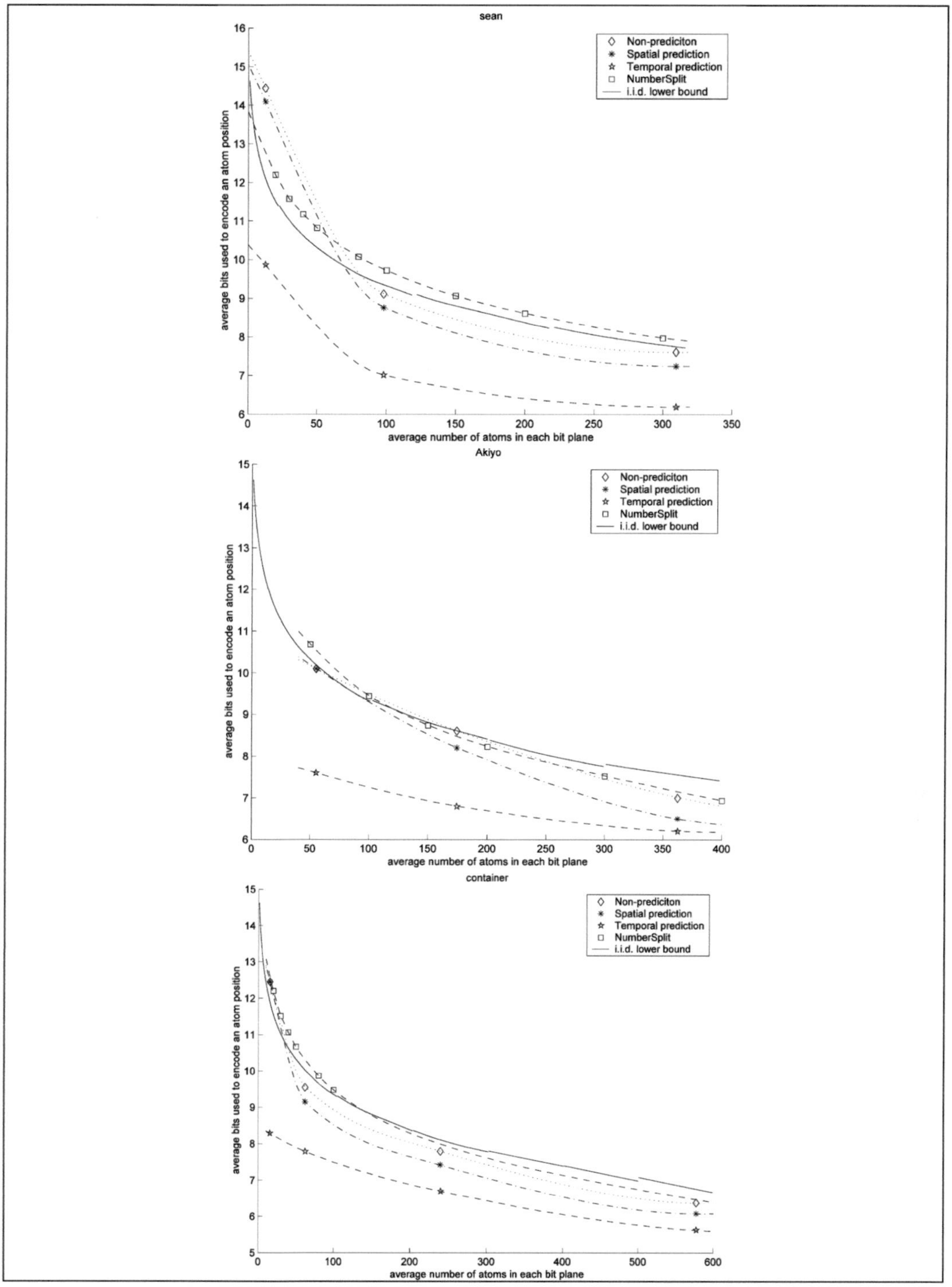

Fig. 3. Comparison of atom position encoding efficiency of quadtree, quadtree prediction and *NumberSplit*. Sequences from top to bottom are respectively Sean, Akiyo and Container.

The performance of the proposed algorithm depends on the correlation of atoms between bit-planes. A node at a higher level of a quadtree represents a larger block in the bit-plane. It is likely that corresponding higher-level nodes have the same value. This is particularly true when coding slow motion sequences in which larger motion residual errors most likely occur at the boundaries of moving objects. These errors tend to be located in almost the same region of two adjacent frames. As for coding efficiency of our algorithm, in Figure 3 we demonstrate and compare the average bits used to encode each atom position over Sean, Akiyo and Container sequences using 10 frames/sec in a QCIF format and a ten second testing time. The first three bit-planes for each frame in Sean and Akiyo are encoded while the first four bit-planes are encoded in each frame of the Container sequence. These bit-planes are encoded using either temporal bit-plane prediction, spatial bit-plane prediction, or no prediction. The X-axis in the figure is the average number of atoms for each bit-plane and the Y-axis is the average number of bits that encodes each atom position for each bit-plane. From left to right, the first mark in a curve of either quadtree or quadtree prediction corresponds to the first significant bit-plane, the second mark to the second significant bit-plane, and so on. Squares (X,Y) in the *NumberSplit* curve indicate that an average of Y bits is used to encode one atom position. All atoms are partitioned into groups of X atoms. The clustering parameter f in *NumberSplit* is set to 0.5.
The coding efficiency of temporal bit-plane prediction is evidently superior to all the others including that derived from theoretical lower bound. This bound, obtained by assuming that atoms are uniformly and identically distributed, can be out-performed if an algorithm can effectively take advantage of non-uniformity in atom distributions. The performances of quadtree without prediction and the *NumberSplit* algorithm have similar results. Quadtree results using spatial bit-plane prediction are slightly better than those without.

4.3 Progressive atom coding algorithm

This section provides the final framework that combines the set partitioning scheme for atom modula and atom positions encoding. We alternatively apply the following two phases on each bit-plane in a residual frame after initially setting the required parameter which would be the most significant bit-plane in a video. In the refinement phase, atom modula in the *AtomList* are refined by adding one extra bit of information. In the sorting phase, new significant atoms are found in the current bit-plane and are then appended to the *AtomList*. The following gives the algorithmic description of the framework.

1. **Initialization :** Set the $AtomList$ as empty. Let n be the most significant bit-plane for motion residual frames of our video.

2. **Refinement Phase :** produce a bit stream corresponding to one extra bit from the modulus of each atom in the $AtomList$.

3. **Sorting Phase :** use the $Quadtree\_Prediction$ algorithm to generate a set of new

atoms whose absolute values of inner products are within $[2^n, 2^{n+1})$ and then include the new atoms to the end of the $AtomList$.

3.1 If the bit-plane-shift parameter $b > 0$, then encode the values in bit-planes $n - 1, \cdots, n - b$ of the new significant atoms.

4. **Next Bit-Plane :** decrease n by 1 and go to Step 2.

Note that the above algorithm is not the same as that proposed in (Shapiro, 1993; Said & Pearlman, 1996). Compared to theirs, our algorithm allows more than one bit-plane atom modulus to be encoded at the sorting pass for each new significant atom. Parameter b in step 3.1, which gives the number of extra bit-planes from the current bit-plane, is used in encoding the modulus of a new significant atom. The position of each atom is encoded only in the pass in which the atom becomes significant and then the atom's modulus is refined by successive passes through the refinement phase. Encoding the position of a new significant atom requires more bits than in refining the atom's modulus. The purpose of encoding more than one bit-plane for a new significant atom is to increase the distortion-reduction δD of atom modulus to compensate for the relative large rate R in encoding the new significant atom.
Let the largest atom modulus be normalized to 1 and let m atoms be newly significant at the k-th significant bit-plane. The total bits spent is at most R_m+mb, where R_m is the bits for the atoms and mb is the bits for coding extra modula of the atoms. In matching pursuit video coding, $\frac{R_m}{m}$ >>b is satisfied for new significant atoms in a bit-plane and reasonable b. Using b extra bit-planes when coding a new significant atom reduces a fraction of at most 2^b distortion over that without using an extra bit-plane (with approximately the same number of bits). This yields an increase of PSNR for encoding new significant atoms. An atom newly significant at the k-th significant bit-plane has a normalized modulus error of at most 2^{-k} and, with bit-plane-shift parameter b, the distortion becomes $2^{-(k+b)}$. Encoding the modulus of a new significant atom with more than one bit-plane is a feature in our low bit rate video coding. The efficacy of this feature in FGS at low bit rates is illustrated in the next section. Figure 4 gives the order in which bit-planes are included in the sorting and refinement phases of our algorithm. The process of sorting and refining bit-planes of the left subfigure is b =0 which is the same as that in (Shapiro, 1993; Said & Pearlman, 1996). In the right subfigure, three bit-planes of atom modula are encoded at the sorting phase, while one bit-plane is encoded at the enhancement phase.

5. FGS matching pursuit video codec

A video streaming encoder compresses and stores video streams and simultaneously transmits them on demand through a scalability-aware transport mechanism to a large amount of users (Chou & Miao, 2006). There are many video scalable encoder applications. Among them, the FGS MPEG-4 video approach has attracted the most attention as it has achieved a fine balance between coding efficiency and coding complexity for producing

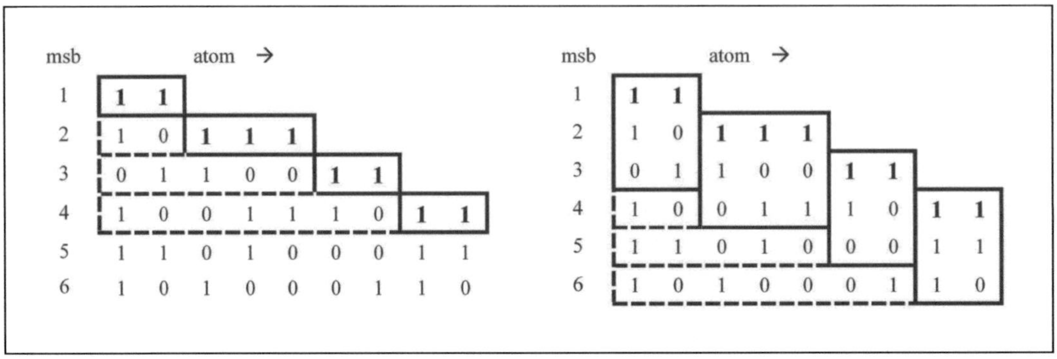

Fig. 4. Modulus sorting and refinement comparison using different b after 4 passes. Left: b = 0. Right: b = 2. Bit-plane values included in sorting and in refinement phases are indicated by solid boxes and dashed boxes respectively.

scalable bit streams. A basic FGS framework requires two layers: the base layer and the enhancement layer. The base layer includes a motion prediction and has an encoder with highly efficient coding in low bit rates. Any decoder must be able to decode the base-layer bit stream. In principle, any FGS method can be used to produce streaming bit-streams for the enhancement layer. The bit-plane-based DCT FGS encoding method is still the most widely used.

5.1 Proposed FGS

Our proposed two-layer FGS matching pursuit video codec is shown in Figure 5. Our base layer encoder, shown at the top subfigure, performs motion compensation and encodes motion residual frames using a matching pursuit. Although an MP-based video encoder is more complex, its decoder is comparably less complex than other methods. Both the base layer and the enhancement layer of our matching pursuit FGS coders use the progressive atom encoding algorithm proposed in previous section in which the atom position is encoded by the Quadtree Prediction algorithm. The position encoding algorithm must store both a quadtree

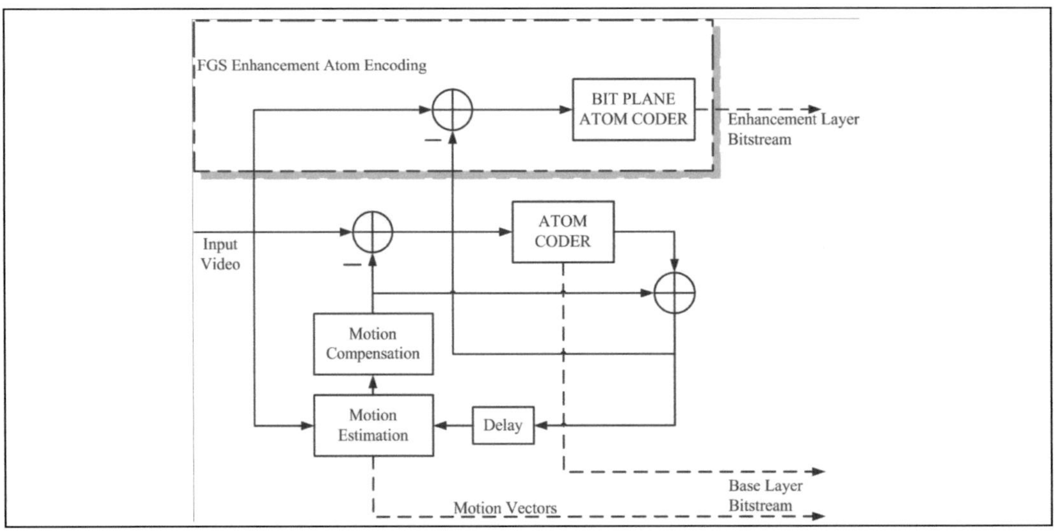

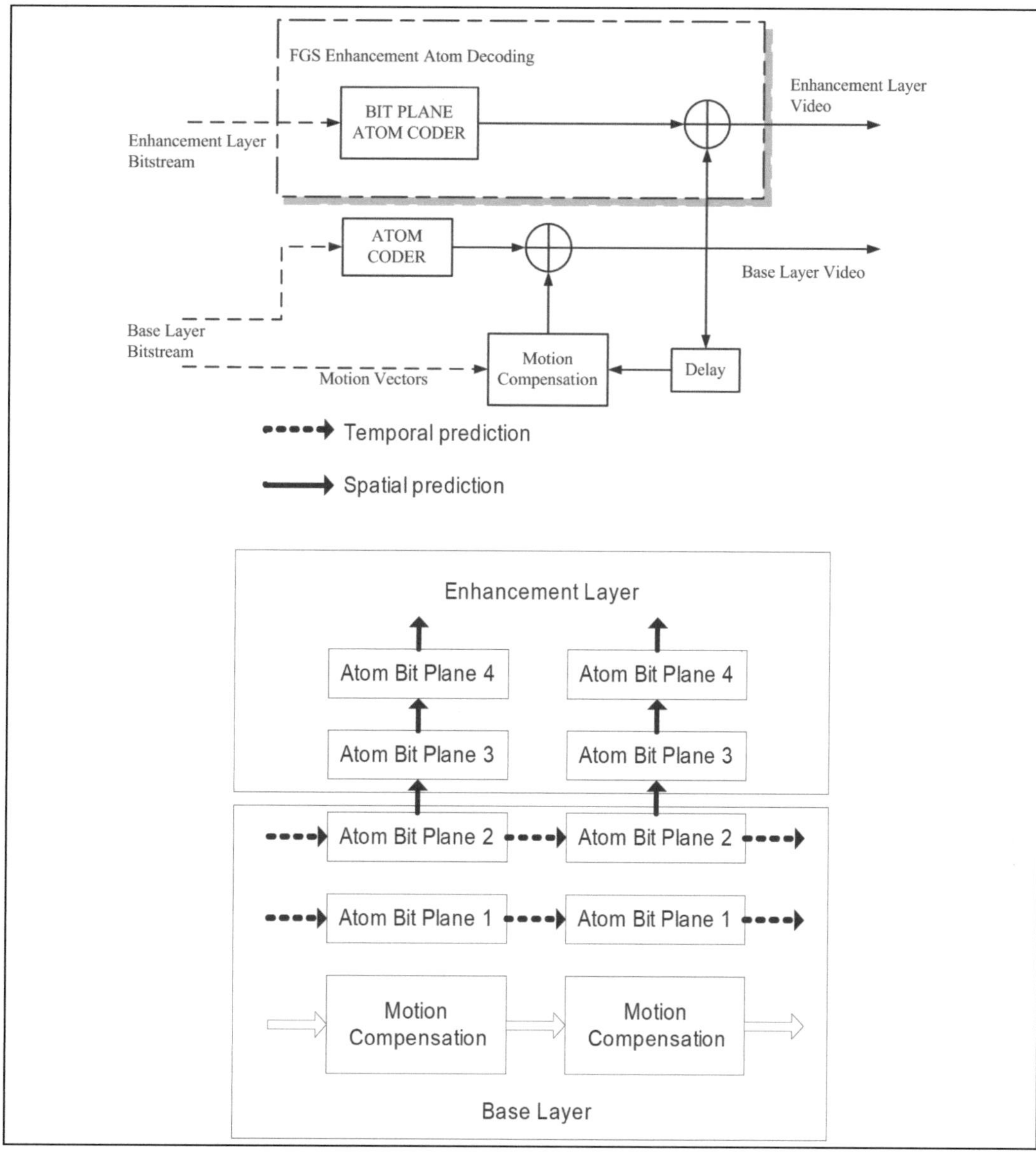

Fig. 5. Our FGS matching pursuit codec. Top: Encoder. Middle: Decoder. Bottom: Atom positions encoded by bit-plane-based predictions.

for each base layer bit-plane in the previous frame (in order to perform temporal prediction), and a quadtree for the union of previous bit-planes at the current frame (to perform spatial prediction). Representing the quadtree of an N pixels bit-plane takes at most $\frac{4N}{3}$ bits. If we operate at a bit rate with two bit-planes as base layer, we would need at most 4N bits for storage. Although slightly more storage is required, the entropy-coder is a two symbol adaptive arithmetic code which is easily implemented at a decoder site. The bottom subfigure of Figure 5 illustrates an example of our bit-plane-based FGS to encode atom position. Temporal prediction is carried out only in base layer bit-planes while spatial prediction is carried out in enhancement layer bit-planes. A bit-plane in the enhancement layer is predicted from all the previous bit-planes from the same frame. The spatial or temporal bit-plane predictions are based on operations on quadtrees. The PSNR can be lifted by finely quantizing atom modula of new significant atoms by setting parameter b. Figure 6 shows experimental results of PSNR performance at low bit rates with different b.

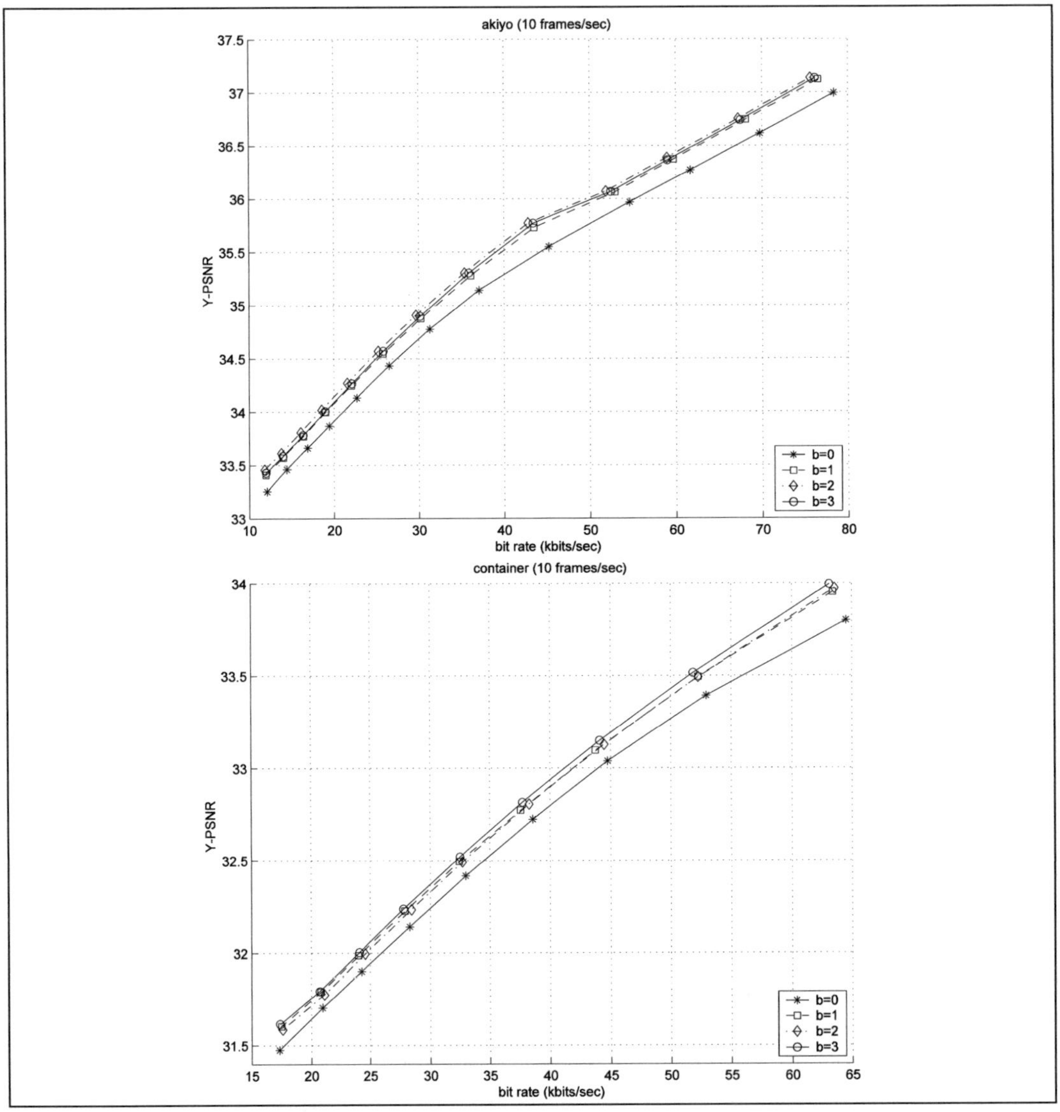

Fig. 6. PSNR at low bit rates by setting different b. Top: Akiyo. Bottom: Container. There is an average 0.2 dB improvement if b is set to either 2 or 3.

5.2 Performance evaluations and comparisons

The performance of our matching pursuit FGS at various bit rates in terms of luminance PSNR (Y-PSNR) are compared with those of DCT FGS. Our FGS DCT-based codec follows

Amendment 2 of the MPEG-4 FGS DCT-based video codec in encoding the enhancement layer of a residual frame (ISO/IEC 14496-2, 2001). In all the following experiments, we divide a frame into blocks and select an atom from only one block at each iteration (Neff & Zakhor, 1997). We use the weighted energy block search algorithm, with weights provided in (Al-Shaykh et al., 1999), to find atoms. The first two parts of this section compare performances of our bit-plane-based matching pursuit FGS to bit-plane-based DCT FGS at different low bit rates. The third part provides the evaluation of our FGS to a bit-plane-based non-scalable matching pursuit video coding.

5.2.1 Comparison of MP and DCT FGS using the same residual image

For a fair comparison of coding efficiency of residual images between bit-plane-based MP FGS and DCT FGS, different codecs should encode the same residual images using the same number of bits. We set up the experiments so that the base layer of the current frame is obtained from the base layer of the previous frame using only motion compensation. In other words, a frame is estimated from the previous base layer using motion compensation and the residual is the enhancement layer of the frame. Accordingly, the differences in encoding residual images by the codecs will not be involved in predicting the following frames, and the codecs will encode the same residual images.
Figure 7 shows Y-PSNR comparisons of our matching pursuit FGS codec with that of the DCT FGS codec using various sequences in QCIF at 10 frames/sec. Because both codecs encode the same residuals in the enhancement layer, as indicated in the Figure 7, the performance of bit-plane-based matching pursuit FGS is better than that of DCT FGS in encoding residuals at low bit rates. The slope corresponding to the matching pursuit bit-plane encoder is higher than that of the DCT bit-plane at bit rates close to the base layer bit rate in each sequence, and it yields that the curve of matching pursuit is above that of DCT in each sequence. This may be because matching pursuit first picked up a few locally energy-concentrated patterns, causing a high reduction in distortions, so that the matching pursuit slope is initially higher than that of the DCT slope. The slopes of the two curves become approximately the same as the bit rate increases. For the Akiyo sequence, at 100 kbps, the largest PSNR gain of the matching pursuit bit-plane encoder over the DCT bit-plane encoder is about 0.8 dB.

5.2.2 Comparisons at the base layer and the enhancement layer

We evaluated the coding efficiency of both layers in matching pursuit FGS and DCT FGS by comparing their Y-PSNR at various low bit rates. Both codecs have the same intra-frame (I-frame) encoded by the DCT method. The other frames are all inter-frame (P-frame). For all comparisons, the base layer of the FGS MP-based codec includes either one or two most significant bit-planes. The base layer bit rates of the FGS DCT-based codec is determined by using a fixed quantization step (QP) for all frames in the sequence. This assures that the base layer's bit rates of the two codecs are as close as possible. The frame rate of all sequences is 10 frames/sec and the format for all sequences is QCIF.
The average Y-PSNR versus the bit rates is plotted in Figure 8. Base layer performance corresponds to the beginning points whose X-axes are at the lowest bit rates in the curves. In all experiments, the Y-PSNR of our MP-based codec is better than that of the DCT-based codec, both in the base layer and enhancement layer. The average base layer improvement is about 0.7 dB. Also, the Y-PSNR of the matching pursuit FGS increases faster than that of the DCT FGS as bit rates increase.

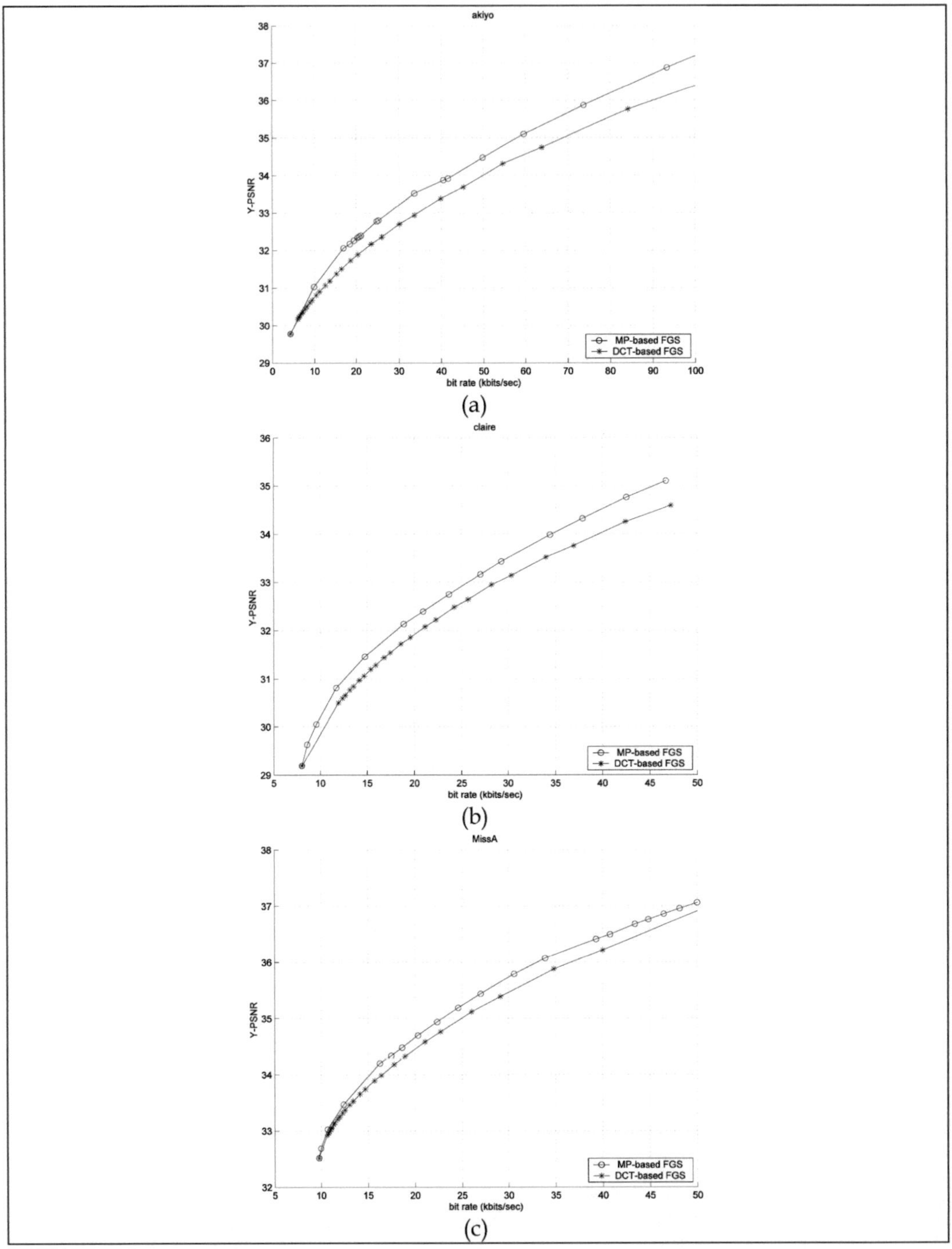

Fig. 7. Comparison of the same residual images encoded by bit-plane-based matching pursuit and bit-plane-based DCT method for (a) 10 seconds Akiyo, (b) 5 seconds Claire, and (c) 3 seconds Miss America sequences. The frame rate is 10 frame/sec and bit-plane-shift parameter b =3.

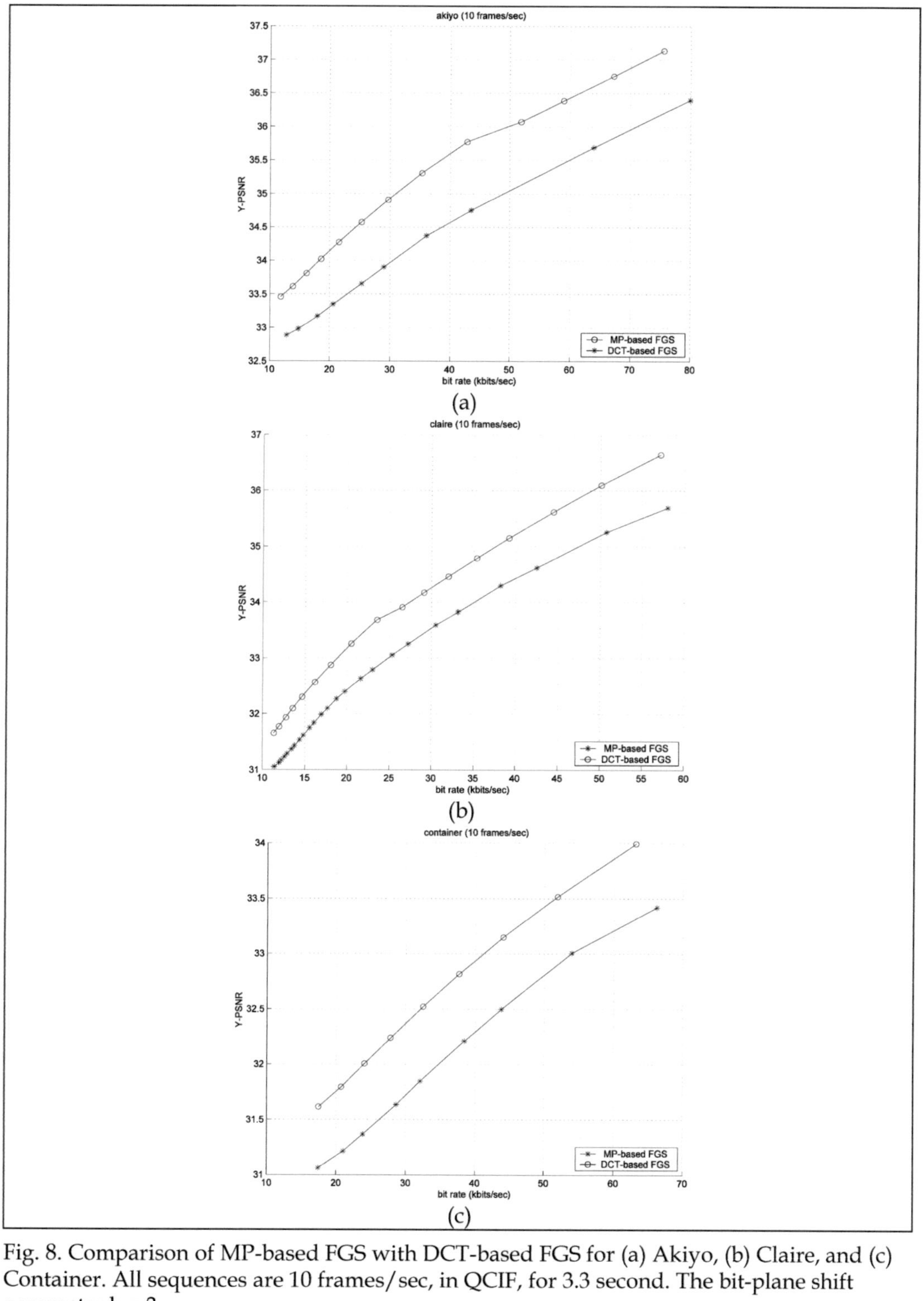

Fig. 8. Comparison of MP-based FGS with DCT-based FGS for (a) Akiyo, (b) Claire, and (c) Container. All sequences are 10 frames/sec, in QCIF, for 3.3 second. The bit-plane shift parameter b = 3.

5.2.3 Evaluating bit-plane representation and prediction of FGS

Here we use different bit-plane numbers as our base layer and compare performances with a bit-plane-based non-scalable codec at low bit rates. Note that our bit-plane-based non-scalable codec does not optimize at a particular bit rate and it is not the best non-scalable matching pursuit codec. Nevertheless, it provides a reference we can use to evaluate important aspects of our FGS.

Figure 9 gives the PSNR performance versus bit rates of the Akiyo and Container sequences. The curve corresponding to the top envelope of each subfigure is the performance of our non-scalable codec in which all the bit-planes are temporally predicted. The previous reconstructed frame from all the bits is used to perform motion compensation for the current frame. The rest of the curves, from the bottom to the top, correspond to performance using one bit-plane, two bit-planes and three bit-planes as our base layer.

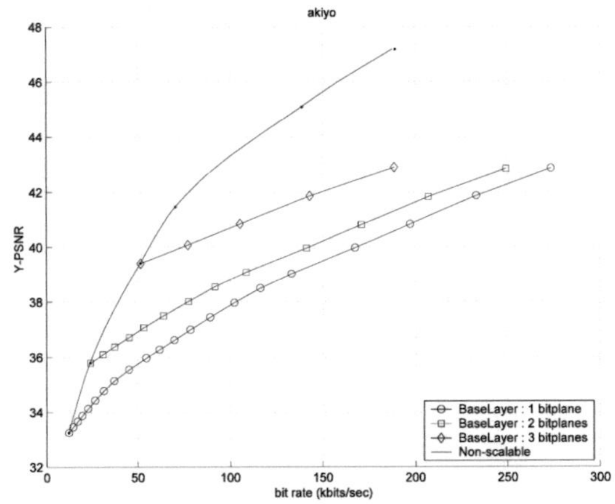

(a)

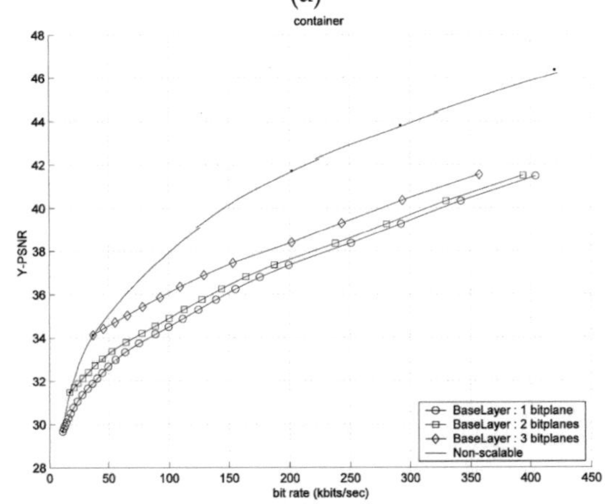

(b)

Fig. 9. Comparison of our FGS with various bit-plane numbers as base layers to a bit-planed-based non-scalable codec. Sequences: (a) Akiyo and (b) Container, are 10 frames/sec, in QCIF, for 3.3 second.

The efficacy of using bit-plane prediction and motion compensation manifests at relatively lower bit rates when the PSNR gap between consecutive curves is comparably large. The curve using one bit-plane as base layer shows the greatest PSNR increase when bit rates are close to the base layer. This is because matching pursuit selected a few atoms with energy concentrated in the first two significant bit-planes and, therefore, caused a higher slope increase at lower bit rates. The gap between curves continues to decrease until higher bit rates are reached at which point the curves are almost parallel.

6. Conclusions

Because channel capacity varies according to network traffic and the capacity of each receiver, fine granular scalability of video coding has emerged as an important area in multimedia streaming research. We propose an FGS video codec based on matching pursuits and bit-plane coding. The proposed FGS algorithm uses the spatial and temporal dependence between bit-planes to exploit the redundancy in the bit-planes. The efficiency of our algorithm in encoding atom positions lies in using a quadtree to represent a bit-plane and to perform bit-plane prediction. The experiment results demonstrate that this algorithm can reduce the number of bits required to encode the atom positions by 1 to 2 bits. The PSNR of the proposed algorithm is compared to and out-performs that of the DCT-based FGS algorithm.

7. References

O. Al-Shaykh, E. Miloslavsky, T. Nomura, R. Neff, and A. Zakhor. (Feb. 1999) Video compression using matching pursuits. IEEE Trans. on Circuits and Systems for Video Technology, 9(1):123–143.

P. A. Chou and Z. Miao. (2006) Rate-distortion optimized streaming of packetized media. IEEE trans. on Multimedia, Vol 8, No.2, pages 390-404.

P. Czerepi´nski, C. Davies, N. Canagarajah, and D. Bull. Matching pursuits video coding: dictionaries and fast implentation. IEEE Trans. on Circuits and Systems for Video Technology, 10(7):1103–1115, Oct. 2000.

G. Davis. (1994) Adaptive Nonlinear Approximations. PhD thesis, Department of Mathematics, New York University.

K. Engan, S.O. Aase, and J.H. Hus. (Oct. 2000) Multi-frame compression: Theory and design. EURASIP Signal Processing, 80(10):2121–2140.

B. Girod, M. Kalman, Y. J. Liang, and R. Zhang. (Sept. 2002) Advances in channel-adaptive video streaming. Journal of Wirelesss Communications on Mobile Computing, 2(6):573– 584.

ISO/IEC 14496-2:2001. Streaming Video Profile.

ISO/IEC JTC1/SC29/WG11, Doc. M10569/S03.(March 2004) Scalable extension of H.264/AVC,

B. Jeon and S. Oh. (April 2003)Fast matching pursuit with vector norm comparison. IEEE Trans. on Circuits and Systems for Video Technology, 13(4):338-342.

J. Le and S. Lei. (July 1999) An embedded still image coder with rate-distortion optimization. 8(7):913–924.

W. Li. (March 2001) Overview of fine granularity scalability in MPEG-4 video standard. IEEE Trans. on Circuits and Systems for Video Technology, 11(3):301–317.

J.L. Lin, W.L. Hwang, and S.C. Pei. (Jan. 2005) SNR scalability based on bitplane coding of matching pursuit atoms at low bit rates: fine-grained and two-layer. IEEE Trans. on Circuits and Systems for Video Technology, 15(1):3–14.

J.L. Lin, W.L. Hwang, and S.C. Pei. (May 2006) Video compression based on orthonormal matching pursuits. In Proceedings of the IEEE International Symposium on Circuits and Systems (ISCAS).

J.L. Lin, W.L. Hwang, and S.C. Pei. (March 2006) Multiple blocks matching pursuit update for low bit rate video coding. IEEE Trans. on Circuits and Systems for Video Technology, Vol.16, No. 3, pp.331-337.

J.L. Lin, W.L. Hwang, and S.C. Pei. (2007) A combined dictionary approximation and maximum atom extraction design for matching pursuit speed-up. IEEE Trans. on Circuits and Systems for Video Technology, Vol.17, No. 12, pp.1679-1689.

G. Mallat and Z. Zhang. (Dec. 1993) Matching pursuits with time-frequency dictionaries. IEEE trans. on Signal Processing, 41:3397–3415.

S. McCanne, M. Vetterli, and V. Jacobson. (Aug. 1997) Low-complexity video coding for receiver-driven layered multicast. IEEE Journal of Selected Areas in Communications, 15(6):982–1001.

R. Neff, T. Nomura, and A. Zakhor. (1998) Decoder complexity and performance comparison of matching pursuit and DCT-based MEPG-4 video codecs. In Proceedings of the IEEE International Conference on Image Processing (ICIP), pages 783–787.

R. Neff and A. Zakhor. (Feb. 1997) Very low bit-rate video coding based on matching pursuits. IEEE Trans. on Circuits and Systems for Video Technology, 7:158–171.

R. Neff and A. Zakhor. (Sept. 2000) Modulus quantization for matching pursuit video coding. IEEE Trans. on Circuits and Systems for Video Technology, 10(6):895–912.

R. Neff and A. Zakhor. (Jan. 2002) Matching pursuit video coding–part I: dictioanry approximation. IEEE Trans. on Circuits and Systems for Video Technology, 12(1):13–26.

J.-R. Ohm, M. van der Schaar, and J. W. Woods. (Oct. 2004) Interframe wavelet coding-motion picture representation for universal scalability. Signal Processing: Image Communication, 19(9):877–908.

D.W. Redmill, D.R. Bull, and P. Czerepi´nski. Video coding using a fast non-separable matching pursuits algorithm. In Proceedings of the IEEE International Conference on Image Processing (ICIP), pages 769–773, 1998.

K. Rose and S. L. Regunathan. (July 2001) Toward optimality in scalable predictive coding. 10(7):965–976.

A. Said and W. A. Pearlman. (June 1996) A new fast and efficient image codec based on set partitioning in hierarchical trees. IEEE Trans. on Circuits and Systems for Video Technology, 6(3):243–250.

J. M. Shapiro. (Dec. 1993)Embedded image coding using zerotrees of wavelet coefficients. IEEE trans. on Signal Processing, 41(12):3445–3462.

E. Shusterman and M. Feder. (March 1994) Image compression via improved quadtree decomposi-tion algorithms. 3(2):207–215.

X. Tang and A. Zakhor. (June 2002) Matching pursuits multiple description coding for wireless video. IEEE Trans. on Circuits and Systems for Video Technology, 12(6):566–575.

M. Vetterli and T. Kalker. (1994) Matching pursuit for compression and application to motion compensated video coding. In Proceedings of the IEEE International Conference on Image Processing (ICIP), pages 725–729.

C. De Vleeschouwer and B. Macq. (Oct. 1999) Subband dictionaries for low-cost matching pursuits of video residues. IEEE Trans. on Circuits and Systems for Video Technology, 9(7):984–993.

C. De Vleeschouwer and B. Macq. (Dec. 2000) SNR scalability based on matching pursuits. IEEE trans. on Multimedia, 2(4):198–208.

C. De Vleeschouwer and A. Zakhor. (June 2002) Atom modulus quantization for matching pursuit video coding. In Proceedings of the IEEE International Conference on Image Processing (ICIP), volume 3, pages 681–684.

5

Motion Estimation at the Decoder

Sven Klomp and Jörn Ostermann
Leibniz Universität Hannover
Germany

1. Introduction

All existing video coding standards, such as MPEG-1,2,4 or ITU-T H.26x, perform motion estimation at the encoder in order to exploit temporal dependencies within the video sequence. The estimated motion vectors are transmitted and used by the decoder to assemble a prediction of the current frame. Since only the prediction error and the motion information are transmitted, instead of intra coding the pixel values, compression is achieved. Due to block-based motion estimation, accurate compensation at object borders can only be achieved with small block sizes. Large blocks may contain several objects which move in different directions. Thus, accurate motion estimation and compensation is not possible, as shown by Klomp et al. (2010a) using prediction error variance, and small block sizes are favourable. However, the smaller the block, the more motion vectors have to be transmitted, resulting in a contradiction to bit rate reduction.

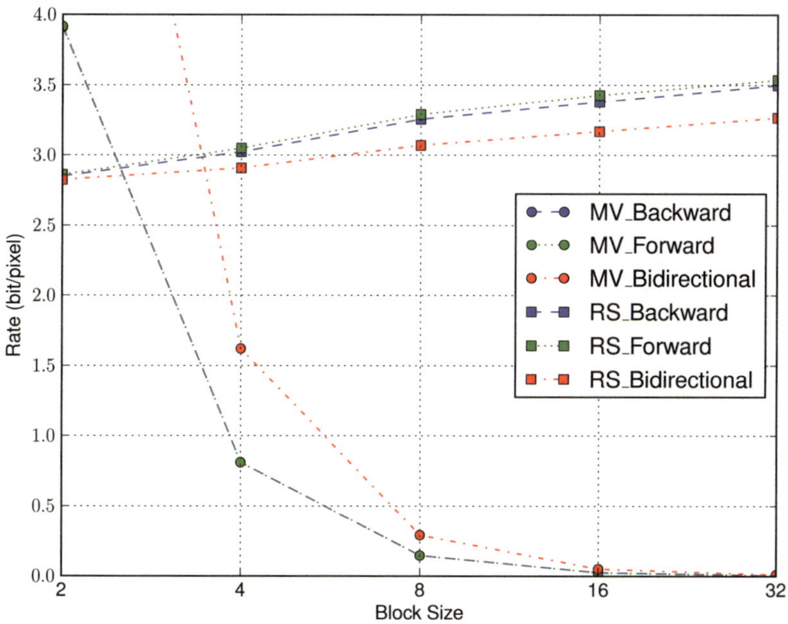

Fig. 1. Data rates of residual (RS) and motion vectors (MV) for different motion compensation techniques (Kimono sequence).

These characteristics can be observed in Figure 1, where the rates for the residual and the motion vectors are plotted for different block sizes and three prediction techniques. Backward motion compensation generates a prediction by only using the frame temporal before the current frame to be coded, whereas forward motion compensation only uses the following frame. Bidirectional motion compensation averages the motion compensated blocks from both frames to form the prediction, which is typical for B frames. As expected, the rate for the residual decreases with smaller block sizes. Bidirectional motion compensation performs best, but also needs more bits to code the motion vectors. The motion vector rates for forward and backward motion estimation are almost identical. For large block sizes, the rate for the motion vectors is negligible, but increases significantly towards small blocks. It can be observed that the block size has a significant impact on the compression performance and is, therefore, adaptively chosen for each macroblock and limited to 4×4 pixels in the ITU-T and ISO/IEC (2003) standard H.264 / AVC.

Increasing computational power allows to implement more sophisticated algorithms, even at the decoder. Recent studies have shown that motion estimation algorithms at the decoder can significantly improve compression efficiency. The estimated motion is already known at the decoder and the transmission of the motion vectors can be omitted.

A first attempt to estimate the motion at the decoder was proposed by Suzuki et al. (2006), where additional macroblock and sub-macroblock modes were added to H.264 / AVC. Those modes predict a block by performing template matching at the decoder, instead of using transmitted motion vectors. This approach was further improved by calculating a weighted average of multiple candidates (Suzuki et al., 2007).

In contrast, Kamp et al. (2008) proposed to adapt the existing P modes instead of introducing additional modes. The encoder decides to either code the motion vector explicitly or to use the derived vector by a rate-distortion optimised mode decision. This so-called decoder-side motion vector derivation (DMVD) estimates the motion vector by matching a template of already reconstructed pixels in the reference frames at different positions. In case DMVD is selected, only the decision has to be signalled and no motion vector is transmitted. The system was later extended to support DMVD also within B macroblock modes (Kamp & Wien, 2010).

Decoder-side motion estimation (DSME), proposed by Klomp et al. (2009), is another approach to reduce the rate for the motion vectors. Temporal interpolation is used to generate a prediction of the current frame at the decoder. This DSME frame is stored and can be used as additional reference for the conventional coding tools. The motion estimated by the conventional tools should be zero, as the DSME frame is already motion compensated and thus, the motion vectors are very efficient to code.

The rest of this chapter is organised as follows: Section 2 recapitulates inter frame coding used in H.264 / AVC. Detailed descriptions of the DMVD and DSME approaches are given in Section 3 and 4, respectively. Experimental results are presented in Section 5. The chapter comes to a close with conclusions in Section 6.

2. Conventional inter frame coding

This section gives a rough overview of conventional inter frame coding used in the ITU-T and ISO/IEC (2003) standard H.264 / AVC, to get a better understanding of the design changes introduced by DMVD and DSME, as described in Section 3 and 4, respectively.

In H.264 / AVC, one frame is divided into so-called macroblocks with the size of 16×16 pixels. In contrast to intra coding, where the current macroblock is predicted by only using already decoded data from within the current frame, inter coding uses reference frames for

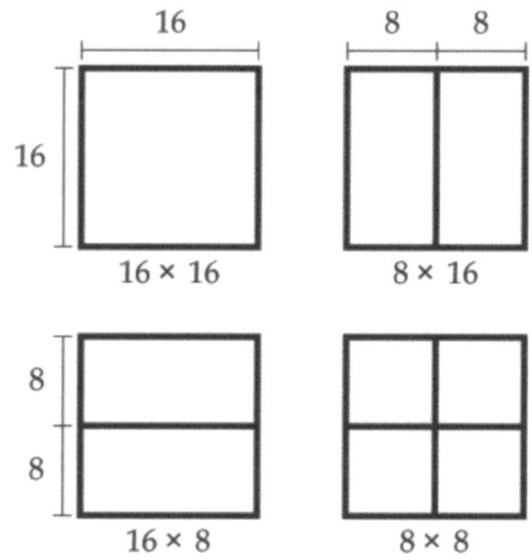

Fig. 2. Macroblock partitions used for inter coding.

motion compensated prediction. As mentioned before, the bit rate to code one block depends on its size. Therefore, a macroblock can be partitioned into smaller blocks in inter coding, to get the best trade-off between residual rate and the rate needed for coding the motion vectors, as depicted in Figure 2. Additionally, a 8×8 macroblock can be further divided into sub-partitions of sizes 8×4, 4×8 and 4×4.

At the encoder, the motion vector for each macroblock (sub-)partition is estimated and a rate-distortion optimised decision, as proposed by Sullivan & Wiegand (1998), is made on what partition structure should be used to minimise the rate for the residual and the motion vectors. Since the partitions are small compared to the size of moving objects within the sequence, it is most likely that neighbouring partitions have similar motion vectors. Thus, H.264 / AVC predicts the motion vector of the current block with the motion vectors from up to three neighbouring blocks, as depicted in Figure 3.

The prediction algorithm is described in more detail by Richardson (2003). This prediction is subtracted from the actual motion vector and only the difference is coded into the bitstream. The details on coding the residual is not of interest for DMVD nor DSME and is omitted in this description.

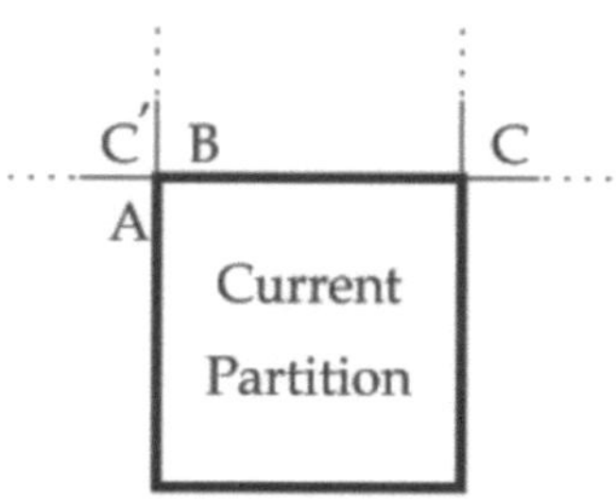

Fig. 3. Motion vectors of block A, B and C are used for motion vector prediction. For DMVD predictive search, A and C (C' if C is unavailable) are used for motion derivation.

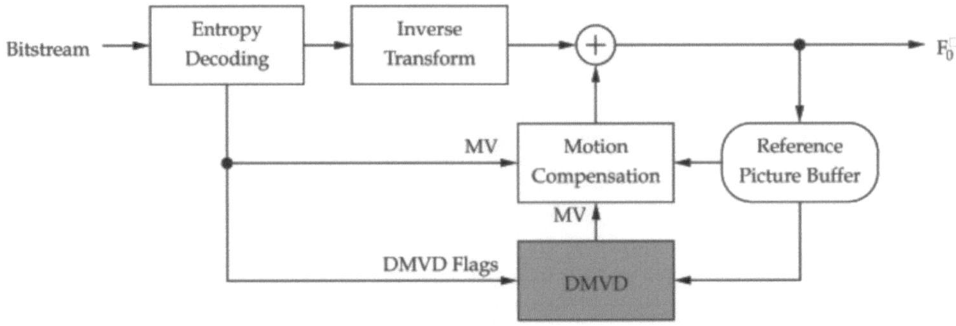

Fig. 4. Simplified block diagram of a conventional hybrid decoder with DMVD modifications, as proposed by Kamp et al. (2008), highlighted in gray.

3. Decoder-side motion vector derivation

The main idea of DMVD is to reduce the rate for the motion information by deriving the motion vectors at the decoder. In case the derivation is successful, no motion information has to be coded into the bitstream and compression is achieved. However, the derived motion vector is not always correct and might impair the compression efficiency due to large prediction error. Therefore, DMVD should be selected adaptively for each macroblock by performing a rate-distortion optimised decision at the encoder, similar to the Lagrangian optimisation described by Sullivan & Wiegand (1998). To transmit this decision to the decoder, Kamp et al. (2008) added additional flags within the H.264 / AVC macroblock layer syntax to signal either the use of the motion vector derived with DMVD, or the use of an explicitly coded motion vector: One flag for the 16×16 macroblock type is used to signal whether the motion vector is coded into the bitstream or whether DMVD is used. Two flags are sent for the two partitions of the 16×8 and 8×16 macroblock types. Furthermore, the sub-types of the 8×8 partitions are coded with one flag for each sub-block. These flags are interpreted in the entropy decoder as shown in Figure 4.
If DMVD flags are set, the motion vector is derived at the decoder and used for motion compensation. Otherwise, an explicitly transmitted motion vector is decoded and used for compensation. Kamp, Ballé & Wien (2009) have shown that the performance can be further improved by using multi-hypothesis prediction. Instead of deriving one motion vector and using the corresponding block as prediction, the two best motion vectors are derived to improve the prediction accuracy. The corresponding blocks of these motion vectors are averaged to form the improved prediction. The following section describes the motion vector derivation process in more detail.

3.1 Template-based motion derivation

For the template-based motion derivation, it is assumed that the objects of the sequence are larger than one block partition. Thus, pixels neighbouring the current block belong to the same object. If the motion of these pixels is known, it can be used for the motion compensation of the current block.
Current video coding standards have in common that the macroblocks within a frame are coded line by line. Therefore, the decoded pixel values above and left of the current macroblock are, in most cases, available. These values can be used to estimate the motion of the current block. Kamp et al. (2008) proposed to use an L-shaped template with a thickness of four pixels, which is matched in the reference frames. However, a full search within all

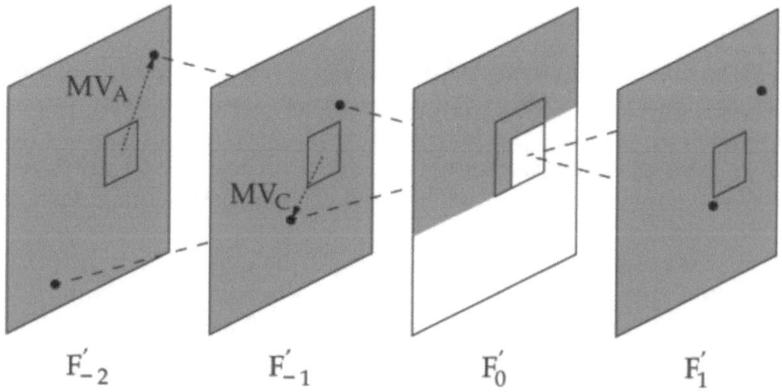

Fig. 5. L-shaped template used for motion search of the current block. Already decoded frame regions are shown in grey. The candidates (black circles) for template matching are derived from motion vectors of two neighbouring blocks (MV_A, MV_C) using linear scaling.

reference frames would induce a high amount of additional complexity at the decoder, and is, therefore, not feasible. For this reason, the template is matched for a smaller search range. It is assumed that the H.264 / AVC motion vector predictor (MVP) is already a good starting point and, thus, is used as the centre of the search range for each reference frame. MVP uses the motion vectors of up to three already decoded partitions next to the current block (Figure 3, block A, B and C) to calculate a prediction of the current motion vector.
The search range around the predicted motion vector is set to four pixels with sub-pel refinement, which introduces high complexity to the decoder. The position with the smallest sum of absolute differences (SAD) is chosen as the derived motion vector.
The complexity of the motion search can be significantly reduced by using a candidate-based approach: A set of candidate motion vectors are selected and the SAD is only calculated at these positions, in order to find the best motion vector. The number of candidates should be small to achieve noticeable complexity reduction.
Kamp, Bross & Wien (2009) proposed to use the motion vectors of neighbouring blocks as candidates for motion vector derivation. More precisely, the motion vectors from block A and C, as depicted in Figure 3, are used. In the case that block C is not available, C' is used. However, the neighbouring blocks may use different reference frames and thus, the motion vectors should be scaled according to the temporal distance of the reference frame. In Figure 5, it is assumed that three reference frames are available and that block A and C use frame F'_{-2} and F'_{-1} as reference, respectively. The two vectors are scaled, resulting in six candidates for the template matching.
Kamp, Bross & Wien (2009) observed that a sub-pel refinement results in improved predictions, although the candidates can already have fractional-pel accuracy. The refinement is performed for each candidate by performing a full-search with quarter-pel accuracy and a search range of only one pixel.
Out of these candidates, the two vectors with the smallest SAD are used to calculate the prediction as described before. Thereafter, the remaining prediction error is coded conventionally using the H.264 / AVC tools.

4. Decoder-side motion estimation

In contrast to decoder-side motion vector derivation, where the aim is to eliminate the need of transmitting motion information to the decoder, decoder-side motion estimation tries to achieve compression by providing an additional reference frame that can be used for frame prediction. Klomp et al. (2009) implemented DSME on top of a H.264 / AVC coder. A simplified block diagram of a conventional hybrid encoder with highlighted DSME changes is depicted in Figure 6.

The reference picture buffer, containing already coded pictures, feeds the previous frame F'_{-1} and the future frame F'_1 that are temporally the closest to the current frame F_0, to the DSME block. The block interpolates between the two frames to create a prediction $\hat{F}_0$ of the current frame. Any temporal interpolation algorithm can be adopted into this architecture, as shown by Klomp et al. (2009) and Munderloh et al. (2010) for block-based and mesh-based motion estimation, respectively.

Since no information regarding the motion between F_0 and the two reference frames F'_{-1} and F'_1 is available at the decoder, linear motion is assumed. Thus, the motion vector between F'_{-1} and F_0 is equal to the motion vector between F_0 and F'_1, and can be expressed by the halved motion between F'_{-1} and F'_1. This assumption can be treated as valid because of the high frame rates of modern video content. After each block of the current frame is interpolated, it is inserted into the reference picture buffer. The tools of the conventional encoder are now able to use this frame for prediction and coding in addition to the other reference frames stored in the reference picture buffer.

Since no distinction is made between the inserted DSME frame and the other reference frames, the encoder transmits the motion vector difference, as described by Richardson (2003), also for a block using the DSME frame $\hat{F}_0$. However, the motion vector estimated by the encoder should be zero, as $\hat{F}_0$ is already motion compensated, and thus, the motion vector difference is very efficient to code. This approach has the advantage that the DSME frame can also be used in cases where the assumption of linear motion is wrong, as shown in Figure 7:

The DSME algorithm estimates the motion between the two reference frames and inserts the interpolated block in the centre of $\hat{F}_0$ because of the assumption of linear motion. However, the

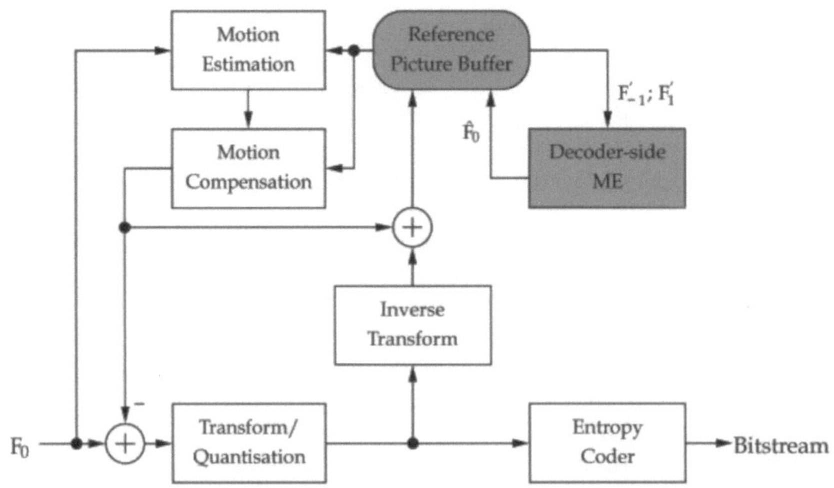

Fig. 6. Simplified block diagram of a conventional hybrid encoder with DSME modifications, as proposed by Klomp et al. (2009), highlighted in grey.

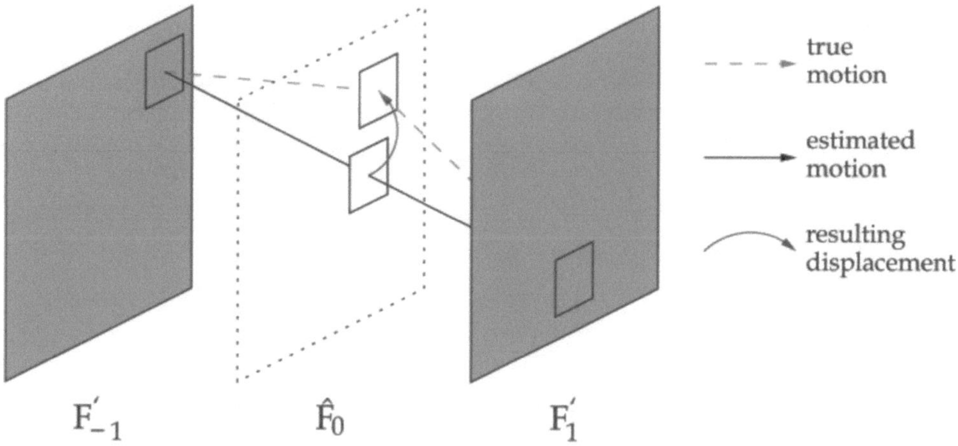

Fig. 7. Displaced interpolation due to nonlinear motion.

true motion drawn with dashed arrows is not linear and the correct position of the block is in the upper right corner. Nevertheless, the encoder can still use that block by applying motion compensation at the DSME frame and transmitting the resulting displacement as depicted in Figure 7.

The most important part of the DSME block is the motion estimation algorithm, since the performance of the proposed system is mainly affected by the accuracy of the motion vectors. Accurate motion vectors result in a good interpolation of the current frame, which will then be selected more often as a reference by the encoder tools. Conventional block matching algorithms, as used in e.g. H.264 / AVC, are not applicable to decoder-side motion estimation, since they only minimise some cost function like the sum of the absolute/squared differences (SAD/SSD) and do not search for true motion. Thus, an adapted motion estimation algorithm is needed, which is described in detail in Section 4.1.

Since the used algorithm interpolates between two frames, the approach is only applicable to B frames, in which a future frame is available at the decoder. However, the design is very flexible and extrapolation from previous frames can easily be implemented to allow DSME also for P frames.

4.1 Motion vector search

As explained in the previous section, the motion estimation algorithm of the DSME block shown in Figure 6 has a significant impact on the coding performance. In this approach, the motion is estimated by minimising the sum of the squared differences (SSD) between the two reference frames F'_{-1} and F'_1. The 6-tap Wiener filter proposed by Werner (1996), which is similar to filter standardised in H.264 / AVC, is used to interpolate sub-pixel values needed to estimate motion vectors with half-pel accuracy.

However, a false local minimum might be found if the block size is small and the search range large, as shown in Figure 8. Thus, the motion compensated interpolation fails, resulting in a distorted frame $\hat{F}_0$ (Figure 9).

To prevent inaccurate motion vectors, the hierarchical motion estimation scheme proposed by Klomp et al. (2010b) is used (Figure 10). The algorithm starts by using a block size of 64×64 pixels and a search range of 128 pixel. For the following iterations, the search range is decreased for each hierarchy level, since the coarse motion was already estimated in previous

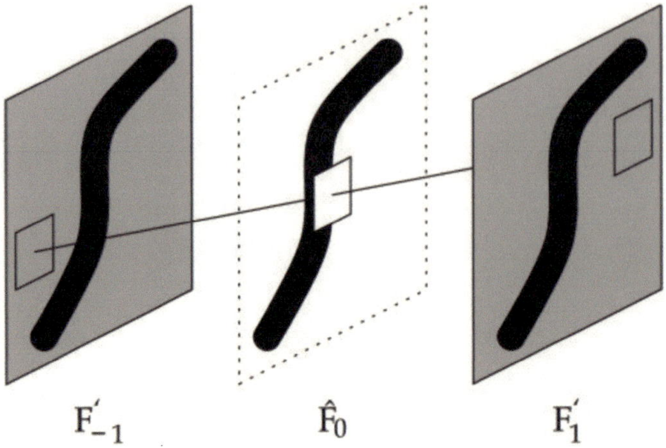

Fig. 8. Bidirectional motion compensation can fail due to large search range and homogeneous background.

levels. The two reference frames F'_{-1} and F'_1, which are used to estimate the motion, are low-pass filtered in the first iteration to prevent local minima due to the large search range. For all other iterations, the unfiltered reference frames are used, since the search ranges are smaller as previously mentioned.

At each hierarchy level, the motion vectors between the previous and the next frame (F'_{-1}, F'_1) are estimated using a conventional block matching algorithm by minimising the SSD. For smaller blocks, the matching window of the motion estimation is slightly larger than the block size during motion compensation to be more robust against image noise. This parameter is set individually for each level.

The search area used for the motion estimation in the current hierarchy level depends on the current search range and the motion vectors of the previous hierarchy level, as depicted in Figure 11: The nine neighbouring motion vectors of the previous level are applied to the current block and define a set of starting points. The search area used for motion estimation is

Fig. 9. Detail of the interpolated frame $\hat{F}_0$ of the PeopleOnStreet sequence. Failed motion compensation is highlighted in red.

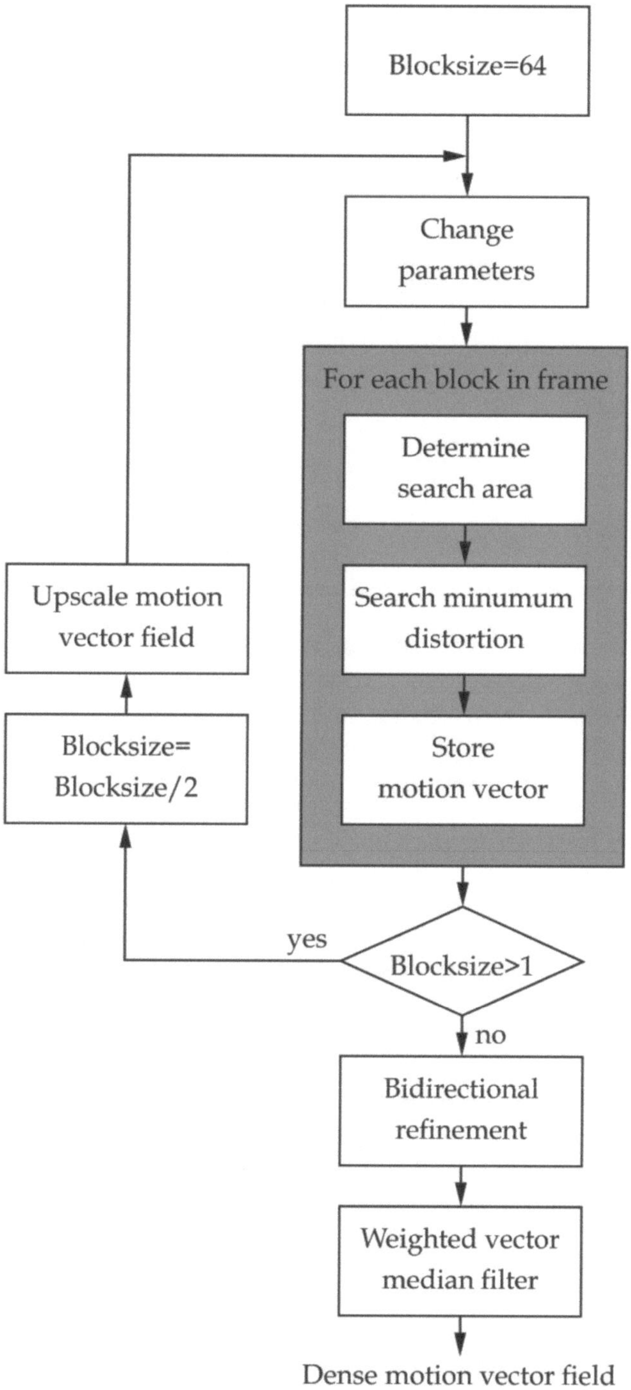

Fig. 10. Block diagram of the hierarchical motion estimation algorithm.

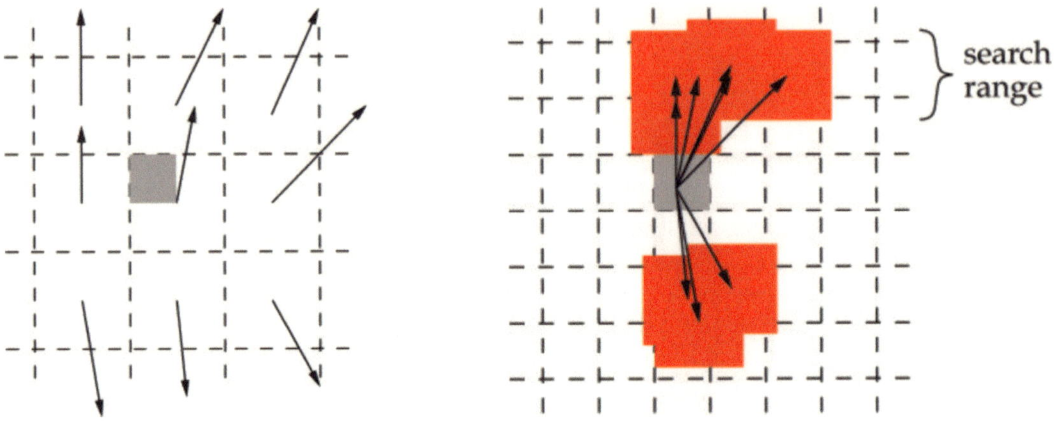

(a) Previous level H_{n-1} (b) Current level H_n

Fig. 11. Search area (red) derived from previous hierarchy level.

calculated by applying the search range to each starting point. Thus, the current block is able to follow the motion of every neighbouring block while still using small search ranges, which significantly reduces the amount of SSD computations compared to the search algorithm used by Klomp et al. (2009).

If the last iteration of the forward motion search is finished, the motion vectors are aligned to the block grid of the current frame. A bi-directional refinement is performed, in which the best sub-pel position is calculated for each motion vector. Thereafter, the vector field is smoothed using a vector median filter weighted by the mean of absolute differences (MAD) of the displaced blocks, as proposed by Alparone et al. (1996), in order to eliminate outliers.

After the motion vector field is estimated, the intermediate frame is interpolated in two steps. First, motion vectors is halved resulting in to motion vector pointing from the current frame to the corresponding blocks in the previous and next frame as depicted in Figure 7. The same 6-tap Wiener filter as used for motion estimation is selected to calculate pixel values at sub-pel positions. Second, the pixel values from the two reference frames are averaged and produce the interpolated frame. Using the pixel values from both frames reduces noise caused by the quantisation of the reference frames and also the camera noise. If only one reference frame is motion compensated and used as interpolated frame would give worse quality and, thus, impair the coding performance.

Thereafter, the interpolated frame is fed into the reference picture buffer an can be used by all H.264 / AVC coding tools as already explained in Section 4. The following section evaluates the coding performance of this approach and gives a comparison with DMVD.

5. Experimental results

To evaluate the performance, seven test sequences are coded using three approaches: Decoder-side motion vector derivation (DMVD), decoder-side motion estimation (DSME) and the underlying ITU-T / ISO/IEC standard H.264 / AVC as reference. These sequences are also used by ITU-T and ISO/IEC (2010) to evaluate tools for a new video coding standard. To allow random access every second, the intra frame period is individually set for each test sequence according to the frame rate. Every eighth frames is coded as P frame. The remaining frames are coded as hierarchical B frames resulting in the following GOP structure: I-b-B-b-B-b-B-b-P.

Sequence	DMVD	DSME
Kimono, 1080p, 24Hz	-9.8 %	-4.9 %
BasketballDrive, 1080p, 50Hz	-5.7 %	-5.7 %
BQTerrace, 1080p, 60Hz	-8.8 %	-4.7 %
PeopleOnStreet, 2560x1600, 30Hz	-9.0 %	-13.0 %
Cactus, 1080p, 50Hz	-5.6 %	-8.2 %
ParkScene, 1080p, 24Hz	-8.9 %	-8.4 %
Traffic, 2560x1600, 30Hz	-7.6 %	-9.7 %

Table 1. BD rate gains for DMVD, DSME compared to H.264 / AVC reference for several high-definition sequences.

The operational rate-distortion curves for four distinctive sequences are plotted in Figure 12 to 15. To obtain an objective measurement of the average rate gains, Bjøntegaard (2001) proposed a method where a third order polynomial is fit into four data points of the rate distortion curve. The so-called Bjøntegaard Delta (BD) rate gains for all seven test sequences are provided in Table 1.

The Kimono sequence used to evaluate the compression performance consist of a global camera pan with a moving person in front of trees. As shown in Figure 12, DMVD has a slightly better performance compared to DSME for the lowest rate point. However, the gain of DSME decreases for higher rates while the gain of DMVD is almost constant for all rate points. Therefore, the BD rate gain of 9.8% for DMVD is twice as big as the gain for DSME, as shown in Table 1.

The BasketballDrive sequence was captured during a Basketball match. It contains some motion blur due to the fast movements of the players. Coding this sequence also results in compression improvements for both approaches, although fast motion and occlusion due to non-rigid objects occur. DSME outperforms DMVD for lower bit rates as shown in Figure 13. Again, the compression performance of DSME decreases for higher bit rates and DMVD gives better results for those rates. Nevertheless, the average rate gains for DMVD and DSME are both 5.7%.

The gain of the DSME approach for BQTerrace (Figure 14) is with 4.7% the lowest for all sequences. The motion estimation fails at the water surface and flames due to the non-rigid motion and missing texture. DMVD can handle these characteristics slightly better.

Sequences with very high resolution can gain even more by using DMVD and DSME, as shown in Figure 15. The PeopleOnStreet sequence is a 4k $\times$ 2k sequence captured with a static camera and contains people crossing a street. The sequence was cropped to 2560 $\times$ 1600 pixels to limit the computational resources for the experiments. DMVD achieves 9% bit rate reduction for this sequence. The average gain is even higher for DSME: 13% bit rate reduction is achieved, since the motion can be estimated very accurately due to the high amount of detail in this high resolution sequence.

The rate-distortion plots for the different sequences have in common that the gain of DSME decreases towards higher rates. The improved quality of the key frames F'_{-1} and F'_1 have almost no influence on the DSME frame estimation accuracy. Thus, the conventional coding tools select more often the other high quality reference frames instead of the interpolated DSME frame. This characteristic can also be observed in Figure 16.

The amount of the macroblocks, which use the DSME frame for prediction, are plotted for the different rate points. The DSME usage is highest for rate point one, which corresponds to the lowest bit rate. For larger rate points, and thus, increasing bit rate and quality, the amount

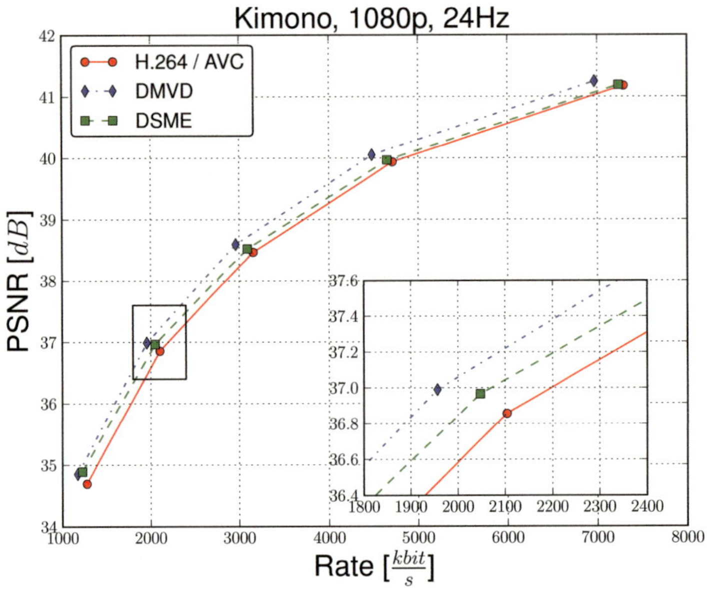

Fig. 12. Rate-Distortion performance of DMVD and DSME for the Kimono sequence.

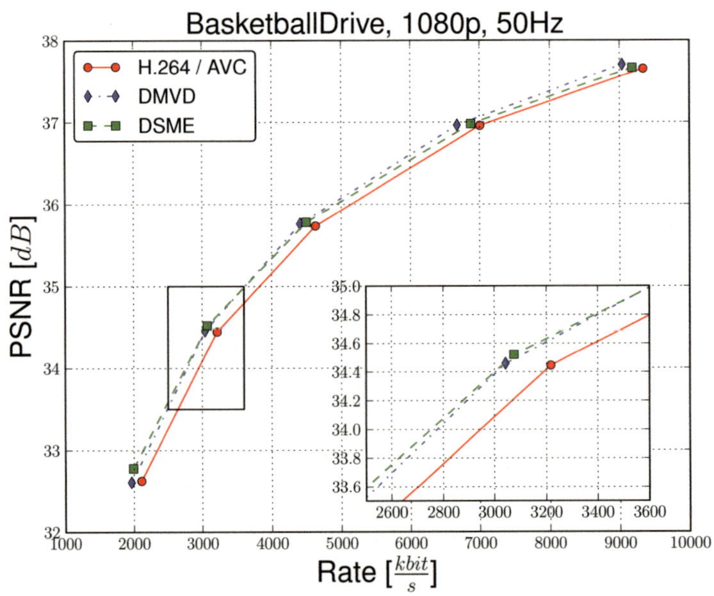

Fig. 13. Rate-Distortion performance of DMVD and DSME for the BasketballDrive sequence.

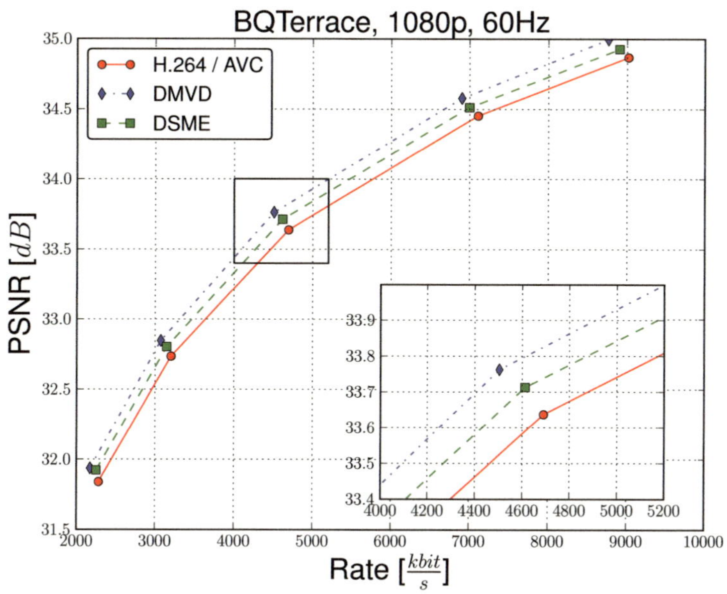

Fig. 14. Rate-Distortion performance of DMVD and DSME for the BQTerrace sequence.

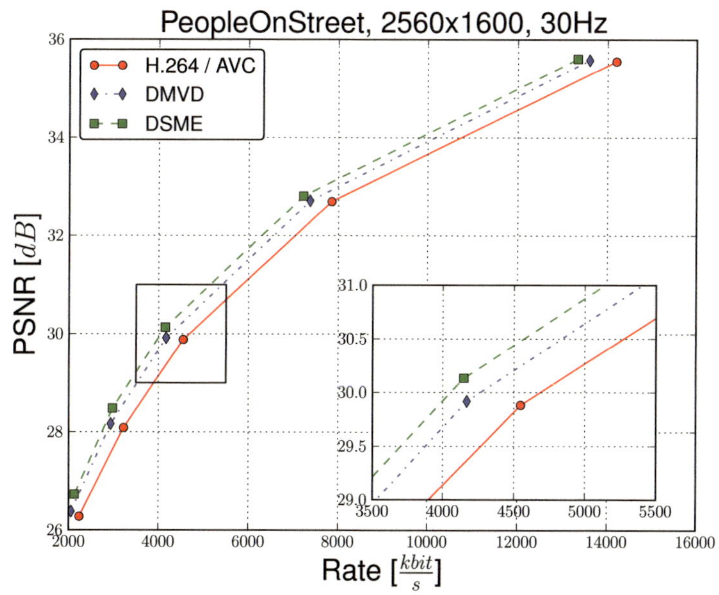

Fig. 15. Rate-Distortion performance of DMVD and DSME for the PeopleOnStreet sequence.

declines. Therefore, the performance of DSME and the H.264 / AVC reference converges. Furthermore, the reduced rate for the motion vectors has a smaller impact at high rate points. In contrast, DMVD achieves high gains for all rate points. Since DMVD uses already decoded pixel values for template matching, it can benefit from the improved quality of the current frame.

Figure 16 is also a good indicator of the overall DSME performance: For the well performing PeopleOnStreet sequence, almost 50% of the macroblocks and sub-macroblocks use the DSME frame for prediction. In contrast, the DSME usage while coding the BQTerrace sequence is around 30%.

The performance gains of the three remaining sequences of the test set have similar characteristics as shown in Table 1. DSME outperforms DMVD for the Cactus and Traffic sequences. Only for ParkScene is the gain of DMVD slightly better than DSME.

6. Conclusions

Two very promising approaches, which improve the compression efficiency of current video coding standards by estimating motion at the decoder, were described. Decoder-side motion vector (DMVD) derivation calculates a prediction of the current block at the decoder by using already decoded data. Thus, no motion vectors have to be transmitted and compression is achieved. Decoder-side motion estimation (DSME) is a frame based approach. The motion is estimated for the whole frame at once and used for motion compensated interpolation of the current frame to be coded. Thereafter, this interpolated frame can then be used as an additional reference for the conventional coding tools. Compression is achieved, since the interpolated frame is already an accurate prediction of the current frame.

DMVD achieves an average bit rate reduction of 7.9%. The average gain of DSME is with 7.8%

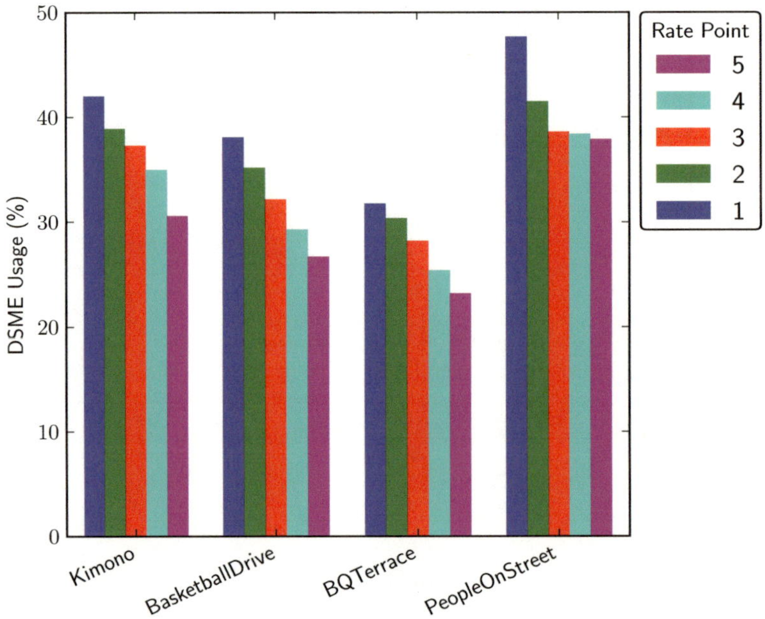

Fig. 16. Usage of the DSME frame as reference for H.264 / AVC inter prediction for different rate points.

almost the same. Interestingly, DSME outperforms DMVD for some sequences, although both approaches try to utilise similar sequence characteristics to achieve compression.
The improved compression efficiency comes along with increased computational complexity. Especially DMVD introduces high complexity due to the hierarchical motion estimation approach. However, hold-type displays, like liquid crystal displays (LCD) and plasma displays, perform motion estimation and temporal interpolation in real-time for frame rate up conversion (Choi et al., 2000). Using such algorithms, the computational complexity of DSME can be reduced.
In 2010, ITU-T Study Group 16 (VCEG) and ISO/IEC JTC 1/SC 29/WG 11 (MPEG) created the Joint Collaborative Team on Video Coding (JCT-VC) to develop a new generation video coding standard that will further reduce the data rate needed for high quality video coding, as compared to the current state-of-the-art H.264 / AVC standard. This new coding standardisation initiative is being referred to as High Efficiency Video Coding (HEVC). Due to the promising rate gains achieved with additional motion estimation algorithms at the decoder, JCT-VC initiated a tool experiment in this research field (Wien & Chiu, 2010). The goal of this tool experiment is to evaluate if techniques based on motion compensation at the decoder should be included into the HEVC standard.

7. References

Alparone, L., Barni, M., Bartolini, F. & Cappellini, V. (1996). Adaptive weighted vector-median filters for motion fields smoothing, *Proceedings of the IEEE International Conference on Acoustics, Speech and Signal Processing*, Georgia, USA.

Bjøntegaard, G. (2001). Calculation of average PSNR differences between RD curves, *ITU-T SG16/Q6 Output Document VCEG-M33*, Austin, Texas.

Choi, B.-T., Lee, S.-H. & Ko, S.-J. (2000). New frame rate up-conversion using bi-directional motion estimation, *IEEE Transactions on Consumer Electronics* 46(3): 603 –609.

ITU-T and ISO/IEC (2003). Draft ITU-T recommendation and final draft international standard of joint video specification, *ITU-T Rec.H.264 and ISO/IEC14496-10AVC* .

ITU-T and ISO/IEC (2010). Joint call for proposals on video compression technology, *ISO/IEC JTC1/SC29/WG11 MPEG Output Document N11113*, Kyoto.

Kamp, S., Ballé, J. & Wien, M. (2009). Multihypothesis prediction using decoder side motion vector derivation in inter frame video coding, *Proceedings of SPIE Visual Communications and Image Processing*, SPIE, Bellingham, San José, CA, USA.

Kamp, S., Bross, B. & Wien, M. (2009). Fast decoder side motion vector derivation for inter frame video coding, *Proceedings of International Picture Coding Symposium*, IEEE, Piscataway, Chicago, IL, USA.

Kamp, S., Evertz, M. & Wien, M. (2008). Decoder side motion vector derivation for inter frame video coding, *Proceedings of the IEEE International Conference on Image Processing*, IEEE, Piscataway, San Diego, CA, USA, pp. 1120–1123.

Kamp, S. & Wien, M. (2010). Decoder-side motion vector derivation for hybrid video inter coding, *Proceedings of the IEEE International Conference on Multimedia and Expo*, Singapore.

Klomp, S., Munderloh, M. & Ostermann, J. (2010a). Block size dependent error model for motion compensation, *Proceedings of the IEEE International Conference on Image Processing*, Hong Kong, pp. 969–972.

Klomp, S., Munderloh, M. & Ostermann, J. (2010b). Decoder–side hierarchical motion estimation for dense vector elds, *Proceedings of the Picture Coding Symposium*, Nagoya,

Japan. Japan, pp. 362-366. Accepted for publication.

Klomp, S., Munderloh, M., Vatis, Y. & Ostermann, J. (2009). Decoder-side block motion estimation for H.264 / MPEG-4 AVC based video coding, *Proceedings of the IEEE International Symposium on Circuits and Systems*, Taipei, Taiwan, pp. 1641–1644.

Munderloh, M., Klomp, S. & Ostermann, J. (2010). Mesh-based decoder-side motion estimation, *Proceedings of the IEEE International Conference on Image Processing*, Hong Kong, pp. 2049–2052.

Richardson, I. E. G. (2003). *H.264 and MPEG-4 Video Compression*, John Wiley & Sons Ltd., West Sussex, England, chapter 6.4.5.3.

Sullivan, G. J. & Wiegand, T. (1998). Rate-distortion optimization for video compression, *IEEE Signal Processing Magazine* 15(11): 74–90.

Suzuki, Y., Boon, C. S. & Kato, S. (2006). Block-based reduced resolution inter frame coding with template matching prediction, *Proceedings of the IEEE International Conference on Image Processing*, Atlanta, USA, pp. 1701 – 1704.

Suzuki, Y., Boon, C. S. & Tan, T. K. (2007). Inter frame coding with template matching averaging, *Proceedings of the IEEE International Conference on Image Processing*, San Antonio, TX, USA, pp. III 409 – 412.

Werner, O. (1996). Drift analysis and drift reduction for multiresolution hybrid video coding, *Signal Processing: Image Communication* 8(5): 387–409.

Wien, M. & Chiu, Y.-J. (2010). Tool experiment 1: Decoder-side motion vector derivation, *JCT-VC Output Document JCTVC-A301*, Dresden, Germany.

Part 3

Video Compression and Wavelet Based Coding

6

Asymmetrical Principal Component Analysis Theory and its Applications to Facial Video Coding

Ulrik Söderström and Haibo Li
Digital Media Lab, Dept. of Applied Physics and Electronics, Umeå University
Sweden

1. Introduction

The use of video telephony has not become a big success but it still has potential to become widespread. Video communication is becoming a well-used application for both personal use and corporations. This kind of communication is used in conversations between people and is essential for saving travel bills for companies. Less traveling also saves the environment and is therefore expected to be an important factor in the future. Even if the available bandwidth will increase it is desirable to use as low bandwidth as possible for communication since less bandwidth means lower cost, more availability in networks and less sensitivity to network delays. As more video is transmitted over networks, lower bandwidth need for video transmission means that more users can make use of video at the same time. Low bandwidth means low power consumption for transmission while low encoding and decoding complexity means low power consumption when the video is encoded and decoded. The impact of power consumption is expected to become much more important in the future as the availability of power is decreased and pollution from energy production needs to be halted.

Every human face is contained within a space called the face space. Every face can be recognized, represented or synthesized with this space. Principal component analysis (PCA) [Jolliffe (1986)] can be used to create a compact representation of this space. This enables PCA to be used for highly efficient video coding and other image processing tasks. The faces in the face space all have the same facial expression but PCA can also be used to create a space with different facial expressions for a single person. This is referred to as the personal face space, facial mimic space or personal mimic space [Ohba et al. (1998)]. This space consists of faces for a single person but with several different facial expressions. According to the American psychologist Paul Ekman it is enough to model six basic emotions to actually model all facial expressions [Ekman & Friesen (1975); Ekman (1982)]. The six basic emotions; happiness, sadness, surprise, fear, anger and disgust (Fig. 1), are blended in different ways to create all other possible expressions.

The combination of basic emotions is not directly applicable for linear processing with images so more than six dimensions are needed. We have previously evaluated exactly how many dimensions that are needed to reach a certain representation quality [Söderström & Li (2010)]. Efficient use of PCA for modeling of any data requires that the global motion is removed from the data set. For facial video this motion corresponds to motion of the entire head, e.g., positional shift and facial rotation. The motion that is modeled with PCA is the local

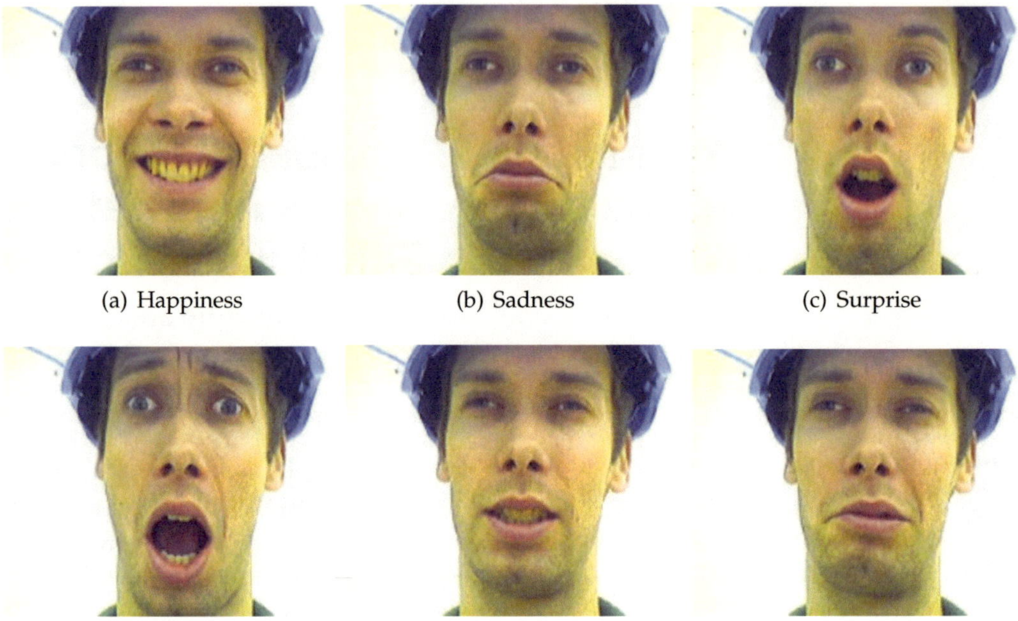

(a) Happiness (b) Sadness (c) Surprise

(d) Fear (e) Anger (f) Disgust

Fig. 1. The six basic emotions.

motion, i.e., the changes in the face, the facial mimic. The global motion can be removed with hardware techniques, e.g., hands-free video equipment [Söderström & Li (2005a)] or software implementations such as facial detection and feature tracking.

PCA provides a natural way for scaling video regarding quality. For the same encoding the decoder can select how many dimensions of the space that are used for decoding and thus scale the quality of the reconstructed video. The built-in scalability of PCA is easily utilized in video compression.

The operations with PCA involves all pixels, K, in a frame. When PCA is used for video compression the complexity for encoding and decoding is linearly dependent on K. It is desirable to have a low complexity for encoding but it is also desirable to have a high spatial resolution on the decoded video. A technique that allows the use of different areas for encoding and decoding is needed.

PCA extracts the most important information in the data based on the variance of the data. When it comes to video frames PCA extracts the most important information based on the pixel variance. The pixel variance is examined in section 5.1. Some pixels may have a high variance but no semantic importance for the facial mimic. These pixels will degrade the model efficiency for the facial mimic. To prevent that these high variance semantically unimportant pixels have effect on the model a region of interest (ROI) can be cropped or extracted from the video frames.

In this article we will examine how part of the frames can be used for encoding while we decode the entire frames. The usage of only a part of the frame for encoding while using full frame decoding is called asymmetrical PCA (aPCA) and it has been introduced by Söderström and Li [Söderström & Li (2008)]. In this work we will focus on different extractions and different sizes of the ROI.

The user can determine the important area in a video sequence or it can automatically be extracted using low-level processing of the frames. We present five different methods for extracting a ROI from video sequences where the face of a person is the most prominent information. An example of how the variance of the individual pixels vary is presented. This example clearly shows the motivation behind using a ROI instead of the entire frame. An example that visualizes the quality of the individual pixels is presented. This example shows that the quality for the semantically important pixels actually is increased when less information is used for encoding; if the correct information is used. Previously we presented how aPCA is used to reduce the encoding complexity [Söderström & Li (2008)]. Here we describe how aPCA can be used to reduce the decoding complexity as well.
Research related to this work is discussed in the next section and video coding based on principal component analysis (PCA) is explained in section 3. Asymmetrical PCA (aPCA) and how it is used to reduce encoder and decoder complexity is explained in section 4. Practical experiments of ROI extraction and usage with aPCA are explained in section 5 and the article is concluded in section 6.

2. Related work

Facial mimic representation has previously been used to encode sequences of faces [Torres & Prado (2002); Torres & Delp (2000)] and head-and-shoulders [Söderström & Li (2005a; 2007)]. These attempts try to represent facial video with a high quality at a very low bitrate. General video coding do not use PCA; the reigning transform is Discrete Cosine Transform (DCT) [Schäfer et al. (2003); Wiegand et al. (2003)]. Representation of facial video through DCT does not provide sufficiently high compression by itself and is therefore combined with motion estimation (temporal compression). DCT and block-matching requires several DCT-coefficients to encode the frames and several possible movements of the blocks between the frames. Consequently, the best codec available today does not provide high quality video at very low bitrates even if the video is suitable for high compression.
Video frames can also be represented as a collection of features from an alphabet. This is how a language functions; a small amount of letters can be ordered in different ways to create all the words in a language. By building an alphabet for video features it should be possible to model all video frames as a combination of these features. The encoder calculates which features that a frame consists of and transmit this information to the decoder which reassembles the frame based on the features. Since only information about which features the frame consists of is transmitted such an approach reach very low bitrates. A technique that uses such an alphabet is Matching Pursuit (MP) [Neff & Zakhor (1997)].
Facial images can be represented by other techniques then with video. A wireframe that has the same shape as a human face is used by several techniques. To make the wireframe move as a face it is sufficient to transmit information about the changes in the wireframe. To give the wireframe a more natural look it is texture-mapped with a facial image. Techniques that make use of a wireframe to model facial images are for example MPEG4 facial animation [Ostermann (1998)] and model based coding [Aizawa & Huang (1995); Forchheimer et al. (1983)]. Both of these techniques reach very low bitrate and can maintain high spatial resolution and framerate. A statistical shape model of a face is used by Active Appearance Model (AAM) [Cootes et al. (1998)]. AAM also use statistics for the pixel intensity to improve the robustness of the method.
All these representation techniques have serious drawbacks for efficient usage in visual communication. Pighin *et al.* provides a good explanation why high visual quality is

important and why video is superior to animations [Pighin et al. (1998)]. The face simply exhibits so many tiny creases and wrinkles that it is impossible to model with animations or low spatial resolution. To resolve this issue the framerate can be sacrificed instead. Wang and Cohen presented a solution where high quality images are used for teleconferencing over low bandwidth networks with a framerate of one frame each 2-3 seconds [Wang & Cohen (2005)]. But high framerate and high spatial resolution are important for several visual tasks; framerate for some, resolution for others and some tasks require both [Lee & Eleftheriadis (1996)]. Any technique that want to provide video at very low bitrates must be able to provide video with high spatial resolution, high framerate and have natural-looking appearance.

Methods that are presented in Video coding (Second generation approach) [Torres & Kunt (1996)] make use of certain features for encoding instead of the entire video frame. This idea is in line with aPCA since only part of the information is used for encoding in this technique. Scalable video coding (SVC) has high usage for video content that is received by heterogenous devices. The ability to display a certain spatial resolution and/or visual quality might be completely different if the video is received by a cellular phone or a desktop computer. The available bandwidth can also limit the video quality for certain users. The encoder must encode the video into layers for the decoder to be able to decode the video in layered fashion. Layered encoding has therefore been given much attention in the research community. A review of the scalable extension for H.264 is provided by Schwarz *et.al.* [Schwarz et al. (2007)].

3. Principal component analysis video coding

First, we introduce video compression with regular principal component analysis (PCA) [Jolliffe (1986)]. Any object can be decomposed into principal components and represented as a linear mixture of these components. The space containing the facial images is called Eigenspace Φ and there as many dimensions of this space as there are frames in the original data set. When this space is extracted from a video sequence showing the basic emotions it is actually a personal mimic space. The Eigenspace Φ={ϕ_1 ϕ_2 ... ϕ_N} is constructed as

$$\phi_j = \sum_i b_{ij}(\mathbf{I}_i - \mathbf{I}_{\underline{0}}) \tag{1}$$

where b_{ij} are values from the Eigenvectors of the covariance matrix $\{(\mathbf{I}_i - \mathbf{I}_{\underline{0}})^T(\mathbf{I}_j - \mathbf{I}_{\underline{0}})\}$. $\mathbf{I}_{\underline{0}}$ is the mean of all video frames and is constructed as:

$$\mathbf{I}_{\underline{0}} = \frac{1}{N}\sum_{j=1}^{N} \mathbf{I}_j \tag{2}$$

Projection coefficients $\{\alpha_j\}$=$\{\alpha_1\ \alpha_2\ ...\ \alpha_N\}$ can be extracted for each video frame through projection:

$$\alpha_j = \phi_j(\mathbf{I} - \mathbf{I}_{\underline{0}})^T \tag{3}$$

Each of the video frames can then be represented as a sum of the mean of all pixels and the weighted principal components. This representation is error-free if all N principal components are used.

$$\mathbf{I} = \mathbf{I}_{\underline{0}} + \sum_{j=1}^{N} \alpha_j \phi_j \tag{4}$$

Since the model is very compact many principal components can be discarded with a negligible quality loss and a sum with fewer principal components M can represent the image.

$$\hat{\mathbf{I}} = \mathbf{I}_{\underline{0}} + \sum_{j=1}^{M} \alpha_j \phi_j \quad (5)$$

where M is a selected number of principal components used for reconstruction ($M < N$).
The extent of the error incurred by using fewer components (M) than (N) is examined in [Söderström & Li (2010)]. With the model it is possible to encode entire video frames to only a few coefficients $\{\alpha_j\}$ and reconstruct the frames with high quality. A detailed description and examples can be found in [Söderström & Li (2005a;b)].
PCA video coding provides natural scalable video since the quality is directly dependent on the number of coefficients M that are used for decoding. The decoder can scale the quality of the video frame by frame by selecting the amount of coefficients used for decoding. This gives the decoder large freedom to scale the video without the encoder having to encode the video into scalable layers. The scalability is built-in in the reconstruction process and the decoder can easily scale the quality for each individual frame.

4. Asymmetrical principal component analysis video coding

There are two major issues with the use of full frame encoding:

1. The information in the principal components are based on all pixels in the frame. Pixels that are part of the background or are unimportant for the facial mimic may have large importance on the model. The model is affected by semantically unimportant pixels.
2. The complexity of encoding, decoding and model extraction is directly dependent on the spatial resolution of the frames, i.e., the number of pixels, K, in the frames. Video frames with high spatial resolution will require more computations than frames with low resolution.

When the frame is decoded it is a benefit of having large spatial resolution (frame size) since this provides better visual quality. A small frame should be used for encoding and a large frame for decoding to optimize the complexity and quality of encoding and decoding. This is possible to achieve through the use of pseudo principal components; information where not all the data are principal components. Parts of the video frames are considered to be important; they are regarded as foreground $\mathbf{I}^f$.

$$\mathbf{I}^f = crop(\mathbf{I}) \quad (6)$$

The Eigenspace for the foreground Φ^f=$\{\phi_1^f \ \phi_2^f \ \ldots \ \phi_N^f\}$ is constructed according to the following formula:

$$\phi_j^f = \sum_i b_{ij}^f (\mathbf{I}_i^f - \mathbf{I}_{\underline{0}}^f) \quad (7)$$

where b_{ij}^f are values from the Eigenvectors of the covariance matrix $\{(\mathbf{I}_i^f - \mathbf{I}_{\underline{0}}^f)^T(\mathbf{I}_j^f - \mathbf{I}_{\underline{0}}^f)\}$ and $\mathbf{I}_{\underline{0}}^f$ is the mean of the foreground. Encoding and decoding is performed as:

$$\alpha_j^f = (\phi_j^f)(\mathbf{I}^f - \mathbf{I}_{\underline{0}}^f)^T \quad (8)$$

$$\hat{\mathbf{I}}^f = \mathbf{I}_{\underline{0}}^f + \sum_{j=1}^{M} \alpha_j^f \phi_j^f \tag{9}$$

where $\{\alpha_j^f\}$ are coefficients extracted using information from the foreground $\mathbf{I}^f$. The reconstructed frame $\hat{\mathbf{I}}^f$ has smaller size and contains less information than a full size frame. A space which is spanned by components where only the foreground is orthogonal can be created. The components spanning this space are called pseudo principal components and this space has the same size as a full frame:

$$\phi_j^p = \sum_i b_{ij}^f (\mathbf{I}_i - \mathbf{I}_{\underline{0}}) \tag{10}$$

From the coefficients $\{\alpha_j^f\}$ it is possible to reconstruct the entire frame:

$$\hat{\mathbf{I}} = \mathbf{I}_{\underline{0}} + \sum_{j=1}^{M} \alpha_j^f \phi_j^p \tag{11}$$

where M is the selected number of pseudo components used for reconstruction. A full frame video can be reconstructed (Eq. 11) using the projection coefficients from only the foreground of the video (Eq. 8) so the foreground is used for encoding and the entire frame is decoded. It is easy to prove that

$$\hat{\mathbf{I}}^f = crop(\hat{\mathbf{I}}) \tag{12}$$

since $\phi_j^f = crop(\phi_j^p)$ and $\mathbf{I}_{\underline{0}}^f = crop(\mathbf{I}_{\underline{0}})$.
aPCA provides the decoder with the freedom to decide the spatial size of the encoded area without the encoder having to do any special processing of the frames. Reduction in spatial resolution is not a size reduction of the entire frame; parts of the frame can be decoded with full spatial resolution. No quality is lost in the decoded parts; it is up to the decoder to choose how much and which parts of the frame it wants to decode. The bitstream is exactly the same regardless of what video size the decoder wants to decode. With aPCA the decoder can scale the reconstructed video regarding spatial resolution and area.

4.1 Reduction of complexity for the encoder

The complexity for encoding is directly dependent on the spatial resolution of the frame that should be encoded. The important factor for complexity is $K * M$, where K is the number of pixels and M is the chosen number of Eigenvectors. When aPCA is used the number of pixels k in the selected area gives a factor of $n = \frac{K}{k}$ in resolution reduction. The number of computations are at the same time decreased by $n * M$.

4.2 Reduction of complexity for the decoder

The complexity for decoding can be reduced when a part of the frame is used for both encoding and decoding. In the formulas above we only use the pseudo principal components for the full frame ϕ_j^p for decoding but if both Φ^p and Φ^f are used for decoding the complexity can be reduced. Only a few principal components of Φ^p are used to reconstruct the entire frame. More principal components from Φ^f are used to add details to the foreground.

	Reconstructed Quality (PSNR) [dB]		
ϕ	Y	U	V
1	28,0	33,6	40,2
5	32,7	35,8	42,2
10	35,2	36,2	42,7
15	36,6	36,4	43,0
20	37,7	36,5	43,1
25	38,4	36,5	43,2

Table 1. Reference results. Video encoded with PCA using the entire frame **I**.

$$\hat{\mathbf{I}} = \mathbf{I}_{\underline{0}} + \sum_{j=1}^{L} \alpha_j^f \phi_j^p + \sum_{j=L+1}^{M} \alpha_j^f \phi_j^f \tag{13}$$

The result is reconstructed frames with slightly lower quality for the background but with the same quality for the foreground $\mathbf{I}^f$ as if only Φ_j^p was used for reconstruction. The quality of the background is decided by parameter L: a high L-value will increase the information used for background reconstruction and increase the decoder complexity. A low L-value has the opposite effect. The reduction in complexity (compression ratio CR) is calculated as:

$$CR = \frac{K(M+1)}{(1+L)K + (M-L)k} \tag{14}$$

When $k << K$ the compression ratio can be approximated to $CR \approx \frac{M+1}{L+1}$. A significant result is that spatial scalability is achieved naturally; the decoder can decide the size of the decoded frames without any intervention from the encoder.

5. Asymmetrical principal component analysis video coding: practical implementations

In this section we show several examples of using aPCA for compression of facial video sequences. We show five examples, all for facial video sequences. As a reference we present the quality for encoding the video sequences with regular PCA in Table 1. This is equal to using the Eigenspace Φ for both encoding and decoding of video sequences.

5.1 Experiment I: Encoding with the mouth as foreground, decoding with the entire frame

The mouth is the most prominent facial part regarding facial mimic. By representing the shape of the mouth the entire facial mimic can be represented quite well. In this experiment, the foreground $\mathbf{I}^f$ consists of the mouth area and $\mathbf{I}$ is the entire frame (Fig. 2). $\mathbf{I}^f$ has a spatial size of 80x64 and $\mathbf{I}$ is 240x176 pixels large.

PCA extracts the most important information in a video sequence based on the variance of the pixels. This means that a pixel with high variance is important and low variance means the opposite. When the entire image is used some pixels which belong to the background may have high variance and be considered important. But these pixels have no semantical importance for the facial mimic and only degrades the model for the facial mimic. Asymmetrical principal component analysis (aPCA) [Söderström & Li (2008)] allow the use of foreground, i.e., important area, for encoding and decoding of entire frames. Fig. 3 shows the variance of the individual pixels in one of the video sequences used in Experiment I. The

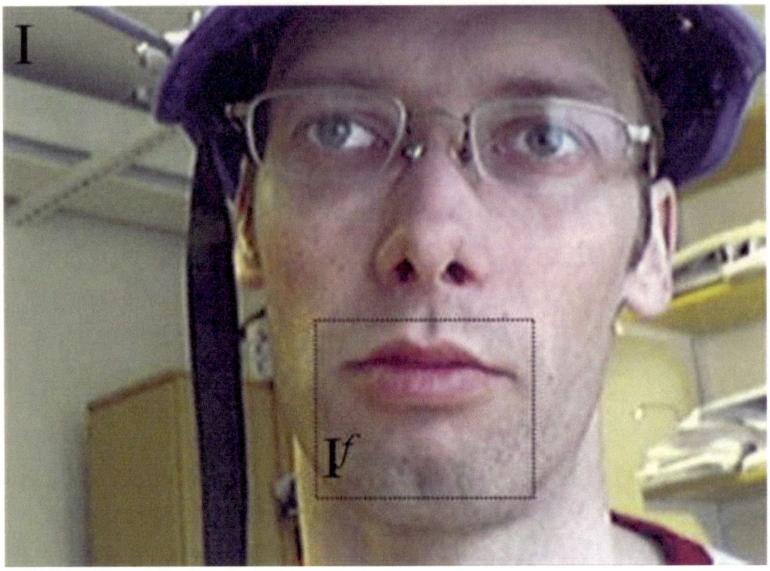

Fig. 2. The entire video frame and the foreground $\mathbf{I}^f$ used for Experiment I.

variance is noted in a heat-scale so white means low variance and yellow means high variance. It is clear that pixels from the background have high variance and are considered important by PCA. By only choosing the pixels that we know are semantically important we can increase the modeling efficiency of the facial mimic. With the use of aPCA it is still possible to decode the entire frames so no spatial resolution is lost.

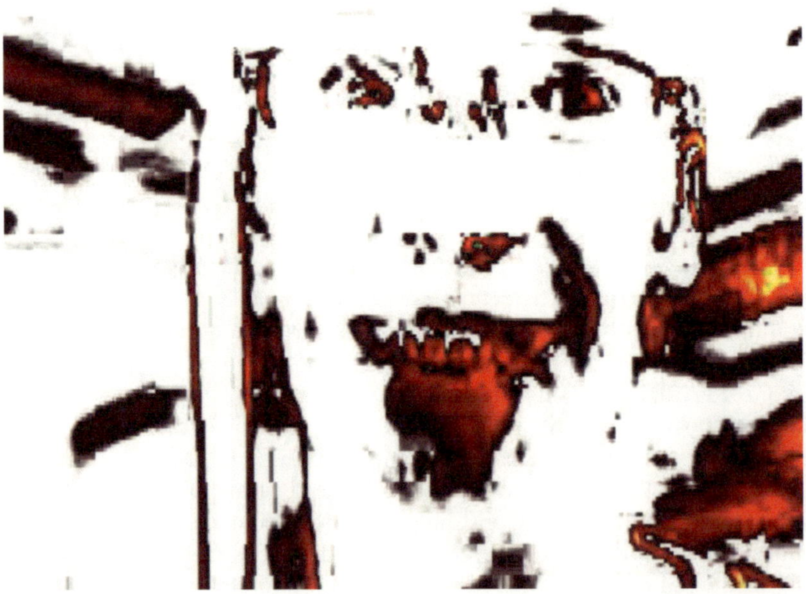

Fig. 3. Variance for the individual pixels in a video sequence. *White = low variance Yellow = high variance*

	Lowered rec. qual. (PSNR) [dB]		
ϕ	Y	U	V
5	-1,4	-0,3	-0,2
10	-1,8	-0,3	-0,2
15	-2,0	-0,2	-0,2
20	-2,0	-0,1	-0,2
25	-2,1	-0,1	-0,2

Table 2. Average lowered reconstruction quality for 10 video sequences for a foreground $\mathbf{I}^f$ consisting of the mouth area (Experiment I).

The reconstruction quality is measured compared to the reconstruction quality when the entire frame **I** is used for encoding (Table 1). We also compare the complexity for encoding with **I** and $\mathbf{I}^f$. The reduction in complexity is calculated as the number of saved pixels. Since we use YUV subsampling 4:1:1 the number of pixels in $\mathbf{I}^f$ is 7680 and **I** consists of 63360 pixels. The reduction in complexity is then slightly more than 8 times. Table 2 shows the average reduction in reconstruction quality for 10 video sequences.
The quality for the pixels in the foreground is improved and the pixels which not are part of the foreground is reconstructed with lower quality when $\mathbf{I}^f$ is used for encoding. The reconstruction quality for each individual pixel in one video sequence is shown in Fig. 4. This figures clearly shows the advantage of aPCA compared to regular PCA. Semantically important pixels are reconstructed with higher quality while unimportant pixels have less reconstruction quality with aPCA compared to PCA.

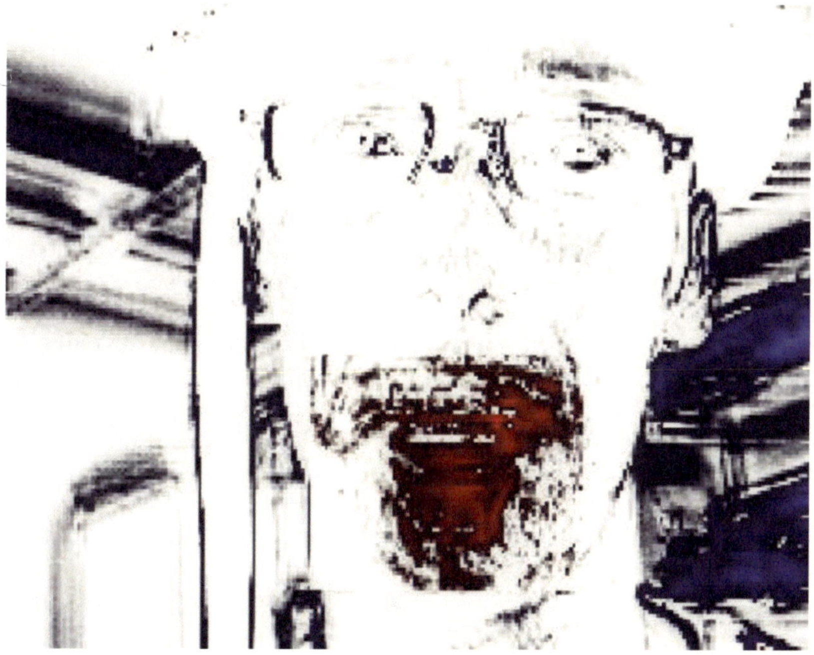

Fig. 4. Individual pixel PSNR for encoding with foreground $\mathbf{I}^f$ compared to encoding with the entire frame **I** *red*=improved PSNR *blue*=reduced PSNR.

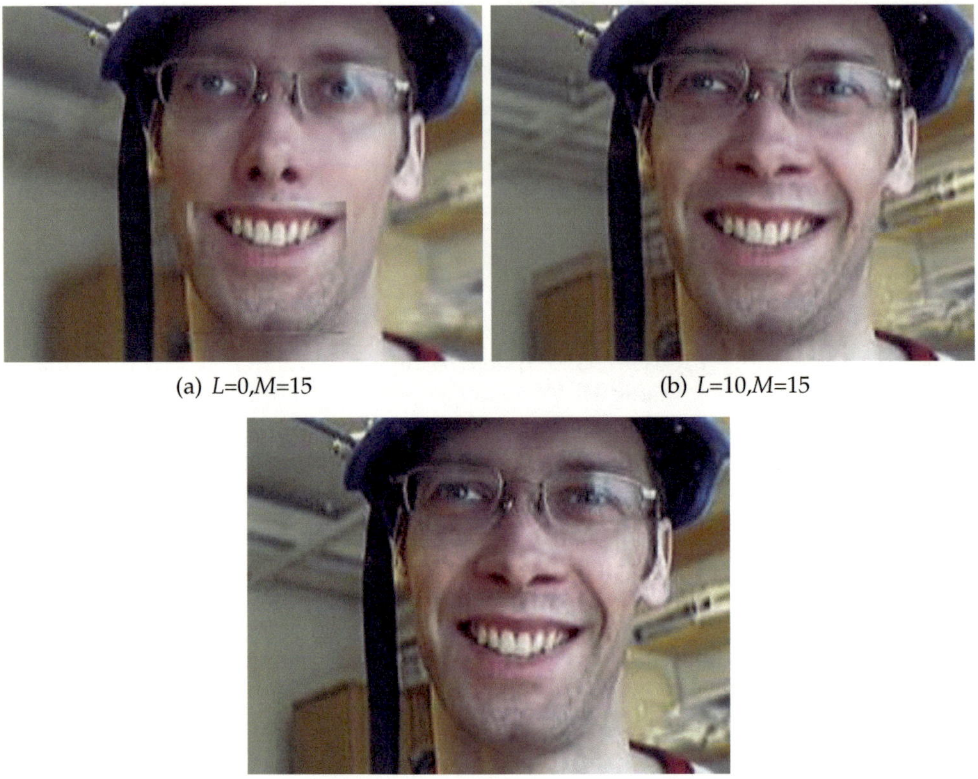

(a) L=0,M=15 (b) L=10,M=15

(c) L=15,M=15

Fig. 5. Reconstructed frames with different setups for Experiment II.

5.2 Experiment II: Encoding with the mouth as foreground, decoding with the entire frame and the mouth area

In this section we show how the complexity for the decoder can be reduced by focusing on the reconstruction quality of the foreground. According to the equations in section 4.2 we reconstruct the frame with different background qualities. Fig. 5 show example frames for different L-values when M is 15.

Table 1 showed the average reconstruction result for encoding with the entire frame **I**. The reduction in reconstruction quality compared to those values are shown in Table 3. The PSNR for the foreground is the same regardless of the value of L since M always is 15 for the results in the table. The complexity reduction is also noted in Table 3. The complexity is calculated for a mouth area of 80x64 pixels and a total frame size of 240x176 pixels with M=15.

5.3 Experiment III: Encoding with the mouth and eyes as foreground, decoding with the entire frame

The facial mimic is dependent on more than the mouth area; the facial mimic of a person can be modelled accurately by modeling the mouth and the eyes. The mimic also contains small changes in the nose region but most of the information is conveyed in the mouth and eye regions. By building a model containing the changes of the mouth and the eyes we can model the facial mimic and we don't need to model any information without semantical importance.

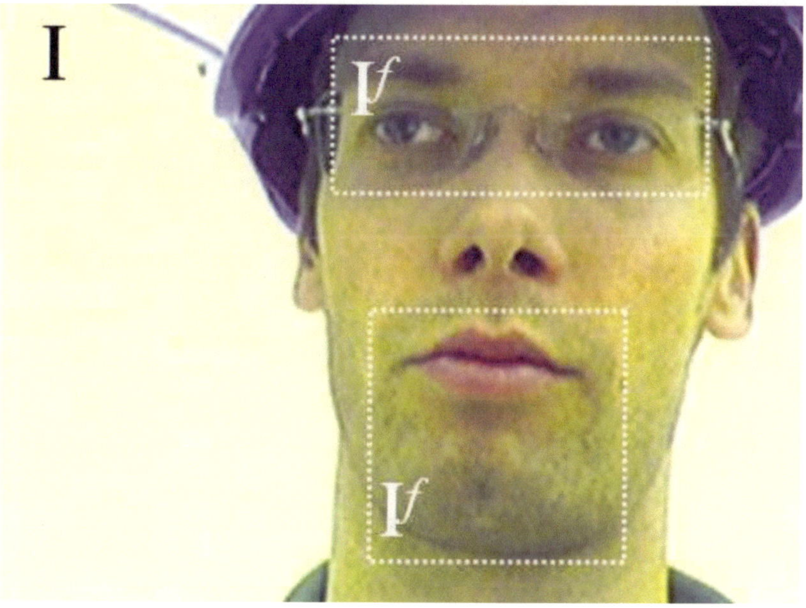

Fig. 6. Foreground $\mathbf{I}^f$ with the eyes and the mouth.

The areas which are chosen as foreground are shown in Fig. 6. The area around both eyes and the mouth are used as foreground $\mathbf{I}^f$ while the entire frame $\mathbf{I}$ is used for decoding. $\mathbf{I}^f$ has a spatial size of 176x64 and $\mathbf{I}$ still has a size of 240x176. The complexity for encoding is increased with an average of 55 % compared to only using the mouth area as foreground (Experiment I) but the complexity is still reduced $\approx$ 4 times compared to using the entire frame for encoding. The quality is also increased compared to experiment I (Table 4) and more accurate information about the eyes can be modeled.

5.4 Experiment IV: Encoding with features extracted through edge detection and dilation, decoding with the entire frame

In the previous three experiments we have chosen the foreground area based on prior knowledge about the facial mimic. In the following two experiments we will show how to select the region of interest automatically. In this experiment we choose one frame from a video sequence and use this to extract the foreground $\mathbf{I}^f$.

1. A representative frame is selected. This frame should contain a highly expressive appearance of the face.

	Lowered rec. qual. (PSNR) [dB]			
ϕ	Y	U	V	CR factor
1	-1,5	-0,7	-0,5	5,6
5	-1,4	-0,5	-0,4	2,4
10	-1,3	-0,3	-0,2	1,4
15	-1,2	-0,3	-0,2	1

Table 3. Average lowered reconstruction quality for 10 video sequences using the mouth and eyes as foreground. (Experiment II) The complexity reduction (CR) factor is also shown and is calculated with M=15. In this calculation L is equal to Φ.

	Lowered rec. qual. (PSNR) [dB]		
ϕ	Y	U	V
5	-1,1	-0,2	-0,2
10	-1,5	-0,2	-0,1
15	-1,5	-0,2	-0,1
20	-1,6	-0,1	-0,1
25	-1,6	0	-0,2

Table 4. Average lowered reconstruction quality for 10 video sequences using an area around the mouth and the eyes for encoding (Experiment III).

2. Face detection detects the face in the selected frame.
3. Edge detection extracts all the edges in the face for the selected frame.
4. Dilation is used on the edge image to make the edges thicker. Every pixel in the dilated image which is 1 (white) is used for encoding.

The face detection method we use is described in [Le & Li (2004)]. The resulting area is similar to the area around the eyes and the mouth in the previous experiment. The result is shown in Table 5.

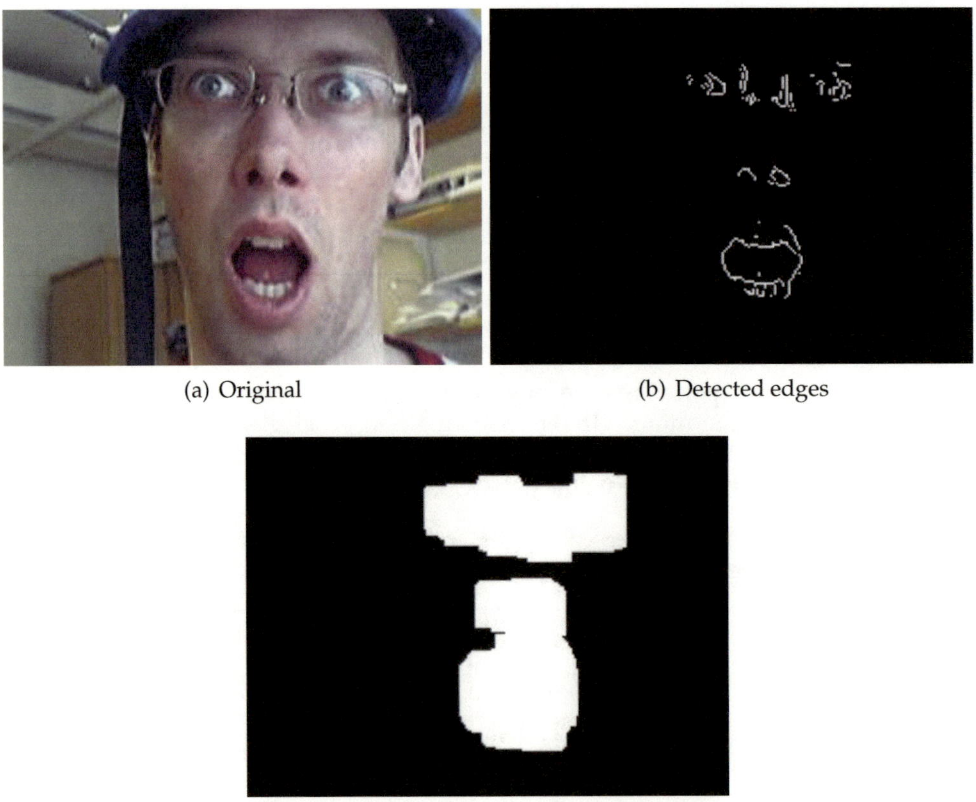

(a) Original (b) Detected edges

(c) Dilated edges (White pixels are foreground $\mathbf{I}^f$)

Fig. 7. Region of interest extraction with edge detection and dilation.

	Lowered rec. qual. (PSNR) [dB]		
ϕ	Y	U	V
5	-1,1	-0,2	-0,2
10	-1,4	-0,2	-0,2
15	-1,5	-0,1	-0,2
20	-1,6	-0,1	-0,1
25	-1,6	0	-0,1

Table 5. Average lowered reconstruction quality for 10 video sequences using a foreground $\mathbf{I}^f$ from Experiment IV.

The average size of this area for 10 video sequences is lower than the previous experiment. It is 11364 pixels large and this would correspond to an square area with the size of $\approx$ 118x64. This corresponds to a reduction in encoding complexity of $\approx$ 5,6 times compared to using the entire frame **I**.

5.5 Experiment V: Encoding with edge detected features as foreground, decoding with the entire frame

Another way to automatically extract the foreground is to use feature detection without dilation. This is a fully automatical procedure since no key frame is selected manually.

1. Face detection [Le & Li (2004)] detects the face in each frame.
2. Edge detection extracts all the edges in the face for each frame.
3. Every edge is gathered in one edge image. Where there is an edge in at least one of the frames there will be an edge in the total frame. Every pixel with an edge in any frame is used for encoding.

The complexity is on average reduced 11,6 times when the area extracted in this way is used for encoding compared to using the entire frame and $\approx$ 3 times compared to using the area around the mouth and the eyes from Experiment III. The reconstruction quality is shown in Table 6.

The reconstruction quality is almost the same for all cases when information from both the eyes and the mouth is used for encoding. When only the mouth is used for encoding the quality is lower. The complexity is at the same time reduced for all the different aPCA implementations. It is reduced heavily when the area is extracted from edges (Experiment V).

	Lowered rec. qual. (PSNR) [dB]		
ϕ	Y	U	V
5	-1,2	-0,3	-0,3
10	-1,6	-0,3	-0,1
15	-1,7	-0,2	-0,2
20	-1,7	-0,2	-0,2
25	-1,7	-0,3	-0,2

Table 6. Average lowered reconstruction quality for 10 video sequences using combined edges from all frames in a video for foreground extraction (Experiment V).

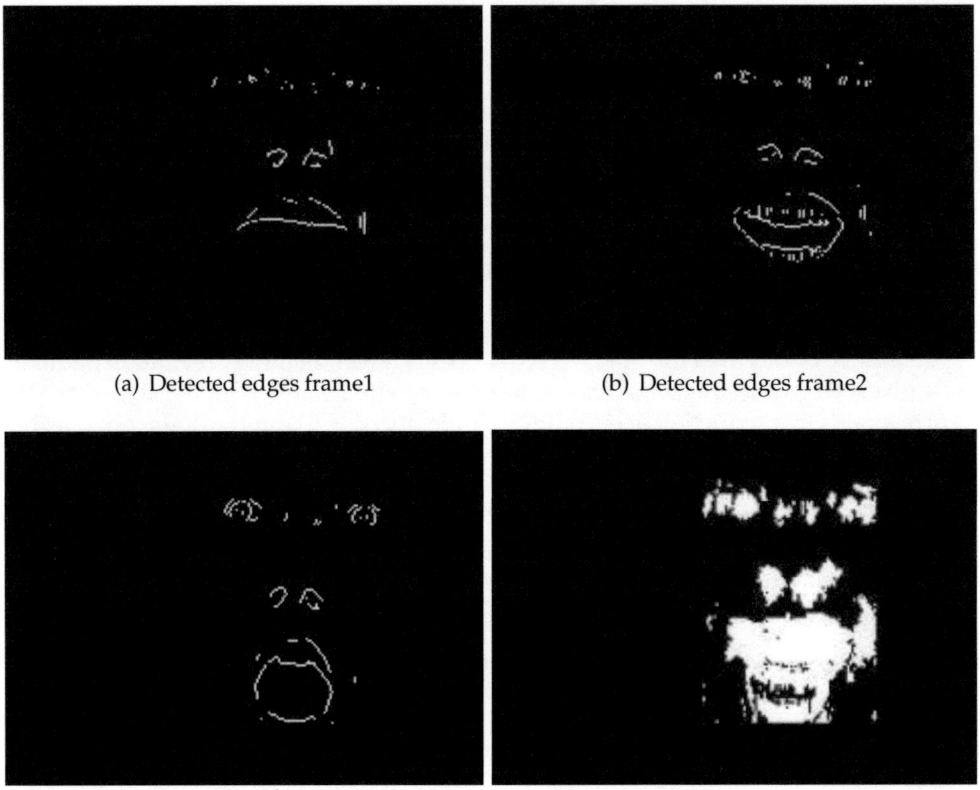

(a) Detected edges frame1 (b) Detected edges frame2

(c) Detected edges frame3 (d) Detected edges in all frames

Fig. 8. Region of interest extraction with edge detection on all frames.

6. Conclusion

We show some of the potential of asymmetrical principal component analysis (aPCA) for compression of facial video sequences. It can efficiently be used to reduce the complexity of encoding and decoding with only a slight decrease in reconstruction quality. The complexity for encoding can be reduced more than 10 times and the complexity for decoding is also reduced at the same time as the objective quality is lowered slightly, i.e., 1,5 dB (PSNR). aPCA is also very adaptive for heterogenous decoding since a decoder can select which size of video frames it wants to decode with the encoder using the same video for encoding. PCA provides natural scalability of the quality and aPCA also provides scalability in spatial resolution with the same encoding. The freedom of assembling the reconstructed frames differently also provides the decoder with the freedom to select different quality for different parts of the frame.

Low bitrate video is far from realized for arbitrary video. Regular video encoding has not reached these low bitrates and previous solutions to low bitrate facial video/representation do not have a natural-looking appearance. aPCA has a major role to play here since it can provide natural-looking video with very low bitrate and low encoding and decoding complexity.

7. References

Aizawa, K. & Huang, T. (1995). Model-based image coding: Advanced video coding techniques for very low bit-rate applications, *Proc. of the IEEE* 83(2): 259–271.

Cootes, T., Edwards, G. & Taylor, C. (1998). Active appearance models, *In Proc. European Conference on Computer Vision. (ECCV)*, Vol. 2, pp. 484–498.

Ekman, P. (1982). *Emotion in the Human Face*, Cambridge University Press, New York.

Ekman, P. & Friesen, W. (1975). *Unmasking the face. A guide to recognizing emotions from facial clues*, Prentice-Hall, Englewood Cliffs, New Jersey.

Forchheimer, R., Fahlander, O. & Kronander, T. (1983). Low bit-rate coding through animation, *In Proc. International Picture Coding Symposium PCS–83*, pp. 113–114.

Jolliffe, I. (1986). *Principal Component Analysis*, Springer-Verlag, New York.

Le, H.-S. & Li, H. (2004). Face identification from one single sample face image, *Proc. of the IEEE Int. Conf. on Image Processing (ICIP)*.

Lee, J. & Eleftheriadis, A. (1996). Spatio-temporal model-assisted compatible coding for low and very low bitrate video telephony, *Proceedings, 3rd IEEE International Conference on Image Processing (ICIP 96)*, Lausanne, Switzerland, pp. II.429–II.432.

Neff, R. & Zakhor, A. (1997). Very low bit-rate video coding based on matching pursuits, *IEEE Transactions on Circuits and Systems for Video Technology* 7(1): 158–171.

Ohba, K., Clary, G., Tsukada, T., Kotoku, T. & Tanie, K. (1998). Facial expression communication with fes, *International conference on Pattern Recognition*, pp. 1378–1381.

Ostermann, J. (1998). Animation of synthetic faces in mpeg-4, *Proc. of Computer Animation, IEEE Computer Society*, pp. 49–55.

Pighin, F., Hecker, J., Lishchinski, D., Szeliski, R. & Salesin, D. H. (1998). Synthesizing realistic facial expression from photographs, *SIGGRAPH Proceedings*, pp. 75–84.

Schäfer, R., Wiegand, T. & Schwarz, H. (2003). The emerging h.264 avc standard, *EBU Technical Review* 293.

Schwarz, H., Marpe, D. & Wiegand, T. (2007). Overview of the scalable video coding extension of the h.264/avc standard, *Circuits and Systems for Video Technology, IEEE Transactions on* 17(9): 1103–1120.

Söderström, U. & Li, H. (2005a). Full-frame video coding for facial video sequences based on principal component analysis, *Proceedings of Irish Machine Vision and Image Processing Conference (IMVIP)*, pp. 25–32. online: www.medialab.tfe.umu.se.

Söderström, U. & Li, H. (2005b). Very low bitrate full-frame facial video coding based on principal component analysis, Signal and Image Processing Conference (SIP'05). online: www.medialab.tfe.umu.se.

Söderström, U. & Li, H. (2007). Eigenspace compression for very low bitrate transmission of facial video, *IASTED International conference on Signal Processing, Pattern Recognition and Application (SPPRA)*.

Söderström, U. & Li, H. (2008). Asymmetrical principal component analysis for video coding, *Electronics letters* 44(4): 276–277.

Söderström, U. & Li, H. (2010). Representation bound for human facial mimic with the aid of principal component analysis, *International Journal of Image and Graphics (IJIG)* 10(3): 343–363.

Torres, L. & Delp, E. (2000). New trends in image and video compression, *Proceedings of the European Signal Processing Conference (EUSIPCO)*, Tampere, Finland.

Torres, L. & Kunt, M. (1996). *Video Coding (The Second Generation Approach)*, Kluwer Academic Publishers.

Torres, L. & Prado, D. (2002). A proposal for high compression of faces in video sequences using adaptive eigenspaces, *Proceedings International Conference on Image Processing* 1: I–189– I–192.

Wang, J. & Cohen, M. F. (2005). Very low frame-rate video streaming for face-to-face teleconference, *DCC '05: Proceedings of the Data Compression Conference*, pp. 309–318.

Wiegand, T., Sullivan, G., Bjontegaard, G. & Luthra, A. (2003). Overview of the h.264/avc video coding standard, *IEEE Trans. Circuits Syst. Video Technol.*, 13(7): 560–576.

7

Distributed Video Coding: Principles and Evaluation of Wavelet-Based Schemes

Riccardo Bernardini, Roberto Rinaldo and Pamela Zontone
University of Udine
Italy

1. Introduction

The current scenario considered for video coding and transmission, as assumed by the MPEG standards, uses complex encoding algorithms, including motion compensation and multi-hypothesis rate-distortion optimized procedures, to achieve high compression efficiency. This is the right solution when the encoding is carried out by high performance devices, while the receivers (e.g., handheld devices or mobile phones) should be kept as simple and cheap as possible. This scenario is rapidly evolving into a new one, where users have the interest to produce and transmit video and multimedia, possibly using their mobile and battery operated lightweight devices. Of course, this calls for new multimedia coding paradigms, where the *encoder* is as simple as possible to reduce the computational power requested for compression and radio transmission. Similar constraints should be considered in monitoring or surveillance applications, where a number of video sensors, with limited computational power, cooperate to send video information to a receiving station.
Distributed Source Coding (DSC) refers to the compression of two or more correlated sources that do not communicate with each other (hence the term distributed coding). These sources send their information to a central decoder that performs joint decoding. In this situation, the challenging problem is to achieve the same efficiency (the joint entropy of correlated sources) while not requiring sources to communicate with each other.
The Slepian-Wolf Theorem is a celebrated result of information theory which assures that this unexpected result is indeed achievable. In other words, it is possible to code two correlated sources (X, Y) one independently of the other, and achieve the same performance obtainable when a coder can exploit knowledge of both. For instance, in a conventional video coder, two consecutive frames can be compressed by computing the motion compensated difference between the first and the second frame, then transmitting the first frame in intra-mode and the inter-mode coded difference frame. The Slepian-Wolf result assures that, in principle, we can achieve the same coding efficiency by coding the two frames independently, i.e., without performing a costly motion compensation operation.

1.1 Chapter organization and contribution

The following chapter will be subdivided into the following sections.

1. An overview of the Slepian-Wolf and Wyner-Ziv theorems, with a short summary of essential Information theoretic concepts;

2. a review of the state-of-the-art in Distributed Source Coding and Distributed Video Coding (DVC), with references to the latest advancements;
3. a presentation of some original work by the authors on the design and evaluation of wavelet-based video coding;
4. an overview of applications of the DVC paradigm to other aspects besides video coding. In particular, we will present results relative to robust transmission of video using an auxiliary DVC stream;
5. conclusions, advantages and limitations of the DVC paradigm.

In particular, we will introduce an original distributed video coder based on processing the wavelet transform with a modulo-reduction function. The reduced wavelet coefficients are compressed with a wavelet coder. At the receiver side, the statistical properties between similar frames are used to recover the compressed frame. A second contribution is the analysis and the comparison of DVC schemes in two different scenarios: in the first scenario the information frames are separated from the other frames, and they are compressed following the original framework considered for Wyner-Ziv coding. In the second scenario, all the frames are available at the encoder making this an interesting proposal for the design of a low-complexity video coder, with no motion compensation, where the information frames are coded using DSC techniques. The whole set of experiments show that the proposed schemes - that do not use any feedback channel - have good performance when compared to similar asymmetric video compression schemes considered in the literature. Finally, we will consider an original error-resilient scheme that employs distributed video coding tools. A bitstream, produced by any standard motion-compensated predictive codec, is sent over an error-prone channel. A Wyner-Ziv encoded auxiliary bitstream is sent as redundant information to serve as a forward error correction code. We propose the use of an extended version of the Recursive Optimal per-Pixel Estimate (ROPE) algorithm to establish how many parity bits should be sent to the decoder in order to correct the decoded and concealed frames. At the decoder side, error concealed reconstructed frames and parity bits are used by the Wyner-Ziv decoder, and each corrected frame is used as a reference by future frames, thus reducing drift. Tests with video sequences and realistic loss patterns are reported. Experimental results show that the proposed scheme performs well when compared to other schemes that use Forward Error Correcting (FEC) codes or the H.264 standard intra-macroblock refresh procedure.

2. Foundation of Distributed Source Coding

In this section we will introduce in detail two major results provided by Information Theory that prove that, under the DSC paradigm, it is still possible to achieve or to approach, in total generality, the optimal performance of a joint coder: the Slepian-Wolf theorem and the Wyner-Ziv theorem. We first introduce the main ideas behind distributed source coding by means of examples.

2.1 A glimpse at Distributed Source Coding

Consider the case of N distributed sensors that communicate with a data collection center using a radio link. Data recorded by each sensor, at each time instant, can be modelled as a set of $X_1, ..., X_N$, random variables, and it is reasonable to expect that there is a strong correlation between data at each sensor. In the case of two sensors X and Y, suppose we can model Y as a random variable with equiprobable integer values in the set $\{0, ..., 7\}$ while $d = X - Y$, the difference between the values recorded by the two sensors, can be modelled as a variable assuming values in $\{0, ..., 3\}$ with equal probability. Assuming d and Y independent, X would have a probability mass function as depicted in Fig. 1,

$$p_X(k) = \sum_{h=0}^{7} Pr[d = k - h, Y = h] = \sum_{h=0}^{7} p_d(k-h)\, p_Y(h).$$

We know from Shannon's theory (6) that the entropy of X

$$H(X) \triangleq -\sum_k p_X(k) \log_2(p_X(k))$$

represents the minimum average number of bits per source symbol necessary to represent the source. In this case, $H(X)$ is obviously greater than the entropy $H(Y) = 3$ bit of Y (the eight equiprobable values of Y can be coded most efficiently with 3 bits). A simple calculation would show that $H(X) \simeq 3.328$ bit.

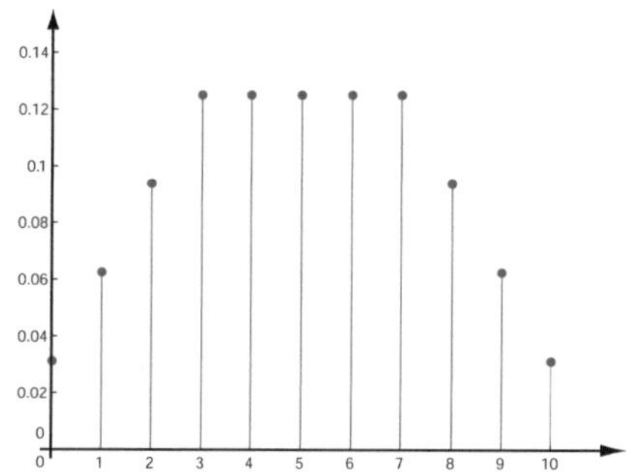

Fig. 1. The probability mass function of X.

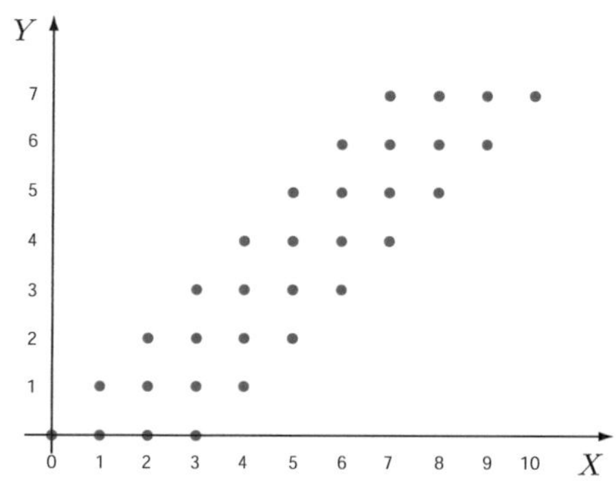

Fig. 2. Support of the probability mass function of (X, Y).

The pair (X, Y) assumes 32 equiprobable values in the set represented in Fig. 2, with associated 5 bit entropy. As it is well known, supposing pairs (X, Y) are generated independently, $H(X, Y) = 5$ bit represents a lower bound for the number of bits (per source pair) with which we can represent sequences of pairs generated by the two sources. If a coder has access both

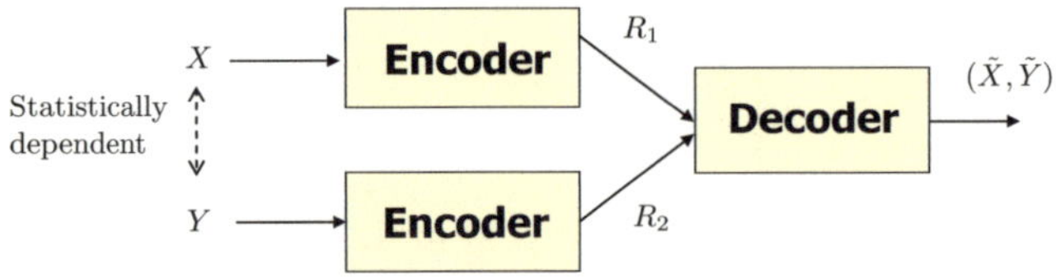

Fig. 3. Distributed Source Coding. Correlated variables X and Y are compressed independently and sent to a joint decoder.

to X and Y, the way to code (X,Y) is obvious: one can use 3 bits to represent the 8 values of Y, and other 2 bits to represent $d = X - Y$.
How can we proceed if the coders for X e Y cannot communicate, as in Fig. 3? Are we forced to use an efficient coding procedure for X and Y, separately, and use $R_1 = H(X)$ and $R_2 = H(Y)$ bit per symbol, respectively? Note that this procedure is inefficient to code the pair, since $H(X,Y) \leq H(X) + H(Y)$.
Fig. 4 illustrates a coding procedure which allows optimal coding even if the two coders do not communicate with each other and act separately. In particular, one can use a unique code (in the figure, a different shape symbol) for the subsets $\{0,4,8\}$, $\{1,5,9\}$, $\{2,6,10\}$, $\{3,7\}$, of the X alphabet. For each value of X, its coder transmits to the decoder the index (the shape symbol) of the subset to which the value of X belongs. With four subsets, 2 bits are sufficient. Observe from the figure that, for each value of Y, we have 4 possible values of X, each one belonging to a *different* subset. Thus, if we know at the decoder the value of Y (represented with R_2=3 bit), and the index of the subset to which X belongs (2 bit), it is possible to uniquely decode the *pair* (X,Y). Note that the two coders act independently, and each of them transmits the index corresponding to the actual value of Y, or the subset index for the actual value of X in each experiment. In particular, we have $R_1 = H(X|Y) = 2$ bit and $R_2 = H(Y) = 3$ bit.
Fig. 5 shows a different example, where the pair (X,Y) assumes 16 equiprobable values (the joint entropy is therefore $H(X,Y) = 4$ bit), and one uses a distributed coding procedure that associates a different code symbol J to the subsets $\{-1,-5\}$, $\{-3,-7\}$, $\{1,5\}$, $\{3,7\}$ of Y, using two bits, and one symbol I for the subsets $\{-7,1\}$, $\{-5,3\}$, $\{-3,5\}$, $\{-1,7\}$ of X values, using other 2 bits. From the pair of code symbols (I,J), one can uniquely identify (X,Y), but the two coders can act independently . Note that in this case we have $R_1 > H(X|Y) = 1$ bit, $R_2 > H(Y|X) = 1$ bit, and $R_1 + R_2 = H(X,Y) = 4$ bit.
In these two examples, one necessary requirement is that each pair (X,Y) can be uniquely identified by (i,j), where $i \in I$ and $j \in J$ identify the labels for subsets of X and Y values, respectively. Note that, in order for the procedure to work, the total number of label pairs $|I||J|$ must be at least as large as the number of (X,Y) pairs with non-zero probability. Moreover, for each value of X (respectively, Y), there must be a sufficient number of labels J (respectively, I) to uniquely identify the non-zero probability corresponding pairs (X,Y). In addition, the key point is to associate a code symbol to a subset (or *bin*) of values of one variable that are sufficiently far apart, so that its exact value can be discriminated once the value (or set of possible values) of the other variable is also known.
The preceding considerations can be justified by a general result of Information Theory derived by Slepian and Wolf in 1973 (7), which we describe below.

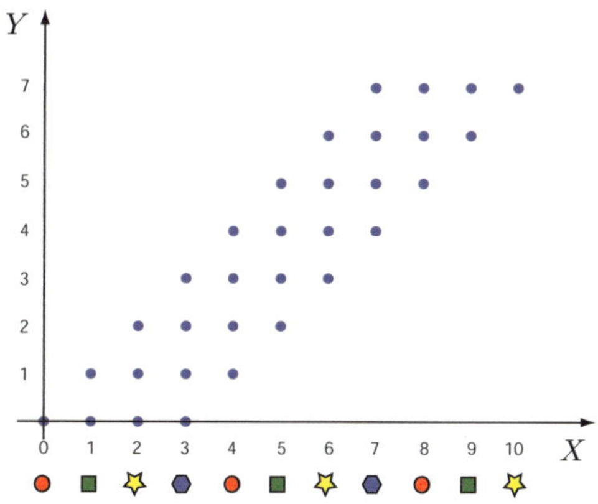

Fig. 4. A "distributed" code for (X, Y).

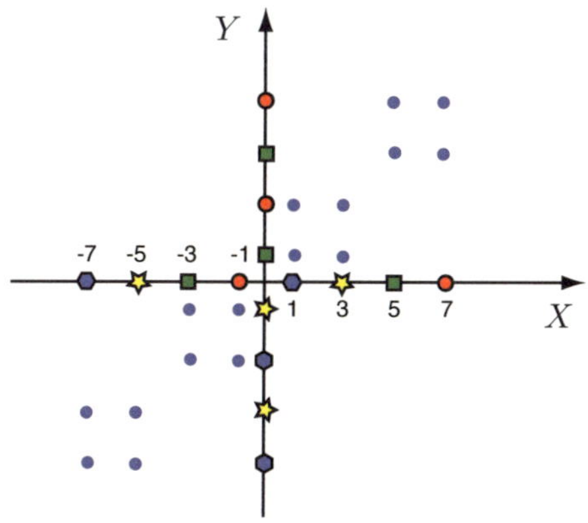

Fig. 5. A "distributed" code for (X, Y).

2.2 The Slepian-Wolf theorem

Let $(X_i, Y_i)_{i=1}^{\infty}$ be a sequence of independent and identically distributed (i.i.d) drawings of a pair of correlated discrete random variables X and Y. For lossless reconstruction, a rate given by the joint entropy $H(X, Y)$ is sufficient if we perform joint coding. The Slepian-Wolf theorem refers to the case of X and Y separately encoded but jointly decoded, i.e., the encoder of each source is constrained to operate without knowledge of the other source, while the decoder has available both encoded message streams (see Fig. 3). It appears that the rate at which we can code the two sources in this case is $H(X) + H(Y)$, which is greater than $H(X, Y)$ if X and Y are not independent.
Let X take values in the set $\mathcal{A}_X = \{1, 2, \ldots, A_X\}$ and Y in the set $\mathcal{A}_Y = \{1, 2, \ldots, A_Y\}$. Denote their joint probability distribution by

$$p_{X,Y}(x, y) = P(X = x, Y = y) \quad x \in \mathcal{A}_X,\ y \in \mathcal{A}_Y.$$

Next, let $(X_1, Y_1), (X_2, Y_2), \cdots, (X_n, Y_n)$ be a sequence of n independent realizations of the pair of random variables (X, Y). Denote by $\mathbf{X}^n$ the block sequence of n-characters $X_1, X_2, \cdots, X_n$ produced by the source X, and by $\mathbf{Y}^n$ the block sequence $Y_1, Y_2, \cdots, Y_n$ produced by the other source. The probability distribution for this correlated pair of vectors is

$$p_{\mathbf{X}^n,\mathbf{Y}^n}(\mathbf{x}^n,\mathbf{y}^n) = P(\mathbf{X}^n = \mathbf{x}^n, \mathbf{Y}^n = \mathbf{y}^n) = \prod_{i=1}^{n} p_{X,Y}(x_i, y_i) \tag{1}$$

$$\mathbf{x}^n = (x_1, x_2, \cdots, x_n) \in \mathcal{A}_X^n$$
$$\mathbf{y}^n = (y_1, y_2, \cdots, y_n) \in \mathcal{A}_Y^n$$

where $\mathcal{A}_X^n$ is the set of A_X^n distinct n-vectors whose components are in $\mathcal{A}_X$ and $\mathcal{A}_Y^n$ is defined analogously.
The first encoder (see Fig. 3) maps the input $\mathbf{X}^n$ to the index $I = C_1(\mathbf{X}^n)$, where $I \in \mathcal{M}_X = \{1, 2, \cdots, M_X\}$; similarly, the other encoder maps the input $\mathbf{Y}^n$ to the index $J = C_2(\mathbf{Y}^n)$, where $J \in \mathcal{M}_Y = \{1, 2, \cdots, M_Y\}$. I and J are called *encoded-X message number* and *encoded-Y message number*, respectively (7). At the decoder side, the joint decoder is a function $g : \mathcal{M}_X \times \mathcal{M}_Y \rightarrow \mathcal{A}_X^n \times \mathcal{A}_Y^n$ such that

$$g(C_1(\mathbf{X}^n), C_2(\mathbf{Y}^n)) = (\tilde{\mathbf{X}}^n, \tilde{\mathbf{Y}}^n).$$

Let P_e^n be the probability of decoding error, i.e., $P_e^n = P[(\mathbf{X}^n, \mathbf{Y}^n) \neq (\tilde{\mathbf{X}}^n, \tilde{\mathbf{Y}}^n)]$.
Associated with these encoders and the joint decoder are rates $R_1 = (1/n)\log M_X$ and $R_2 = (1/n)\log M_Y$. We think of the two encoders as producing the integers I and J after n correlated source pairs (X, Y) have been generated. R_1 units of information per source character are sufficient to transmit I to the joint decoder and R_2 units are sufficient to transmit J. The decoder then produces the estimates $\tilde{\mathbf{X}}^n$ and $\tilde{\mathbf{Y}}^n$ of the input sequences $\mathbf{X}^n$ and $\mathbf{Y}^n$.
The pair of rates R_1 and R_2 is said to be an *admissible rate point* (7) if for every $\epsilon > 0$ there exist for some $n = n(\epsilon)$ encoders and decoders (considering the case with two decoders as well) with $M_X = \lfloor \exp(nR_1) \rfloor$ and $M_Y = \lfloor \exp(nR_2) \rfloor$ such that $P_e^n < \epsilon$. Here the symbol $\lfloor \cdot \rfloor$ denotes the largest integer not greater than the argument of the function. In other words, the pair of rates R_1 and R_2 is an admissible rate point if it is possible to construct a sequence of codes with rate R_1 for $\mathbf{X}^n$ and rate R_2 for $\mathbf{Y}^n$, such that $P_e^n \rightarrow 0$ with $n \rightarrow \infty$.
The *achievable rate region* is the closure of the set of admissible rate points.
The **Slepian-Wolf theorem** says that if R_1 is the rate corresponding to the coding of X and R_2 to the coding of Y (see Fig. 3), the *achievable rate region* of DSC is given by:

$$R_1 \geq H(X|Y), \tag{2}$$
$$R_2 \geq H(Y|X), \tag{3}$$
$$R_1 + R_2 \geq H(X, Y). \tag{4}$$

Fig. 6 shows the achievable region for the Slepian-Wolf theorem. The Slepian-Wolf theorem suggests, therefore, that it is possible to compress statistically dependent signals, in a distributed scenario, to the same rate as with a system where the signals are compressed jointly.
The proof of the Slepian-Wolf theorem uses, as it is common in Information Theory, the concepts of typical set and of random coding. We give here the main ideas, while a complete development can be found, for instance, in (6). As a matter of fact, it can be shown, using the Law of Large Numbers, that, for large n, there are basically $2^{nH(X)}$ highly probable (*typical*) $\mathbf{X}^n$ sequences, while the other possible source sequences are generated with vanishing

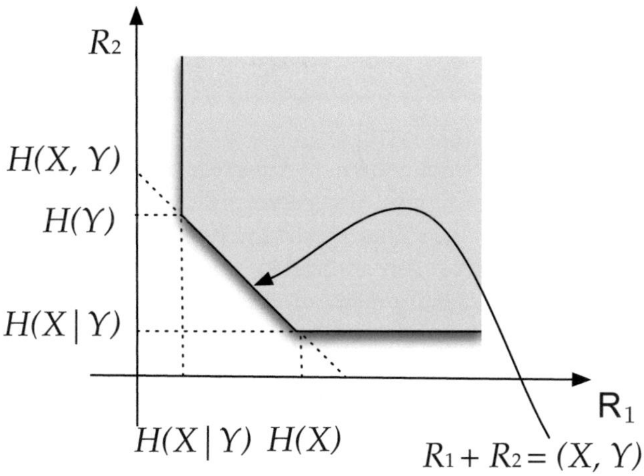

Fig. 6. Achievable rate region for two sources in Distributed Source Coding.

probability. Along the same lines, there are $2^{nH(Y)}$ sequences $\mathbf{Y}^n$, and only $2^{nH(X,Y)}$ jointly typical sequences $(\mathbf{X}^n, \mathbf{Y}^n)$. Furthermore, for each typical $\mathbf{X}^n = \mathbf{x}^n$, there are about $2^{nH(Y|X)}$ jointly typical $\mathbf{Y}^n$ and $2^{nH(X|Y)}$ jointly typical sequences for each $\mathbf{Y}^n = \mathbf{y}^n$. The requirements of the Theorem become therefore obvious: the number 2^{nR_1} of I labels and 2^{nR_2} of J labels have to be large enough so that $(i, j), i \in I, j \in J$, can identify uniquely each typical $(\mathbf{X}^n, \mathbf{Y}^n)$ (this is ensured by Eq. (4)). Moreover, since the codes are assigned by separate coders, for each typical value of $\mathbf{X}^n$ (respectively, $\mathbf{Y}^n$), there must be at least $2^{nH(Y|X)}$ possible labels (respectively, $2^{nH(X|Y)}$). This is indeed ensured by conditions in Eq. (2) and Eq. (3). Note that, in the examples of the previous section, we had similar requirements to code each random pair. In addition, the conditions of the Theorem assure that, as n increases, there are exponentially many more labels than sequences in the typical sets, so that choosing the codes at random will provide unique labelling with high probability.

In Slepian-Wolf coding schemes, it is practical to design codes to approach one corner point of the achievable region (Fig. 6), e.g., with $R_1 = H(X|Y)$ and $R_2 = H(Y)$. This problem is known as the problem of source coding X with *side information* Y at the decoder, and it can be referred to as an *asymmetric scenario*. In this asymmetric context, therefore, the aim is to code X at a rate that approaches $H(X|Y)$ based on the correlation model between X and Y and not using the specific Y at the encoder.

2.3 Practical schemes for Distributed Coding

Wyner first realized the close connection between DSC and channel coding (9), suggesting the use of linear channel codes as a constructive approach for Slepian-Wolf coding (10). The basic idea in Wyner's work was to partition the space of all possible source outcomes into disjoint bins that are the cosets of some good linear channel code for the specific correlation model between X and Y.

If we take two binary symmetric sources and we consider an (n, k) binary linear block code, there are 2^{n-k} different syndromes, each one indexing a different bin of 2^k binary words of length n. Each bin is a coset code of the block code, which means that the distance properties of the original code are preserved in each bin. In particular, the Hamming distance between any two source binary words in the coset (i.e., the number of symbols in which the two codewords differ) is at least equal to the *minimum distance* of the linear code, a characteristic that has to be established at design time. As a matter of fact, a linear code with minimum distance $d = 2t + 1$ can successfully correct any error vector $\mathbf{e}$ with t symbol errors in the received noisy codeword.

As we will see below, a practical scheme for distributed coding consists in sending to the receiver, for a sequence of n input bits, the corresponding $(n-k)$ syndrome bits, thus achieving a compression radio $\frac{n}{n-k}$. This approach was only recently used for practical Slepian-Wolf code schemes based on conventional channel codes. If the correlation model between X and Y can be seen as a binary channel, this syndrome concept can be extended to all binary linear codes such as Turbo and LDPC codes.

In a typical transmission system, given an (n,k) systematic linear channel code with the $(n-k) \times n$ parity-check matrix $\mathbf{H}$, and using this channel code for error correction, the length-k input message is transformed into a length-n message $\mathbf{X}$ by appending $n-k$ parity bits. The codeword $\mathbf{X}$ has now length n and $n-k$ syndrome bits are computed as $\mathbf{s} = \mathbf{X}\mathbf{H}^T$.

We transmit the codeword $\mathbf{X}$ and we receive a vector $\mathbf{Y} = \mathbf{X} + \mathbf{e}$, where $\mathbf{e}$ is the error vector which indicates the positions where the received vector $\mathbf{Y}$ differs from the transmitted one $\mathbf{X}$. As it is well known, knowledge of the syndrome $\mathbf{s}$ allows to determine the minimum weight $\mathbf{e} = g(\mathbf{s})$ such that $\mathbf{Y} = \mathbf{X} + \mathbf{e}$. At the receiver side, if $g(\mathbf{Y}\mathbf{H}^T) = g((\mathbf{X}+\mathbf{e})\mathbf{H}^T) = g(\mathbf{e}\mathbf{H}^T)$ is the decoding function based on the syndrome, we can write therefore $\mathbf{e} = g(\mathbf{e}\mathbf{H}^T)$ with probability close to 1 and recover from this the original codeword $\mathbf{X}$.

We see now how a similar procedure can be used to code $\mathbf{X}$ and recover it from the side-information $\mathbf{Y}$ in a distributed coding scenario. A length-n vector $\mathbf{X}$ of source symbols is compressed as the $n-k$ bit syndrome $\mathbf{s} = \mathbf{X}\mathbf{H}^T$ of a linear code. The syndrome is sent to the receiver, where the side information $\mathbf{Y}$ is available. Suppose the correlation model implies that, to each n-length source binary word $\mathbf{X}$, corresponds the side-information vector $\mathbf{Y} = \mathbf{X} + \mathbf{e}$, where $\mathbf{e}$ is an error vector that can be corrected by the code with probability close to 1. Then, it is possible to reconstruct $\mathbf{X}$ with the knowledge of the syndrome $\mathbf{s}$ and $\mathbf{Y}$. In fact, if $g(\cdot)$ denotes the decoding function based on the syndrome, we can calculate the difference $\mathbf{Y}\mathbf{H}^T - \mathbf{s} = (\mathbf{Y}\mathbf{H}^T - \mathbf{X}\mathbf{H}^T) = (\mathbf{Y} - \mathbf{X})\mathbf{H}^T = \mathbf{e}\mathbf{H}^T$, derive $\mathbf{e} = g(\mathbf{e}\mathbf{H}^T)$ and finally determine $\mathbf{X} = \mathbf{Y} - \mathbf{e}$.

In summary, the source messages can be partitioned by means of a linear channel code, in such a way that all the messages with the same syndrome are assigned to the same coset. The messages in the coset are sufficiently far apart, since they are separated, at least, by the minimum distance of the code. The receiver identifies the coset from knowledge of the syndrome. Furthermore, using the side-information, it can discriminate the actual source message, as soon as the differences between the side-information and the source message can be corrected by the code. An alternative partition can be obtained by assigning to the same coset all the messages that generate the same parity bits. This last approach is known to be suboptimal (11) since there is no guarantee that these cosets have the good geometrical properties of the syndrome-based cosets in terms of minimum distance of the elements in each coset.

A practical correlation model that is often assumed between binary X and Y is the binary symmetric model where the correlation between X and Y is modeled by a binary symmetric channel (BSC) with cross-over probability p. We know that for this channel $H(X|Y) = H(p) = -p\log_2 p - (1-p)\log_2(1-p)$. Although this model looks simple, the Slepian- Wolf coding problem is not trivial.

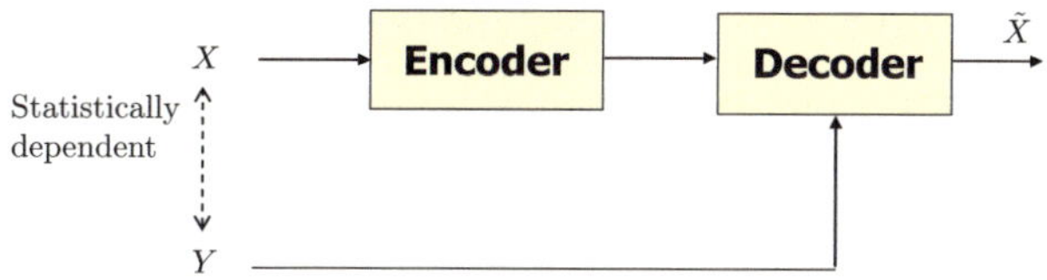

Fig. 7. Asymmetric scenario: source coding of X with *side information* Y.

2.4 Wyner-Ziv theorem

The Slepian-Wolf theorem is focused on the case of lossless compression of two correlated sources. The counterpart of this theorem for lossy source coding is the Wyner and Ziv's theorem on source coding with side information (8). The theorem considers the problem of how many bits are needed to encode X under the constraint that the average distortion between X and the coded version $\tilde{X}$ does not exceed a given distortion level, assuming the side information available at the decoder but not at the encoder (see Fig. 7). In detail, let $(X_i, Y_i)_{i=1}^{\infty}$ be a sequence of independent and identically distributed (i.i.d) drawings of a pair of correlated discrete random variables X and Y. Let X take values in the set $\mathcal{A}_X = \{1, 2, \ldots, A_X\}$. Denote by $\mathbf{X}^n$ the blocks of n-characters $X_1, X_2, \cdots, X_n$ that are coded into a binary stream of rate R, which can in turn be decoded as a sequence $\tilde{\mathbf{X}}^n$. The average distortion level is $1/n \sum_{i=1}^{n} E[d(X_i, \tilde{X}_i)]$, where $d(x, \tilde{x}) \geq 0, x \in \mathcal{A}_X$, is a pre-assigned distortion measure.

Let $R^*(D)$ be the infimum of rates R such that communication is possible at an average distortion level not exceeding $D + \varepsilon$ (with $\varepsilon > 0$ arbitrarily small and with a suitably large n) when only the decoder has access to the side information $\mathbf{Y}^n$; let $R_{X|Y}(D)$ be the rate-distortion function which results when the encoder as well as the decoder has access to the side information. In (8) it is shown that when $D > 0$ then

$$R^*(D) > R_{X|Y}(D).$$

Therefore, knowledge of the side information at the encoder allows the transmission of $\mathbf{X}^n$ at a given distortion level using a smaller transmission rate.

With this theorem, we can notice that a Wyner-Ziv scheme suffers some rate loss when compared to lossy coding of X when the side information Y is available at both the encoder and the decoder. One exception is when X and Y are jointly gaussian and the MSE (Mean Squared Error) distortion measure is used. There is no rate loss with Wyner-Ziv coding in this case, which is of special interest in practice; in fact, as a first approximation, many images and video sources can be modeled as jointly gaussian, and so may be the case for measured values in sensor networks applications.

Finally, it is easy to show that, in case of discrete variables and zero distortion, we obtain the Slepian-Wolf theorem:

$$R^*(0) = R_{X|Y}(0) = H(X|Y).$$

3. State-of-the-art in DSC and DVC

Recently, several schemes based on the Slepian-Wolf (and its continuous variable counterpart – Wyner-Ziv) theorem have been proposed for distributed video coding (DVC). In general, the current implementations consider X as a noisy version of Y. Typically, X and Y are constructed as the bitplanes of some representation of the source (in the pixel, or transform domain) so that efficient binary codes (like Turbo or LDPC codes) can be used. In particular,

1. one coder transmits information (with a standard coding scheme), from which the decoder can calculate the side-information Y;
2. an independent coder protects X by means of an error correction code;
3. the independent coder transmits the code syndrome or parity bits to represent X;
4. the receiver, by exploiting the protection properties of the error correction code, recovers X from its "noisy" version Y and the code syndrome or parity bits (see Fig. 8).

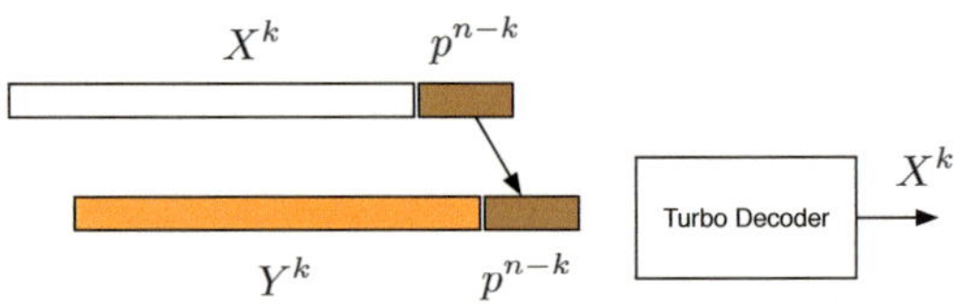

Fig. 8. Distributed coding using the parity bits of an efficient Turbo binary code.

This paradigm has been implemented in some practical schemes presented in the literature. In (12), Pradhan and Ramchandran presented a syndrome-based framework that employs trellis-coded quantization and trellis channel codes, successively extended to a video coding system called PRISM (13). The idea is to consider every video frame as a different source; DSC allows the encoding of the frames without performing motion estimation at the encoder, with performance similar to a standard video coder that exploits the temporal correlation between consecutive frames. Hence, this scheme requires a light encoder and a complex decoder.
Other works are based on channel codes such as Turbo Codes and LDPC codes (14; 15). In particular, in (14) Aaron et al. apply a Wyner-Ziv coding to the pixel values of a video sequence. The reference scheme of (14) , with two separate coders and a joint decoder, assumes that the video sequence is divided into Key frames (i.e., the even frames of the sequence), and Wyner-Ziv (WZ) frames (the odd frames). One coder codes the Key frames without knowledge of the WZ frames and sends them to the decoder. The decoder computes a prediction of the WZ frames that will be used as side information in the distributed coding paradigm. Such an approach is extended to the transform domain in (15). The DCT transform enables the coder to exploit the statistical dependencies within a frame, and so better rate-distortion performance can be achieved. In general, LDPC codes show some performance advantage with respect to Turbo codes. More recently, in (24) a probability updating technique (PUT) to enhance the Turbo coding performance in the context of Wyner-Ziv video coding has been presented.
The algorithms to generate the side information at the decoder influence significantly the rate-distortion performance of the Wyner-Ziv video coding schemes. The techniques described in (28; 29) were selected for the DISCOVER mono-view codec (21). The architecture of this codec is based on the scheme proposed in (15) but many improvements have been added in order to enhance the performance of the basic building blocks. However, as in the original scheme, a feedback channel is still used to request more parity bits until the decoder reconstruction is successful. An improved side information generation method using field coding has been also proposed in (23). WZ frames are divided into the top and bottom fields

as the field coding of a conventional video codec. Top fields are coded with the generation method presented in (28) and bottom fields are reconstructed using the information of the already decoded top fields. Hash-based motion estimation approaches have been presented in (26; 27). In these schemes additional bits are sent by the WZ encoder to aid the decoder in estimating the motion and generate the side information.

Other possible schemes have been presented in the literature. In (16) the pixels of a frame are divided into two sub frames: the key sub frame, consisting of the odd vertical pixel lines, is conventionally encoded and it is used at the decoder to compute the side information that will be used to reconstruct the Wyner-Ziv sub frame (the even vertical pixel lines of the original frame). In (17) Tagliasacchi et al. propose another WZ sub frame coding. The WZ frames are split in two parts: the first part is decoded using the side information only (obtained from the Key frames). The second part is instead decoded using the side information and the previously decoded WZ sub frame.

Wavelet based coding schemes have the potential advantage to naturally allow multiresolution and embedded coding. A wavelet domain DVC scheme has been proposed in (30). A pair of lattice vector quantizers (LVQ) is used to subtract the dependence between wavelets coefficients. The Authors extend the motion compensation refinement concept of pixel domain to wavelet domain and propose a new search strategy for vector reconstruction. In (31), a wavelet domain DVC scheme based on the zero-tree entropy (ZTE) coding is then presented. The wavelet coefficients are quantized using scalar quantization and reorganized in terms of the zero-tree structure. Only the significant coefficients are encoded with a Turbo coder and the punctured parity bit are transmitted. In (32), the Authors exploit the multiresolution properties of the wavelet decomposition to refine motion estimation at the receiver, in order to improve the quality of the side information.

In (18) a scalable video coding scheme is proposed, which performs the DSC between the base and the enhancement layer. In (19), instead, the DSC principles are applied to hyperspectral images. A technique for Wyner-Ziv coding on multispectral images based on a set theory is investigated in (20). Recent advances in multi-view distributed video coding have been also reported in (25).

4. Wavelet-based video coding schemes

In this section we present and compare different Distributed Video Coding (DVC) schemes based on the use of the wavelet transform, which naturally allows for spatial and other forms of scalability. The results presented here summarize the content of (1–4).

The video frames are separated into Key frames, i.e., the ones that are coded using standard techniques and sent to the receiver, and Wyner-Ziv (WZ) frames, which are coded using the distributed coding paradigm. For the results we present below, the Key frames are the even frames of the sequence, while the WZ frames are the odd ones, as in (14).

Two scenarios have been considered (see Fig. 10). In the first, the WZ frames are encoded independently of the Key frames, and the Key frames are encoded and decoded using a conventional intraframe codec. This is the original framework considered for Wyner-Ziv coding, e.g., in (14; 15). In the second scenario, all frames (Key frames and WZ frames) are available at the encoder. This scenario is interesting for the design of a low-complexity video coder, with no motion compensation, and where half of the frames (the WZ frames) are coded using distributed source coding techniques. This framework is considered, for example, in (33).

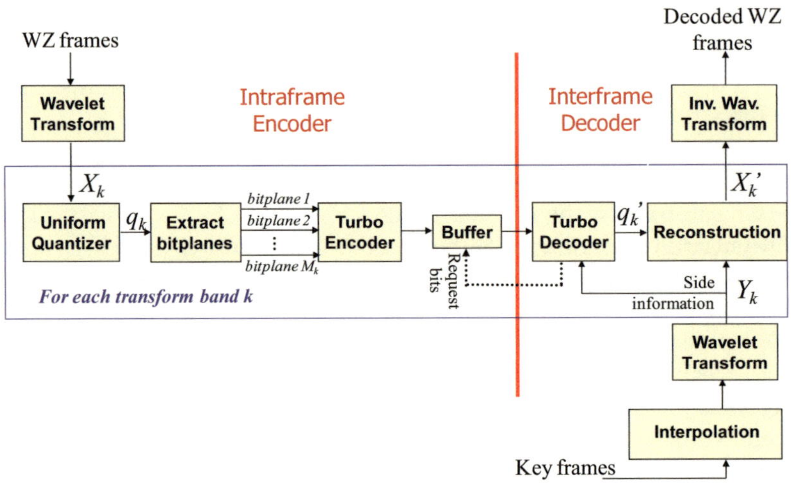

Fig. 9. The reference wavelet based DVC scheme.

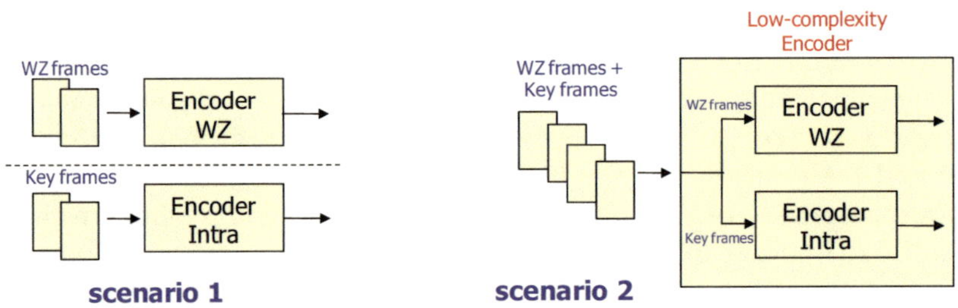

Fig. 10. The considered scenarios.

The reference scheme, which we describe below, is an extension of the one considered in (15), and operates in the wavelet domain, according to the scheme of Fig. 9.

4.1 Wyner-ziv wavelet domain scheme

This scheme operates on the Wavelet Transform of the WZ frames. A three level, ten band wavelet transform is considered for QCIF sequences (see Fig. 11.a). At the encoder, the wavelet transform coefficients are grouped together to form coefficient subbands. Each subband is then quantized using a midtread uniform quantizer where the quantization step is set to be equal for all the subbands (this is the optimal solution for orthogonal transforms). Bits are assigned according to a modified sign/module labeling procedure (4). For each subband, the bitplanes are then independently coded using a *Rate Compatible Punctured Turbo* (RCPT) coder. Using different puncturing schemes, it is possible to send incremental subsets of parity bits, thus allowing to vary the protection offered by the coder to the bitstream.
At the decoder, the side information is generated from the Key frames using temporal interpolation based on Motion Compensated (MC) interpolation with symmetric motion vectors (34). The purpose of this procedure is to reconstruct at the receiver a good approximation of each WZ frame, which will be used by the decoder as side information. The parity bits sent by the encoder are used to recover the bitplanes of the wavelet transform of the WZ frames from those of the side-information.

This scheme uses a feedback channel, and to allow the decoder to request additional parity bits until correct decoding is possible, we consider the transmission of a 16 bit CRC code for each bitplane. If the transmitted CRC does not match with the decoded bitplane, the decoder requests additional parity bits from the encoder buffer until the reconstructed bitplane matches the CRC and the decoding is declared to be successful.
As in (15), the iterative turbo decoder uses information about already decoded bitplanes to improve a-priori knowledge while decoding the next bitplane. Moreover, since the WZ frames are typically quantized more coarsely than the Key frames, the decoder implements a Maximum Likelihood reconstruction strategy, where the WZ wavelet coefficient is reconstructed as the value in the quantization interval, determined on the basis of the WZ decoded bitplanes, which is closest to the value of the side-information. The scheme considered in this section has performance similar to the one of (15), with the possible advantage that the use of the wavelet transform naturally allows for various forms of scalability.

4.2 Hybrid wavelet domain Wyner-ziv scheme with rate estimation

One of the drawbacks of the scheme described above, is that it requires a feedback channel to request additional parity bits, until successfully decoding is achieved (with a residual decoding error probability if the CRC fails). The use of the feedback channel may not be possible in certain applications, e.g., interactive applications, live streaming or multicast transmission, because of the excessive delay that is introduced by the procedure.

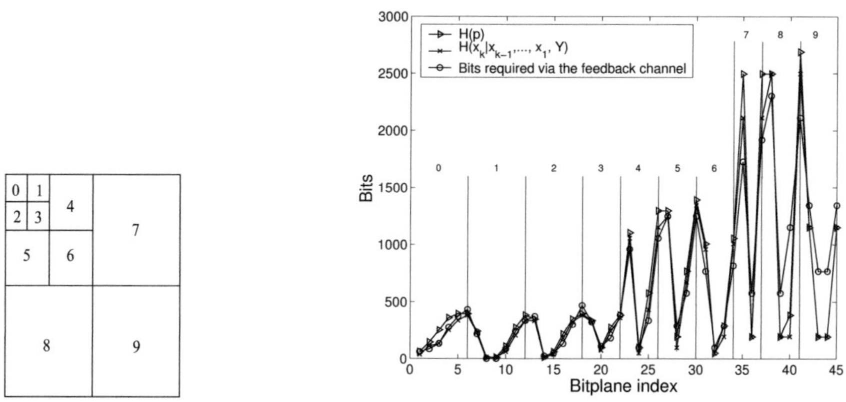

(a) (b)

Fig. 11. (a) The 3-level wavelet transform; (b) bitrate prediction using the statistical models.

Here we present a scheme that does not use a feedback channel, and includes a procedure to estimate the required bitrate for WZ frames at the encoder. Since the decoder cannot make requests to the WZ encoder, it is necessary that the latter estimates the required parity bits for each wavelet coefficient bitplane.
In particular, we propose that the WZ wavelet coefficients in each subband are related to those of the corresponding side information according to the model $X = Y + e$, where Y and e are independent random variables, and e has a Laplacian distribution, i.e., e has a probability density function

$$f_e(a) = \frac{\alpha}{2} e^{-\alpha|a|}. \tag{5}$$

Let us denote with x_k the k-th bitplane of X, with x_1 being the most significant bit. We show in (4) that, as suggested by the Slepian-Wolf theorem, the conditional entropy

$$H(x_k|x_{k-1}, \ldots, x_1, Y) \tag{6}$$

provides a good estimate of the required WZ bitrate for the bitplanes of coefficients belonging to the lower resolution subbands (in particular, subbands 0-6 in Fig. 11.a). Note that $H(x_k|x_{k-1}, \ldots, x_1, Y)$ can be computed at the encoder using the model $X = Y + e$, by estimating α in Eq. (5) based on an approximation $\widetilde{Y}$ of the side-information that will be constructed at the receiver.

In particular, in the first scenario (see Fig. 10), the Key frames are not available at the encoder. Therefore, we compute the average of the WZ frames closest to the current frame, and approximate the side information as the wavelet coefficients $\widetilde{Y}$ of this average. In the second scenario, $\widetilde{Y}$ is the wavelet coefficient of the average of the Key frames closest to the current frame. The two scenarios differ only for the side information $\widetilde{Y}$ which is constructed at the transmitter for rate estimation.

We show in (4) that the entropy $H(p)$ corresponding to the bitplane crossover probability $p = \mathrm{P}[x_k \neq y_k]$ (1; 35; 36) also provides an acceptable estimate of the required bitrate, with $H(p)$ assuming a more conservative larger value. Note that, if one assumes the binary symmetric channel model $x_k = y_k + q_k$, where q_k is independent on y_k, $\mathrm{P}[q_k = 1] = p$, and the sum is modulo 2, we have $H(p) = H(x_k|y_k)$. This is consistent with Eq. (6), where dependence from WZ and side information bitplanes, other than the current bitplane, is neglected. Entropy $H(x_k|y_k)$ or probability p can be computed from x_k, which is known at the encoder, and y_k, calculated from an approximation $\widetilde{Y}$ of the side information.

For high resolution subbands (subbands 7-9 in Fig. 11.a), the models tend to underestimate the required bitrate thus leading to incorrect decoding. Therefore, a hybrid procedure where the quantized high resolution subbands are entropy coded using low-complexity intra-coding procedures (37) is proposed. For the lower resolution subband, $H(p)$ of the bitplane crossover probability $p = \mathrm{P}[x_k \neq y_k]$ (1; 35; 36) is used as the estimate. As an example, Fig. 11.b shows the required bits for each bitplane of all wavelet subbands for one frame of the QCIF sequence *Teeny*, quantized with a quantization step $\Delta = 32$. The vertical lines and the index from 0 to 9 separate the bitplanes of different subbands. In the figure $H(p)$, the entropy and the bitrate actually requested via the feedback channel are shown.

4.3 DVC via modulo reduction

In (1; 4) we propose an alternative procedure for DVC that does not use Turbo codes and does not require feedback from the receiver. As seen in Fig. 12, it comprises three steps: 1) reduction modulo M of the unquantized original wavelet coefficient X to obtain the *reduced variable* $\overline{X} = \Phi_M(X) \triangleq X \bmod M$ (see Fig. 13); 2) lossy coding of $\overline{X}$. The reduced coefficients can be compressed by means of an efficient wavelet coder. In our implementation we use the low complexity coder presented in (37), but other choices are possible; 3) at the receiver, maximum likelihood (ML) decoding of X from quantized $\overline{X}$ and side information Y. As before, the side information Y is generated by temporal interpolation based on Motion Compensated (MC) interpolation with symmetric motion vectors (34). In (4) it is discussed how to choose M to guarantee the recovery of X, after detailing the reconstruction procedure.

The idea behind this scheme can be understood with the help of Fig. 13. The original coefficient X is reduced modulo M to obtain $\overline{X}$, thus producing values in $[-M/2, M/2]$.

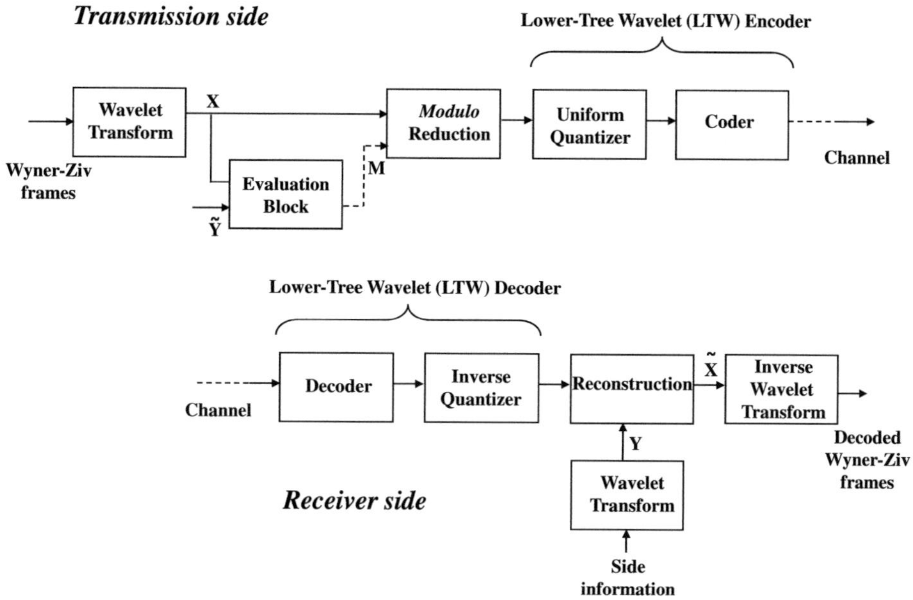

Fig. 12. The proposed scheme with the Evaluation block.

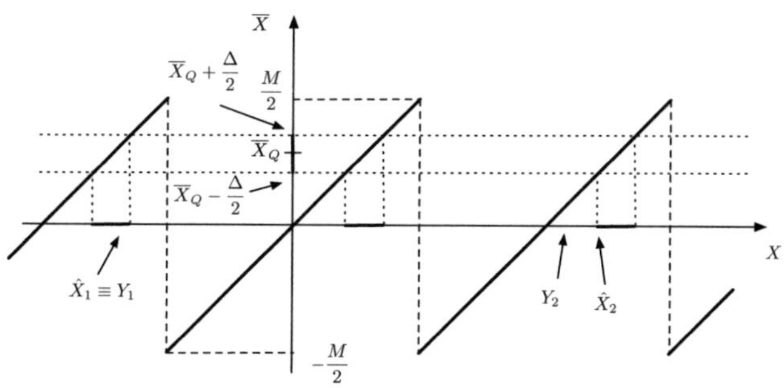

Fig. 13. Construction of the reduced variable $\overline{X}$, and examples of the reconstruction rule at the receiver.

The reduced range values $\overline{X}$ can therefore be quantized and coded more efficiently than the original coefficients. Knowledge of the quantized $\overline{X}$ value $\overline{X}_Q$ at the receiver, allows to conclude that the original X belongs to the set $I_Q + nM$, $n \in Z$, given by the translations of the correct quantization interval for X. Finally, one selects n so that the reconstructed X belongs to the set $I_Q + nM$ and is closest to the side-information Y at the receiver.
It is worth giving the rationale behind this scheme by comparing it with a syndrome-based Wyner-Ziv scheme. In a WZ scheme, instead of transmitting each bitplane of X, we transmit a *syndrome* which allows the receiver to deduce that the encoded binary word belongs to a *coset*; similarly, in the proposed scheme, from the knowledge of $\overline{X}$ one can deduce that X belongs to the *coset* $\Phi_M^{-1}(\overline{X}) = \{\overline{X} + nM;\ n \in Z\}$ (see Fig. 13; we neglect here the effect of quantization). The reduced value $\overline{X}$ can be interpreted as an *analog syndrome* of X. At the receiver, ML reconstruction estimates X by choosing the element of $\Phi_M^{-1}(\overline{X})$ that is closest to the side information Y. Disregarding quantization, it is clear that no error occurs if $|X - Y| < M/2$.
In the usual syndrome-based Wyner-Ziv paradigm, the number of bits of the syndrome must be large enough to allow for the correction of all the "flipped" bits in the bitplanes of X and of the side information. If the syndrome length is not sufficient, X is recovered with an error; similarly, in the proposed scheme, the value of M is chosen large enough to grant for the reconstruction, and if the value of M is underestimated, errors will occur. The major difference between this scheme and a classical WZ scheme is that having an *analog syndrome* allows us to move the quantizer *after* the syndrome computation and use any lossy scheme to encode the reduced values.

4.4 Experimental results for wavetet-based DVC

To have an idea of the performance which can be obtained with DVC schemes, we report here some experiments with the wavelet-based schemes considered above. Further experiments and details can be found in (4).
We consider 299 frames of the QCIF *Foreman* sequence, and 73 frames of the QCIF *Teeny* sequence, coded at 30 frames/s. Only the performance relative to the luminance component of the WZ frames (i.e., the even frames) is considered. The Key frames (i.e., odd frames) are compressed at the encoder with the H.264/AVC standard coder. We set a quantization parameter QP in order to have an average PSNR, for the Key frames, of about 33 dB.
The Turbo code is a Rate Compatible Turbo Punctured (RCPT) code with a puncturing period equal to 33 (15). The Wavelet transform is computed by using the well known 9/7 biorthogonal Daubechies filters, using a three level pyramid. As mentioned before, the difference between the two considered scenarios determines how the approximation $\widetilde{Y}$ is calculated at the transmitter. To this respect, we recall that motion compensation is used at the receiver only. We consider the results relative to the use of the reference scheme presented in Section 4.1 (WD WZ), the scheme with rate estimation described in Section 4.2 (WD WZ RE), and the scheme using modulo reduction of Section 4.3 (MR). We also report the results relative to a simple scheme where the WZ frames are intra-coded, but the actual reconstruction is computed as the X value that belongs to the coded quantization interval and is closest to the side-information Y at the receiver (MLJD in the figures). We consider also a scheme where the WZ schemes are intra-coded (IC), and, for scenario 2, a scheme where the frame difference between consecutive frames is intra-coded. Finally, we also report the performance

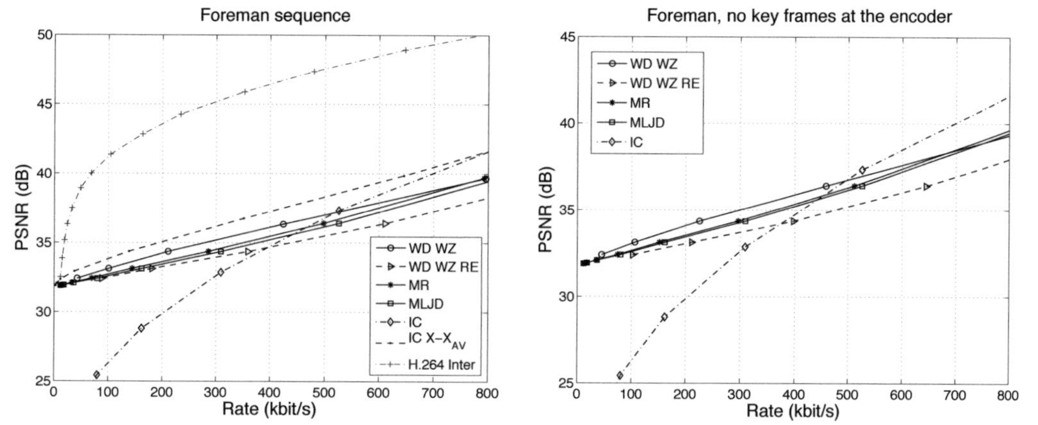

(a) (b)

Fig. 14. (a) Rate-PSNR performance for the *Foreman* sequence (scenario 2), the Key frames are compressed using a QP = 35. (b) Rate-PSNR performance for the *Foreman* sequence (scenario 1), the Key frames are not available at the encoder and they are compressed using a QP = 35.

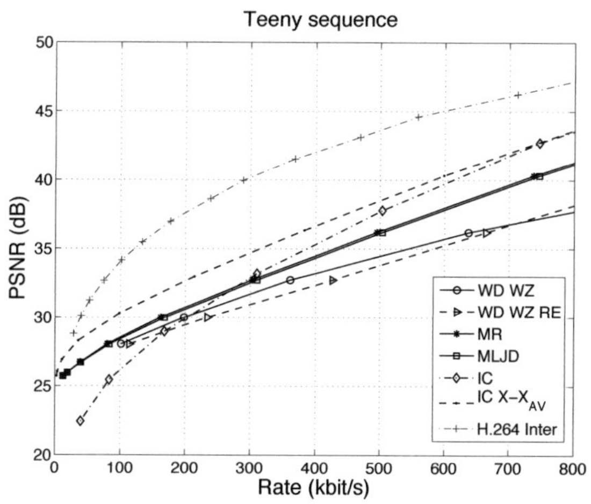

Fig. 15. Rate-PSNR performance for the *Teeny* sequence (scenario 2), the Key frames are compressed using a QP = 5.

of a standard H.264 video coder with inter-frame coding. In this case, the WZ frames are encoded as B frames (predicted from the previous and next frame with motion compensation). As we can see from the figures, for scenario 2, intra coding of the difference $X - X_{AV}$ with joint decoding performs much better than the other schemes. As mentioned, the intra coder can be implemented in this case with low complexity (37), with a clear performance advantage with respect to the DVC schemes considered in this paper and in related papers in the literature. However, note that this scheme can not be used in scenario 1. Among the other schemes, the WZ Wavelet Domain scheme with feedback from the receiver has the best performance at some bit-rates, while we notice some performance loss when the rate is estimated at the encoder. The modulo reduction scheme has comparable or better performance, with a slight advantage (around 0.3 dB) over the MLJD scheme. In Fig. 15, one can notice that, for the high motion video sequence *Teeny*, the performance of the DVC schemes based on channel codes degrades. In all cases, the performance loss with respect to H.264 in inter-mode is significant.

5. Robust transmission of video using an auxiliary DVC stream

As another application of the Distributed Coding paradigm, we summarize in this section the results presented in (2). In particular, we consider the problem of protecting a video stream from data losses, that may be caused by transmission errors. Error protection is achieved by producing an auxiliary redundant stream encoded according to the Wyner-Ziv (WZ) video coding paradigm. This auxiliary scheme can protect a primary stream encoded with any motion-compensated predictive codec.

Along similar lines as those described in the previous sections, the proposed scheme works in the transform domain, and protects the most significant bitplanes of the Discrete Cosine Transform (DCT) coefficients. It uses LDPC codes to compute the syndrome bits of the auxiliary stream.

At the receiver side, the primary stream is decoded and motion-compensated error concealment is applied, in order to do partial recovery of the transmission errors. The concealed reconstructed frame is used as side information by the Wyner-Ziv decoder, which performs LDPC decoding based on the received syndrome bits. The prior information that can be obtained at the decoder, based on the observed error pattern, can be also used to efficiently help LDPC decoding.

One key point of the proposed procedure is that, in order to allocate the appropriate number of syndrome bits, one has to define an appropriate model relating X and Y and, in particular, one has to estimate the variance of their difference, as it was done, in a different context, in the procedure described in Section 4.2. To this purpose, a modified version of the ROPE algorithm (Recursive Optimal per-Pixel Estimate of end-to-end distortion) (38), that works in the DCT domain, is introduced. The proposed EDDD algorithm (Expected Distortion of Decoded DCT coefficients) provides an estimate of the channel induced distortion for each frame and DCT subband. This information is then used to determine the model parameters and estimate the number of syndrome bits to be produced by the Wyner-Ziv encoder.

The proposed sheme was compared with one where Forward Error Correction (FEC) codes are used. The FEC scheme adopts (N, K) Reed-Solomon channel codes. Moreover, the scheme was also compared to the use of the intra-macroblock refresh procedure, which is a non-normative tool in the standard H.264/AVC which increases the robustness to transmission errors (39). Experimental results (see Fig. 16) show that the proposed scheme has comparable or better performance, especially at high packet loss probability, than a scheme using FEC codes. One possible advantage of the proposed solution, is that it naturally allows for rate adaptivity and unequal error protection (UEP) achieved at the frame, DCT band and bitplane granularity.

In addition, the proposed scheme outperforms the intra-macroblock refresh procedure. Note that the latter requires to be applied either at encoding time, or to transcode a pre-encoded bitstream to perform mode switching. Conversely, in the proposed scheme, one can deal with a pre-encoded sequence and simply add Wyner-Ziv bits for protection, maintaining the original bitstream unaltered.

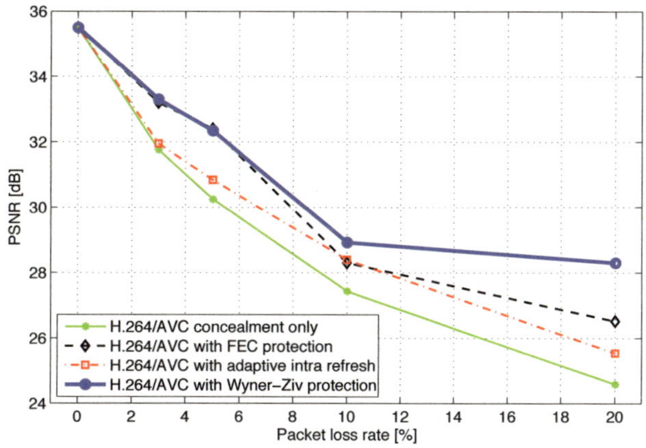

Fig. 16. PSNR vs. PLR for the *Foreman* sequence.

6. Conclusions

In this chapter, we presented the main concepts relative to Distributed Source Coding (DSC), and presented its application to video coding (DVC) and to error protection for video transmission. Although distributed coding is a well known result in Information Theory, its practical implementation, in particular for video coding, is rather recent. DVC is particularly attractive because it can simplify the video compression algorithm, which, as seen, becomes in principle a channel coding procedure. This allows to shift the complexity from the encoder to the decoder, which now has to compute the side-information, typically using a costly motion compensation procedure. Moreover, since decoding exploits a statistical, rather than deterministic, dependence between the source and the side information, it is possible that the decoding process is tolerant to errors and more robust than in a conventional decoder. This makes DVC an interesting option for emerging applications where geographically separated sources capture correlated video.

Experiments show, however, that some conventional techniques (e.g., intra coding with joint decoding and intra coding of the difference between the current frame and the one obtained by averaging the closest Key frames), which do not or partially use the distributed coding paradigm, can have comparable or better performance than the considered DVC schemes, at least for some sequences and bit-rates. In addition, an H.264 interframe coding has significantly better performance than the considered DVC schemes. However, DVC can have a role in some applications, especially when a good quality side information can be constructed at the decoder.

7. References

[1] R. Bernardini, R. Rinaldo, and P. Zontone, "Wavelet domain distributed coding for video", *Proc. International Conference on Image Processing 2006,* Atlanta, USA, October 2006, pp. 245-248.

[2] R. Bernardini, M. Fumagalli, M. Naccari, R. Rinaldo, M. Tagliasacchi, S. Tubaro and P. Zontone, "Error Concealment Using a DVC Approach for Video Streaming Applications", *Proc. Eusipco 2007,* Poznań, Poland, pp. 668-672, Sept. 2007.

[3] Riccardo Bernardini, Roberto Rinaldo, Pamela Zontone, Andrea Vitali, "Performance Evaluation of Distributed Video Coding Schemes", *Proc. IEEE International Conference on Signal Processing 2008*, Las Vegas, Nevada, USA, pp. 709-712, Apr. 2008.
[4] R. Bernardini, R. Rinaldo, A. Vitali, P. Zontone (2009), "Performance evaluation of wavelet-based distributed video coding schemes," SIGNAL, IMAGE AND VIDEO PROCESSING, ISSN: 1863-1703, doi: 10.1007/s11760-009-0141-4.
[5] R. Bernardini, M. Naccari, R. Rinaldo, M. Tagliasacchi, S. Tubaro and P. Zontone, "Rate allocation for robust video streaming based on distributed video coding," *Signal Processing: Image Communication*, Volume 23 , Issue 5, June 2008, pp. 391–403 .
[6] T. Cover and J. Thomas, "Elements of Information Theory", New York, Wiley, pp. 158-167, 1991.
[7] D. Slepian and J. K. Wolf, "Noiseless Coding of correlated information sources," *IEEE Transactions on Information Theory*, vol. 19, n. 4, pp. 471–480, 1973.
[8] A. Wyner and J. Ziv, "The rate-distortion function for source coding with side information at the decoder," *IEEE Transactions on Information Theory*, vol. 22, n. 1, pp. 1–10, 1976.
[9] Zixiang Xiong, Angelos D. Liveris, and Samuel Cheng, "Distributed source coding for sensor networks," *IEEE Signal Processing Magazine*, pp. 80–94, 2004.
[10] A. Wyner, "Recent results in the Shannon Theory," *IEEE Transactions on Information Theory*, vol. 20, n. 1, pp. 2–10, 1974.
[11] A. D. Liveris, Z. Xiong, and C. N. Georghiades, "Distributed compression of binary sources using conventional parallel and serial concatenated convolutional codes," *Proceedings of the IEEE Data Compression Conference*, 2003.
[12] S. S. Pradhan and K. Ramchandran, "Distributed source coding using syndromes (DISCUS): Design and construction," *IEEE Transactions on Information Theory*, vol. 49, pp. 626–643, Mar. 2003.
[13] R. Puri, A. Majumbar, P. Ishwar, and K. Ramchandran, "Distributed video coding in wireless sensor networks," *Signal Processing Magazine, IEEE*, vol. 23, pp. 94–106, July 2006.
[14] A. Aaron, R. Zhang, and B. Girod, "Wyner-ziv coding of motion video," in *Proc. Asilomar Conference on Signals and Systems*, (Pacific Grove, California), Nov. 2002.
[15] A. Aaron, S. Rane, E. Setton, and B. Girod, "Transform-domain wyner-ziv codec for video," in *Visual Communications and Image Processing*, San Jose, CA, Jan. 2004.
[16] A. Adikari, W. Fernando, H. K. Arachchi, and W. Weerakkody, "Wyner-ziv coding with temporal and spatial correlations for motion video," in *IEEE Electrical and Computer Engineering, Canadian Conference*, May 2006.
[17] M. Tagliasacchi, A. Trapanese, S. Tubaro, J. Ascenso, C. Brites, and F. Pereira, "Exploitation spatial redundancy in pixel domain wyner-ziv video coding," in *IEEE International Conference on Image Processing*, Atlanta, GA, October 2006.
[18] H. Wang and A. Ortega, "Scalable predictive coding by nested quantization with layered side information," in *Proc. of IEEE International Conference on Image Processing*, 2004.
[19] M. Barni, D. Papini, A. Abrardo, and E. Magli, "Distributed source coding of hyperspectral images," in *Proc. of IEEE International Geoscience and Remote Sensing Symposyum (IGARSS)*, 2005.
[20] X. Li, "Distributed coding of multispectral images: a set theoretic approach," in *Proc. of IEEE International Conference on Image Processing*, 2004.

[21] X. Artigas, J. Ascenso, M. Dalai, S. Klomp, D. Kubasov, and M. Ouaret, "The discover codec: Architecture, techniques and evaluation," in *Picture Coding Symposium (PCS)*, Lisboa, Portugal, Nov. 2007.

[22] W. Liu, L. Dong, and W. Zeng, "Motion refinement based progressive sideinformation estimation for wynerziv video coding," *to appear in IEEE Trans. Circuits and Systems for Video Technologies*, 2010.

[23] C-H Han, Y-I Jeon, S-W Lee and H-S Kang, "Improved Side Information Generation Using Field Coding for Wyner-Ziv Codec", *2nd International Congress on Image and Signal Processing*, Tianjin, October 2009.

[24] C. Brites and F. Pereira, "Probability Updating for Decoder and Encoder Rate Control Turbo based Wyner-Ziv Video Coding", *Proc. of IEEE International Conf. on Image Processing*, Hong Kong, China, September 2010.

[25] F. Dufaux, M. Ouaret and T. Ebrahimi, "Recent advances in multi-view distributed video coding", *Proc. of SPIE Mobile Multimedia/Image Processing for Military and Security applications*, 2007.

[26] A. Aaron, S. Rane, and B. Girod, "Wyner-ziv Video Coding with Hash-based Motion Compensation at the Receiver", *IEEE International Conference on Image Processing*, Singapore, October 2004.

[27] J. Ascenso and F. Pereira, "Adaptive hash-based side information exploitation for efficient Wyner-Ziv video coding", *IEEE International Conference on Image Processing*, Saint Antonio, USA, September 2007.

[28] J. Ascenso and C. Brites and F. Pereira, "Improving Frame Interpolation With Spatial Motion Smoothing for Pixel Domain Distributed Video Coding", 5th *EURASIP Conference on Speech and Image Processing*, July 2005.

[29] J. Ascenso, C. Brites and F. Pereira, "Content Adaptive Wyner-Ziv Video Coding Driven by Motion Activity," *IEEE International Conference on Image Processing*, Atlanta, USA, October 2006.

[30] A. Wang, Y. Zhao, and L. Wei, "Wavelet-Domain Distributed Video Coding with Motion-Compensated refinement", *Proc. ICIP 2006*, Atlanta USA, Oct. 2006, pp. 241–244.

[31] X. Guo, Y. Lu, F. Wu, and W. Gao, "Distributed Video Coding using Wavelet", *Proc. ISCAS 2006*, Island of Kos, Greece, May 2006, pp. 5427-5430.

[32] W. Liu, L. Dong and W. Zeng, "Estimating side-information for Wyner-Ziv video coding using resolution-progressive decoding and extensive motion exploration", *Proc. IEEE International Conference on Acoustics, Speech, and Signal Processing (ICASSP)*, April 2009, pp. 721–724.

[33] M. Tagliasacchi, A. Trapanese, S. Tubaro, J. Ascenso, C. Brites, and F. Pereira, "Intra Mode Decision Based on Spatio-temporal Cues in Pixel Domain Wyner-Ziv Video Coding", *IEEE International Conference on Acoustic, Speech and Signal Processing*, Toulouse, May 2006.

[34] D. Alfonso, D. Bagni, D. Moglia, "Bi-directionally motion-compensated frame-rate up-conversion for H.264/AVC decoder", ELMAR Symposium, June 2005, Zadar, Croatia.

[35] D. Kubasov, K. Lajnef and C. Guillemot, "A Hybrid Encoder/Decoder Rate Control for Wyner-Ziv Video Coding with a Feedback Channel, *Proc. of MMSP, IEEE International Workshop on Multimedia Signal Processing*, Chania, Crete, Greece, October, 2007, pp. 251-254.

[36] C. Guillemot, F. Pereira, L. Torres, T. Ebrahimi, R. Leonardi, and J. Ostermann, "Distributed Monoview and Multiview Video Coding", *Signal Processing Magazine, IEEE*, Sept. 2007, Vol. 24, Issue 5, pp. 67-76.

[37] J. Oliver, M.P. Malumbres, "Low-Complexity multiresolution image compression using wavelet lower trees", *IEEE Transactions on Circuits and Systems for Video Technology*, Vol. 16, Nov. 2006, pp. 1437–1444.

[38] R. Zhang, S. L. Regunathan, and K. Rose, "Video coding with optimal inter/intra-mode switching for packet loss resilience", *IEEE J. Sel. Areas Commun.*, vol. 18, no. 6, pp. 966–976, June 2000.

[39] ITU-T, *Information Technology - Coding of audio-visual objects - Part 10: advanced video coding*, 2003, Final Draft International Standard, ISO-IEC FDIS 14 496-10.

8

Correlation Noise Estimation in Distributed Video Coding

Jürgen Slowack[1], Jozef Škorupa[1], Stefaan Mys[1], Nikos Deligiannis[2], Peter Lambert[1], Adrian Munteanu[2] and Rik Van de Walle[1]
[1]*Ghent University – IBBT*
Department of Electronics and Information Systems (ELIS) – Multimedia Lab
Gaston Crommenlaan 8 bus 201, B-9000 Ghent
[2]*Vrije Universiteit Brussel (VUB) – IBBT*
Electronics and Informatics Department (ETRO)
Pleinlaan 2, B-1050 Brussels
[1,2]*Belgium*

1. Introduction

Video compression is achieved by exploiting spatial and temporal redundancies in the frame sequence. In typical systems, the encoder is made responsible for exploiting the redundancies by predicting the current frame to be coded from previously coded information (such as other frames and/or blocks). Next, the residual between the frame to be coded and its prediction is transformed, quantized, and entropy coded. As the quality of the prediction has a large influence on the coding performance, high performing but computationally expensive algorithms for generating the prediction have been developed. As a result, typical video coding architectures show an imbalance, with an encoder that is significantly more complex than the decoder.

A new way for performing video coding has been introduced in the last decade. This new paradigm, called distributed video coding (DVC), shifts the complexity from the encoder to the decoder. Such a setup facilitates a different range of applications where the main focus and constraints are on the video (capturing and) coding devices, instead of on the decoding (and displaying) devices. Some examples of target applications include video conferencing with mobile devices, wireless sensor networks and multi-view video entertainment.

The aforementioned shift in complexity is realized by making the decoder responsible for generating the prediction, hereby relieving the encoder from this complex task. While the encoder has the ability to select the best prediction based on a comparison with the original to be coded, the decoder can not perform this comparison as it has only access to already decoded information, and not to the original. This complicates the decoder's task to estimate an accurate motion field compared to conventional predictive video coding.

In distributed video coding, the prediction generated at the decoder (called the side information) often contains a significant amount of errors in comparison to the original video frames. Therefore, the errors are corrected using error correcting information sent by the encoder (such as turbo or LDPC codes). For efficient use of these error correcting bits, soft channel information is needed at the decoder concerning the quality of the generated side

information Y with respect to the original X present at the encoder. More specifically, the decoder needs information expressing the correlation between X and Y. This correlation needs to be estimated since X is available only at the encoder, while Y is available only at the decoder.
The accuracy of estimating the correlation between X and Y has a large impact on compression performance in distributed video coding. When using a less accurate model, more rate from the encoder will be needed in order to correct the errors in Y and reliably decode X. Hence, one way to improve DVC compression performance is by focusing on the correlation model and by improving the accuracy of estimating it in practical DVC systems.
The correlation between X and Y is usually expressed through the difference $N = X - Y$, referred to as the correlation noise. Modeling the distribution of N is difficult because of its non-stationary characteristics, both in the temporal and spatial direction. This is illustrated by means of an example in Figure 1. In this example, the decoded frames at index 39 and 41 are used by the decoder to generate an estimation of the frame at index 40, following the techniques described in the context of the well-known DVC system called DISCOVER (Artigas et al. (2007)). When analyzing the correlation noise N in Figure 1, one can observe that N is spatially non-stationary, meaning that different spatial regions feature different error distributions. Some regions are well predicted (such as the grass in the background), while the prediction accuracy for other regions is rather poor. Similar non-stationary behavior can be observed in the temporal direction as well. Other sequences lead to similar conclusions, as illustrated by Figure 2 for the Table Tennis sequence. Due to these highly varying statistics, accurately estimating the distribution of N has proved to be a challenging task in distributed video coding.
In this chapter we describe several techniques that improve upon current approaches for correlation estimation in DVC. First, in Section 2, details are provided for the DVC architecture based on which our designs are built. This description is followed by a discussion on the current literature concerning correlation noise estimation, in Section 3. Next, two techniques that improve upon existing approaches are presented. The first technique (described in Section 4) incorporates knowledge about the quantization noise, which improves the accuracy of the correlation model, particularly at low rates. In the second improvement, we compensate for inaccurate assumptions made when generating the side information, as discussed in Section 5. The results achieved by both approaches are promising, and they underline the importance of accurate correlation modeling in DVC. Final conclusions of our work are given in Section 6.

2. Introducing the DVC architecture

Figure 3 depicts the DVC codec that is used as a starting point for the techniques presented in this chapter. The architecture is largely based on the pioneering architecture developed by Aaron et al. (2004a), and on its popular extension developed in the context of DISCOVER by Artigas et al. (2007). The latter can still be considered among the current state-of-the-art in DVC, and it provides a benchmark as its executables are available online[1].
The operation of the codec in Figure 3 is as follows. First, the frame sequence is partitioned into key frames I and Wyner-Ziv frames W, using a fixed GOP structure for the entire sequence (e.g., a GOP of length four would be: I-W-W-W-I-...). The key frames are coded without using other frames as references, i.e., applying H.264/AVC intra coding. Each

[1] http://www.discoverdvc.org

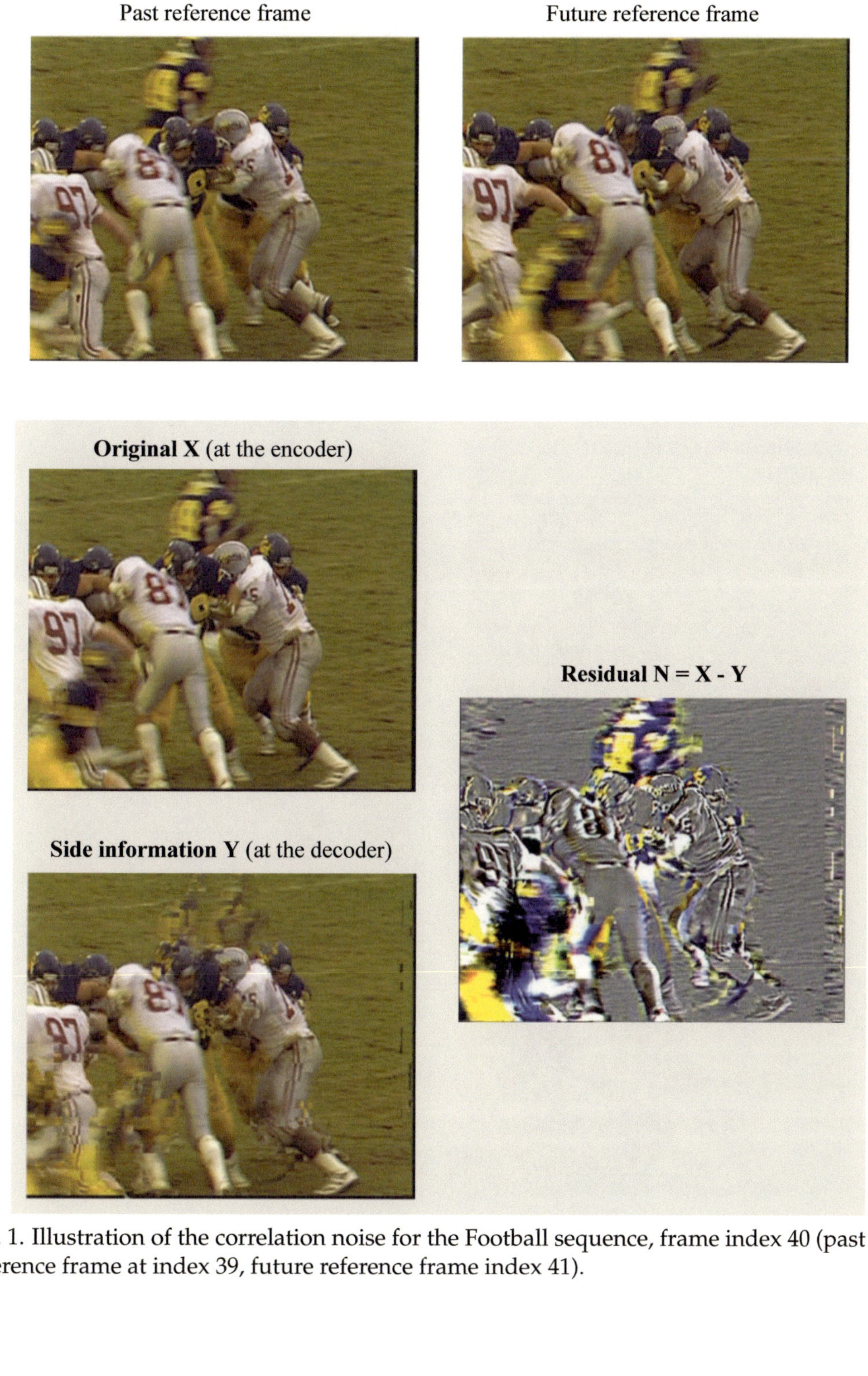

Fig. 1. Illustration of the correlation noise for the Football sequence, frame index 40 (past reference frame at index 39, future reference frame index 41).

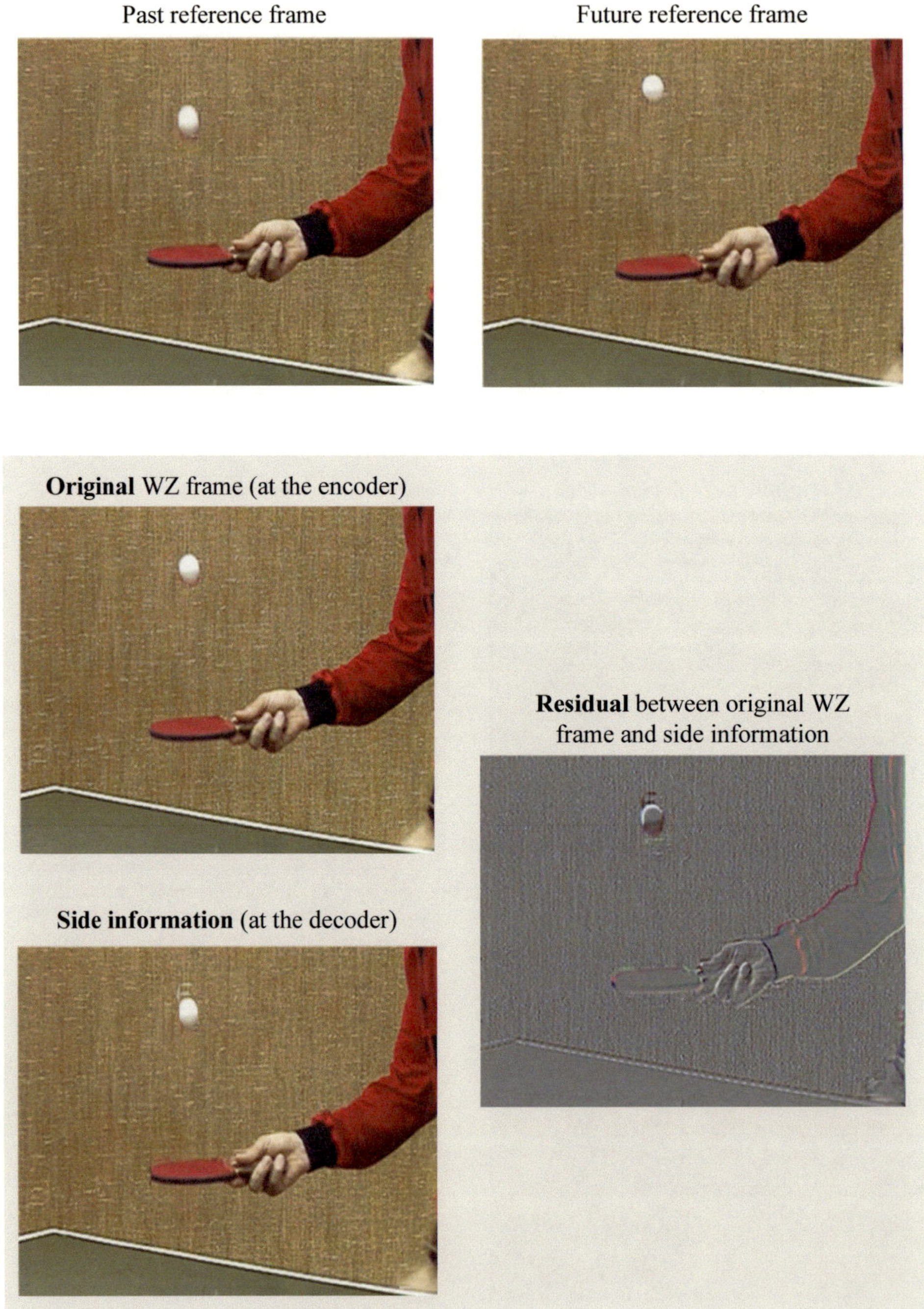

Fig. 2. Illustration of the correlation noise for the Table Tennis sequence, frame index 2 (past reference frame at index 1, future reference frame index 3).

Wyner-Ziv frame is partitioned into non-overlapping blocks of 4-by-4 pixels, and each block is transformed using a discrete cosine transform (DCT). Next, for all blocks, the resulting DCT coefficients at the same spatial index k (with $0 \leq k \leq 15$) are grouped into coefficient bands X_k. For example, each fourth coefficient in each block will be collected, forming the fourth coefficient band X_3. Next, each band is quantized to Q_k using a quantizer with 2^{M_k} quantization bins. The zero bin of this quantizer is 1.5 times larger than the other bins, for all coefficient bands except for the first (DC band). Subsequently, for each band, bits at identical positions are grouped into bitplanes BP_i^k. For example, all most significant bits of all DC coefficients will form bitplane BP_0^0. Finally, for each bitplane, parity bits are generated by a turbo coder (Lin & Costello (2004)) and stored in a buffer. These bits will be sent in portions to the decoder upon request.

At the decoder, key frames are decoded into I' by applying H.264/AVC intra decoding. We note that, in our notation, $'$ is used to indicate decoded frames. Side information is generated for each Wyner-Ziv frame, using already decoded frames as references. A hierarchical GOP structure is used, meaning that the sequence $I_1 - W_1 - W_2 - W_3 - I_2$ is coded and decoded in the following order: $I_1 - I_2 - W_2 - W_1 - W_3$. For example, the side information for W_1 will be generated using I_1' as a past reference frame, and W_2' as a future reference frame (Aaron et al. (2003)). Several techniques for generating the side information have been proposed in the literature. In our architecture, we follow the method adopted in DISCOVER (Artigas et al. (2007)).

After generating the side information Y, the correlation between X and Y is modeled. This correlation model – forming the main subject in this chapter – will be described in detail in Section 3.1, and it will be further extended in the remainder of this chapter.

The turbo decoder uses the correlation model in a Viterbi-like decoding procedure. To this extent, the turbo decoder requests parity bits (also called Wyner-Ziv bits) from the encoder's buffer via the feedback channel, until reliable decoding is achieved (Škorupa et al. (2009)).

When turbo decoding terminates, the bitplanes are multiplexed. This operation is the inverse of the bitplane extraction process performed at the encoder. As a result, the turbo decoder returns for each coefficient the index of the quantization bin containing the original value with very high probability. The following step – called reconstruction – is to select one particular value in this bin as the decoded value of the coefficient. The reconstruction method used here is the so-called centroid reconstruction, as described by Kubasov et al. (2007). After reconstruction, the result is inverse transformed, yielding the decoded Wyner-Ziv frame W'.

3. Related work on correlation estimation

The correlation between X and Y is commonly modeled using a Laplace distribution (Aaron et al. (2004a); Brites & Pereira (2008); Kubasov et al. (2007)), or a Gaussian distribution (Macchiavello et al. (2009)). The Laplace distribution is used by the majority of researchers as a good trade-off between model accuracy and complexity.

Using the Laplace distribution, the correlation between X and Y is described through a conditional probability density function of the form:

$$f_{X|Y}(x|y) = \frac{\alpha}{2} e^{-\alpha|x-y|}. \tag{1}$$

At the decoder, the realization of the side information, y, is available, and so only the distribution scale parameter α needs to be estimated. The relation between α and the variance σ^2 is given by:

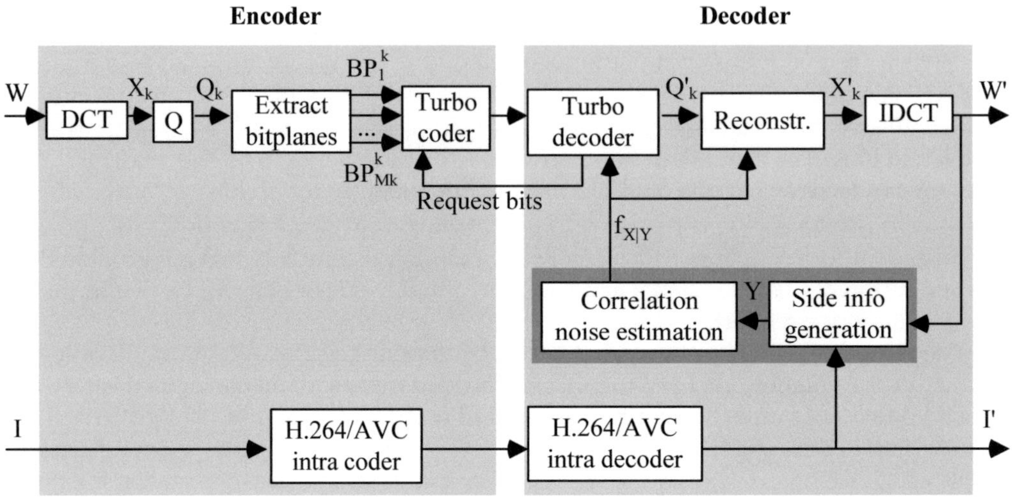

Fig. 3. The DVC architecture used as a starting point for the designs presented in this chapter.

$$\alpha = \frac{\sqrt{2}}{\sigma}. \tag{2}$$

Initially, stationary models and/or offline approaches have been used in the literature to estimate α. For example, in Stanford's DVC system, parameters for each coefficient band are obtained through an initial training stage performed on several sequences (Aaron et al. (2004a;b); Girod et al. (2005)). A temporally and spatially stationary model is adopted as the same parameter set is used throughout the entire sequence. Other offline techniques allow access to X at the decoder for obtaining correlation information (Trapanese et al. (2005)).
While these techniques are impractical or lack flexibility, efficient online techniques have been proposed only recently. An important contribution in this context is due to Brites & Pereira (2008), who propose offline and online methods both in the pixel-domain and transform-domain. Since each block in the side information is generated as the average between a past reference block and a future reference block, the similarity between these two reference blocks is used to estimate the correlation between the original X and its estimation Y. If the side information generation process is unable to find good matches between past and future reference blocks, then X and Y are assumed to be poorly correlated. On the other hand, if there is a good match, the correlation between X and Y is assumed to be strong. As such, this technique allows online estimation of the correlation noise by analyzing similarities between past and future motion-compensated frames.
An alternative solution has been proposed in our own work (Škorupa et al. (2008)). This technique – described further on in detail – also uses the motion-compensated residual between the past and future reference frames for estimating the correlation noise. However, one of the major differences with the previous technique is that the transform-domain noise is estimated by converting the pixel-domain noise estimates. The results show increased performance compared to the work of Brites & Pereira (2008).
Converting pixel-domain correlation noise estimates to their transform-domain equivalents has been proposed as well by Fan, Au & Cheung (2009). In the latter, instead of using the

motion-compensated residual, the authors exploit information available from the previously decoded Wyner-Ziv frame as well as the previously decoded coefficient bands.
Information from decoded coefficient bands is used also by Huang & Forchhammer (2009), aiming to improve the method proposed by Brites & Pereira (2008). The decoded information is used to classify coefficients, applying different estimators for different categories.
As discussed further, the techniques for correlation noise estimation described in the literature have a few shortcomings, especially the ones that exclusively rely on the motion-compensated residual. Therefore, in this chapter, two techniques are presented that improve upon previous approaches in the literature, including our previous work on correlation noise estimation (Škorupa et al. (2008)). To this extent, we first describe in detail this method in the following subsection.

3.1 From pixel-domain to transform-domain correlation estimation (Škorupa et al.)

Using common techniques for side information generation such as the ones used in DISCOVER (Artigas et al. (2007)), each block in the side information frame Y is created through motion compensation. More precisely, each block in Y is created as the average of a block in a decoded frame X'_B in the past (i.e., a frame at a lower frame-index relative to the current frame) and a block in a decoded frame X'_F in the future (i.e., a frame at a higher frame-index). The reference blocks are obtained by following the calculated past and future motion vectors denoted by (dx_B, dy_B) and (dx_F, dy_F), respectively.
As in the work of Brites & Pereira (2008), the similarity between past and future blocks is used to estimate the correlation noise. If the difference between the reference blocks is low, the corresponding block in the side information is assumed to be of high quality. On the other hand, if the difference between both blocks is large then it is likely that side information generation failed to obtain a reliable estimate.
Let R denote the motion-compensated residual given by:

$$R(x,y) = X'_B(x + dx_B, y + dy_B) - X'_F(x + dx_F, y + dy_F). \tag{3}$$

As such, there exists a relation between the correlation noise N and the motion-compensated residual R. This relation is illustrated by means of an example in Figure 4, which contains the result from coding frame 93 of the Foreman sequence (I-W-I-W GOP structure). This example shows that there is strong resemblance between R and N. Good matches between past and future reference blocks (i.e., low values for R) indeed often correspond to low values for N. Hence, although N can not be determined at the decoder in a practical DVC system, due to the absence of X, R can be calculated, since it only involves decoded reference frames. Therefore, similar to the work of Brites & Pereira (2008), we use R as basis for estimating N. However, the actual estimate of N differs in our method, as we first generate a pixel-domain estimation and then convert this result to the transform domain.
Using R, for each block at index k in the side information, the central moment is calculated:

$$Mom_k(R) = E_k\left[|R(x,y)|^{0.5}\right], \tag{4}$$

where E_k denotes the expectation taken only over the block at index k in the frame. Likewise, the average central moment $Mom(R)$ is obtained through expectation over the entire residual frame R:

$$Mom(R) = E\left[|R(x,y)|^{0.5}\right]. \tag{5}$$

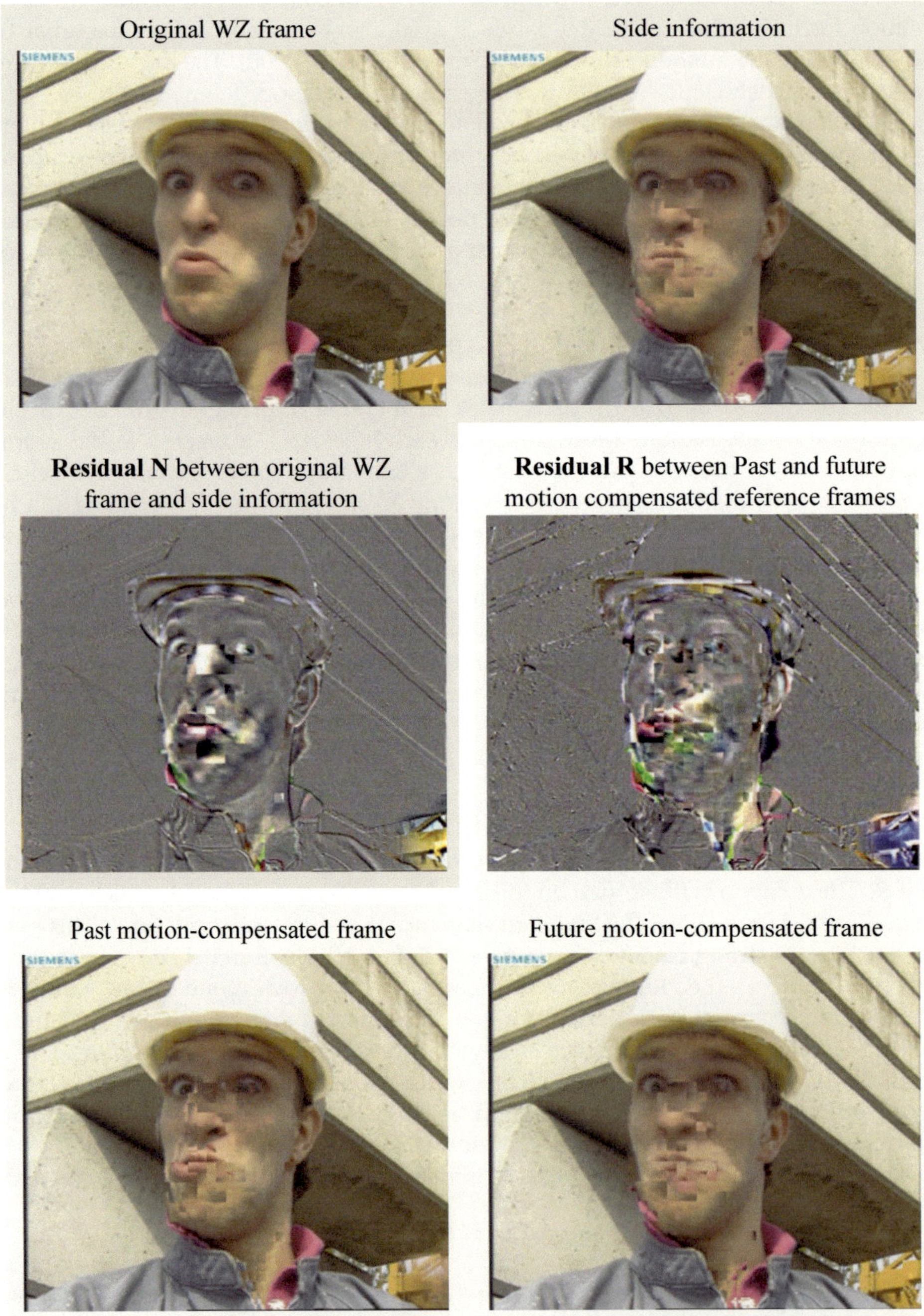

Fig. 4. Correlation noise *N* compared to the motion compensated residual *R* (fine quantization, intra quantization parameter of 10 is employed for the reference frames).

$s_{i,j}$	j			
i	4.25	2.06	1.16	0.77
	2.06	1.00	0.56	0.38
	1.16	0.56	0.32	0.21
	0.77	0.38	0.21	0.14

Table 1. Scaling parameters $s_{i,j}$ for pixel to transform-domain conversion of the α parameter estimation, following the techniques proposed in our previous work (Škorupa et al. (2008)).

The central moment of the correlation noise N for the block at index k is then estimated as:

$$\widetilde{Mom}_k(N) = \frac{Mom_k(R) + Mom(R)}{2}. \tag{6}$$

The rationale behind this formula is that it estimates the central moment of N for the block at index k by combining local and global information from R.
Finally, for each pixel in the block at index k, the following expression is used to estimate α:

$$\alpha_k^P = \frac{\pi}{4\widetilde{Mom}_k(N)^2}, \tag{7}$$

where the upper-index P indicates that this α parameter is defined in the pixel-domain. The lower index k differentiates between different blocks in the same frame, so as to cope with the spatial non-stationarities discussed before.
To convert the pixel-domain α parameter to its (DCT) transform-domain equivalent, a scaling step is applied. As such, the α parameter of the coefficient at index (i,j) in block k is given by:

$$\alpha_{k,(i,j)}^T = \frac{\alpha_k^P}{\sqrt{s_{i,j}}}, \tag{8}$$

with $s_{i,j}$ defined as in Table 1 ($0 \leq i \leq 3$ and $0 \leq j \leq 3$). For more information about this scaling operation we refer to Škorupa et al. (2008).
For future reference in the extensions provided in this chapter, we define the average pixel-domain α as:

$$\alpha^P = \frac{\pi}{4\widetilde{Mom}(N)^2}, \tag{9}$$

where $\widetilde{Mom}(N)$ denotes the frame-average of $\widetilde{Mom}_k(N)$. We also define its transform-domain counterpart as:

$$\alpha_{(i,j)}^T = \frac{\alpha^P}{\sqrt{s_{i,j}}}. \tag{10}$$

4. Accounting for quantization noise

As a first extension in this chapter, the model for correlation noise estimation is refined by accounting for the quantization noise. The technique is based on the observation that the quantization noise in the decoded reference frames X_B' and X_F' has a different impact on R than it has on N. As a result, inaccuracies occur in the previous method for correlation noise estimation when the quantization noise is high (i.e., for coarse quantization).

For fine quantization (Figure 4) of the intra-frames, the residual R and the correlation noise N show strong resemblance. In well-predicted areas both N and R depict low (i.e. mid-gray) values. On the other hand, R still provides reasonably accurate information about the average mismatch in areas that are poorly predicted. Hence, for fine quantization of the intra-frames, R can indeed be used to estimate N.

However, as shown in Figure 5, when the intra frames are coarsely quantized, there is a mismatch between R and N. In specific, the distribution of N has a much larger variance than the distribution of R. This is a consequence of the quantization noise present in the reference frames. Due to this noise, some of the fine detail is lost in the past and future reference frames. However, the side information generation process is still able to find good matches between past and future blocks, since the details have been erased in a similar way in both frames. As a result, the residual R is typically low, and the side information Y that is constructed through interpolation does not contain some of the fine details either. Consequently, the lost details can be found in N, but not in R, resulting in higher energy for N compared to the energy in R. For example, one can observe in Figure 5 that some of the texture details of the concrete in the background are present in N but not in R.

Our current technique (proposed in Škorupa et al. (2008) and described in Section 3.1) compensates insufficiently for quantization noise. To illustrate this, measurements have been performed for the luma DC component of Foreman (CIF, first 101 frames, I-W-I-W GOP structure). The distribution of N measured offline has been compared against the average noise distribution estimated online using the method described in Section 3.1. The results are presented in Figure 6, including the measured distribution of R. These results show that – for coarse quantization (i.e., IQP 40) – there is a clear mismatch between the measured distribution of N and its estimated distribution based on R.

4.1 Proposed solution

As a solution to this problem, statistics about the quantization noise are determined at the encoder. This information is then sent to the decoder, where it is used to improve the estimation of N.

For high resolution quantization, i.e., when the width of the quantization bin is small compared to the variance of the distribution of the signal, the average distortion due to uniform quantization can be approximated by the distortion of a random variable that is uniformly distributed over the quantization bin, which has a variance of $d^2/12$, where d denotes the bin width (Gersho & Gray (1992)). In our case, this approximation is inaccurate since medium and low rates are specifically targeted. At these rates, the quantization noise depends on the distribution of the signal, hence it is sequence-dependent, and non-stationary (in time and space[2]). Therefore, the quantization noise of the intra frames is calculated at the encoder (Section 4.1.1) and this information is used at the decoder to improve the estimation of the correlation noise (Section 4.1.2).

4.1.1 Encoder-side

For each coefficient band, the variance of the quantization noise of the intra frames is estimated by calculating the variance of the difference between the transformed original intra frame and the transformed intra decoded version. The computational overhead remains low,

[2] In the technique proposed here, the average quantization noise will be calculated per frame, hereby ignoring spatial differences. Accounting for spatial differences comes at the cost of increased signaling overhead.

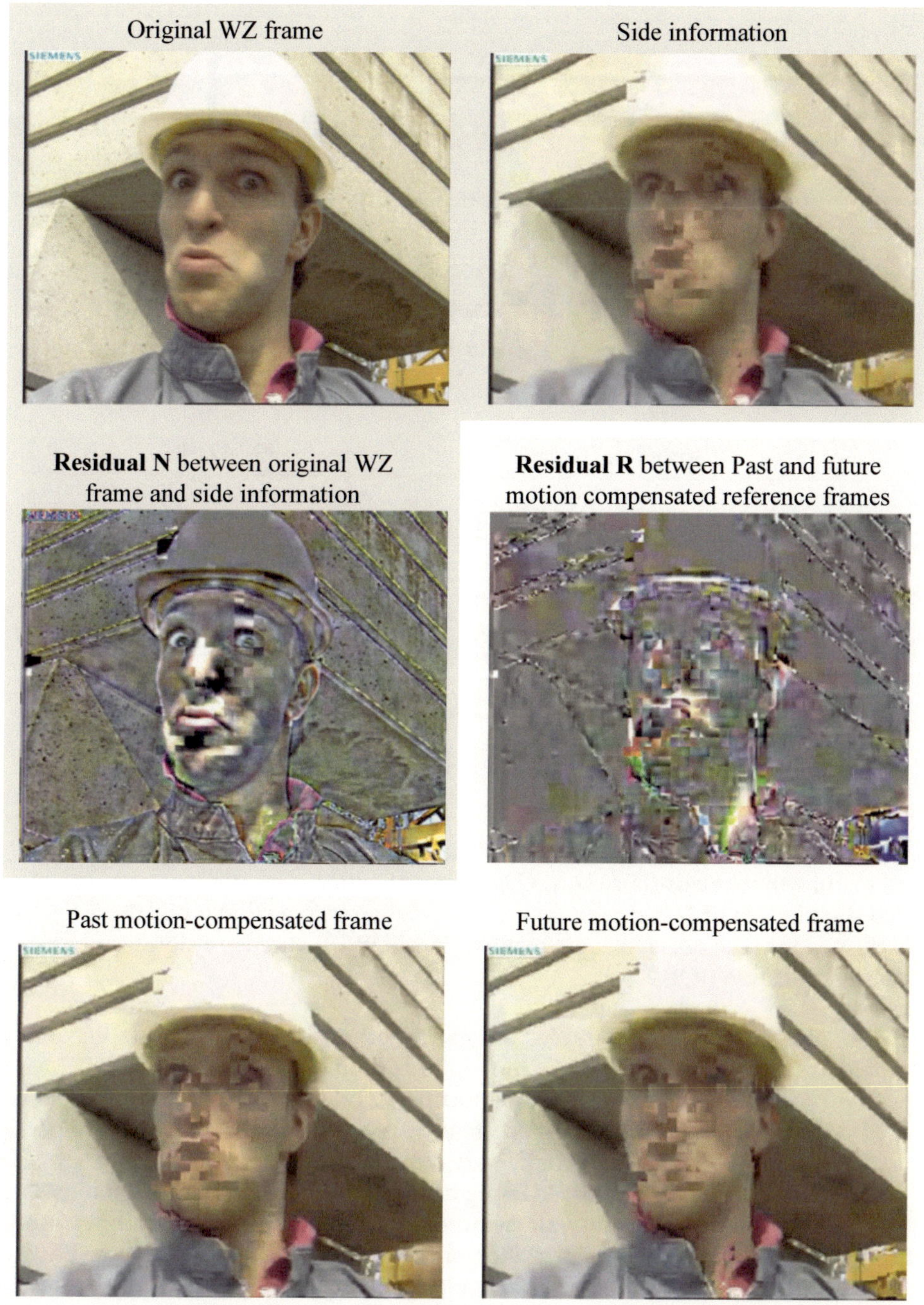

Fig. 5. Correlation noise N compared to the motion compensated residual R, for coarse quantization, i.e. an intra quantization parameter (IQP) of 40 is employed for the intra frames. In this case, some of the residual texture in N is not present in R, since quantization has removed this information from the reference frames.

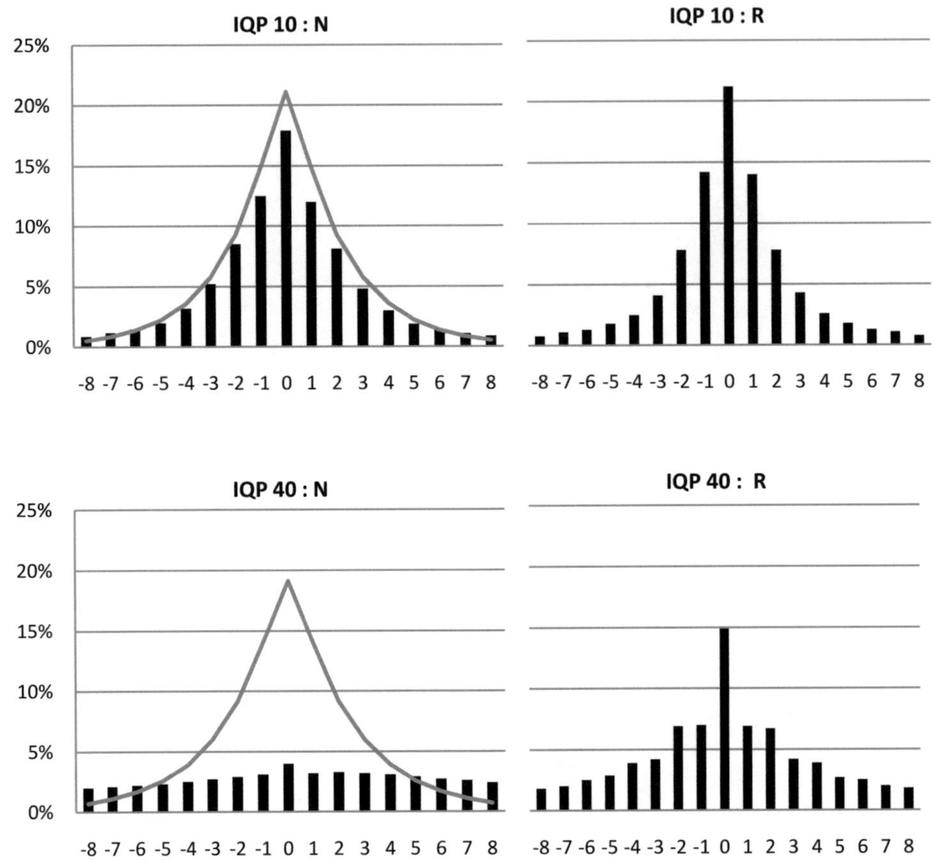

Fig. 6. Measured distribution of N and R, for the luma DC component of Foreman, for different quantization levels (H.264/AVC intra quantization parameter given). The average estimated distribution of N is drawn on top. Clearly, we can see that while the estimated noise is close to the true noise for fine quantization (IQP 10), there is a significant mismatch for coarse quantization (IQP 40).

since H.264/AVC intra decoded frames are generated anyway by the intra encoder in the context of mode decision and rate-distortion optimization.

To limit the overhead of sending the quantization noise variances to the decoder, some additional processing steps are performed. Firstly, it was observed that the variances of the chroma components (U and V) are usually very similar. Therefore, only the average of both is used. Next, the variances are quantized using a uniform quantizer having 2^M bins. It can be assumed that the variances are never much larger than the variance of a random variable that is uniformly distributed over the quantization bin, so that the quantizer range can be restricted to the interval $[0, d^2/12]$; d can be easily calculated from the H.264/AVC intra quantization parameter. For M, the largest integer is taken that is not greater than 5 and for which d is at least 1. Since a 4-by-4 DCT transformation is used, the result of processing the variances is that at most $5 \cdot (16 + 16) = 160$ bits need to be sent to the decoder per I frame.

Since the quantization noise statistics do not always change drastically from intra frame to intra frame, information is only sent if the average difference between the newly quantized

variances and the previously-sent quantized values is at least 0.5. This ensures that only significant updates are communicated.
In our experiments, the above processing steps proved to be efficient. The overhead of sending the quantization noise information to the decoder only accounts for maximum 0.05% of the total bit rate, for each rate point.

4.1.2 Decoder-side

At the decoder, the coded variances for the intra frames are received from the encoder, and reconstructed. Next, the decoder uses these variances to improve the modeling of the correlation noise between a particular Wyner-Ziv frame and the associated side information Y. As in most DVC systems, quantization of the intra and Wyner-Ziv frames is chosen in such a way that all frames have more or less the same quality. Therefore, it is assumed that the decoded intra frames and Wyner-Ziv frames are all affected by approximately the same noise. In addition, the quantization noise corrupting Y is similar to the noise in the reference frames, so that the quantization noise variances $\left(\sigma^{Q}_{(i,j)}\right)^2$ received from the encoder can be applied to the side information Y.
Now that an approximation of the quantization noise in Y has been obtained, this needs to be combined with the noise induced by motion, deformation, illumination changes, etc. Since the current methods for correlation noise estimation provide a good approximation when quantization noise is low (as shown before), both methods are combined. The standard deviation σ of the correlation noise N associated with a coefficient at index (i,j) in block k, is thus estimated as:

$$\sigma = \sigma^{T}_{k,(i,j)} + C \cdot \sigma^{Q}_{(i,j)}, \tag{11}$$

with

$$C = \begin{cases} 1 - \dfrac{\sigma^{T}_{(i,j)}}{2\sigma^{Q}_{(i,j)}} & , \text{if } \dfrac{\sigma^{T}_{(i,j)}}{2\sigma^{Q}_{(i,j)}} < 1 \\ 0 & , \text{otherwise} \end{cases} \tag{12}$$

where $\sigma^{T}_{k,(i,j)}$ and $\sigma^{T}_{(i,j)}$ relate to Equation 8 and Equation 10, respectively, since:

$$\sigma^{T}_{k,(i,j)} = \frac{\sqrt{2}}{\alpha^{T}_{k,(i,j)}}, \tag{13}$$

and

$$\sigma^{T}_{(i,j)} = \frac{\sqrt{2}}{\alpha^{T}_{(i,j)}}. \tag{14}$$

To justify this experimentally derived formula, similar measurements are performed as before. Comparing the new model for correlation noise estimation to the actual correlation noise in Figure 7 clearly shows that our estimation has become significantly more accurate.

4.2 Results

In order to quantify the impact of the proposed model on the coding performance, tests have been performed on sequences with different motion characteristics, including Mother and

		Proposed		Previous work		BJM delta rate	
		PSNR (dB)	rate (kbps)	PSNR (dB)	rate (kbps)	PSNR (dB)	rate (%)
MD	Q0	41.8	513	41.8	540	41	-6.1
	Q1	38.9	261	38.9	288	38	-11.6
	Q2	36.4	129	36.3	151	36	-16.6
	Q3	34.3	69	34.2	88	35	-19.5
Tab. Tennis	Q0	37.5	1666	37.5	1668	37	0.1
	Q1	33.4	827	33.3	835	33	-2.0
	Q2	30.2	405	30.1	421	30	-6.4
	Q3	27.8	216	27.7	235	28	-10.3
Foreman	Q0	38.2	1434	38.1	1445	38	-1.4
	Q1	34.8	708	34.7	722	34	-3.9
	Q2	31.6	357	31.4	374	31	-7.2
	Q3	28.7	188	28.6	201	29	-9.1

Table 2. Average results per Wyner-Ziv frame, for Mother and Daughter (MD), Table Tennis (Tab. Tennis), and Foreman. Bjøntegaard delta rate metrics (BJM) illustrate the evolution of the gain for different levels of quality (negative values indicate decrease in bit rate).

Daughter, Foreman, and Table Tennis. All are in CIF resolution, 30 fps, and with a GOP length of 4. The results are given in Table 2 for the Wyner-Ziv frames only.

The Bjøntegaard (2002) delta metric is used to illustrate the rate difference at a given level of quality. This metric shows that our new technique performs particularly well at low rates (i.e., coarse quantization), with average rate gains up to 19.5% per Wyner-Ziv frame for Mother and Daughter.

The results show that the gain for Mother and Daughter is larger than for Table Tennis and Foreman. This is because Mother and Daughter is a sequence with low motion characteristics, hence, the side information generation process is able to find very good matches, resulting in small values for R and consequently for $\sigma^T_{k,(i,j)}$ (and $\sigma^T_{(i,j)}$). Therefore, $\sigma^Q_{(i,j)}$ is relatively large, which results in a large impact on σ. For sequences with high motion content, $\sigma^T_{k,(i,j)}$ and $\sigma^T_{(i,j)}$ are larger so that the impact of our update is smaller.

The results obtained for our technique are interesting, but some areas still need further exploring. For example, we have assumed so far that the quantization noise in the decoded intra frames and the decoded Wyner-Ziv frames is similar. This might not always be true since the reconstruction of the intra frames and the reconstruction of the Wyner-Ziv frames is performed using different techniques.

4.3 Conclusions

The results of this section show that relying only on the motion-compensated residual between the reference frames (used for generating the side information) does not always deliver an accurate estimation of the correlation noise. Instead, we have shown that the quantization distortion in the reference frames needs to be taken into account as well in order to improve the accuracy of the noise estimates. Exploiting this information has resulted in significant performance gains, in particular at medium and low rates.

On the one hand, the results in this section underline the importance of accurate correlation noise modeling in DVC. On the other hand, the results encourage researchers to investigate

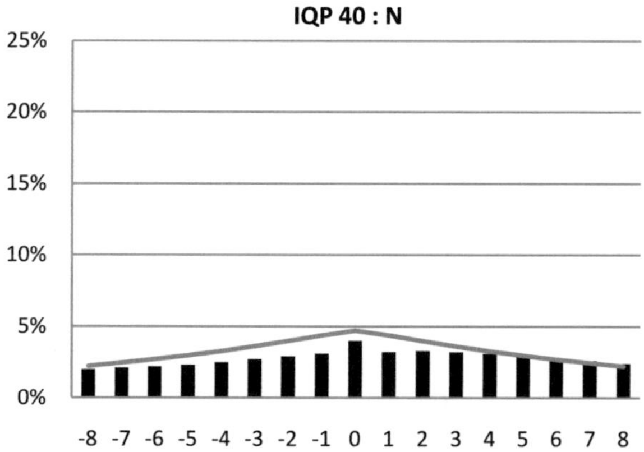

Fig. 7. The new method for correlation noise estimation is more accurate for coarse quantization (i.e. low rates).

other sources of information to improve the noise estimation accuracy, and develop new correlation noise models.

5. Compensating for motion estimation inaccuracies

This section details a second major contribution of this chapter, where the correlation model is further improved by compensating for the inaccuracies in the generation of the side information. This is achieved by using a correlation model based on multiple predictors, as detailed next.

Current techniques for side information generation commonly assume that the motion between the past and future reference frames can be approximated as linear. This assumption is made in, for example, Stanford's DVC architecture (Aaron et al. (2004a)) as well as in DISCOVER (Artigas et al. (2007)). Even in cases where more complex motion models are used, motion interpolation is still performed in a linear fashion. For example, Kubasov & Guillemot (2006) use mesh-based techniques to obtain a model of the motion between the past and future reference frame. The side information is then created through linear interpolation along the motion trajectories described by this model, assuming uniform motion between the reference frames.

The assumption that the motion between the reference frames can be approximated as linear becomes less valid when the distance between the reference frames increases. This is illustrated for a GOP of size eight. Side information has been generated for the 5th frame of the Foreman sequence, using the first frame as a past reference, and the 9th frame as a future reference. When analyzing the residual between the side information and the original frame in Figure 8, it is clear that a lot of errors need to be corrected, increasing significantly the Wyner-Ziv rate. Judging from the quality of the side information itself, it could already be expected that the accuracy of estimating the face is low. However, the residual also reveals that errors need to be corrected in the background as well. More specifically, we can see that edges in the side information are not predicted accurately. This is due to non-linear camera motion.

To compensate for inaccuracies in side information generation, most recent techniques apply a refinement approach. Decoding is performed partially, and the partially decoded frame is used to improve the quality of the side information. The improved side information is

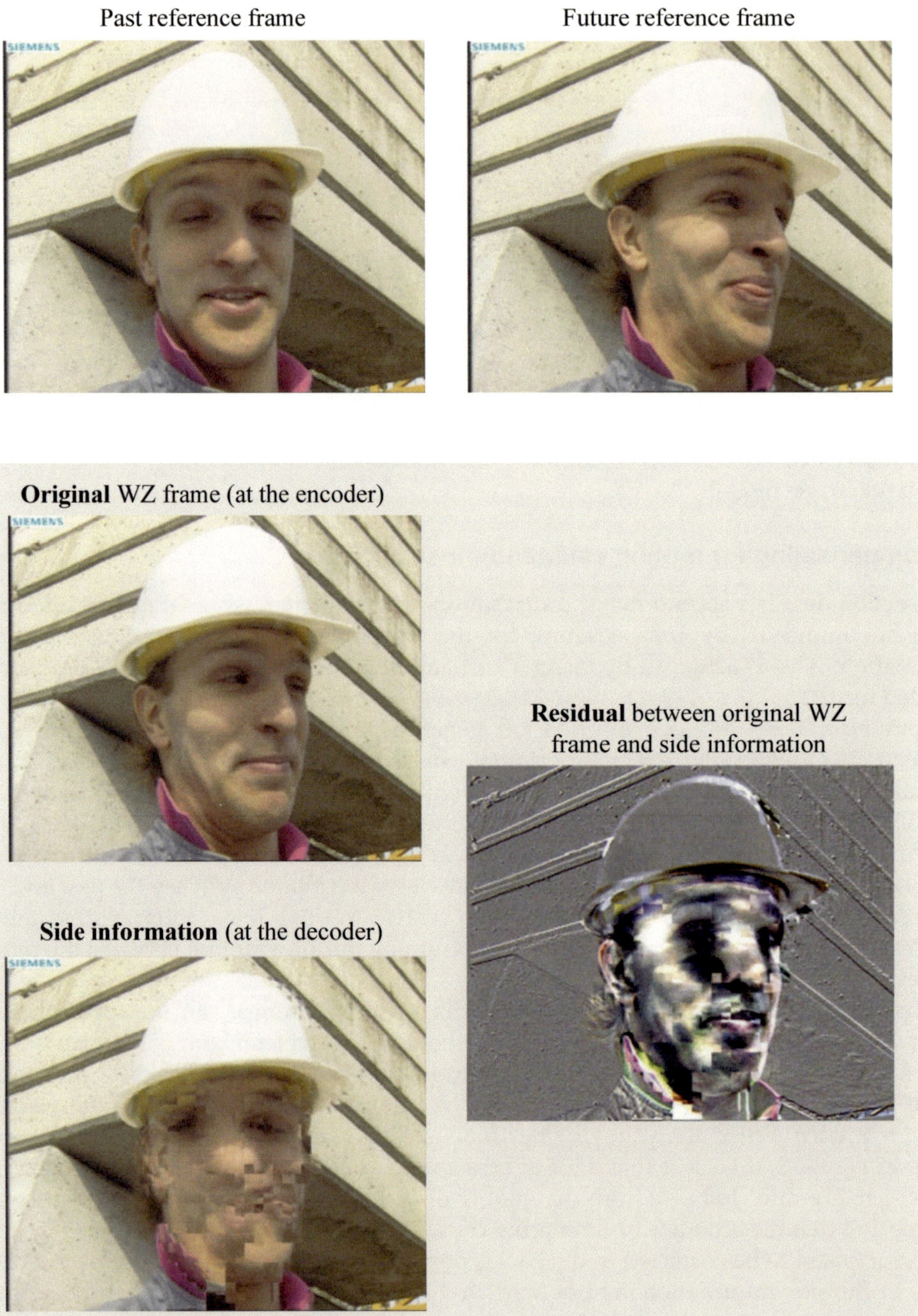

Fig. 8. Especially for large GOP's, the assumption of linear motion becomes less valid.

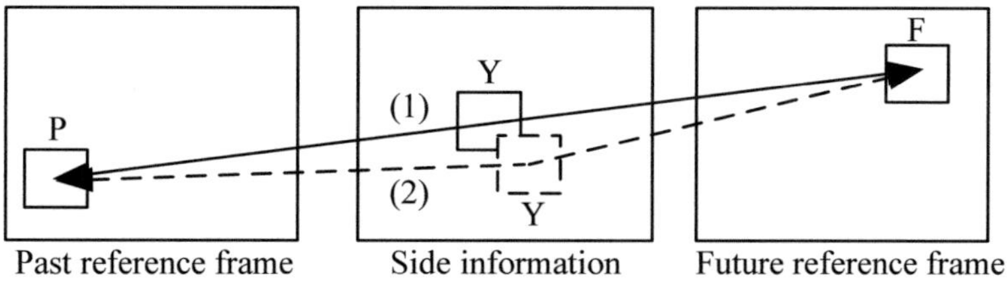

Fig. 9. The linear motion vector (1) could be inaccurate in the sense that the interpolation between P and F should be located on a different spatial position (2) than the one given by a linear motion vector (1).

then used for further decoding. For example, Martins et al. (2009) propose to refine the side information after each coefficient band has been decoded. A layered approach is used by Fan et al. (2009), dividing each frame into a low-resolution base layer and higher resolution refinement layers. The decoded base layer is used for improving side information accuracy of the following, higher resolution refinement layer, and so on. Information about the (partially) decoded frame can also be used to re-evaluate the side information generation process, for example, by identifying "suspicious" (i.e. possibly wrong) motion vectors (Ye et al. (2009)). While these techniques show good results, what they have in common is that they can compensate for mistakes only *after* some information has been decoded. Therefore, in this section, a technique is proposed where some of these uncertainties are quantified *prior to decoding*. This is realized by extending the correlation model, improving the performance with an additional 8% gain in bit rate.

5.1 Proposed technique

The main idea is to compensate for inaccuracies by using more than one prediction for each block. We recall that a particular block in the side information Y is generated by averaging past and future reference blocks P and F respectively, using a linear motion vector. However, if the motion is non-linear, then the prediction should appear on a different spatial position in the side information (Figure 9). Hence, to predict a block at position (x_0, y_0), the block at position (x_0, y_0) in Y can be used, together with some of the surrounding blocks in Y. This strategy can also be beneficial in other cases with complex motion such as occlusion and deformation. Before explaining this method, a description of the codec is provided.

5.1.1 Codec description

The proposed codec is depicted in Figure 10, highlighting the extensions that enable compensation for motion estimation inaccuracies.

As before, the techniques for side information generation are adopted from DISCOVER. The output of this process is the side information Y, and for each block, the (linear) motion vector MV_{SI}, as well as the residual R_{SI} between the past and future reference blocks. This information is used as input for the proposed extensions. First, for each block, multiple predictors are generated (Section 5.1.2). Next, each of these predictors is assigned a weight (Section 5.1.3), and the correlation between the predictors and the original is modeled (Section 5.1.4). This distribution is used by the turbo decoder, which requests bits until the decoded result is sufficiently reliable. Finally, the quantized coefficients are reconstructed (Section 5.1.5) and inverse transformed to obtain the decoded frame W'.

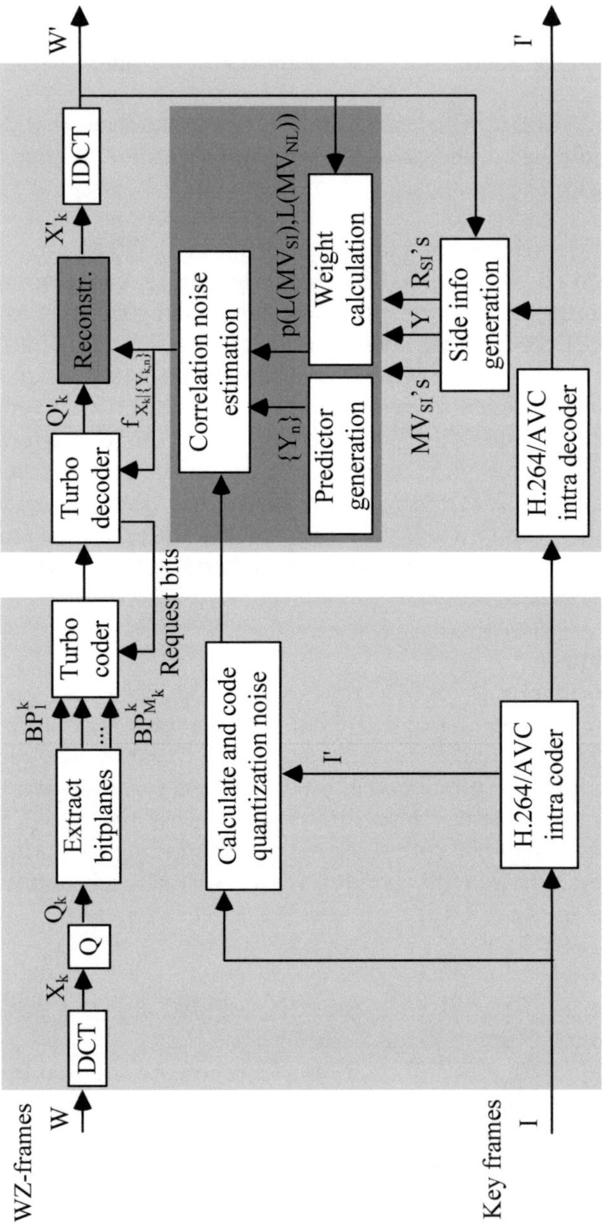

Fig. 10. The DVC codec featuring a correlation model that compensates for quantization noise and motion estimation inaccuracies.

5.1.2 Generation of predictors

A block at position (x_0,y_0) is predicted using multiple predictors, obtained from the side information frame Y. The first predictor is the predictor corresponding to linear motion, i.e., the block at the co-located position in Y. To compensate for motion inaccuracies such as non-linear motion, surrounding blocks in Y are taken into account as well. As a compromise between complexity and performance, eight additional predictors are used, namely the ones corresponding to positions $(x_0 \pm m, y_0 \pm m)$ in Y $(m \in \{0,1\})$. This results in a total of 9 predictors per block.
Not every predictor is equally likely, so that weights are calculated for each predictor, as explained in the following section.

5.1.3 Online calculation of the predictor weights

Each of the 9 predictors is assigned a weight, according to the probability that this predictor is the best one out of the set. This probability is estimated using the results from previously decoded frames. In a previously decoded frame W', given the previous side information Y, the best predictor for a block is obtained using the following procedure.
Each block in W' is compared to each of the 9 predictors in Y. More specifically, the mean absolute difference (MAD) is calculated between the block at a certain position (x_0,y_0) in W' and the co-located block in Y. This MAD indicates the amount of errors corrected when using the linear predictor. Likewise, the MAD for other predictors is calculated, for example, comparing the block at position (x_0,y_0) in W' to the block at position (x_0+1, y_0+1) in Y etc. The predictor with the lowest MAD is then considered the best one out of the set.
However, a non-linear predictor is only considered best in case its MAD is lower than 0.9 times the MAD of the linear predictor. Otherwise, the linear predictor is considered to be the best. This criterion is used to ensure that only significant improvements over the linear predictor are taken into account. For example, in a region with not much texture, one of the non-linear predictors could have a lower MAD than the linear predictor, because the quantization noise in this predictor has distorted the block in such a way that it resembles better the decoded result. To avoid these situations, the MAD of a non-linear predictor must be lower than 0.9 times the MAD of the linear predictor. The value of 0.9 has been experimentally obtained.
Given the best predictor, a histogram table is updated, based on a characterization of the predictor using two parameters.
The first parameter is the amplitude of the motion. For example, the linear predictor could be highly reliable in static regions (e.g. in the background), but its reliability could be much lower for fast moving objects in the foreground. To discriminate between such cases, the amplitude of the (linear) motion vector MV_{SI} is used. To this extent, the following amplitude metric $L()$ is defined:

$$L((x,y)) = max(|x|,|y|). \tag{15}$$

The second parameter discriminates between different predictors, through the amplitude of the non-linearity of the predictor. Denote MV_{NL} as the predictor offset compared to the linear predictor. For example, if the linear predictor corresponds to the block at position (x_0,y_0) in Y, then the predictor at position (x_0+1, y_0-1) in Y has $MV_{NL} = (1,-1)$.
Due to the use of the amplitude metric for this second parameter, all 8 non-linear predictors have a value of one for $L(MV_{NL})$. Only the linear-motion predictor has a different value, namely zero. As such, the statistics of the predictor having $MV_{NL} = (1,-1)$ are assumed to be similar to those of the predictor having $MV_{NL} = (0,1)$. This simplification can be refined

in future work, for example, by assigning higher weights to the non-linear predictors in the direction of the motion MV_{SI}.
Given the best predictor and its parameters $L(MV_{SI})$ and $L(MV_{NL})$, the histogram table T is updated. This table only covers the statistics of the current frame. All elements have been initialized to zero before any updating takes place. The parameters $L(MV_{SI})$ and $L(MV_{NL})$ serve as coordinates in T, and the corresponding value in T is incremented by one, for the best predictor.
After all blocks in W' have been processed, the result is combined with the result from previously decoded frames, by updating global statistics:

$$p_{i,j} = K \cdot p_{i,j} + (1 - K) \cdot \frac{T(i,j)}{\sum_k T(i,k)}, \tag{16}$$

where $p_{i,j}$ is a shorthand for $p(L(MV_{SI}) = i, L(MV_{NL}) = j)$. The update parameter K is set to 0.8. This value – which has been obtained through experiments – remains fixed for all test sequences. A more detailed study of the update parameter is left as future work.
The global statistics are used for calculating the weights for the predictors in the following Wyner-Ziv frame to be decoded. More specifically, the weight $w_{i,j}$ for a predictor characterized by $L(MV_{SI}) = i$, and $L(MV_{NL}) = j$ is calculated as:

$$w_{i,j} = \frac{p_{i,j}}{N_j}, \tag{17}$$

where N_j denotes the number of predictors (for that block) having a value of j for $L(MV_{NL})$. Hence, N_j equals one for the linear-motion predictor, and 8 for the remaining ones.

5.1.4 The correlation model

The goal is to model the correlation between the original X and the set of predictors denoted $\{Y_n\}$ (with $0 \le n \le 8$). This is modeled in the (DCT) transform-domain. For each 4-by-4 block in the original frame, 16 distributions are generated, i.e., one for each coefficient X_k (with $0 \le k \le 15$). The predictors are transformed, and all coefficients at the same index are grouped. Denote the predictors for X_k as $\{Y_{k,n}\}$.
As explained previously in this chapter, the correlation between the original and the side information is commonly modeled using a Laplace distribution. Hence, with multiple predictors, the conditional distribution $f_{X_k|\{Y_{k,n}\}}$ is modeled as a combination of weighted Laplace distributions, i.e.:

$$f_{X_k|\{Y_{k,n}\}}(x|\{y_{k,n}\}) = \sum_m w_m \cdot \frac{\alpha}{2} e^{-\alpha|x - y_{k,m}|}, \tag{18}$$

where $y_{k,m}$ indicates the k-th coefficient of the m-th predictor. w_m is the weight of the m-th predictor.
The scaling parameter α is calculated based on the reference residual of the linear predictor, using the techniques proposed in Section 4.

5.1.5 Coefficient reconstruction

After turbo decoding, the quantization bin q'_k containing the original value (with very high probability) is known at the decoder. The following step is to choose a value in this quantization bin as the decoded coefficient X'_k. This is done through optimal centroid reconstruction for multiple predictors (Kubasov et al. (2007)):

$$X'_k = \frac{\sum_m w_m \int_{q'_L}^{q'_H} x \cdot \frac{\alpha}{2} e^{-\alpha|x-y_{k,m}|} dx}{\sum_m w_m \int_{q'_L}^{q'_H} \frac{\alpha}{2} e^{-\alpha|x-y_{k,m}|} dx}, \tag{19}$$

where q'_L and q'_H indicate the low and high border of q'_k, respectively.

5.2 Results

Tests have been conducted on three different sequences: Foreman, Football and Coastguard. All are in CIF resolution, at a frame rate of 30 frames per second. A GOP of size 8 is used, and only the luma component is coded to enable a comparison with the DISCOVER codec. The system is also compared to our previous improvement described in Section 4, which uses only one predictor per block.

The results in Figure 11 indicate improvements over both systems. The gains are the largest for sequences with complex motion such as Football and Foreman, where the linear predictor does not always provide an accurate prediction. In these cases, using multiple predictors to compensate for inaccuracies shows average Bjøntegaard (2002) quality gains up to 0.4 dB over our approach in the previous section, and 1.0 dB over DISCOVER (both for Football and Foreman).

The gain diminishes for sequences with rather simple motion characteristics such as Coastguard. For such sequences, an accurate prediction is already provided by the linear-motion predictor, and little is gained by using additional predictors. Over our approach in the previous section, average quality gains of 0.1 dB are reported, and 1.4 dB over DISCOVER.

6. Conclusions

Modeling the correlation between the original frame available at the encoder and its prediction available at the decoder, is an important but difficult problem in DVC. While most current techniques rely on the motion-compensated residual between the reference frames, in this chapter, two techniques have been proposed that improve the modeling accuracy over the conventional approaches by using more than this residual.

The first technique exploits information about the quantization of the reference frames. In brief, information about the quantization of the key frames is sent from the encoder to the decoder. Using this information the correlation model at the decoder is refined, yielding high gains at medium and low rates. This method can be further improved, for example, by estimating the quantization noise at the decoder-side instead of sending this information from encoder to decoder. Another extension could be to account for spatial variation of the quantization noise.

The second technique presented in this chapter applies a correlation model with multiple predictors. In this solution we compensated for uncertainties in the assumption of linear motion between the reference frames by considering surrounding positions as well. Fair compression gains were reported especially for sequences featuring complex motion characteristics. We believe that this model can be further extended, for example, by explicitly dealing with occlusions.

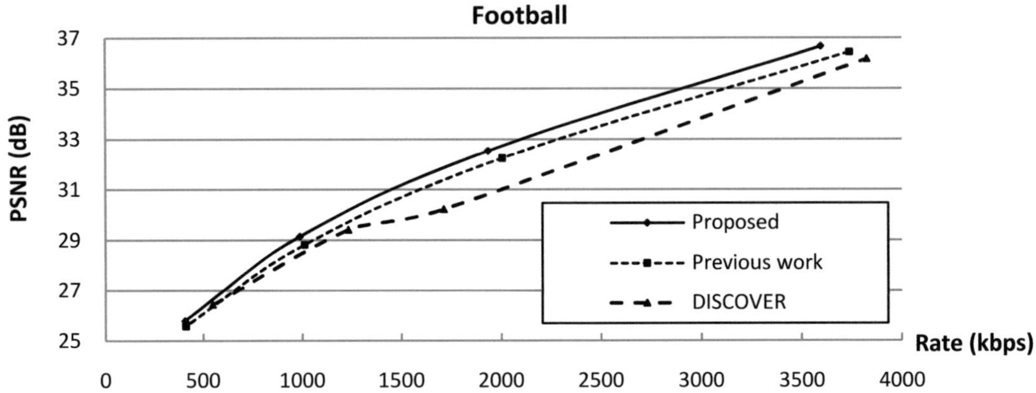

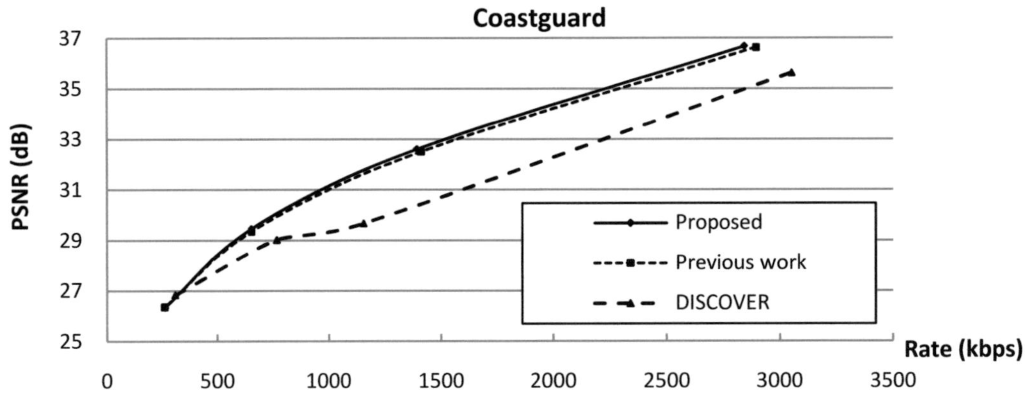

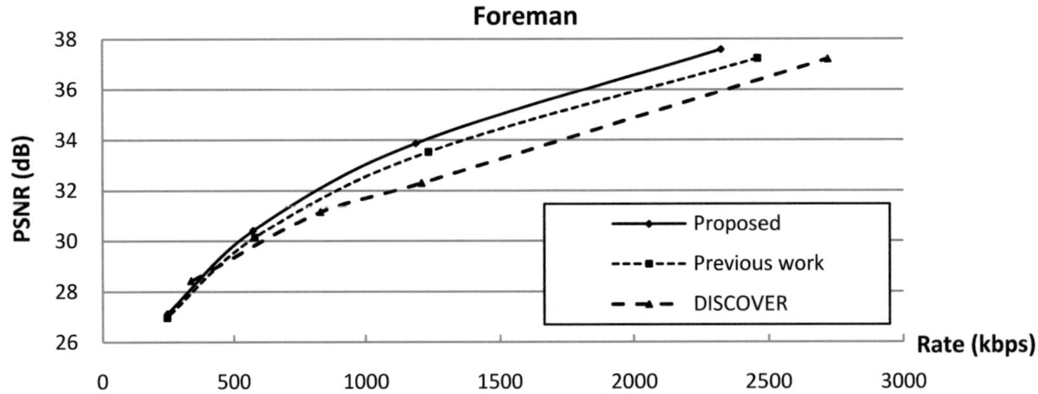

Fig. 11. Average quality gains of 0.4 dB are reported over our approach in the previous section, for both Football and Foreman. As expected, the gain diminishes for sequences with regular motion characteristics, such as Coastguard.

7. References

Aaron, A., Rane, S., Setton, E. & Girod, B. (2004). Transform-domain Wyner-Ziv codec for video, *Proc. SPIE Visual Communications and Image Processing*, Vol. 5308, pp. 520–528.

Aaron, A., Setton, E. & Girod, B. (2003). Towards practical Wyner-Ziv coding of video, *Proc. IEEE International Conference on Image Processing (ICIP)*, pp. 869–872.

Aaron, A., Zhang, R. & Girod, B. (2004). Wyner-Ziv video coding with hash-based motion compensation at the receiver, *Proc. IEEE International Conference on Image Processing (ICIP)*, pp. 3097–3100.

Artigas, X., Ascenso, J., Dalai, M., Klomp, S., Kubasov, D. & Ouaret, M. (2007). The DISCOVER codec: Architecture, techniques and evaluation, *Proc. Picture Coding Symposium (PCS)*.

Bjøntegaard, G. (2002). Calculation of average PSNR differences between RD-curves, *Technical report*, VCEG. Contribution VCEG-M33.

Brites, C. & Pereira, F. (2008). Correlation noise modeling for efficient pixel and transform domain Wyner-Ziv video coding, *IEEE Transactions on Circuits and Systems for Video Technology* 18: 1177–1190.

Fan, X., Au, O. C. & Cheung, N. M. (2009). Adaptive correlation estimation for general Wyner-Ziv video coding, *IEEE International Conference on Image Processing (ICIP)*.

Fan, X., Au, O. C., Cheung, N. M., Chen, Y. & Zhou, J. (2009). Successive refinement based Wyner-Ziv video compression, *Signal Processing: Image Communcation* . doi:10.1016/j.image.2009.09.004.

Gersho, A. & Gray, R. M. (1992). *Vector quantization and signal compression*, Kluwer Academic Publishers.

Girod, B., Aaron, A., Rane, S. & Rebollo-Monedero, D. (2005). Distributed Video Coding, *Proc. IEEE, Special Issue on Video Coding and Delivery*, Vol. 93, pp. 71–83.

Huang, X. & Forchhammer, S. (2009). Improved virtual channel noise model for transform domain Wyner-Ziv video coding, *Proc. IEEE International Conference on Acoustics, Speech and Signal Processing (ICASSP)*, pp. 921–924.

Kubasov, D. & Guillemot, C. (2006). Mesh-based motion-compensated interpolation for side information extraction in Distributed Video Coding, *Proc. IEEE International Conference on Image Processing (ICIP)*.

Kubasov, D., Lajnef, K. & Guillemot, C. (2007). A hybrid encoder/decoder rate control for a Wyner-Ziv video codec with a feedback channel, *IEEE MultiMedia Signal Processing Workshop*, pp. 251–254.

Kubasov, D., Nayak, J. & Guillemot, C. (2007). Optimal reconstruction in Wyner-Ziv video coding with multiple side information, *IEEE MultiMedia Signal Processing Workshop*, pp. 183–186.

Lin, S. & Costello, D. J. (2004). *Error control coding*, 2 edn, Prentice Hall.

Macchiavello, B., Mukherjee, D. & Querioz, R. L. (2009). Iterative side-information generation in a mixed resolution wyner-ziv framework, *IEEE Transactions on Circuits and Systems for Video Technology* 19(10): 1409–1423.

Martins, R., Brites, C., Ascenso, J. & Pereira, F. (2009). Refining side information for improved transform domain wyner-ziv video coding, *IEEE Transactions on Circuits and Systems for Video Technology* 19(9): 1327–1341.

Trapanese, A., Tagliasacchi, M., Tubaro, S., Ascenso, J., Brites, C. & Pereira, F. (2005). Improved correlation noise statistics modeling in frame-based pixel domain Wyner-Ziv video coding, *International Workshop on Very Low Bitrate Video*.

Škorupa, J., Slowack, J., Mys, S., Lambert, P., Grecos, C. & Van de Walle, R. (2009). Stopping criterions for turbo coding in a Wyner-Ziv video codec, *Proc. Picture Coding Symposium (PCS)*.

Škorupa, J., Slowack, J., Mys, S., Lambert, P. & Van de Walle, R. (2008). Accurate correlation modeling for transform-domain Wyner-Ziv video coding, *Proc. Pacific-Rim Conference on Multimedia (PCM)*, pp. 1–10.

Ye, S., Ouaret, M., Dufaux, F. & Ebrahimi, T. (2009). Improved side information generation for distributed video coding by exploiting spatial and temporal correlations, *EURASIP Journal on Image and Video Processing* 2009. Article ID 683510.

9

Non-Predictive Multistage Lattice Vector Quantization Video Coding

M. F. M. Salleh[1] and J. Soraghan[2]
[1]*Universiti Sains Malaysia*
[2]*University of Strathclyde*
[1]*Malaysia*
[2]*United Kingdom*

1. Introduction

In recent years, the demand for mobile multimedia applications has increased tremendously. Since the volume of the application data such as video is high and the bandwidth of mobile channels is limited, efficient compression techniques are very much required (Ghanbari, 2003) (Sikora, 2005). This research area has attracted many researchers since the last 40 years, and many related works have been done as reviewed in (Sikora, 2005).

Generally, video compression technique aims to reduce both the spatial and temporal redundancy of a video sequence. The motion estimation and compensation is a very efficient technique to exploit the temporal redundancy of the video sequence (Sikora, 2005). Thus, it has been used in video coding standards for application in mobile communications such as in H.263 (H.263, 2000) and H.264 (Ostermann et al., 2004). Although this process offers significant gain in coding efficiency, the encoded bitstream suffers from channel errors during transmission in mobile channels which reduces the reconstructed frame quality at the receiver.

Motion JPEG2000 (ISO/IEC, 2002), uses Intra-frame video coding only which eliminates the prediction step uses in motion estimation process in the temporal domain. It offers less design complexity, reduces computational load and increases robustness in wireless environments (Dufaux & Ebrahimi, 2004). In another work done in (Akbari & Soraghan, 2003), a video coding scheme has been developed to omit the prediction step in temporal domain for robust video transmission in noisy mobile environment. In that work, the similar high frequency subbands from each frame within a Group of Frame (GOP) are joined to produce a number of group data. Each of the group data is processed using an Adaptive Joint Subband Vector Quantization (AJSVQ). The Adaptive Vector Quantization (AVQ) technique has been developed based on the work presented in (Voukelatos & Soraghan, 97).

In the past years, there have been considerable research efforts in Lattice Vector Quantization (LVQ) for image and video compression schemes (Conway & Sloane, 1988) (Barlaud et al., 94) (Kossentini & Smith, 99) (Sampson et al., 95) (Weiping et al., 97) (Kuo et Al., 2002) (Man et. al., 2002) (Feideropoulou et. al., 2007). The choice for LVQ has been for its property to reduce complexity of a vector quantizer. In video coding, the works have been inclined towards using LVQ with motion estimation and compensation process as explained in (Sampson et al., 95) (Weiping, et. al., 97) (Kuo et al., 2002) (Feideropoulou et al., 2007). However, only the work in (Man et. al., 2002) has been introduced to omit the motion estimation and compensation techniques and yet incorporates LVQ in the encoding process. The prediction step is omitted by the wavelet transform on the temporal domain, thus reducing the computational load in the video coding scheme. The LVQ is applied on the coefficients of the transformed data. The work is reported to achieve a good balance between coding efficiency and error resilience.

In our related work (Salleh & Soraghan, 2005) (Salleh & Soraghan, 2006) (Salleh & Soraghan, 2007), multistage lattice vector quantization (MLVQ) has been introduced. This technique has the capability to capture the quantization errors. For every pass of quantization process the errors are magnified by multiplication with the current scaling factor. The advantage of this process is that, it offers reduction in quantization errors and hence enhances reconstruction of frame quality as well it offers robustness for video transmission over mobile channels.

This chapter presents a video coding scheme that utilizes MLVQ algorithm to exploit the spatial-temporal video redundancy. Since LVQ reduces computational load of the codebook generation, this paves the way for the video coding scheme to have multistage processes (multistage lattice VQ). The Unequal Error Protection (UEP) and Equal Error Protection (EEP) schemes are also developed for robust video transmission. Results of the video coding scheme in erroneous Hilly Terrain (HT) and Bad Urban (BU) mobile environments are significantly better than H.263 codec using the TETRA channel simulator (ETSI, 1995). The performance under the same settings is comparable to H.264 codec for some test video sequences.

2. Background

The following subsections discuss briefly the basic concept of lattice vector quantization as well as a brief discussion about quad-tree coding. The use of vector quantization for lossy compression has been very common since the last decade. Lattice vector quantization technique offers great advantage in term of coding simplicity due to its regular structure (Conway & Sloane, 1988).

2.1 Lattice vector quantization

In lattice vector quantization (LVQ), the input data are mapped to the lattice points of a certain chosen lattice type. The lattice points or codeword may be selected from the coset points or the truncated lattice points (Gersho & Gray, 1992). The coset of a lattice is the set of points obtained after a specific vector is added to each lattice point. The input vectors surrounding these lattice points are group together as if there are in the same *voronoi* region. Some of the background of lattices, the quantizing algorithms for the chosen lattice type and the design of the lattice quantizer's codebook are now presented.

2.1.1 Lattice type

A lattice is a regular arrangement of points in k-space that includes the origin or the zero-vector. A lattice is defined as a set of linearly independent vectors [Conway and Sloane, 1988];

$$\Lambda = \{X : X = a_1 u_1 + a_2 u_2 + ... + a_n u_n\} \tag{1}$$

where $\Lambda \in \Re^k$, $n \le k$, a_i and u_i are integers for i=1, 2,….,n . The vector set $\{u_i\}$ is called the basis vectors of lattice Λ and it is convenient to express them as a generating matrix $U = [u_1, u_2, ..., u_n]$.
As an example consider a two-dimensional lattice Λ_2 with basis vectors as:

$$\Lambda_2 = \{X : X = a_{11}u_1 + a_{12}u_1 ; a_{21}u_2 + a_{22}u_2\}$$

Also let us assume that

$$a_{11} = 0, a_{12} = \sqrt{3}, a_{21} = 2, a_{22} = 1$$

The generating matrix is given by:

$$U = [u_1, u_2] = \begin{bmatrix} 0 & \sqrt{3} \\ 2 & 1 \end{bmatrix}$$

The vector X represents a two dimensional coordinate system where each point can be represented $X = (x_1, x_2)$. Thus, it can be written that

$$x_1 = \sqrt{3}m_2$$

$$x_2 = 2m_1 + m_2$$

where m_1 and m_2 are any integer value. Figure 1 shows the lattice structure defined by this example.

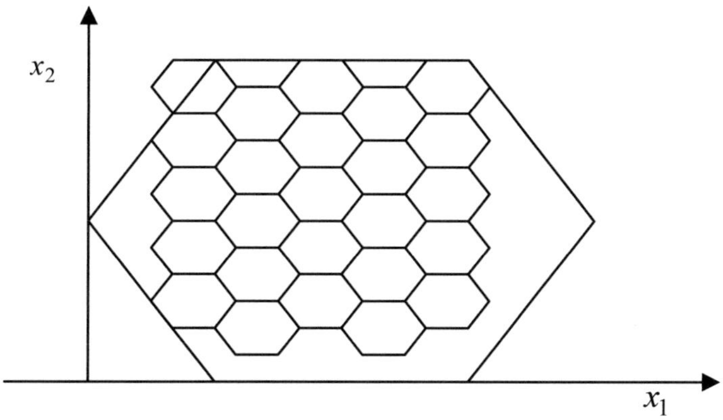

Fig. 1. Two-dimensional hexagonal lattice

The reciprocal or dual lattice Λ^* consists of all points Y in the subspace of $\Re^k$ spanned by $u_1, u_2, ..., u_n$ such that the inner product $X.Y = x_1y_1 + ... + x_ky_k$ is an integer for all $x \in \Lambda$ (Conway & Sloane, 1988). When the lattices are contained in their duals, there exist the cosets representatives $r_0, ..., r_{d-1}$ such that

$$\Lambda^* = \bigcup_{i=0}^{d-1} (r_i + \Lambda) \tag{2}$$

where d is the determinant of Λ. In a different approach, the dual lattice is obtained by taking the transpose of the inverse generating matrix given by $\left(U^{-1}\right)^{t}$ once the generating matrix is known (Gibson & Sayood, 1988).

The Z^n or cubic lattice is the simplest form of a lattice structure. It consists of all the points in the coordinate system with a certain lattice dimension. Other lattices such as $D_n(n \geq 2)$, $A_n(n \geq 1)$, $E_n[n = 6,7,8]$ and their dual are the densest known sphere packing and covering in dimension $n \leq 8$ (Conway & Sloane, 1988). Thus, they can be used for an efficient lattice vector quantizer. The D_n lattice is defined by the following (Conway & Sloane, 1988):

$$D_n = (x_1, x_2, \ldots\ldots, x_n) \in Z^n \tag{3}$$

$$where \sum_{i=1}^{n} x_i = even$$

Its dual i.e. D_n^* is the union of four cosets of D_n:

$$D_n^* = \bigcup_{i=0}^{3} (r_i + D_n) \tag{4}$$

$$where\ r_0 = \left(0^n\right),\ r_1 = \left(\frac{1}{2}^n\right),\ r_2 = \left(0^{n-1}, 1\right),\ r_3 = \left(\frac{1}{2}^{n-1}, -\frac{1}{2}\right)$$

The A_n lattice for $n \geq 1$ consists the points of $(x_0, x_1, \ldots\ldots, x_n)$ with the integer coordinates sum to zero (Conway & Sloane, 1982). The lattice quantization for A_n is done in $n+1$ dimensions and the final result is obtained after reverting the dimension back to n (Gibson & Sayood, 1988), (Conway & Sloane, 1982). Its lattice A_n^* consists of the union of $n+1$ cosets of A_n (Conway & Sloane, 1982):

$$A_n^* = \bigcup_{i=0}^{n} (r_i + A_n) \tag{5}$$

The expression for E_n lattice with $n = 6,7,8$ is explained in as the following:

$$E_8 = \left(\frac{1}{2}, \frac{1}{2}, \frac{1}{2}, \frac{1}{2}, \frac{1}{2}, \frac{1}{2}, \frac{1}{2}, \frac{1}{2}\right) + D_8 \tag{6}$$

The dual lattice is given by the same definition i.e. $E_8^* = E_8$.
The lattice E_7 is defined as the following:

$$E_7 = A_7 \bigcup \left(\left(-\frac{1}{2}^4, \frac{1}{2}^4 \right) + A_7 \right) \tag{7}$$

The dual lattice is given by the following:

$$E_7^* = \bigcup \left(\left(-\frac{3}{4}^2, \frac{1}{4}^6 \right) + E_7 \right) = \bigcup_{i=0}^{3} (s_i + A_7) \tag{8}$$

$$where\ s_i = \left(\left(\frac{-j}{4}\right)^{2i}, \left(\frac{i}{4}\right)^{2j} \right),\ i+j=4$$

Besides, other important lattices have also been considered for many applications such as the Coxeter-Todd (K_{12}) lattice, Barnes-Wall lattice (Λ_{16}) and Leech lattice (Λ_{24}). These lattices are the densest known sphere packing and coverings in their respective dimension (Conway & Sloane, 1988), (Gibson & Sayood, 1988).

2.3 Quad-tree coding

Significant data often sifted from a set of data or subband using quad-tree coding technique. Often, a treshold is used for this purpose. If the data energy is higher than the threshold value, the block remains in the subband otherwise the block is replaced with zeros. This process continues until all the blocks in the subband are checked. At the end that particular subband has some zero coefficients as well as some preserved significant coefficients or the subband has been sifted. Then, the significant coefficients in the sifted subbands are searched and saved as a unit following a top down quadtree structure. Thus, there are two outcomes of this process namely; the significant units and the MAP sequence which tells the location of the significant subband coefficients. The pseudo code shown in Figure 2 illustrates the search of the preserved significant coefficients procedure on a particular sifted subband:

```
1.  Obtain maximum quad-tree level based on subband rectangular size
2.  FOR quad-tree level = 1 to maximum
        a.  call for TEST UNIT
        b.  save MAP sequence and significant unit
3.  END
TEST UNIT:
1.  Divide the subband into 4 descendent subregions
2.  FOR descendent subregion = 1 to 4
    a.  IF descendent subregion has nonzero components
    b.  Attach "1" to MAP sequence, and further split the descendent subregion into
        another 4 equal descendent subregions
          i.  IF size of subregion equal block size
          ii. save block into significant unit
      ELSE
    a.  Attach "0" to MAP sequence and stop splitting the descendent subregion, and
        return to one level up of the quad-tree levels.
    b.  Return MAP sequence and significant unit
3.  END
```

Fig. 2. Search procedure of the significant coefficients

Figure 3 and Figure 4 show construction of a top down quad-tree structure of the MAP sequence out of a sifted subband. The symbol X in Figure 3 shows the nonzero value of subband coefficients. The quad-tree structure produces a degree of compression to the MAP sequence as shown in Figure 4.

0	X	0	0	***0***	***0***	0	0
X	***0***	0	0	***0***	***0***	0	0
0	0	***0***	***0***	0	0	***0***	***0***
0	0	***0***	***0***	0	0	***0***	***0***
0	***0***	0	0	***0***	***0***	0	0
0	X	0	0	***0***	***0***	0	0
0	0	***0***	***0***	0	0	***0***	***0***
0	0	***0***	***0***	0	0	***0***	***0***

Fig. 3. Part of a sifted subband

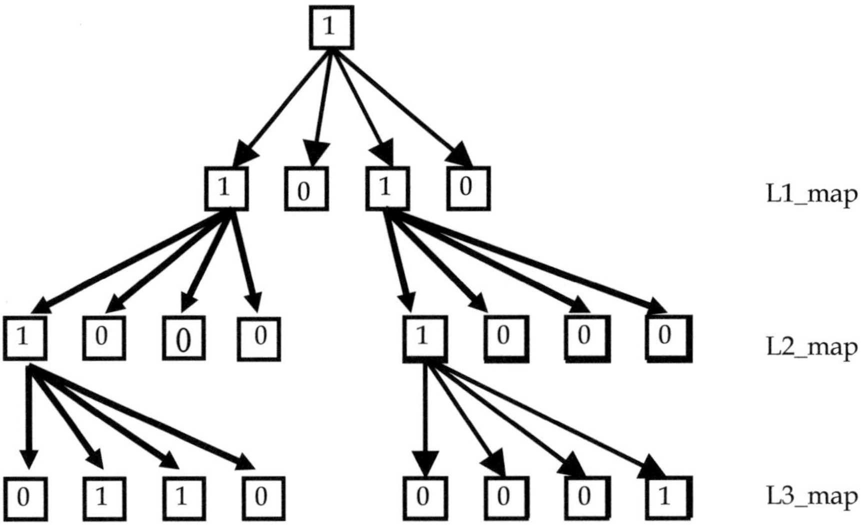

Fig. 4. Corresponding quad-tree representation of MAP sequence

3. Multistage lattice vector quantization video codec

In this section, the implementation of the proposed video codec based on the MLVQ technique is presented. The same high frequency subbands are grouped and their significant coefficients are processed by the MLVQ algorithm for lossy compression. The encoding procedure for MLVQ is also presented in the following subsections.

3.1 Overview MLVQ video codec

The block diagram of the MLVQ video codec is shown in Figure 5. The video codec takes a video sequence and passes it to a frame buffer. The buffer dispatches n frames at a time to m DWT blocks, thus effectively group the video sequence into a group of n frames. Each of these m DWT blocks performs 2-D discrete wavelet transform using JPEG2000 wavelet

(Lawson & Zhu, 2002). Then, the same high frequency subbands from each frame are joined together.
The coefficients of the high frequency subbands from each group are first subdivided into a predefine unit block size of $N \times N$, which ultimately defines the size of vector dimension. Then the significant vectors are searched or identified in each subband group by comparing the individual vector's energy with a threshold value. The preserved significant vectors from the subband group are then passed to the multistage lattice VQ (MLVQ) process for lossy compression. The MLVQ process produces two outputs i.e. the scale list and index sequence. The index sequence is then entropy coded using the Golomb coding (Golomb, 66). The location information of the significant units is defined as the MAP sequence (Man et al., 99) represented in the form of binary ones and zeros. If the coefficient block size is significant the MAP data is one otherwise it is zero. The lowest frequency subband group is compressed using the lossless coding. The non-predictive MLVQ video coder operates at a fixed frame rate and a fixed output bit rate by allocating a constant number of bits to all the frames of the input video sequence.

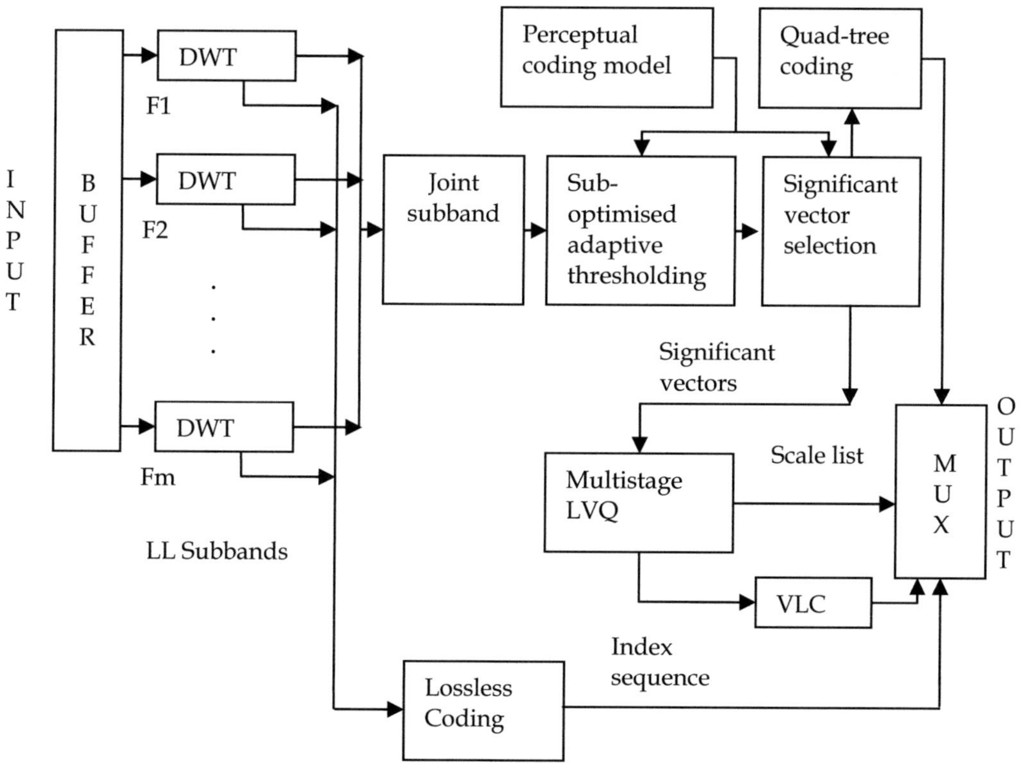

Fig. 5. Non-predictive MLVQ video encoder

3.2 Joining high frequency subbands

A video sequence contains high temporal redundancy due to the similarity of the successive frames content. One way to reduce the temporal redundancy is to get the difference frame between the successive frames in a group of picture (GOP). In many video coding standards that use motion estimation and compensation, this redundancy is exploited via the

prediction process. However, this technique produces a video coding scheme that is not robust, particularly in mobile environments. Moreover, motion estimation technique involves high computational loads and design complexity. The advantage of joining the high frequency subbands within the GOP is that, if one or more of the code joint high frequency subbands bitstream are corrupted, the GOP can still be reconstructed using the other joint subbands as well as the low frequency subbands. Unlike video standards which employed motion estimation, the lost of motion vector data results in the lost of the prediction frames leaving only the intra frames for reconstruction.
The non-predictive MLVQ video codec joins the same subbands within the GOP results in $3L_{\max}$ groups of subbands as illustrated in Figure 6 below. In this case $L_{\max}$ denotes the number of DWT level. The significant coefficients of each subband group are then selected using the quad-tree coding. The preserved significant coefficients of each subband group are then coded using the multistage lattice vector quantization (MLVQ) encoding process. Applying the MLVQ encoding to the preserved significant coefficients of the subband groups exploits the spatial and temporal redundancy of the video sequence.

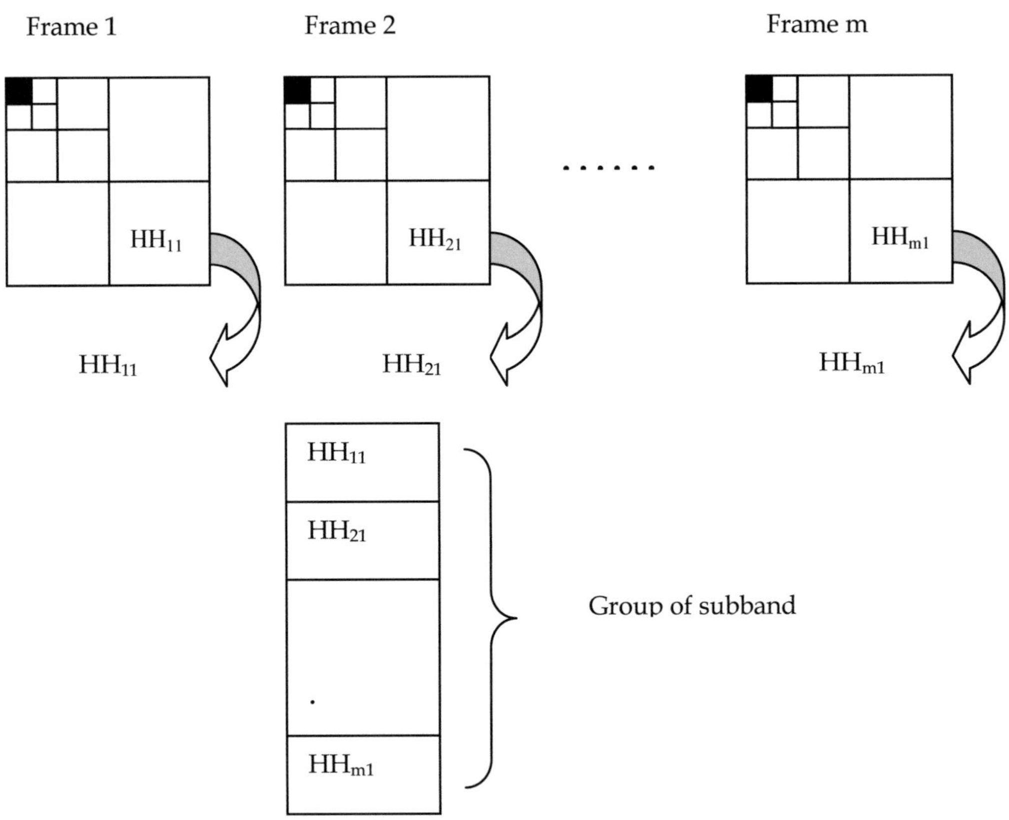

Fig. 6. Joining subband significant coefficients in a GOP

3.3 Single pass LVQ encoder

The significant coefficients or vectors of every joint subband are quantized and output as the scale list and index list. In this work, the Z_n lattice quantizer has been chosen to quantize the significant vectors. The Z_n spherical codebook is enumerated by theta series. The spherical codebook is chosen since the data to be quantized are the preserved coefficients relative to a threshold, rather than the entire wavelet coefficients of the high frequency subbands. They do not exhibit the Laplacian distribution which requires a pyramidal codebook. In this work, a four-dimensional Z_4 lattice codebook has been chosen due its simple codebook construction. The codebook is derived with the first energy level $(m=1)$ has 8 lattice points or vectors, second level $(m=2)$ has 24 vectors, and third level $(m=3)$ has 32 vectors. Therefore, a total of 64 codewords are in the codebook which can be represented by 6-bit index.

Spherical Z_n LVQ Encoding Procedure

The significant vectors are quantized using the Z_n spherical LVQ. The encoding procedure of a single stage or pass LVQ process is summarized below:

1. *Scale the input vectors.*
   a. *Obtained an energy list from the input vector list. Let E_i be the individual element in the energy list set. $E_i = \sum_j^N X_j^2$ where j is the column and i is the row of a matrix respectively while N is the dimension of the vector.*
   b. *Find the maximum energy from the list $(E_{\max})$.*
   c. *Define the energy list normalized factor β $((0<\beta\le 1))$, where 1 indicates the maximum energy.*
   d. *Define selected energy: $E_s = \lfloor E_{\max} \times \beta \rfloor$ where $\lfloor . \rfloor$ is a floor function.*
   e. *Scaling factor: $\alpha = \sqrt{\frac{E_s}{m}}$*
   f. *Scale vectors are obtained by dividing each input vectors by the scaling factor α.*
2. *The scaled vectors are quantized using the Z_n lattice quantizing algorithm.*
3. *The output vectors of this algorithm are checked to make sure that they are confined in the chosen spherical codebook radius m.*
4. *If the output vectors exceed the codebook radius m then they are rescaled and remapped to the nearest valid codeword to produce the final quantized vectors (QV).*

In lattice VQ, the vectors can be scaled in such a way that the resulting scaled vector will reside in one of the three combinations of regions i.e. the granular region, overlap regions, or both. The normalized factor β serves as the indicator as where the scaled vectors would reside in one of these three regions. If the value of β is 1 all the scaled vectors are in the granular region. For example, if the value is 0.8 the majority of the scaled vectors are in the granular region, and few are in the overlap region. Therefore, the optimum value of β is obtained from experiment. In the experiment the value of β starting from 0.5 up to 0.9 with 0.01 increments are used. Each time the image is reconstructed, and the value of PSNR is the calculated. Therefore, the optimum β is found from the best value of PSNR. This value will be used in the first stage or pass of multistage LVQ and the subsequent LVQ stages the scaled vectors are forced to reside only in granular regions $(\beta=1)$. This is because the quantization errors data have small magnitude variation.

3.4 MLVQ encoder

The multistage LVQ (MLVQ) process is illustrated in Figure 6 using an example of a particular group subband. In each LVQ pass three outputs i.e. the scale factor (α), quantized vectors (QV), and the quantization error vectors (QE) are produced. At every pass, the quantized vectors (QV) are obtained using the spherical Z_n LVQ. If the four-dimensional vectors are quantized, and if the origin is included, the outer lattice point will be removed to accommodate the origin.
The first LVQ stage processes the significant vectors and produces a scale factor (α_1), the quantized vectors (QV_1) or codewords, and the quantization error vectors (QE_1) etc. Then the quantization error vectors (QE_1) are "blown out" by multiplying them with the current stage scale factor (α_1). They are then used as the input vectors for the subsequent LVQ stage, and this process repeats up to stage K. Figure 7 illustrates the resulting K-stage codebook generation and the corresponding indexes of a particular subband. Next, the index sequences of the K-stage codebook are variable length coded.

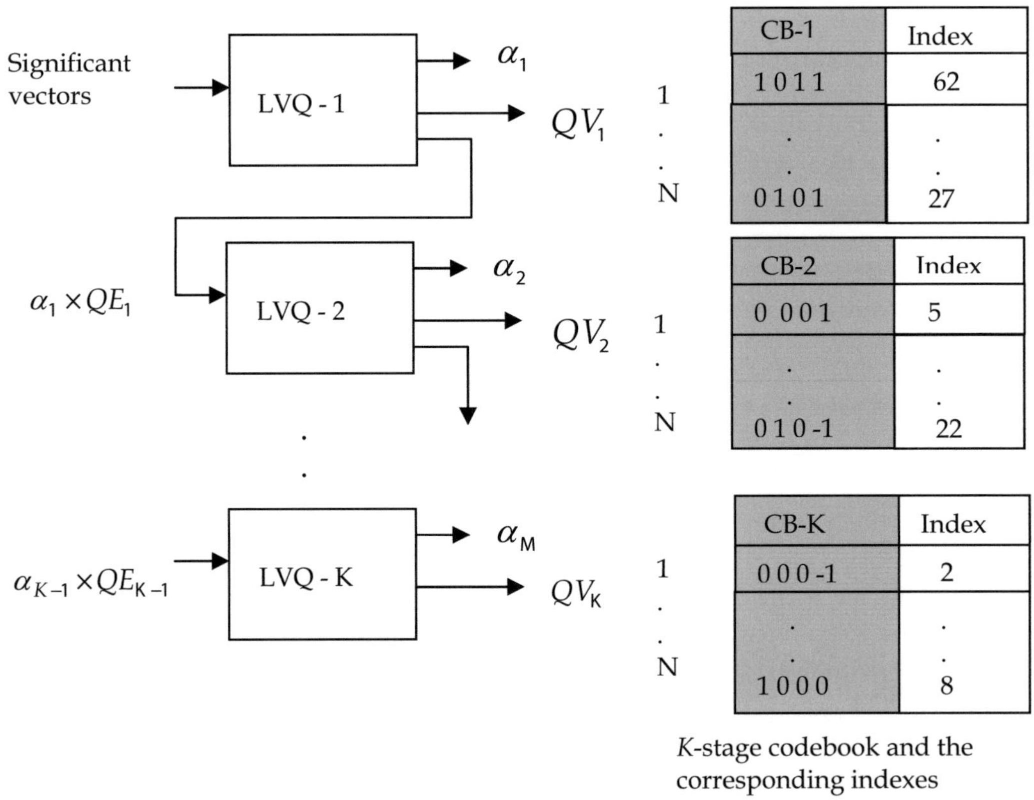

Fig. 7. MLVQ process of a particular subband

The flow diagram of MLVQ algorithm that process all the high frequency subbands as well as a simple bit allocation procedure is described in Figure 8. In this work, a three-level DWT system $(L_{\max} = 3)$ results in nine subbands. The encoding process starts from the lower frequency subbands towards the higher frequency subbands. This is because the lower

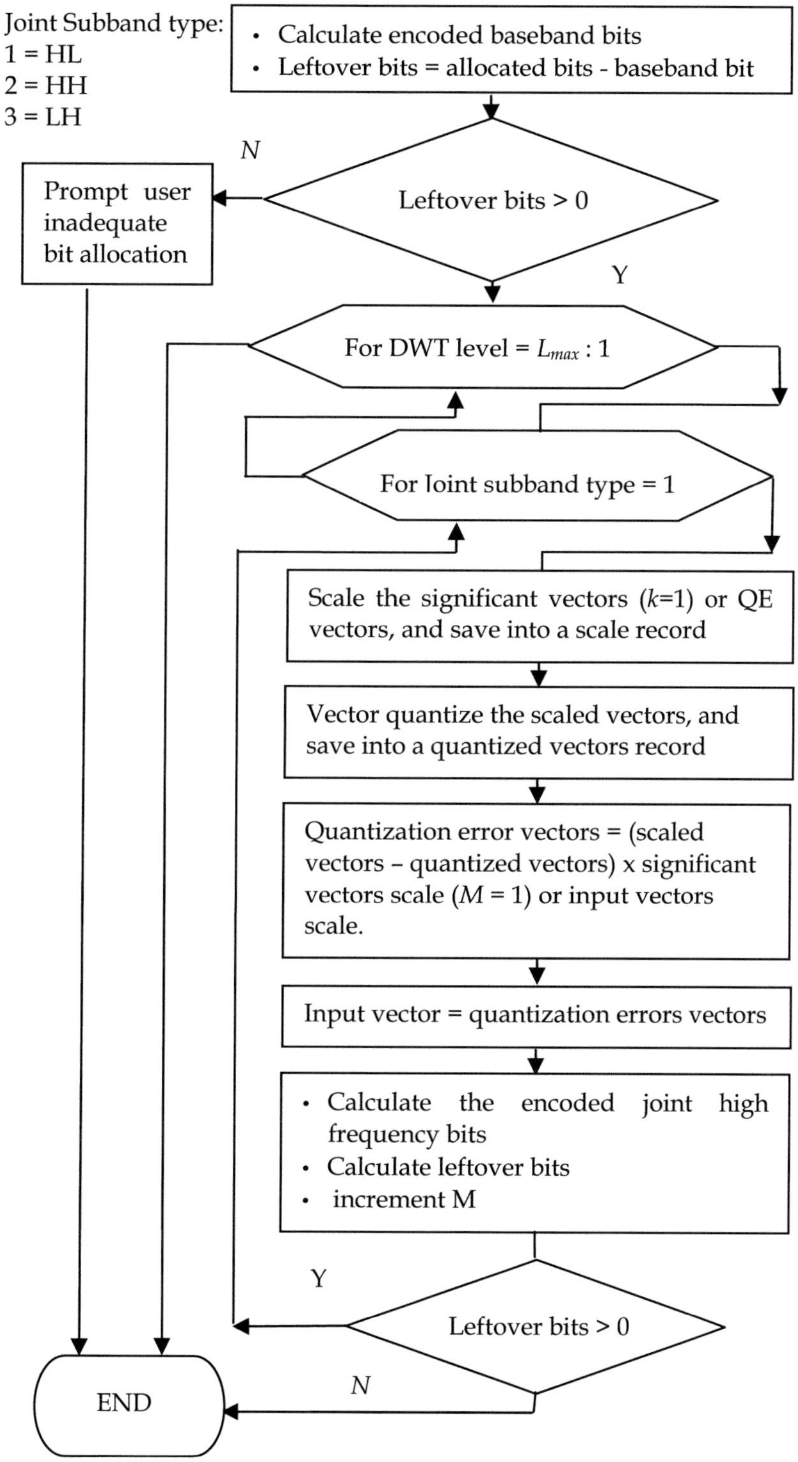

Fig. 8. Flow diagram of MLVQ algorithm

subbands contain more important information and therefore have more impact on the reconstructed image.

In this work, a simple bit allocation procedure is employed. The encoder calculates first the corresponding amount of bit usage for the lower subband. Then, the left over bits for high frequency subbands is obtained by subtracting this amount from the total bit allocated. Subsequently, the high frequency subbands are encoded starting from the joint HL, HH, and LH subbands. In each joint subband the amount of encoded bits used is calculated, and the leftover bit is obtained. The encoding process continues for the subsequence quantization stage if all the three high frequency subbands have been encoded. The process ends when the left over bit is exhausted. In this work, the experimental data has prevailed that the optimum performance of the codec occurs when there are three multistage processes to encode the video sequence.

In this algorithm, the residual data or quantization error vectors are captured and sent to the decoder to increase the reconstruction of frames quality. The quantization errors vectors are produced and *magnified* as the extra set of input vectors to be quantized. The advantage of magnifying the quantization errors vectors is that many vectors which have components near zero can be quantized to many more lattice points during the subsequent LVQ stages. Thus, more quantization errors can be captured and the MLVQ can produce better frame quality.

4. MLVQ video transmission system

The block diagram of the MLVQ video codec for transmission in mobile channel is shown in Figure 9. The *Lossy Video Compression* is the same process as the MLVQ encoder which encodes the video sequence with some compression gain. The compressed bitstream is then classified according to a predefine syntax structure in the *Bitstream Constructor* process. In this stage the bitstream is enciphered into two parts i.e. the header and texture. In the *RS Encoder* process the forward error correction (FEC) codes are added to the bitstream using Reed Solomon codes (Reed & Solomon, 60). In the next stage, the coded header and texture

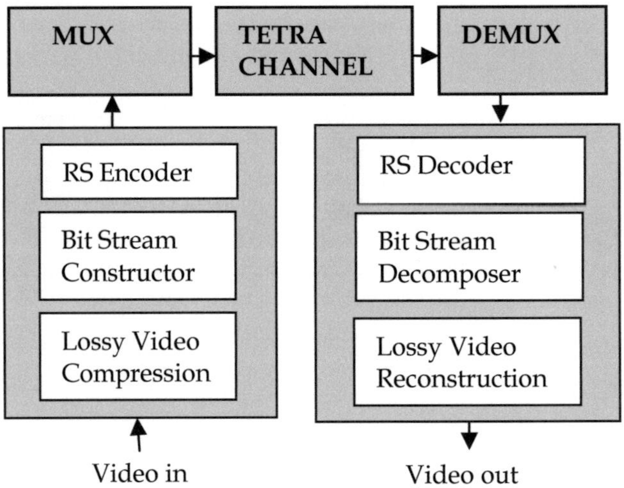

Fig. 9. Block diagram of MLVQ video transmission

are combined together in and alternating structure before they are passed through the TETRA Channel simulator. The received data are first de-multiplexed to the header and texture bitstreams. Then the *RS Decoder* process eliminates the added bit redundancy in the coded bitstreams. Then, the *Bitstream Decomposer* process deciphers the received bitstreams to the meaningful data for video decoding. The final stage is the *Lossy Video Reconstruction* process, where the compressed video sequence is reconstructed. The bitstream syntaxes are protected using the forward error correction codes (FEC) using the RS codes before they are transmitted in mobile channels. In this work, two error resilient schemes are developed i.e. the Equal Error Protection (UEP) and Unequal Error Protection (EEP) schemes.

4.1 Unequal error protection

In this work the shortened Reed Solomon codes are selected for forward error correction due to their burst error and erasure correcting capabilities, which makes them suitable to be used for error correction in mobile applications. Table 1 shows the properties of the shortened RS codes for FEC (Akbari, 2004).

Original Code	Shortened Code	Code rate	Errors/Erasures Corrected
RS (255 , 237)	RS (54 , 36)	2/3	9 errors/18 erasures
RS (255 , 219)	RS (54 , 18)	1/3	18 errors/36 erasures
RS (255 , 215)	RS (54 , 14)	1/4	20 errors/40 erasures

Table 1. RS codes properties (Akbari, 2004).

The UEP scheme applied to the MLVQ codec is shown in Figure 10. The labels S_1 and S_2 represent the streams of different levels of priority produced by the MLVQ encoder. The C_1 and C_2 denote the channel codes being used with rates of r_1 and r_2 respectively, where $r_1 < r_2$.

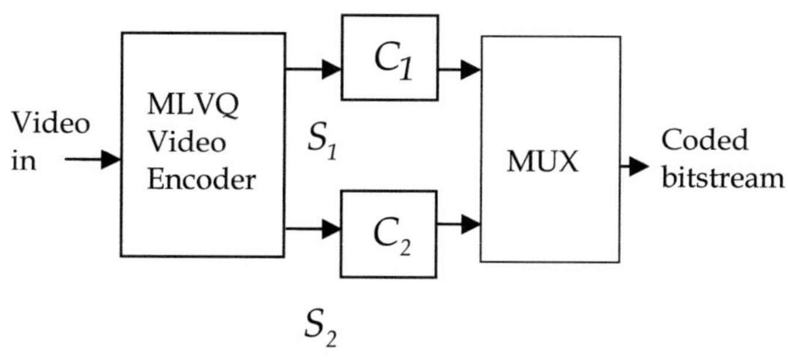

Fig. 10. UEP scheme for MLVQ video codec

The MLVQ video codec bitstream is partitioned into a header and texture syntaxes. The header field contains parameters that can potentially cause decoding failure or loss of synchronisation, while the texture data defines the quality of the decoded frames without having any influence on the decoding process or codec synchronization. The purpose of partitioning the video bitstream is to have the UEP scheme where the header data are protected with more bit redundancy (code rate r_1) and the texture data is protected with less bit redundancy (code rate r_2) where $r_1 < r_2$.

The header data for each group of pictures (GOPs) contains important data for decoding such as picture start code, quad-tree parameters (MAP sequence), index sequence and scale list, which are transmitted through the channel with code rate r_1 . The texture data contain the low frequency subband data are passed through the channel with code rate r_2 . In this work the code rate of $r_1 = 1/4$ and $r_2 = 2/3$ are used UEP scheme. The bit allocation for each group of pictures takes into account the additional bits consumed by the UEP scheme in the following way:

- Suppose F is the allocated bits for a GOP
- First, calculate the LL subands bits used after lossless coding
- Then, computes the bits used to encode the texture data: $bit_{TXT} = bit_{LL} \times \frac{1}{r_2}$
- Then, calculate the left over bits: $bit_{LFOVR} = F - bit_{TXT}$
- Thus, bits requires to encode header is given: $bit_{HDR} = bit_{LFOVR} \times r_1$

4.2 Equal Error Protection (EEP)

The equal error protection (EEP) uses the same amount of bit redundancy to protect both header and texture data. In this work, this scheme is developed for the purpose of comparing the performance of the MLVQ video codec with EEP with the H.263 video standard with EEP scheme. In addition, for further comparison with the current video coding standard, the the EEP scheme for H.264 has also been developed. The bitstream of H.264 format obtained from the JM reference software version 10.1 (JM H.264, http://iphome.hhi.de/suehring/tml/) is protected globally with the RS codes before sending the protected bitstream through TETRA channel. In this work the code rate of 1/3 is used for the protection of the source data for both C_1 and C_2 .

5. Results

This section presents the results of video transmission on error free channel. In this experiment the performance of the proposed MLVQ video codec is compared with the AJSVQ (Akbari & Soraghan, 2003) over noiseless channel in order to show the incremental results. The performance comparison with other video standards is also conducted for various bit rates. Then, the performance comparison between the codecs in mobile channels using the TETRA channel simulator is conducted.

5.1 Transmission in error free channel

The error free channel assumes an ideal channel condition with no lost to video data. All of the test video sequences used are in the form of Quarter Common Intermediate Format (QCIF) format. In this format, the luminance components consist of 144×176 pixels, while the chrominance components have 72×88 pixels. The optimized value found from experiment for the normalized energy factor $(\beta = 0.76)$. This value is used in spherical LVQ encoding scheme of the first stage or pass of the multistage quantization process found after using "Foreman", "Carphone", "Miss America" and "Salesman" video sequences. The value is used throughout the high frequency subbands encoding process. In the subsequent passes of the MLVQ scheme the value is set to one $(\beta = 1.0)$.

A preliminary experiment is conducted as to show the incremental performance of the new MLVQ video codec, where the test video sequence "Miss America" is first encoded using 64kbps at 8 fps and compared to the non-predictive video codecs. In this case, the performance results are compared to the motion JPEG2000 standard and AJSVQ video codec (Akbari & Soraghan, 2003) (Akbari 2003). In order to emulate the motion JPEG2000 video scheme, the individual gray frame of "Miss America" of size 176x144 pixels per frame is coded using the JPEG2000 image still coding standard. Fig. 11 below shows the relative performance of the first frame of "Miss America" sequence between MLVQ and AJSVQ. Other test sequences like "Salesman" and "Carphone" are also used in simulation. Fig. 12 and Fig. 13 show the results taken at various bit rates for frame rate of 12 fps. The results show that in noiseless environment H.264 always has the best performance as compared to the rest of the codecs.

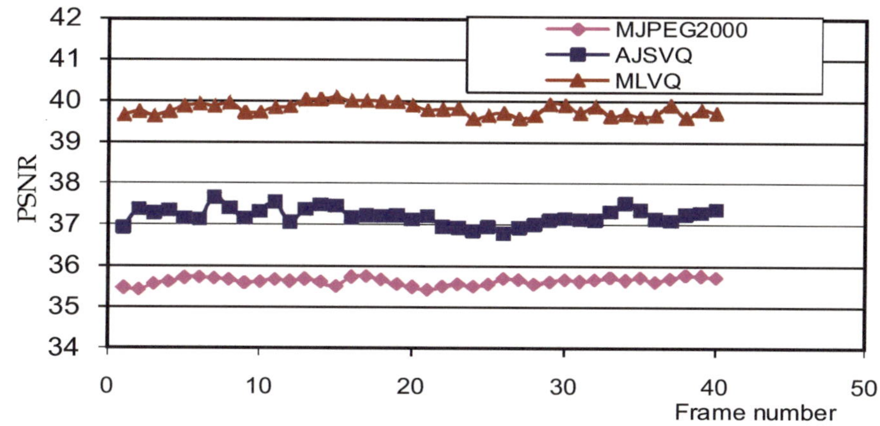

Fig. 11. Relative performance of "Miss America" at 8 fps

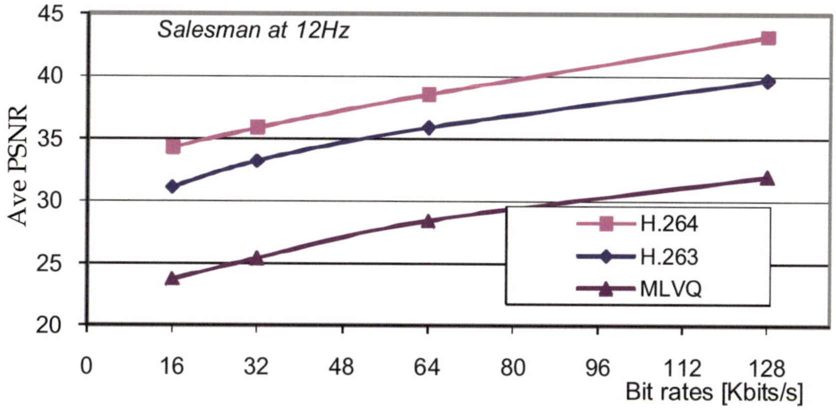

Fig. 12. "Salesman" over noiseless channel

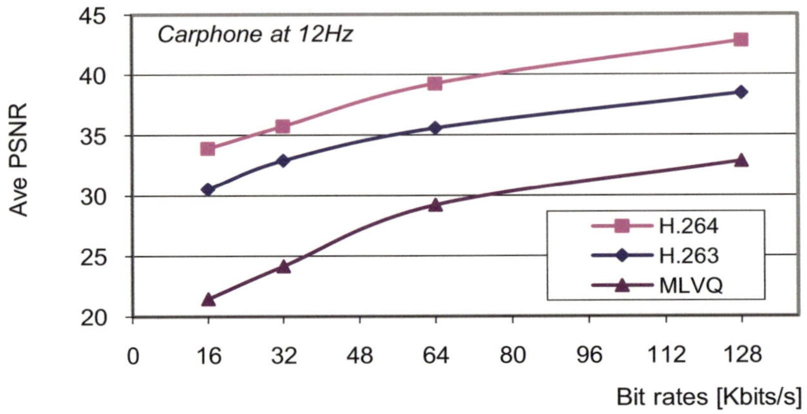

Fig. 13. "Carphone" over noiseless channel

5.2 Transmission in mobile channels

In this subsection, two experimental results will be presented. First, the performance comparison results between the proposed MLVQ video codec with H.263 are presented. Secondly, the comparison performance results of the new codec against H.264 video standard are also presented.

5.3 Comparison with H.263

In this experiment the H.263+ encoder that employs Annexes D (Advanced Prediction Mode), F (Unrestricted Motion Vectors) and G (PB-frames) is used for simulation. The shortened RS codes with code rate of 1/3 and block interleaving at a depth of four with each ECC are utilized to equally protect the compressed H.263 bitstream and mitigate the effects of burst errors. The Bad Urban (BU) and Hilly Terrain (HT) environments with channel SNR equal to 18 dBs of the TETRA channel simulator (ETSI, 95) are used in the experiment. The video is encoded using bit rate 64 kb/s and frame rate of 15 fps throughout this experiment. Fig. 14 and Fig. 15 show the performance of the 'Foreman' and 'Carphone' test sequences particularly on frame rate 15 fps, at 18 dB channel SNR in bad urban (BU) and hilly terrain (HT) mobile environments respectively. The results show the performance of MLVQ with UEP is always better than the MLVQ with EEP. The performance of the MLVQ codec with EEP scheme is also compared to the H.263 with EEP schemes. This gives a fair comparison since both codecs use the same technique for error protection. The performance of MLVQ with UEP scheme is then compared to the MLVQ with EEP scheme to show the improvement gain due to the UEP scheme.

5.4 Comparison with H.264

In this experiment, MLVQ codec with UEP scheme has been chosen since it offers the best performance of forward error correction scheme. The baseline profile of the H.264 standard (JM H.264, http://iphome.hhi.de/suehring/tml/) is used since it is used for application in mobile environment. The baseline profile H.264 is equipped with the error resilient tools

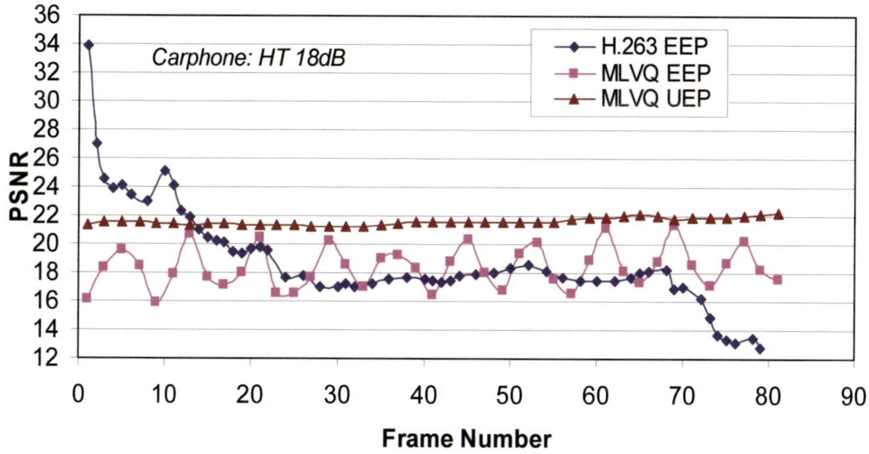

Fig. 14. "Foreman" sequence over BU18 channel, 15 fps.

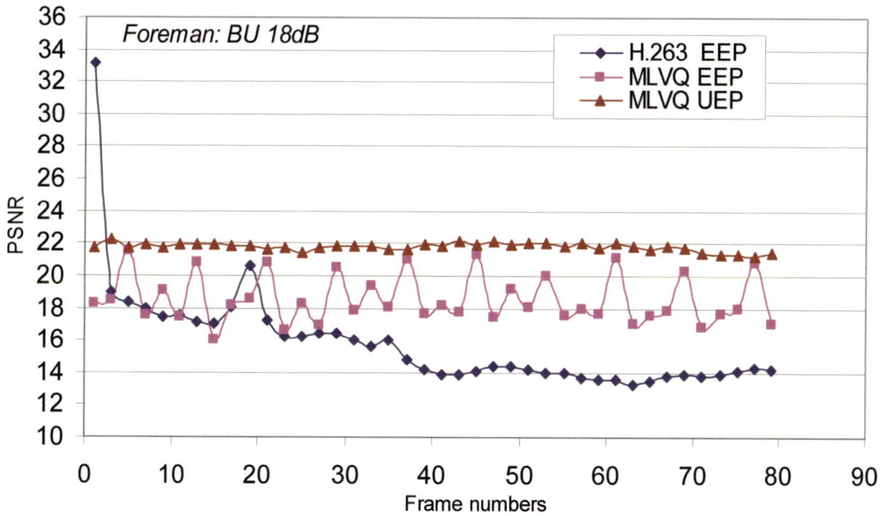

Fig. 15. "Carphone" sequence over HT18 channel, 15 fps.

such as redundant slices, flexible macroblock ordering, macroblock line intra refreshing and feedback channel. However, the baseline profile does not support data partition. Hence, the equal error protection (EEP) scheme with RS code rate ¼ is used for bits error protection before being transmitted in the mobile channels. In this experiment the TETRA Hilly Terrain (HT) channel is used as the mobile environment. The test sequences "Foreman", "Carphone" and "Miss America" with bit rate of 64kbits/s and frame rate at 15 fps are used. In this experiment, the MLVQ codec are compared to the H.264 with error resilient tools enabled. Table 2 below summarizes the error resilient tool used in the experiment.

Error resilient tool features	**H.264 bitstream**
Slice mode	50 MB per slice
Error concealment	No
Redundant slices	No
FMO	Interleave mode
MB line intra refreshing	Yes
Feedback channel	No

Table 2. Error resilient tools used in H.264 video standard

Table 3 shows the average PSNR obtained for the two codecs, where the average PSNR of H.264 is higher than MLVQ codec. This is due to the fact that the PSNR values of the earlier decoded H.264 frames are always higher. As the number of frame gets higher the PSNR values of H.264 are comparable to MLVQ as shown in Figure 16.

Mobile Environment	**Sequence**	**H.264 PSNR**	**MLVQ PSNR**
HT	Carphone	25.36	21.70
	Foreman	24.43	21.80
	Miss America	31.20	29.86

Table 3. Average PSNR of test sequences as compared to H.264 at SNR18dB

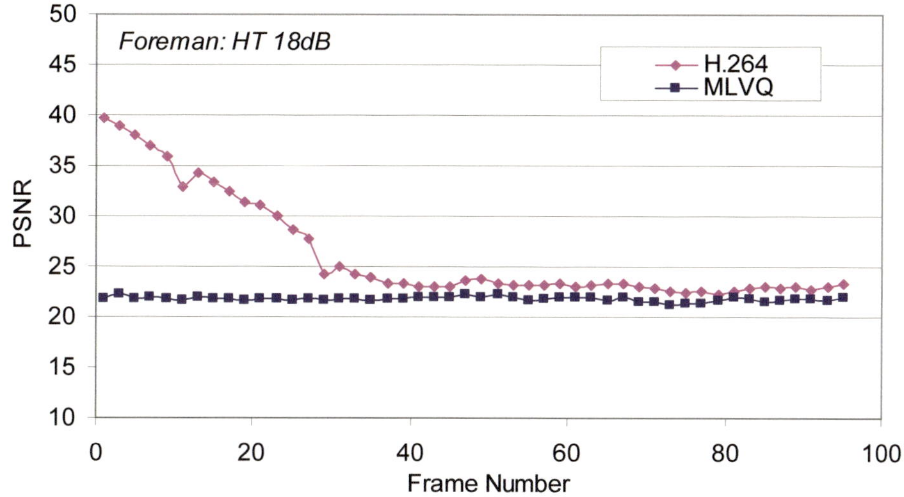

Fig. 16. "Foreman" sequence over HT18 channel

6. Conclusion

In this paper the multistage lattice vector quantization (MLVQ) coding scheme for mobile applications has been presented. The video codec groups the video sequence into a group of m-frames by grouping the high frequency subbands from each frame. The significant coefficients or vectors are then quantized using the MLVQ coding. The lattice vector quantization offers less amount of computation in generating the codebook due to its regular structure. Since the codebook generation does not require any computation, this facilitates the use of multistage quantization process to capture the quantization residual errors. This enhances the reconstructed frame quality. In noiseless environment, MLVQ is always inferior from the H.263 and H.264 standard codecs. However, the performance of the non-predictive MLVQ scheme is superior to the H.263 in mobile environment since the new video codec does not contain any motion vectors data. The non-predictive MLVQ codec performs comparably near to the performance of the latest H.264 video codec in erroneous mobile channels.

7. Future research

The forward error correction adds redundant bits to the coded bitstream, which allows the decoder to correct errors up to certain level. However, this reduces compression ratio. Moreover, the FEC must be designed with the assumption of the worst case scenario. If for example, the coded video is transmitted through an error-free channel, the additional bits are unnecessary. In another situation, where the channel might have highly variable quality the worst case situation also vary. Therefore, this suggests the need to employ the very powerful codes. In other words, these scenarios address a problem of efficient bits allocation for forward error correction technique, while minimizing the reduction of compression ratio. One area of future direction could be to investigate the use of multiple descriptions coding (MDC). In this way, the joint source i.e. the MLVQ video data and the channel coding method could provide an effective way for error resilience with relatively small reduction in compression ratio.

8. References

Adoul, J. P.; and Barth, M. (1988). "Nearest neighbor algorithm for spherical codes from the Leech lattice," *IEEE Trans. Information Theory*, Vol. 34, No. 5, Sept. 1988, pp. 1188-1202, ISSN: 0018-9448.

Akbari, A. S.; and Soraghan, J. J. (2003). "Adaptive joint subband vector quantization codec for handheld videophone applications," *Electronic Letters*, vol. 39, no. 14, July 2003, pp.1044-1046, ISSN: 0013-5194.

Akbari, A. S. (2004). "Fuzzy Multiscale based Image and Video Processing with Applications," PhD Thesis, Institute for Communication and Signal Processing, Department of Electrical and Electronic Engineering, University of Strathclyde, Glasgow, UK, December 2004.

Barlaud, M.; et al., (1994). "Pyramidal Lattice Vector Quantization for Multiscale Image Coding," *IEEE Trans. Image Processing*, Vol. 3, No. 4, July 1994, pp. 367-381, ISSN: 1057-7149.

Y. Be'ery, B. Shahar, and J. Snyders, "Fast decoding of the Leech lattice", *IEEE J. Selected Areas in Comm.*, Vol. 7, No. 6, Aug. 1989, pp. 959 – 967, ISSN: 0733-8716.

Conway, J. H.; and Sloane, N. J. A; (1988). *Sphere Packings, Lattices, and Groups*, Springer-Verlag, ISBN-10: 0387985859, New York.

Conway, J. H.; and Sloane, N. J. A. (1982). "Fast Quantizing and Decoding Algorithms for Lattice Quantizers and Codes," *IEEE Trans. Information Theory*, vol. IT-28, March 1982, pp. 227-232, ISSN: 0018-9448.

Dufaux F.; and Ebrahimi, T. (2004). "Error-Resilient Video Coding Performance Analysis of Motion Jpeg-2000 and MPEG-4," *Proc. of SPIE Visual Communications and Image Processing*, San Jose, CA, January 2004.

ETSI: TETRA Voice and Data, Part 2: (1995). "Air Interface, ETS 300 392-2," November 1995.

Feideropoulou, G.; et al., (2007). "Rotated Constellations for Video Transmission Over Rayleigh Fading Channels," *IEEE Signal Processing Letters*, Vol. 14, No. 9, Sept. 2007, pp. 629 – 632, ISSN: 1070-9908.

Forney Jr., G. D. (1988). "Coset codes. II. binary lattices and related codes," *IEEE Trans. Information Theory*, Vol. 34, No. 5, Sept 1988, pp. 1152 -1187, ISSN: 0018-9448.

Gersho, A.; and Gray, R.M. (1992). *Vector Quantization and Signal Compression*, Kluwer Academic, ISBN-10: 0792391810, New York.

Ghanbari, M. (2003). *Standard Codecs: Image Compression to Advanced Video Coding*, The Institution of Engineering and Technology, ISBN-10: 0852967101, London, UK.

Gibson, J. D.; and Sayood, K. (1988). "Lattice Quantization," *Advances in Electronics and Electron Physics*, Vol. 72, pp. 259-330, P. Hawkes, ed., Academic Press.

Golomb, S. W. (1966) "Run-length Encodings," *IEEE Trans. Inf. Theory*, Vol. IT-12, No. 3, July 1966, pp. 399-401, ISSN: 0018-9448.

ISO/IEC 15444-3:2002, (2002). "Information technology – JPEG2000 image coding system – Part 3: Motion JPEG2000," 2002.

ITU-T Recommendation H.263, (2000). "Video codec for Low bit rate communication," Version 3, November 2000.

JM H.264/AVC Reference Software available at homepage http://iphome.hhi.de/suehring/tml/.

Kuo, C. M. et al., (2002). "Multiresolution Video Coding Based on Kalman Filtering Motion Estimation," *Journal of Visual Communication and Image Representation*, Vol. 13, No. 3, September 2002, pp. 348-362, ISSN: 1047-3203.

Lawson, S.; and Zhu, J. (2002). "Image compression using wavelets and JPEG2000: a tutorial," *Electronics & Communication Engineering Journal*, Vol. 14, No. 3, June 2002, pp. 112-121, *ISSN:* 0954-0695.

Man, H. et al., (1999). "A Family of Efficient and Channel Error Resilient Wavelet/Suband Image Coders," *IEEE Transaction on Circuits and Systems for Video Technology*, Vol.9, No.1, Feb. 1999, pp. 95–108, ISSN: 1051-8215.

Man, H. et al., (2002). "Three-dimensional subband coding techniques for wireless video communications," *IEEE Transaction on Circuits and Systems for Video Technology*, Vol. 12, No. 6, June 2002, pp. 386-397, ISSN: 1051-8215.

Ostermann, et al, (2004). "Video coding with H.264/AVC: Tools, Performance, and Complexity," *IEEE Circuits and System Magazine*, Vol. 4, No. 1, First Quarter 2004, pp. 7-28, ISSN: 0163-6812.

Ran, M.; and Snyders, J. (1998). "Efficient decoding of the Gosset, Coxeter-Todd and the Barnes-Wall Lattices" *Proc. IEEE Int. Symp. Information Theory*, ISBN: 0-7803-5000-6, Cambridge, MA, August 1998, pp. 92, IEEE, New York.

Reed, I. S.; and Solomon, G. (1960). "Polynomial codes over certain finite fields," *Journal of the Society of Industrial and Applied Mathematics*, Vol. 8, June 1960,pp. 300--304, *ISSN*: 03684245.

Salleh, M. F. M.; and Soraghan, J. (2005). "A new multistage lattice VQ (MLVQ) technique for image compression," *CD-ROM Proc. European Signal Processing Conference 2005*, Antalya, Turkey.

Salleh, M. F. M.; and Soraghan, J. (2006). "A new adaptive subband thresholding algorithm for multistage lattice VQ image coding," *Proc. IEEE Int. Conf. Acoustics Speech and Signal Processing (ICASSP 2006)*, Vol. 2, pp. 457-460, ISBN: 1-4244-0469-X, Toulouse France, IEEE, New York.

Salleh, M. F. M.; and Soraghan, J. (2007). "Non-predictive multi-scaled based MLVQ video coding for robust transmission over mobile channels," *Electronics Letters*, Vol. 43, No. 13, June 2007, pp. 711-712, ISSN: 0013-5194.

Sampson, D. G. et al., (1995). "Low bit-rate video coding using wavelet vector quantisation," *IEE Proceedings Vision, Image and Signal Processing*, Vol. 142, No. 3, June 1995, pp. 141 - 148, ISSN: 1350-245X.

Sikora, T. (2005). "Trends and perspectives in image and video coding," *Proceedings of IEEE*, Vol. 93, No. 1, Jan 2005, pp. 6-17, ISSN: 0018-9219.

Sloane, N. J. A. (1981). "Tables of Sphere Packings and Spherical Codes", *IEEE Transactions on Information Theory*, Vol. IT-27, No. 3, May 1981, pp. 327-338, ISSN: 0018-9448.

Voukelatos, S. P.; and Soraghan, J. J. (1997) "Very Low Bit Rate Colour Video Coding Using Adaptive Subband Vector Quantization with Dynamic Bit Allocation," *IEEE Transactions. on Circuits and Systems for Video Technology*, Vol. 7, no. 2, April 1997, pp. 424-428, ISSN: 1051-8215.

Weiping, L. et al., (1997). "A video coding algorithm using vector-based techniques," *IEEE Transactions on Circuits and Systems for Video Technology,* Vol. 7, No. 1, Feb. 1997, pp.146 - 157, ISSN: 1051-8215.

Part 4

Error Resilience in Video Coding

10

Error Resilient Video Coding using Cross-Layer Optimization Approach

Cheolhong An[1]*and Truong Q. Nguyen[2]
[1]*Qualcomm Incorporated*
[2]*University of California San Diego*
U.S.A.

1. Introduction

A communication system can be modeled as Open Systems Interconnection (OSI)-7 layers. Generally, each layer solves its own optimization problem. For example, video coding of the application layer minimizes distortion with or without considering transmission errors for given bit rate constraints. The Transmission Control Protocol (TCP) layer solves fair resource allocation problems given link capacities, and the Internet Protocol (IP) layer minimizes the path cost (e.g. minimum hop or link price). In the Media Access Control (MAC) layer, throughput is maximized for given bit error probability, and the Physical (PHY) layer minimizes the bit error probability or maximizes the bit rate (e.g. diversity and multiplexing of Multiple Input Multiple Output (MIMO)).

However, all the other layers except the application layer are not directly observed by end users. It means that the users evaluate a communication system based on quality of the application layer. Therefore, we need to maximize quality of the application layer cooperating with the other layers since one layer's optimization can affect performance of the other layers. In this chapter, we focus on trade-offs between rate and reliability for given information bit energy per noise power spectral density $\frac{E_b}{N_0}$ (i.e. Signal-to-Noise Ratio (SNR)) with consideration to error resilient video coding feature. Especially, the application oriented cross-layer optimization is considered for transmission of compressed video streams.

For the cross-layer optimization, the basic framework of Network Utility Maximization (NUM) (Kelly et al. (1998)) or extend framework of NUM (Chiang et al. (2007)) can be used. Especially, Lee et al. (2006) incorporate trade-offs between rate and reliability to the extend NUM framework. This framework is applied to decide the number of slices, source code rate, channel code rate, MAC frame length and channel time allocation for multiple access among

---

*Portions reprinted, with permission, from (C. An and T. Q. Nguyen, "**Resource Allocation for Error Resilient Video Coding over AWGN using Optimization Approach**", *the IEEE Transactions on Image Processing*, vol. 17 , pp. 2347-2355, Dec., 2008) ©[2008] IEEE, (C. An and T. Q. Nguyen, "**Resource Allocation for TDMA Video Communication over AWGN using Cross-Layer Optimization Approach**", *the IEEE Transactions on Multimedia*, vol. 10, pp. 1406-1418, Nov., 2008) ©[2008] IEEE, and (C. An and T. Q. Nguyen, "**Analysis of Utility Functions for Video**", in *Proceedings of the IEEE International Conference on Image Processing*, Sep., 2007) ©[2007] IEEE the utility functions. Figure 1 represents the procedure of cross-layer optimization with an objective function of the application layer. Trade-offs between rate and reliability of the other layers are mathematically modeled as constraint functions. Therefore, mathematical models to represent each layer's features are important. We formulate the end-to-end distortion function of error resilient video coding as a utility function and trade-offs relation between rate and reliability of the other layers as constraint functions. If mathematical models are available, an optimization problem can be formulated and convex property of the problem needs to be analyzed for convex optimization problem whose solution is the global optimum (Boyd & Vandenberghe (2004)).

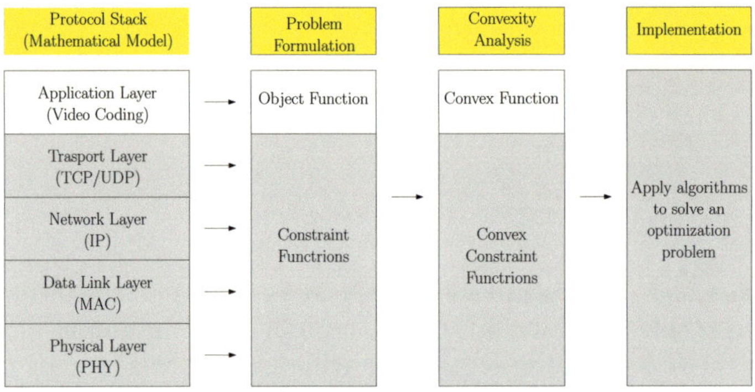

Fig. 1. Procedure of Application-Oriented (AO) cross-layer optimization.

For the convex optimization problem in (1), the objective function $f_0(x)$ must be concave for the maximization, inequality constraint functions $f_i(x)$ must be convex functions and equality functions $h_j(x)$ must be affine in the optimization problem (Boyd & Vandenberghe (2004)):

$$\begin{aligned} &\max_{x} \quad f_0(x) \\ &s.t. \quad f_i(x) \leq 0, \;\; h_j(x) = 0 \quad i,j = 1,...,p \end{aligned} \tag{1}$$

If the problem is not a convex optimization problem, it can be transformed into a convex optimization problem after transformation of optimization variables since convexity and concavity are not intrinsic features of a function. One of simple examples is geometric programming which is not a convex optimization problem. It can be transformed into a convex problem as in Boyd & Vandenberghe (2004). Chiang et al. (2007) showed several other techniques to decouple constraint functions and to transform optimization variables for convex optimization. If the problem is convex, Boyd & Vandenberghe (2004); Palomar & Chiang (2007) presented several algorithms that can be used to solve a convex optimization problem. In this chapter, the primal-dual decomposition method is applied to obtain optimal solutions using the Lagrangian dual decomposition and the (sub)gradient projection method in D.P.Bertsekar (2003); Johansson & Johansson (2005).

In this chapter, the NUM framework is applied to solve resource allocation problems for video communication with elaborate mathematical models and other optimization variables with Automatic Repeat reQuest (ARQ) and Time Division Multiple Access (TDMA). First, we are interested in allocating source code rate, channel code rate, MAC frame length and channel time allocation for multiple access among the utility functions. Many previous researches in Bystrom & Modestino (2000); Cheung & Zakhor (2000); Hochwald & Zeger (1997); K et al.

(2000); Z.He et al. (2002) only focused on finding optimal source code rate and channel code rate without considering MAC functionality such as ARQ and multiple access. Qiao & Choi (2001) adapted MAC frame size and modulation and channel code rate of the PHY layer for maximization of goodput without consideration of error effects of the application layer. Izzat et al. (2005) analyzed importance of MAC frame size to video streaming and Chou & Miao (2006); Haratcherev et al. (2005) addressed source code rate with delay constraint. Haratcherev et al. (2006) applied cross-layer signal method which directly signals the throughput of the link layer to video coding layer to reduce rate control time of video coder, but it does not consider error effects of video coding. In Kalman & Girod (2005), channel time allocation is performed experimentally between two utility functions.

Next, we further extend the framework with consideration of error resilient video coding, especially, the raster scan order picture segmentation known as a slice of a picture (An & Nguyen (2008a)). In H.264 (2009), a slice can contain any number of Macro Blocks (MBs) in a picture with raster scan order unless Flexible MB Ordering (FMO) is used. Segmentation of a picture is a common method for error resilient video coding without limitation of profile (Richardson (2003)). However, it is not well known regarding effects of multiple slices in video coding. Cote et al. (2000); Harmanci & Tekalp (2005) divided slices based on the Rate-Distortion (RD) optimization without considering network packetization and slice error probability. Masala et al. (2004) rearranged some portions of a slice to fit the network packet size in order to increase throughput. As a result, these methods can induce multiple slices loss from one packet loss. Wang et al. (2006) only showed channel-induced distortion with respect to (w.r.t.) slice error probability without considering video coding efficiency. Chiew et al. (2005) used the intra-refresh, multiple reference frames and sliced-coding to prevent error propagation using feedback information from decoder. In Wu & Boyce (2007), the redundant slice feature was proposed to replace corrupted primary slices. The proposed methods mainly focus on usage of slices without considering how many slices are adequate for given network status.

Here, we jointly optimize the number of slices with constraints of the MAC and PHY layers to answer a question how many slices of a picture are sufficient for error protection for given channel error probability. For this work, we analyze source coding efficiency w.r.t. the number of slices because it decreases the error probability of slice but increases the source-coded bit rate if a picture is composed of too many slices. Detail discussion on this trade-off will be presented in subsection 2.2 General guidelines were suggested in Wenger (2003) as follows: a coded slice size is as close as Maximum Transfer Unit (MTU) size of MAC but never bigger than MTU size. This constraint prevents fragmentation of the IP layer. Consequently, one MAC frame carries one IP datagram which contains one slice. It is reasonable to the wired MAC such as Ethernet. However, one MAC frame can be fragmented into smaller frames in order to increase reliability in the wireless MAC such as 802.11 (1999). Therefore, the constraint, that is, a coded slice is as close as MTU size does not prevent MAC fragmentation. In this chapter, we directly decide the optimal MAC frame size which is the length of the fragmented MAC frame. Then a slice is coded as close to the optimal MAC frame length as possible. These constraints are considered as a joint optimization problem with constraints from the PHY and MAC layers.

Previous works do not consider all the protocols from the application layer to the PHY layer. In this chapter, we build all the protocol stacks explicitly or implicitly. The application, the MAC and the PHY layers are explicitly formulated as an optimization problem with the number of slices, source code rate, channel code rate, MAC frame size and channel time allocation as optimization variables. IP, User Datagram Protocol (UDP) and Real-Time Transport Protocol (RTP) are implicitly considered as protocol overheads. The delay and buffering issues of video streaming are implicitly considered with assumption that maximum delay and jitter are guaranteed by the functionality of TDMA MAC. In order to consider RD characteristics of video sequences as well as distortion of channel errors, negative of end-to-end distortion is modeled as a utility function. In this chapter, we consider sum of utility functions as an objective function of an optimization problem for fair resource allocation within the same subscription policy.

2. Mathematical models of protocol layers

In this chapter, a communication system with Additive White Gaussian Noise (AWGN) channel in Figure 2 is considered and formulated as an optimization problem. We jointly optimize three layers of the protocol stack: the application, the data link and the physical layers to decide the optimal number of slices, source code rate, channel code rate, MAC frame size and channel time allocation for a given SNR. The data link layer uses 802.11a-like MAC with Automatic Repeat reQuest (ARQ) and Time Division Multiple Access (TDMA). Acknowledge packets (ACKs) are assumed to be received without any errors because the length of packets is relatively short. In the PHY layer, Binary Phase Shift Keying (BPSK) modulation and high resolution soft decision demodulation are assumed with the perfect bit interleave and deinterleave. For Forward Error Correction (FEC), Rate Compatible Punctured Convolutional code (RCPC) (Hagenauer (1988)) and Viterbi decoder are used. In the application layer, H.264 video encoder and decoder are considered with error resilient video coding. For error resilient video coding, multiple slice coding is used, and previous decoded frame is considered for simple error concealment. We model negative of Mean Square Error (MSE) $-E[(X-\tilde{X})^2]$[1] as a utility function, because the end-to-end distortion $E[(X-\tilde{X})^2]$ is generally used as an objective measure to evaluate quality in video compression. In order to circumvent delay and jitter issues of video streaming, TDMA method instead of Carrier Sense Multiple Access with Collision Avoidance (CSMA/CA) is considered. For multiple access, joint optimization among coordinator and utility functions is performed distributively for the optimal channel time allocation in a coordinated network.

2.1 Analysis of Utility function for Video

video coding is considered for the application layer. The framework of NUM has the maximization of an objective function. In order to match this framework, the maximization of $-E[(X-\tilde{X})^2]$ is equivalent to the minimization of the end-to-end distortion $E[(X-\tilde{X})^2]$ which induces the maximization of Peak Signal-to-Noise Ratio (PSNR)[2]. Let the end-to-end distortion D_t be $E[(X-\tilde{X})^2]$. D_t in (2) can be decomposed into source-induced distortion D_e and channel-induced distortion D_c with assumption that quantization errors and channel errors are uncorrelated with zero mean. Z.He et al. (2002) showed experimentally that they

[1] Original samples X are input data of the video encoder in the transmit side, and reconstructed samples $\tilde{X}$ are output data of the video decoder in the receiver side which are shown in Figure 2.

[2] $PSNR = 10\log_{10}\frac{255^2}{D_t}$ where $D_t = E[(X-\tilde{X})^2]$

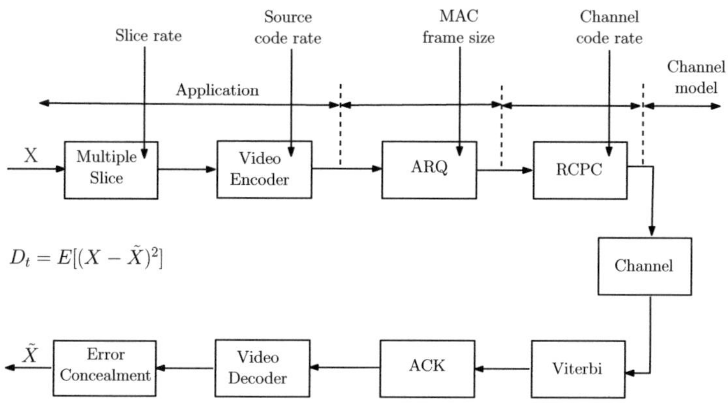

Fig. 2. A communication system model over AWGN.

are uncorrelated:

$$\begin{aligned} D_t &= E[(X-\tilde{X})^2] = E[(X-\hat{X}+\hat{X}-\tilde{X})^2] \\ &= E[(X-\hat{X})^2] + E[(\hat{X}-\tilde{X})^2] + 2E[(X-\hat{X})(\hat{X}-\tilde{X})] \\ &\approx E[(X-\hat{X})^2] + E[(\hat{X}-\tilde{X})^2] = D_e + D_c \end{aligned} \tag{2}$$

where X are original samples, $\hat{X}$ are reconstructed samples at the encoder, and $\tilde{X}$ are reconstructed samples at the decoder. In An & Nguyen (2007), we analyzed utility functions for video. From the information theory, a D-R model [3] in (3) is induced from the Independent Identically Distributed (IID) gaussian process with variance σ^2 in Taubman & Marcellin (2002)

$$D_e(R) = \sigma^2 2^{-2R} \tag{3}$$

where R is the source bit per pixel, and σ^2 is variance of a Discrete Cosine Transform (DCT) coefficient. According to different distributions and quantization methods, the above D-R model can be generalized into (4) by Taubman & Marcellin (2002)

$$D_e(R) = \epsilon^2\sigma^2 2^{-2R} = \beta e^{-\alpha R} \quad (\beta, \alpha > 0) \tag{4}$$

where $\epsilon^2 \approx 1.2$ for the Laplacian distribution. It is generally well known that a D-R model (4) only matches well with experimental results in a high bit rate region. A P-R function $PSNR(R)$ from (4) makes it clear, since $PSNR(R)$ has a linear relation with R as follows :

$$\begin{aligned} PSNR(R) &= 10\log_{10}\frac{255^2}{D_e} \\ &= 10log_{10}\frac{255^2}{\beta e^{-\alpha R}} = a_1 R + a_2 \end{aligned} \tag{5}$$

[3] we use the bit per pixel R instead of the bit per second x_s without index s of each source for the simplicity : $R_s = \frac{x_s}{f_r \times f_w \times f_h}$ where f_r is the number of frames per second and $f_w \times f_h$ is the number of samples per frame.

Figure 3 shows that the linear model (5) does not match well with the experimental $PSNR(R)$ which is highly nonlinear especially in a low bit rate region. Moreover, the video quality of many applications is between 28dB and 45dB which is a highly nonlinear area.

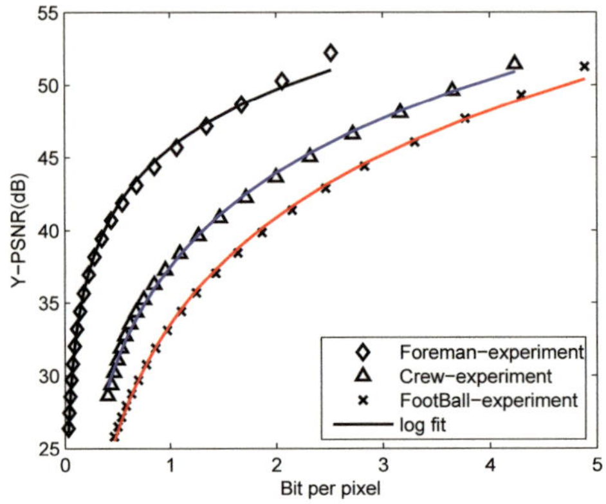

Fig. 3. PSNR vs. bpp for video sequences from An & Nguyen (2008a) (©[2008] IEEE).

A D-R model (6) is an variation of (4) shown in Wu et al. (2006)

$$D_e(R) = \beta e^{-\alpha R^{\gamma}} \quad (\beta > 0,\ \ 0 < \gamma, \alpha < 1) \tag{6}$$

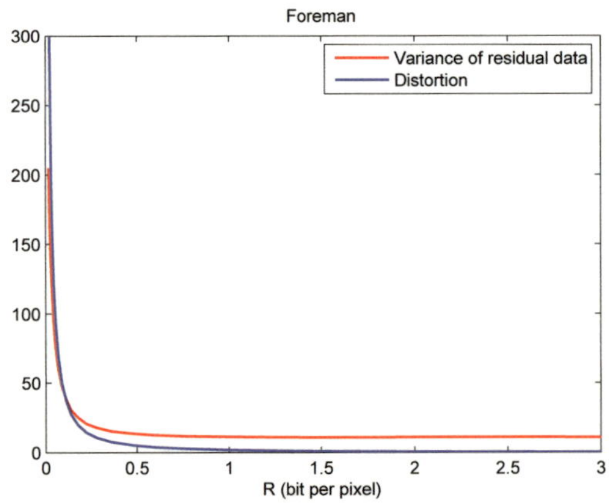

Fig. 4. Variance and distortion with respect to bit per pixel.

The main reason of the mismatch between mathematical models and experimental results is that the distortion in the mathematical models is obtained for a given variance of DCT coefficients. In the image compression techniques such as JPEG and JPEG2000 Taubman & Marcellin (2002), input data of a quantizer are DCT coefficients of natural image pixels. Therefore, variance of input data does not depend on the quantization step size. However, in the video coding techniques such as H.264 (2009), residual data of a current frame, which are difference between original samples and predicted samples from inter or intra prediction, are transformed and quantized. Inter or intra predicted samples are obtained from the neighboring reconstructed samples or previous decoded picture which the sum of predicted samples and quantized residual data. Therefore, residual data have different variance according to the quantization step size which controls bit per pixel R as shown in Figure 4. k. Jain (1989) showed that variance of residual data is highly correlated to variance of DCT coefficients. Consequently, variance of residual data relates to distortion as shown in Figure 4. In a high bit rate region, variance of residual is almost same such that experimental results match well with (4) but in a low rate region variance changes rapidly such that the mathematical models are different from experimental results. Therefore, input variance of a quantizer changes with respect to R such that a D-R model (4) needs to be modified as follows:

$$D_e(R) = \epsilon^2\sigma^2(R)e^{-\alpha R} = \epsilon^2(a_1 e^{-a_2 R} + a_3)e^{-\alpha R}$$
$$= ae^{-bR} + ce^{-dR} \quad (a,b,c,d > 0) \tag{7}$$

PSNR can be considered as a utility function in addition to the distortion. Figure 3 shows that the linear model (5) does not match well with the experimental $PSNR(R)$ of H.264 reference software model (JM (2007)) since it is highly nonlinear especially in the low bit rate region. Therefore, we propose $PSNR(R)$ and its distortion in reference An & Nguyen (2007) as follows:

$$PSNR(R) = m_1 \log(R) + m_2 \quad (m_1, m_2 > 0) \tag{8}$$
$$D_e = a_1 x^{-a_2} \quad (a_1, a_2 > 0) \tag{9}$$

Figure 3 represents that (8) matches well with experimental results of H.264 reference software model (JM (2007)) which is configured with high complexity rate distortion optimization, Universal Variable Length Coding (UVLC), 7 B frames and fast motion search of Enhanced Predictive Zonal Search (EPZS) at main profile. The proposed distortion model is a convex function w.r.t. source code rate x and $\log x$ which is necessary for convex optimization in transform domain. If an original problem is not convex, the problem can be transformed into a convex optimization problem after transformation of optimization variables.
A P-R model (8) is fitted to experimental results (H.264 reference software model JM (2007) is used for this experiment) as shown in Figure 3. They match well with experimental results in the usual operating bit rate ($R < 2$). A D-R model (10), which is induced from (8), is

$$D_e(R) = hR^{-j} \quad (h, j > 0) \tag{10}$$

Channel-induced distortion D_c is generated from channel errors because if there are no errors during the transmission, D_c vanishes since reconstructed samples $\tilde{X}$ in the video decoder is equal to reconstructed samples $\hat{X}$ in the video encoder. Wang et al. (2006) proposed that the channel-induced distortion D_c is

$$D_c = \frac{p}{I_r(1-p)} D_{ECP} \tag{11}$$

where D_{ECP}, I_r and p denote average distortion after error concealment, average intra Macro Block (MB) ratio in a picture and slice error probability of one picture, respectively. Wang et al. (2006) claimed that (11) is approximately valid with sub-pixel motion vectors, deblocking filtering and constrained intra prediction of H.264 (2009). Each video frame is coded as $\frac{x}{V_r}$ bits where V_r is video frame rate. Therefore, slice error probability p of a video frame comprising of one slice is

$$p = 1 - \left(1 - \frac{P_{fr}^{d_{max}}}{8(L - h_{ov})}\right)^{\frac{x}{V_r}} \tag{12}$$

$$\approx \frac{x}{V_r} \cdot \frac{P_{fr}^{d_{max}}}{8(L - h_{ov})} \tag{13}$$

after considering average bit error probability of ARQ in the MAC layer $P_{fr}^{d_{max}}$, which will be explained in subsection 2.5 Here, we assume $\frac{P_{fr}^{d_{max}}}{8(L-h_{ov})} \ll 1$ for an convex optimization problem. This assumption is usually satisfied with ARQ function (d_{max}), adequate frame error probability and MAC frame size.

2.2 Application layer with error resilient video coding

There are many methods to protect a coded video stream in H.264 (Richardson (2003); Wenger (2003)). For example, slice grouping which allocates MBs to a slice group by a slice group map is known as FMO, and redundant slices carry the same MBs with different quality in the base profile of H.264. In the extended profile, one slice can be separated into three partitions according to the importance of MBs, and each partition can be decoded independently. The most basic method for error resilient video coding without limitation of profiles is a picture segment which is known as a slice. A slice consists of any number of MBs in raster scan order within a picture, that is, a slice can include from one MB to maximum MBs of a picture. It also means that a picture is composed of a single slice or multiple slices. The main purpose of the picture segmentation is to enable independent decoding of slices because each slice has its own start code, and it is separately coded. Therefore, loss of some slices of a picture does not affect decoding of the other slices. Consequently, some portions of a picture could still be reconstructed, and they can be used for error concealment of loss parts in a picture. However, Motion Vector (MV) prediction, intra prediction, MB mode prediction and context of entropy coding are restricted for independent decoding which will be discussed later in detail. As a result, multiple slices of a picture reduce video coding efficiency with error resiliency increased.

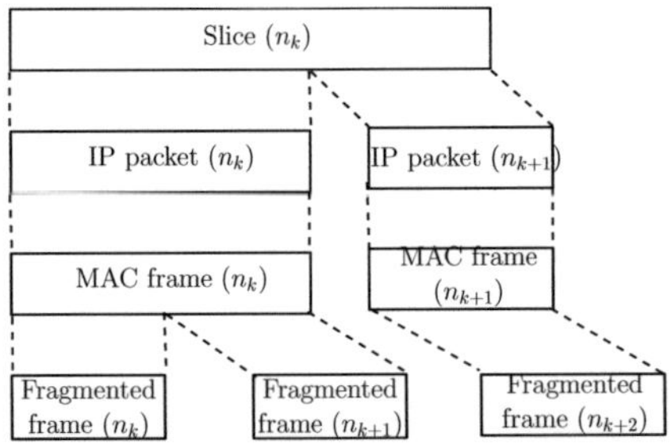

Fig. 5. IP layer fragmentation because a slice length is larger than MTU.

Thus, an essential issue of picture segmentation is how to decide the number of slices of a picture since it has a trade-off between a source-coded rate and error probability of a slice. If the number of slices increases, a source-coded rate increases, but error probability of a slice decreases because coded bits of a slice decrease. However, error probability of a slice is also

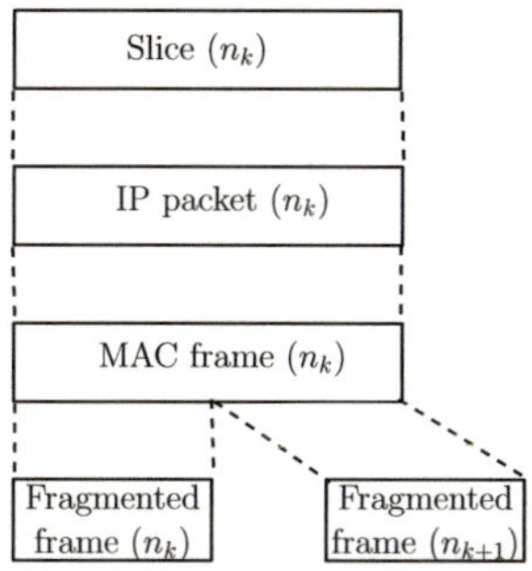

Fig. 6. MAC layer fragmentation even though a slice length is smaller than MTU.

highly related with network packetization. Figure 5 shows that if a slice length is larger than MTU, the IP layer fragments a slice into several IP packets. Thus, error probability of one slice increases because any loss of IP packets induces loss of a slice. Even if a slice length is smaller than MTU, the slice can be partitioned into smaller MAC frames due to the MAC fragmentation in wireless environment which is illustrated in Figure 6. Therefore, we jointly optimize a MAC frame length and slice length with source and channel-coded rate in order to satisfy the following constraint.

Constraint 1: A coded slice is as close as the optimal MAC frame size so that there is no fragmentation of the MAC frame, since the optimal MAC frame is optimal to minimize end-to-end distortion.

Equation (11) is applied to quantify distortion from error probability of a slice, and source-induced distortion D_e is derived from (9). However, (9) does not consider effects of the number of slices, that is, it is modeled as one slice per video frame.

Here, we analyze effects of the number of slices to the source-induced distortion and its bit rate. H.264 reference software model JM (2007) can segment a picture based on the number of MBs or the number of byte. If we choose the former option, each slice can be coded by various bits. Therefore, a picture is segmented by the number of byte to satisfy the Constraint 1. Three parts are mainly affected from multiple slice coding.

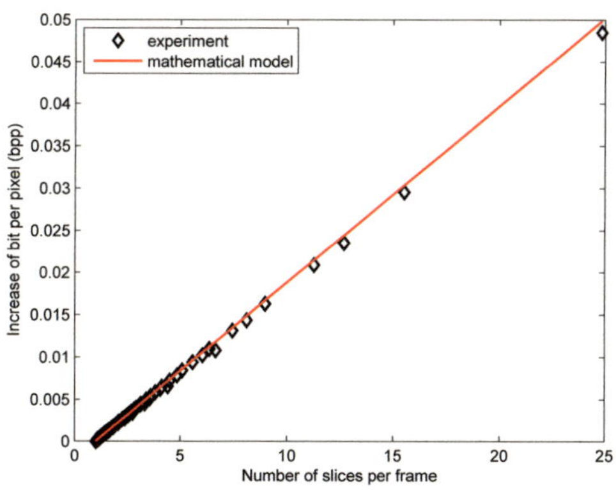

Fig. 7. Slice header bits increase w.r.t. the number of slices from An & Nguyen (2008a) (©[2008] IEEE).

First, coded bits for slice header information increase along with the number of slices because every slice of a picture is needed to be decoded independently. Figure 7 shows that slice header bits increase w.r.t. the number of slices at each different bit rate. Thus, increments of slice header bits X_{SH} do not depend on coded bit rates, but rather the number of slices. Therefore, it is modeled as

$$X_{SH} = \kappa_1(n-1) \tag{14}$$

where κ_1 is a positive constant and n is the number of slices of a picture. If $n = 1$, there is no increase of slice header bits. Figure 7 illustrates that equation (14) matches well with the experimental result.

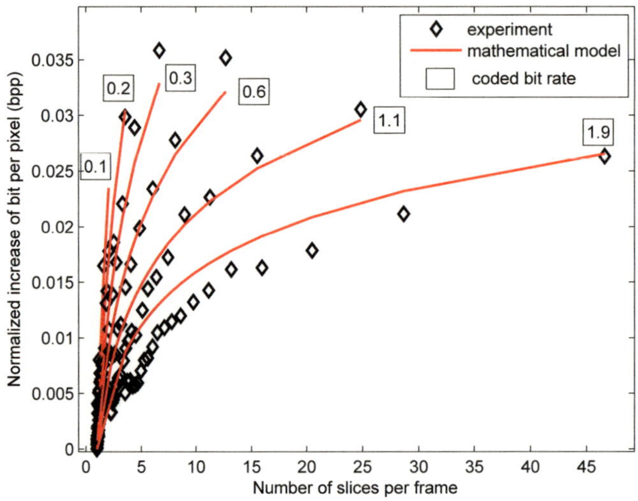

Fig. 8. Sum of other bits increase w.r.t. the number of slices at different bit per pixels from An & Nguyen (2008a) (©[2008] IEEE).

Second, MV prediction, intra prediction, MB mode prediction and context of entropy coding are restricted for independent decoding. If a current MB is at the boundary of different slices, neighboring MBs of the current MB are not available for MV prediction, intra prediction, MB mode prediction and context of entropy coding. Therefore, they increase coded bits for MVs, luminance Y, color residual C and MB mode. Figure 8 illustrates that overall normalized bits except slice header bits increase differently according to both the number of slices and coded bit rates. Furthermore, Figure 8 suggests out that effect of picture segmentation is larger at low bit rates. Consequently, we model bit increments from the restriction of prediction as follows:

$$X_{OT} = \kappa_2\sqrt{x}\log(n) \tag{15}$$

where κ_2 is a positive constant, n is the number of slices of a picture and x is a source-coded bit rate. For $n = 1$, there are no bit increments. The mathematical model and experimental results are shown in Figure 8.
Last, the restriction of MV prediction, intra prediction, MB mode prediction and context of entropy coding induce different coded bits and motion-compensated prediction errors. Thus,

RD optimization of H.264 in (16) can choose different MB modes from MB modes of one sliced picture. It affects both coded bits $Z(\mathbf{m})$ and distortion $D(\mathbf{m})$ from the RD optimization:

$$\min_{\mathbf{m}} D(\mathbf{m}) + \lambda(QP) \cdot Z(\mathbf{m}), \quad \mathbf{m} = (MV, Mode) \tag{16}$$

$$\lambda(QP) = \xi 2^{\frac{(QP-12)}{3}} \tag{17}$$

where ξ and λ are a positive constant and the Lagrange multiplier, respectively. Vector $\mathbf{m}$ contains optimization variables which consist of MV and MB modes. The effects on bit rates are already reflected in (14) and (15). Here, an variation of distortion is discussed. Figure 9 shows variations of PSNR and coded bits according to the number of slices at each bit per pixel (bpp). Although PSNR does not change, bpp increases w.r.t. the number of slices as shown in Figure 9. It results from the fact that the RD optimization of H.264 helps to reduce distortion at the high bit rate region. From the RD optimization (16) and the relation (17) between λ and Quantization Parameter (QP) in Weigand et al. (2003), λ is smaller at high bit rates (small QP) which means that the RD optimization tries to minimize more distortion $D(\mathbf{m})$ than coded bits $Z(\mathbf{m})$. Therefore, the variation of distortion can be diminished. On the contrary, the RD optimization increases distortion at the low bit rate region, but distortion does not change significantly since the distortion of low bit rates is already large and the number of slices is small. From the above results, we assume that the number of slices does not affect source-induced distortion but rather source-coded rates. The bit increments X_{SL} are modeled as the sum of (14) and (15).

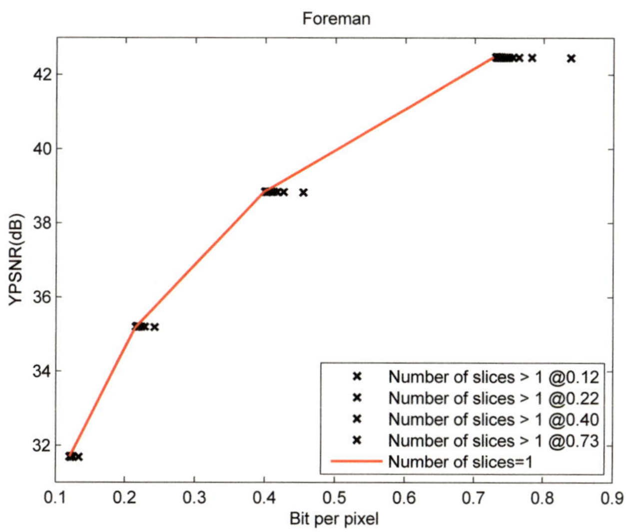

Fig. 9. PSNR vs. the number of slices at each bit per pixel from An & Nguyen (2008a) (©[2008] IEEE).

2.3 Objective function of network utility maximization problem

In this chapter, we use the sum of negative of distortion functions as an objective function for maximization. We may consider the sum of PSNR functions as an objective function. However, these optimization problems have quite different solutions. If we only consider a single utility function as an objective function, the solution of maximization of a PSNR function is equal to the solution of minimization of a distortion function:

$$\arg\max_{x} PSNR(x) = \arg\min_{x} D(x)$$

However, the solution of maximization of the sum of PSNR functions is different from the solution of minimization of the sum of distortion functions:

$$\begin{aligned}
&\arg\max_{\mathbf{x}} -\sum_{s} D_s(x_s) = \arg\min_{\mathbf{x}} \sum_{s} D_s(x_s) \\
&\neq \arg\max_{\mathbf{x}} \sum_{s} PSNR_s(x_s) = \arg\max_{\mathbf{x}} \sum_{s} 10\log\frac{255^2}{D_s(x_s)} \\
&= \arg\min_{\mathbf{x}} \sum_{s} \log D_s(x_s) = \arg\min_{\mathbf{x}} \prod_{s} D_s(x_s)
\end{aligned} \quad (18)$$

Moreover, if we compare average PSNR between two methods, the optimal PSNR (average PSNR) value from solution of the sum of distortion is always smaller than the optimal PSNR value from solution of the sum of PSNR. The average PSNR can be calculated by two definitions.

First, if we find the optimal solution $\mathbf{x}_{\mathbf{d}}^*$ of the sum of distortion, we can calculate PSNR of each utility function and then average these values. However, this average PSNR ($\frac{1}{N}\sum_{s=1}^{N} PSNR_s$) is always smaller than average PSNR from the optimal solution $\mathbf{x}_{\mathbf{p}}^*$ of the sum of PSNR because we solve a convex optimization problem and the solution is global optimal solution, thus any other solutions such as $\mathbf{x}_{\mathbf{d}}^*$ can not achieve larger sum of PSNR (average PSNR) than $\mathbf{x}_{\mathbf{p}}^*$.

Second, if we define average distortion[4] and its PSNR[5] as notes, the average PSNR value $PSNR_d$ is less than or equal to average PSNR which is proved as follows:

$$\begin{aligned}
PSNR_d &= 10\log_{10}\frac{255^2}{\frac{1}{N}\sum_s D_s(x_s)} \\
&= 10\log_{10} 255^2 - 10\log_{10}\frac{1}{N}\sum_{s} D_s(x_s) \\
&\leq 10\log_{10} 255^2 - \frac{10}{N}\sum_{s}\log_{10} D_s(x_s) \\
&= \frac{1}{N}\sum_{s}\left(10\log_{10} 255^2 - 10\log_{10} D_s(x_s)\right) \\
&= \frac{1}{N}\sum_{s} 10\log_{10}\frac{255^2}{D_s(x_s)} = \frac{1}{N}\sum_{s} PSNR_s
\end{aligned}$$

It means that even though we achieve the minimum sum of distortion (average distortion), PSNR of the average distortion is smaller.

Here, we show one example. From Table 1, there are two utility functions and three configurations, and configuration 2 is current distortion and PSNR of two utility functions. If we reallocate bits to maximize sum of PSNR functions or minimize sum of distortion

[4] Average distortion$D_{avg} \triangleq \frac{1}{N}\sum_{s=1}^{N} D_s$, where N is the number of utility functions.

[5] Average PSNR $PSNR_d \triangleq 10\log_{10}\frac{255^2}{D_{avg}}$.

functions, the distortion of U_0 varies slightly and the distortion of U_1 varies significantly because U_0 is currently operating at low distortion and U_1 operates at high distortion. The convex property of a distortion function induces different variation of distortion according to reallocation of bits. If we reduce bits of U_1 and reallocate the bits to U_0, the distortion and its PSNR of two utility functions change from configuration 2 to configuration 1. The other case changes from configuration 2 to configuration 3.

Table 1 shows that if we reallocate bits to maximize sum of PSNR, we should reallocate bits of two utility functions for configuration 1 and if we decide bits of two utility functions to minimize sum of distortion, we should choose the solution of configuration 3. This result matches with the result of (18), because the maximization of the sum of PSNR functions is equivalent to the minimization of multiplication of distortion. The multiplication of distortion are 300, 400 and 450 from configuration 1 to 3. Thus, configuration 1 has the minimum multiplication of distortion which corresponds to the maximum of sum of PSNR.

Which solution is better? Generally, configuration 3 is better than the others for fair resource allocation since variation of PSNR and distortion between utility functions decreases, even though average PSNR is smaller. Consequently, we use the sum of distortion functions as an objective function of NUM problem, even if average PSNR is smaller than average PSNR obtained from the solution of maximization of the sum of PSNR.

Utility function	Config 1	Config 2	Config 3
U_0	5 (41)[a]	10 (38)	15 (36)
U_1	60 (30)	40 (32)	30 (33)
$U_0 + U_1$	65 (71)	50 (70)	45 (69)

[a] Distortion (PSNR[dB])

Table 1. Example of max. PSNR vs. min. Distortion.

2.4 Physical layer model

After Viterbi decoding, Lin & Costello (2004) showed that bit error probability P_b of a binary-input and continuous-output AWGN channel is bounded by

$$P_b < \sum_{d=d_{free}}^{\infty} B_d Q\left(\sqrt{\frac{2drE_b}{N_0}}\right)$$

$$< \sum_{d=d_{free}}^{\infty} B_d e^{-\frac{drE_b}{N_0}}, \quad (Q(x) < e^{-\frac{x^2}{2}}) \tag{19}$$

$$\approx B_{d_{free}} e^{-\frac{d_{free} r E_b}{N_0}} \tag{20}$$

where B_d is the total number of nonzero information bits on all weight-d paths, d_{free} is the free distance of convolutional code, and r is the channel code rate. Equation (20) is derived with the assumption of dominance of first term in (19) at large $\frac{E_b}{N_0}$. However, it is difficult to use these equations as a mathematical model because of the two main reasons, that is, convexity and dependency of parameters B_d and d_{free} with respect to channel code rate r.

First, Figure 10 illustrates the experimental results of RCPC (Hagenauer (1988)) for memory $M = 6$ to show the variation of P_b according to the number of paths d from d_{free} to $d_{free} + 6$.

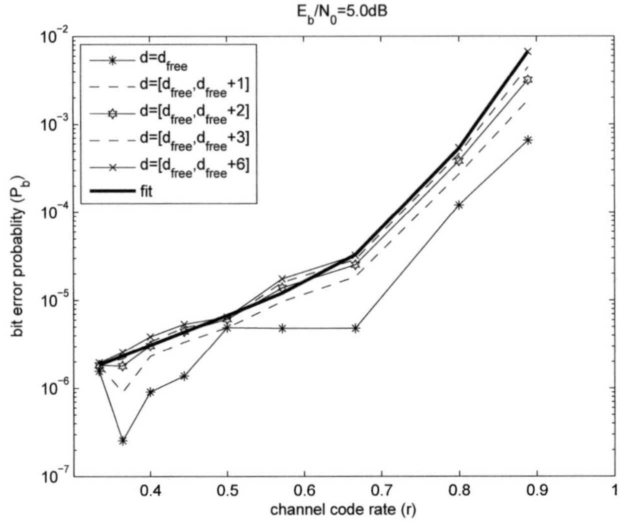

Fig. 10. Bit error probability P_b at $\frac{E_b}{N_0} = 5dB$ from An & Nguyen (2008b) (©[2008] IEEE)

Figure 10 shows that the first term of (19), that is, equation (20) is not dominant at low SNR. From Figure 10, we recognize that P_b is not a convex function of r, especially at high SNR, but it can be mildly assumed to be a convex function at low SNR. This convexity is necessary for the convex optimization which will be discussed in section 3. So we propose a convex model for the bit error probability P_b with respect to r given $\frac{E_b}{N_0}$ and M as follows:

$$P_b = p_1 e^{p_2 r} + p_3 e^{p_4 r} \tag{21}$$

where p_1, p_2, p_3 and p_4 are positive variables which depend on $\frac{E_b}{N_0}$. Equation (21) is a convex-hull mapping of equation (19) where B_d and d_{free} are obtained from Hagenauer (1988). Figure 10 illustrates that the proposed model is close to the experimental results of Hagenauer (1988). However, Figure 10 shows that some R values are not convex hull points but the difference between convex hull points (module curve) and experimental values are not large and mathematical P_b is also lower bound experimental values. Thus, this convexity model is only adequate at low SNR region. Therefore, we confine that SNR is lower than or equal to 7dB.

2.5 MAC layer model

For a MAC frame length of L Bytes, the error probability of a MAC frame P_{fr} is

$$\begin{aligned} P_{fr} &\leq 1 - (1 - P_b)^{8L} \approx 8LP_b, \quad (P_b \ll 1) \\ &= 8L\left(p_1 e^{p_2 r} + p_3 e^{p_4 r}\right) \end{aligned} \tag{22}$$

where (22) is derived with assumption of low bit error probability. If errors occur during the transmission of a MAC frame, the MAC frame is retransmitted up to the number of the maximum retransmission d_{max}. Therefore, the average time T_{avg} to transmit successfully one

MAC frame is

$$T_{avg} = \sum_{i=1}^{d_{max}} P(n=i)\Big((i-1)\tau_f + \tau_s\Big) \tag{23}$$

where $P(n = i)$ is the success probability at i-th times transmission. τ_f and τ_s are one transaction time (time duration from transmitting a data frame to receiving its ACK packet) of fail and success, respectively. In this chapter, we assume $\tau_f = \tau_s = \tau$ since they are almost same in TDMA media access method because given a time slot, the medium can be accessed without waiting. In contrast, CSMA/CA of 802.11 (1999) increases the contention window to two times, if there is an error. Therefore, τ_f usually becomes longer according to the number of retransmission (802.11 (1999)). There is some possibility of not receiving ACK packets which can induce longer waiting time, but we assume that ACK packets are always received without errors because the length of packets is relatively short. Consequently, the average transmission time of one MAC frame T_{avg} is

$$\begin{aligned} T_{avg} &= (1-P_{fr})\tau\Big(1 + 2P_{fr} + 3P_{fr}^2 + \ldots + d_{max}P_{fr}^{d_{max}-1}\Big) \\ &= (1-P_{fr})\tau\left(\frac{1-P_{fr}^{d_{max}}}{(1-P_{fr})^2} - \frac{d_{max}P_{fr}^{d_{max}}}{1-P_{fr}}\right) \\ &= \tau\left(\frac{1-P_{fr}^{d_{max}}}{1-P_{fr}} - d_{max}P_{fr}^{d_{max}}\right) \approx \frac{\tau}{1-P_{fr}}, \quad (P_{fr} \ll 1) \end{aligned} \tag{24}$$

One MAC frame, which has $8L$ bits length, can be transmitted successfully during T_{avg}. Consequently, the average goodput x_{gp} (application layer throughput excluding protocol overheads, retransmitted data packets and so on) is

$$x_{gp} = \frac{8(L-h_{ov})}{T_{avg}} = \frac{8(L-h_{ov})(1-P_{fr})}{\tau} \tag{25}$$

Here, h_{ov} is overhead of a MAC frame including the MAC header, Frame Check Sequence (FCS), service information and tail shown in Figure 11, as well as other protocols (e.g. Internet Protocol). If transmission of one MAC frame fails up to the number of the maximum retransmission d_{max}, the error probability of one MAC frame is $P_{fr}^{d_{max}}$, and one MAC frame encapsulates $8(L-h_{ov})$ of application layer bits. Therefore, the average bit error probability of the application layer after ARQ is $\frac{P_{fr}^{d_{max}}}{8(L-h_{ov})}$.

In this chapter, 802.11 (1999) MAC and 802.11a (1999) PHY are considered for our mathematical model. The transaction time τ shown in Figure 11 is

$$\begin{aligned} \tau &= T_{Preamble} + T_{Sig} + \frac{8LT_{symbol}}{N_{SD} r \log_2 M_o} + 2SIFS + \tau_{ack} \\ &= \frac{1}{N_{SD}}\left(A_0 + \frac{8LT_{symbol}}{r\log_2 M_o} + \frac{8L_{ack}T_{symbol}}{r\log_2 M_o}\right) \end{aligned}$$

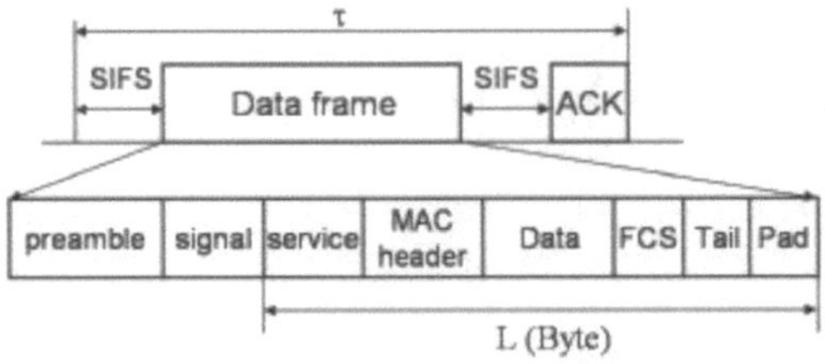

Fig. 11. One transaction and MAC frame structure from An & Nguyen (2008b) (©[2008] IEEE).

where

$$\tau_{ack} = T_{Preamble} + T_{Sig} + \frac{8L_{ack}T_{symbol}}{N_{SD}r\log_2 M_o},$$
$$A_0 = 2N_{SD}(T_{Preamble} + T_{Sig} + SIFS)$$

Here, N_{SD} is the number of Orthogonal Frequency Division Multiplexing (OFDM) data subcarriers. $T_{Preamble}$, T_{Sig} and Short InterFrame Space (SIFS) are the preamble time, the signal time and the short time space between frames, respectively. T_{symbol} is OFDM symbol time. L_{ack} and M_o represent the length of an ACK packet and the M_o-ary modulation, respectively. Consequently, the goodput x_{gp} is

$$x_{gp} = N_{SD}\frac{8(L - h_{ov})(1 - P_{fr})}{A_0 + \frac{8LT_{symbol}}{r\log_2 M_o} + \frac{8L_{ack}T_{symbol}}{r\log_2 M_o}} \tag{26}$$

For TDMA, contention-free period T_{pcf} is divided into some amount of time T_s for each source, i.e., $\sum_s T_s = T_{pcf} - B$ where B is beacon time. During T_s, each source executes transactions with its own source code rate x_s, channel code rate r_s and frame length L_s. Therefore, each source can achieve different error probability of a MAC frame P^s_{fr} and its goodput x^s_{gp}. $T_{pcf} = T_{RI} - T_{dcf}$, where T_{RI} is the repetition interval and T_{dcf} is the contention period. Finally, each source's goodput x^s_{gp} is formulated as follows:

$$x^s_{gp} = t_s \cdot N_{SD}\frac{8(L_s - h_{ov})(1 - P^s_{fr})}{A_0 + \frac{8L_sT_{symbol}}{r_s\log_2 M^s_o} + \frac{8L_{ack}T_{symbol}}{r_s\log_2 M^s_o}} \tag{27}$$

where $t_s = \frac{T_s}{T_{RI} - T_{dcf} - B}$, $\sum_s t_s = 1$ and $t_s \geq 0$.

3. Problem formulation

In this section, we only consider a Basic Service Set (BSS) which consists of a set of nodes controlled by a single coordination function (one node which is named as a coordinator in a BSS performs this function), and we assume that each node in a BSS can transmit directly to its destination node. Note that in 802.11 (1999), all transactions have to pass through Access Point (AP) to reach their destination nodes. However, 802.11e (2005) allows each node to exchange frames directly through the direct link. Therefore, the number of links to reach the destination is only one for each source. For simplicity, a link index for each source is omitted. In reference

An & Nguyen (2008b), we formulated a cross-layer optimization problem with one slice per picture as follows using mathematical models in section 2:

$$\max_{\mathbf{x,p,L,r,t}} \quad -\sum_{s}\left(a_1 x_s^{-a_2} + \frac{p_s}{I_r(1-p_s)} D_{ECP}\right) \tag{28}$$

$$s.t. \quad \frac{x_s}{V_r}\frac{\left[8L_s(p_1 e^{p_2 r_s} + p_3 e^{p_4 r_s})\right]^{d_{max}}}{8(L_s - h_{ov})} \le p_s \tag{29}$$

$$x_s \le t_s \cdot N_{SD}\frac{8(L_s - h_{ov})(1 - P_{fr}^s)}{A_0 + \frac{8L_s T_{symbol}}{r_s \log_2 M_o^s} + \frac{8L_{ack} T_{symbol}}{r_s \log_2 M_o^s}} \tag{30}$$

$$x_s^{min} \le x_s \le x_s^{max}, \; r_s^{min} \le r_s \le r_s^{max}$$

$$L_s^{min} \le L_s \le L_s^{max}, \; p_s^{min} \le p_s \le p_s^{max}$$

$$\sum_s t_s \le 1, \; t_s \ge 0, \; \forall s$$

where $P_{fr}^s = 8L_s(p_1 e^{p_2 r_s} + p_3 e^{p_4 r_s})$ and $s \in S$ and S is a set of utility functions which transmit their video streams. Utility functions $U_s(x_s, p_s)$ in (31) are the negative end-to-end distortion D_t in (28) which was discussed in section 2. The constraint (29) is relaxed from the equality constraint of slice error probability of one video frame comprising one slice. In case of one slice of a picture, slice error function $P_s(x_s, L_s, r_s)$ of (32) is derived in (29) as $\frac{x_s}{V_r}\frac{(8L_s P_b)^{d_{max}}}{8(L_s - h_{ov})}$ where $(8L_s P_b)^{d_{max}}$ is MAC frame error probability after d_{max} ARQ retransmission. Each video frame is coded as $\frac{x_s}{V_r}$ bits where V_r is a video frame rate, and one MAC frame carries $8(L_s - h_{ov})$ information bits. Thus, the number of MAC frames to transfer one video frame is $\frac{x_s}{V_r} \cdot \frac{1}{8(L_s - h_{ov})}$. If one of MAC frames to carry a picture fails, the whole picture (one slice) is lost since a video picture is coded as a single slice. Consequently, slice error probability is a product of the number of MAC frames for a picture and MAC frame error probability. Equation (30) shows that the source bit rate should be less than or equal to the goodput x_{gp} of MAC layer in (27). The main solutions of this problem are the source code rate x, the MAC frame size L and the channel code rate r among the optimization variables. The slice error probability p can be considered as an auxiliary variable. Each optimization variable has its own minimum and maximum constraints which are represented as y_s^{min} and y_s^{max} where $y_s \in \{x_s, L_s, r_s, p_s\}$.
We rewrite the problem (28) for simple notation:

$$\max_{\mathbf{x,p,L,r,t}} \quad \sum_s U(x_s, p_s) \tag{31}$$

$$s.t. \quad P(x_s, L_s, r_s) \le p_s \tag{32}$$

$$x_s \le x_{gp}(t_s, L_s, r_s) \tag{33}$$

$$x_s^{min} \le x_s \le x_s^{max}, \; r_s^{min} \le r_s \le r_s^{max}$$

$$L_s^{min} \le L_s \le L_s^{max}, \; p_s^{min} \le p_s \le p_s^{max}$$

$$\sum_s t_s \le 1, \; t_s \ge 0, \; \forall s$$

The problem (31) can be solved by the primal-dual decomposition, as explained in Palomar & Chiang (2007). First, we consider a primal decomposition of problem (31) by fixing the scheduling of the channel time allocation **t**. Then the problem (31) becomes two optimization problems as follows:

$$\max_{\mathbf{x},\mathbf{p},\mathbf{L},\mathbf{r}} \quad \sum_s U_s(x_s, p_s) \tag{34}$$

$$\text{s.t.} \quad P_s(x_s, L_s, r_s) \leq p_s \tag{35}$$

$$x_s \leq x^s_{gp}(L_s, r_s), \quad \forall s \tag{36}$$

$$x_s^{min} \leq x_s \leq x_s^{max}, \ r_s^{min} \leq r_s \leq r_s^{max}$$

$$L_s^{min} \leq L_s \leq L_s^{max}, \ p_s^{min} \leq p_s \leq p_s^{max}$$

and

$$\max_{\mathbf{t}} \quad \sum_s U_s^*(\mathbf{t}) \tag{37}$$

$$\sum_s t_s \leq 1, \ t_s \geq 0, \quad \forall s$$

where $U_s^*(\mathbf{t})$ is the optimal objective value of each source in (34) for a given **t**. The coupled constraints of (34) are decomposed by taking log of the constraints (35) and (36) and transforming optimization variables as $\tilde{x}_s = \log x_s, \tilde{p}_s = \log p_s, \tilde{L}_s = \log L_s$ and $\tilde{r}_s = \log r_s$ as in Chiang et al. (2007); Lee et al. (2006). Consequently the problem in (34) becomes

$$\max_{\tilde{\mathbf{x}},\tilde{\mathbf{p}},\tilde{\mathbf{L}},\tilde{\mathbf{r}}} \quad \sum_s \tilde{U}_s(\tilde{x}_s, \tilde{p}_s) \tag{38}$$

$$\text{s.t.} \quad \tilde{P}_s(\tilde{x}_s, \tilde{L}_s, \tilde{r}_s) \leq \tilde{p}_s$$

$$\tilde{x}_s \leq \tilde{x}^s_{gp}(\tilde{L}_s, \tilde{r}_s), \quad \forall s$$

$$\tilde{x}_s^{min} \leq \tilde{x}_s \leq \tilde{x}_s^{max}, \ \tilde{r}_s^{min} \leq \tilde{r}_s \leq \tilde{r}_s^{max}$$

$$\tilde{L}_s^{min} \leq \tilde{L}_s \leq \tilde{L}_s^{max}, \ \tilde{p}_s^{min} \leq \tilde{p}_s \leq \tilde{p}_s^{max}$$

where $\log y_s^{min} = \tilde{y}_s^{min}$, $\log y_s^{max} = \tilde{y}_s^{max}$ and $\log y_s = \tilde{y}_s$ and $y_s \in \{x_s, L_s, r_s, p_s\}$, and the functions $\tilde{U}_s(\tilde{x}_s, \tilde{p}_s)$, $\tilde{P}_s(\tilde{x}_s, \tilde{L}_s, \tilde{r}_s)$ and $\tilde{x}^s_{gp}(\tilde{L}_s, \tilde{r}_s)$ can be derived from the complete formulation presented below.

$$\max_{\tilde{\mathbf{x}},\tilde{\mathbf{p}},\tilde{\mathbf{L}},\tilde{\mathbf{r}}} \quad -\sum_s \left(a_1 e^{-a_2 \tilde{x}_s} + \frac{e^{\tilde{p}_s}}{I_r(1 - e^{\tilde{p}_s})} D_{ECP} \right)$$

$$\text{s.t.} \quad \tilde{x}_s + d_{max} \left[\log 8 + \tilde{L}_s + \log(p_1 e^{p_2 e^{\tilde{r}_s}} + p_3 e^{p_4 e^{\tilde{r}_s}}) \right] - \log(e^{\tilde{L}_s} - h_{ov}) - \log(8V_r) \leq \tilde{p}_s$$

$$\tilde{x}_s \leq \log(t_s) + \log(8N_{SD}) + \log(e^{\tilde{L}_s} - h_{ov}) + \tilde{r}_s$$

$$+ \log \left[1 - 8e^{\tilde{L}_s} (p_1 e^{p_2 e^{\tilde{r}_s}} + p_3 e^{p_4 e^{\tilde{r}_s}}) \right] - \log(A_0 e^{\tilde{r}_s} + A_1 e^{\tilde{L}_s} + A_2)$$

$$\tilde{x}_s^{min} \leq \tilde{x}_s \leq \tilde{x}_s^{max}, \quad \tilde{r}_s^{min} \leq \tilde{r}_s \leq \tilde{r}_s^{max}$$
$$\tilde{L}_s^{min} \leq \tilde{L}_s \leq \tilde{L}_s^{max}, \quad \tilde{p}_s^{min} \leq \tilde{p}_s \leq \tilde{p}_s^{max}, \quad \forall s$$

where

$$A_0 = 2N_{SD}(T_{Preamble} + T_{Sig} + SIFS),$$
$$A_1 = \frac{8T_{symbol}}{\log_2 M_o^s} \text{ and } A_2 = \frac{8L_{ack}T_{symbol}}{\log_2 M_o^s}$$

The problem (38) is a convex optimization problem and satisfies the Slater's qualification condition. Therefore, the Lagrangian duality can be used to obtain the optimal solutions (Boyd & Vandenberghe (2004)) which is called as a dual decomposition in Palomar & Chiang (2007). The partial Lagrangian of the problem (38) is

$$\begin{aligned}\mathcal{L}(\tilde{\mathbf{x}}, \tilde{\mathbf{P}}, \tilde{\mathbf{L}}, \tilde{\mathbf{r}}, \breve{}, \mathbf{fl}) &= \sum_s \tilde{U}_s(\tilde{x}_s, \tilde{p}_s) + \sum_s \left[\gamma_s\left(\tilde{p}_s - \tilde{P}_s(\tilde{x}_s, \tilde{L}_s, \tilde{r}_s)\right) + \lambda_s\left(\tilde{x}_{gp}^s(\tilde{L}_s, \tilde{r}_s) - \tilde{x}_s\right)\right] \\ &= \sum_s \mathcal{L}_s(\tilde{x}_s, \tilde{p}_s, \tilde{L}_s, \tilde{r}_s, \lambda_s, \gamma_s)\end{aligned}$$

where λ and γ are Lagrange multipliers. Moreover, the Lagrangian dual function is given as follows:

$$Q(\lambda, \gamma) = \max_{\tilde{\mathbf{x}}, \tilde{\mathbf{p}}, \tilde{\mathbf{L}}, \tilde{\mathbf{r}}} \sum_s \mathcal{L}_s(\tilde{x}_s, \tilde{p}_s, \tilde{L}_s, \tilde{r}_s, \lambda_s, \gamma_s) \tag{39}$$
$$\tilde{x}_s^{min} \leq \tilde{x}_s \leq \tilde{x}_s^{max}, \quad \tilde{r}_s^{min} \leq \tilde{r}_s \leq \tilde{r}_s^{max}$$
$$\tilde{L}_s^{min} \leq \tilde{L}_s \leq \tilde{L}_s^{max}, \quad \tilde{p}_s^{min} \leq \tilde{p}_s \leq \tilde{p}_s^{max}$$

The problem (39) can be solved at each source since the Lagrangian is separable. Therefore, the dual problem is also solved separately as follows:

$$\min_{\lambda \geq 0, \gamma \geq 0} \sum_s Q_s(\lambda_s, \gamma_s) \tag{40}$$

where

$$Q_s(\lambda_s, \gamma_s) = \max_{\tilde{x}_s, \tilde{p}_s, \tilde{L}_s, \tilde{r}_s} \mathcal{L}_s(\tilde{x}_s, \tilde{p}_s, \tilde{L}_s, \tilde{r}_s, \lambda_s, \gamma_s)$$

The dual problem is solved by the gradient projection method if the dual function $Q_s(\lambda_s, \gamma_s)$ is differentiable as in D.P.Bertsekar (2003):

$$\lambda_s^{k+1} = \left[\lambda_s^k - \eta^k \frac{\partial Q_s}{\partial \lambda_s}\right]^+,$$

$$\gamma_s^{k+1} = \left[\gamma_s^k - \eta^k \frac{\partial Q_s}{\partial \gamma_s}\right]^+$$

where η^k is a positive step size at iteration k, and $[\cdot]^+$ denotes the projection onto the nonnegative orthant. The projection operation guarantees that the Lagrange multipliers λ and γ satisfy their nonnegative conditions. In the previous formulation, we solve the optimization problem (34) for given the channel time $\mathbf{t}$. Here, we solve the master primal problem (37) using the subgradient method in D.P.Bertsekar (2003); Johansson & Johansson (2005). The subgradient of $U_s^*(t_s)$ with respect to t_s is given by $\lambda_s^*(t_s)\frac{\partial \tilde{x}_{gp}^s(t_s)}{\partial t_s}$ (Johansson & Johansson (2005)) where $\lambda_s^*(t_s)$ is the optimal Lagrange multiplier associated with the constraint $\tilde{x}_s \leq \tilde{x}_{gp}^s(\tilde{L}_s, \tilde{r}_s)$ in (38) for a given t_s. Therefore, the master primal problem (37) updates the channel time allocation $\mathbf{t}$ as follows:

$$\tilde{\mathbf{t}}^{k+1} = \mathbf{t}^k + \eta^k \begin{bmatrix} \lambda_1^*(t_1)\tilde{x}_{gp}^{\prime 1}(t_1) \\ \vdots \\ \lambda_s^*(t_s)\tilde{x}_{gp}^{\prime s}(t_s) \end{bmatrix}, \quad \mathbf{t}^{k+1} = \left[\tilde{\mathbf{t}}^{k+1}\right]_{\mathcal{P}} \tag{41}$$

where $\tilde{x}_{gp}^{\prime s}(t_s) = \frac{\partial \tilde{x}_{gp}^s(t_s)}{\partial t_s}$ and $[\cdot]_{\mathcal{P}}$ denotes the projection onto the feasible convex set $\mathcal{P} \triangleq \{\mathbf{t} : \mathbf{t} \succeq 0, \sum_s t_s \leq 1\}$. Due to the projection, this subgradient update cannot be performed independently by each source. A coordinator in a BSS can solve the primal problem. The projection onto the feasible convex set can be formulated as another optimization problem as follows:

$$\min_{\mathbf{t}} \parallel \mathbf{t} - \tilde{\mathbf{t}} \parallel^2 \tag{42}$$
$$s.t. \sum_s t_s \leq 1, \ \ t_s \geq 0, \ \ \forall s$$

The problem (42) is formulated from the fact that the projected point $\mathbf{t}$ from $\tilde{\mathbf{t}}$ minimizes the distance between two points. This problem can be solved using the very efficient algorithm in Palomar (2005).
If a picture is segmented as multiple slices, the problem (31) is modified as follows:

$$\max_{\mathbf{x},\mathbf{p},\mathbf{L},\mathbf{r},\mathbf{t},\mathbf{n}} \ \sum_s U(x_s, p_s) \tag{43}$$
$$s.t. \ \ N(x_s, n_s) \leq 8(L_s - h_{ov}) \tag{44}$$
$$P(L_s, r_s) \leq p_s \tag{45}$$
$$x_s + X_{SL}(x_s, n_s) \leq x_{gp}(t_s, L_s, r_s) \tag{46}$$
$$x_s^{min} \leq x_s \leq x_s^{max}, \ \ r_s^{min} \leq r_s \leq r_s^{max}$$
$$L_s^{min} \leq L_s \leq L_s^{max}, \ \ p_s^{min} \leq p_s \leq p_s^{max}$$
$$n_s^{min} \leq n_s \leq n_s^{max}, \ \ \sum_s t_s \leq 1, \ \ t_s \geq 0, \quad \forall s$$

where $X_{SL}(x_s, n_s) = \kappa_1(n_s - 1) + \kappa_2\sqrt{x_s}\log(n_s)$ from (14) and (15), and the slice length $N(x_s, n_s)$ is the number of bits per slice, that is, $\frac{x_s + X_{SL}(x_s,n_s)}{V_r} \cdot \frac{1}{n_s}$. The closeness of a coded slice to the bound in (44) is limited by the optimal MAC frame size which satisfies Constraint 1. This constraint is an active constraint at an optimal solution, that is, the slice length $N(x_s, n_s)$ is equal to information bits of one MAC frame $8(L_s - h_{ov})$. Equation (46) and utility functions in (43) are derived from the experimental results of subsection 2.2 the number of slices does not affect source-induced distortion but rather source-coded bit rates. Therefore, a source-coded bit rate (one sliced source code rate) x_s is increased by bit increments $X_{SL}(x_s, n_s)$ according to the number of slices and a coding bit rate x_s. However, utility functions are not functions of the sum of x_s and $X_{SH}(x_s, n_s)$ in order to maintain distortion at x_s since they do not depend on $X_{SH}(x_s, n_s)$ which are bit increments of the number of slices. If equation (44) is satisfied, the error probability of slices p_s of (45) is just error probability of a MAC frame after ARQ because one MAC frame only carries one slice. Thus, $P(L_s, r_s)$ is $(8L_sP_b^s)^{d_{max}}$. Here, one more optimization variable n is added for the number of slices. The complete mathematical formulation of (43) is described as follows:

$$\max_{\mathbf{x},\mathbf{p},\mathbf{L},\mathbf{r},\mathbf{n},\mathbf{t}} \quad -\sum_s \left(a_1 x_s^{-a_2} + \frac{p_s}{I_r(1-p_s)} D_{ECP} \right) \tag{47}$$

$$s.t. \quad \frac{x_s + \kappa_1(n_s - 1) + \kappa_2\sqrt{x_s}\log(n_s)}{V_r \cdot n_s} \le 8(L_s - h_{ov}) \tag{48}$$

$$\left(8L_s(p_1 e^{p_2 r_s} + p_3 e^{p_4 r_s}) \right)^{d_{max}} \le p_s \tag{49}$$

$$x_s + \kappa_1(n_s - 1) + \kappa_2\sqrt{x_s}\log(n_s) \le t_s \cdot N_{SD} \frac{8(L_s - h_{ov})(1 - P_{fr}^s)}{A_0 + \frac{8L_s T_{symbol}}{r_s \log_2 M_o^s} + \frac{8L_{ack} T_{symbol}}{r_s \log_2 M_o^s}} \tag{50}$$

$$x_s^{min} \le x_s \le x_s^{max}, \quad r_s^{min} \le r_s \le r_s^{max}, \quad L_s^{min} \le L_s \le L_s^{max}$$

$$p_s^{min} \le p_s \le p_s^{max}, \quad n_s^{min} \le n_s \le n_s^{max}, \quad \sum_s t_s \le 1, \quad t_s \ge 0, \quad \forall s$$

where $P_{fr}^s = 8L_s(p_1 e^{p_2 r_s} + p_3 e^{p_4 r_s})$ and $s \in S$, and S is a set of utility functions which transmit their video streams. Utility functions $U(x_s, p_s)$ in (43) are the negative sum of (11) and (9) which was discussed in section 2.2for maximization. The constraints (48) and (49) are relaxed from the equality constraints of a slice length and slice error probability. Equation (50) shows that the source bit rate should be less than or equal to the goodput of MAC layer. The main solutions of this problem are the source code rate x, the MAC frame size L, the channel code rate r, the number of slices n and channel time allocation t among the optimization variables. The slice error probability p can be considered as an auxiliary variable.

The problem (43) is also solved by the primal-dual decomposition method. First, we perform a primal decomposition of the problem (43) by fixing scheduling of the channel time allocation **t**. Then the problem (43) becomes two optimization problems as follows:

$$\max_{\mathbf{x},\mathbf{p},\mathbf{L},\mathbf{r},\mathbf{n}} \quad \sum_s U(x_s, p_s) \tag{51}$$

$$s.t. \quad N(x_s, n_s) \le 8(L_s - h_{ov})$$

$$P(L_s, r_s) \le p_s$$

$$
\begin{aligned}
& x_s + X_{SL}(x_s, n_s) \le x_{gp}(L_s, r_s) \\
& x_s^{min} \le x_s \le x_s^{max}, \ r_s^{min} \le r_s \le r_s^{max} \\
& L_s^{min} \le L_s \le L_s^{max}, \ p_s^{min} \le p_s \le p_s^{max} \\
& n_s^{min} \le n_s \le n_s^{max}
\end{aligned}
\tag{52}
$$

and

$$
\begin{aligned}
\max_{\mathbf{t}} \quad & \sum_s U_s^*(\mathbf{t}) \\
& \sum_s t_s \le 1, \ t_s \ge 0, \quad \forall s
\end{aligned}
\tag{53}
$$

where $U_s^*(\mathbf{t})$ is the optimal objective value of each source in (51) for given $\mathbf{t}$. The problem has strong duality and thus, the Lagrangian duality can be applied to obtain the optimal solutions. The procedure to solve the problem (43) is almost the same as that for the problem (31).

4. Coexistence among utility functions with or without cross-layer optimization

In the practical environment, we consider coexistence among cross-layered utility functions and conventional utility functions which do not support cross-layer optimization. First, a conventional coordinator which does not solve the primal optimization problem (53) cooperates with cross-layered utility functions. In this case, cross-layered utility functions decide optimal solutions by solving the problem (51) for given channel times. This is just one instance of iterative optimization between primal-dual optimization. Second, a coordinator, which solves the primal optimization problem (53), coexists with conventional utility functions. In this case, each utility function needs to feedback its own subgradient $\lambda_s^*(t_s)\frac{\partial \tilde{x}_{gp}^s(t_s)}{\partial t_s}$, which was explained in the previous section, to a coordinator and then the coordinator can update channel time allocation $\mathbf{t}$ as the equations (41).

The issue is how conventional utility functions estimate their subgradient. In this optimization problem, the subgradient is $\frac{\lambda_s^*(t_s^k)}{t_s^k}$ but allocated channel times for utility functions are already available at the coordinator. Therefore, each utility function only needs to feedback its own λ_s^* for a given channel time t_s^k. The remain problem is how to estimate λ_s^* in the conventional utility functions. We can easily estimate an approximate value $\hat{\lambda}_s$ of λ_s^* from RD optimization of H.264 video encoder. The RD optimization is not standard part of H.264 (2009) but the reference software model of H.264 JM (2007) supports the RD optimization for better performance. The RD optimization is formulated as follows:

$$
\min_{\mathbf{m}} \quad \sum_{n=1}^{N} d_n(\mathbf{m}_n) \quad s.t. \quad \sum_{n=1}^{N} x_n(\mathbf{m}_n) \le X_F \tag{54}
$$

where $\mathbf{m}_n = (M_n, \mathbf{MV}_n, QP_n, \mathbf{Ref}_n)$ which is a vector of Macro Block (MB) mode, Motion Vectors (MVs), Quantization Parameter (QP) and reference frames for inter prediction. N is the number of MBs in a frame, and X_F is the bit constraint of a frame. d_n and x_n are distortion and coded bits of the nth MB, respectively. The optimization problem (54) can be solved by the Lagrangian duality as follows:

$$q(\lambda) = \min_{\mathbf{m}} \sum_{n=1}^{N} \Big(d_n(\mathbf{m}_n) + \lambda x_n(\mathbf{m}_n) \Big) - \lambda X_F \tag{55}$$

and its dual problem is

$$\max_{\lambda \geq 0} q(\lambda) \tag{56}$$

If we know the optimal solution of the dual problem (56), we can obtain the solution of the primal problem (54) after solving (55). However, in order to simplify the above optimization problems, the relation between λ and QP was derived in Sullivan & Wiegand (1998); Takagi (2002); Weigand et al. (2003); Wiegand & Girod (2001), and estimation of X_F from QP was studied in Chiang & Zhang (1997); Kim (2003). Thus, the reference software model of H.264 JM (2007) has the following relation:

$$\lambda = \kappa 2^{\frac{(QP-12)}{3}}, \tag{57}$$

$$X_F = \gamma \frac{MAD}{Q_{step}} + \xi \frac{MAD^2}{Q_{step}^2}, \quad Q_{step} = \nu 2^{\frac{QP-12}{6}} \tag{58}$$

where κ is a function of slice types (I, P, B), the number of referenced frames and QP. γ and ξ are estimated using linear regression based on Mean Absolute Difference (MAD) and target bits X_F. ν is a function of QP. Equations (57) and (58) provide an approximate solution for λ of the dual problem (56), that is, QP is estimated from (58) for the given constraint X_F and then λ is induced from (57). Lee et al. (2000); Li et al. (2003) proposed how to estimate target bits X_F from video frame rate, buffer fullness, picture type and some other information.

If average value of the bit constraint X_F is well estimated to match with goodput x_{gp} of (52), average λ of the RD optimization is close to λ^* of subgradient. However, the RD optimization λ is obtained from original variables, but λ^* of subgradient is decided from transformed variables which is denoted in (38). Therefore, we need to find out the relation between transformed domain λ_t and original domain λ. Sullivan & Wiegand (1998) presented $\lambda = -\frac{dD(x)}{dx}$ such that transformed domain $\lambda_t = -\frac{dD(\tilde{x})}{d\tilde{x}} = -\frac{dD(x)}{dx} \cdot \frac{dx}{d\tilde{x}} = \lambda x$, where $\tilde{x} = \log x$.

In summary, the rate control algorithm of the video encoder changes QP not to overflow nor underflow a buffer which means rate of video encoder follows goodput of the network layer, and then λ of original domain is derived from (57). The approximate of subgradient $\hat{\lambda}$ is obtained from multiplication of λ and current coded rate. Average value of the approximate subgradient $\hat{\lambda}$ is transferred to a coordinator to receive updated channel time allocation.

If channel-induced distortion is considered, Reichel et al. (2007) described that λ is changed into $\lambda_{err} = (1-p) \cdot \lambda$. Consequently, conventional utility functions feedback average value of $(1-p) \cdot \lambda \cdot x$ to a coordinator. In order to decide error probability p, there are two ways from the PHY layer to the application layer (bottom-up) and from the application layer to the PHY layer (top-down). In the bottom-up case, error probability of the application layer can be derived from error probability of the network layer after maximizing goodput.

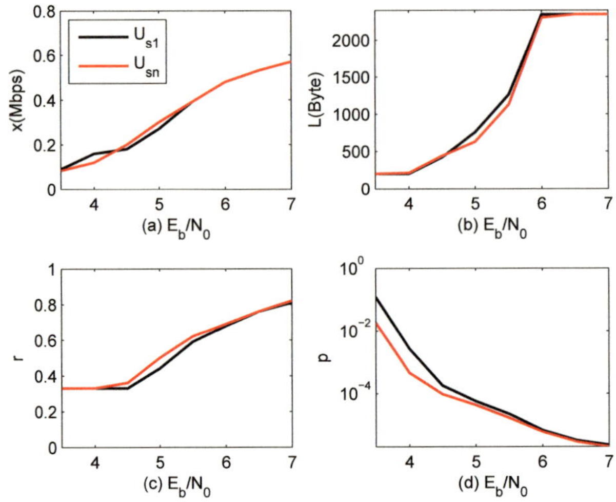

Fig. 12. Optimization variables (x, r, L and p) of a single-sliced utility function and a multiple-sliced utility function from An & Nguyen (2008a) (©[2008] IEEE).

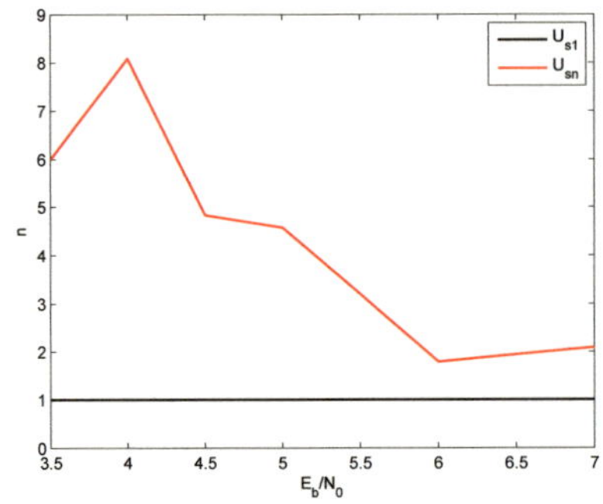

Fig. 13. The optimal number of slices of a multiple-sliced utility function from An & Nguyen (2008a) (©[2008] IEEE).

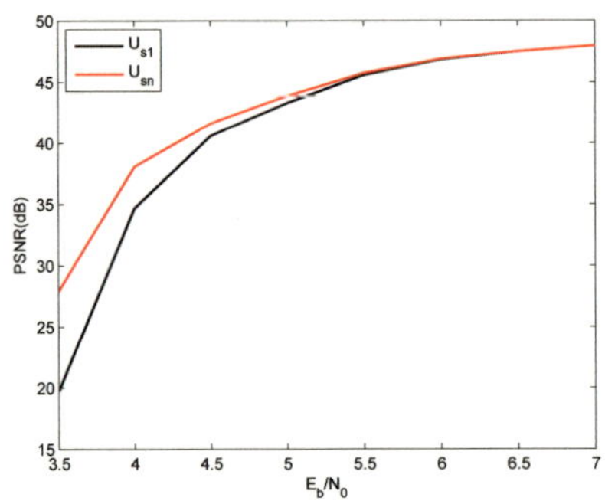

Fig. 14. PSNR of a single-sliced utility function vs. PSNR of a multiple-sliced utility function from An & Nguyen (2008a) (©[2008] IEEE).

5. Numerical Examples

In this chapter, 802.11a-like MAC and 802.11a (1999) PHY are considered for simulations. Main differences from standard 802.11 are TDMA access, fixed modulation, continuous channel code rate and adaptive MAC frame size without MAC fragmentation. The modulation is fixed as BPSK ($M_o^s = 2, \forall s$), and the channel code rate can be changed continuously from the mother code of RCPC to the maximum code rate. The other parameters of the PHY layer are the same as in 802.11a (1999). For simplicity, the maximization of negative end-to-end distortion is solved by the minimization of end-to-end distortion, but we still call the functions as utility functions instead of loss functions.

5.1 Single-sliced utility function vs. Multiple-sliced utility function

In this example, we compare performance of a multiple-sliced utility function U_{sn} with a single-sliced utility function U_{s1}. Here, we only solve the sub-dual problem (51) for U_{sn} and the sub-dual problem in problem (34) for U_{s1} for a given channel time. As a result, the optimal source code rate x, channel code rate r, MAC frame size L and the number of slices n of each utility function are obtained. Figures 12 and 13 show primal optimization variables of two utility functions. From Figure 12 (d), slice error probability p of U_{sn} is smaller than error probability of U_{s1} because the optimal number of slices of U_{sn} is larger as shown in Figure 13. Thus, the source and channel code rate of U_{sn} are higher since less error correction is needed which is shown at $E_b/N_0 > 4.5$ in Figures 12 (a) and (c). However, the source code rate x of U_{sn} is lower at $E_b/N_0 \leq 4.5$ because U_{sn} use channel bit rates for slice coding at the same channel code rate r. From Figure 13, the optimal number of slices increases as SNR decreases which is consistent with general intuition. However, the optimal number of slices is smaller at SNR 3.5 than SNR 4 as shown in Figure 13. The main reason is that the relative bit increments (penalty) w.r.t. the number of slices are larger at low bit rate which is shown in Figure 8 and the optimal source code rate x is decreased to satisfy the network capacity from SNR 3.5 to 4. Figure 14 indicates that gain from the picture segmentation is larger especially at low SNR.

5.2 Channel time allocation for multiple-sliced video coding

In this subsection, we consider channel time allocation for single-sliced and multiple-sliced utility functions. Furthermore, we will present that the optimal channel time allocation highly depends on video contents. For this work, we consider the following simulation environment: there are two BSSs which are completely separate. In each BSS, there are 16 utility functions (single node may have multiple utility functions) which send different video streams. All the utility functions denoted as U_{s1}^s in one BSS code each video picture as a single slice, and utility functions U_{sn}^s in the other BSS use multiple slices for error resilient video coding. All the utility functions operate at SNR 5dB. Multiple-sliced utility functions solve the problem (51), and single-sliced utility functions solve the corresponding subproblem in the problem (34) for given channel times $\mathbf{t}$ which was done in subsection 5.1 Here, the channel times $\mathbf{t}$ are iteratively allocated to utility functions after a coordinator solves the master problem (53). Reallocated channel times are transferred to each node by a beacon signal. Each utility function solves the optimization problem (51) for updated channel times and then feedbacks its subgradient to the coordinator during the contention period. The coordinator updates channel times based on subgradients from all the utility functions within a BSS after solving the problem (53). Thus, a coordinator and utility functions within a BSS keep iteratively solving the optimization problem (53) and (51), respectively.

In order to present dependency between channel times and video contents, utility functions stream different video sequences in two BSSs. However, we only explain multiple-sliced utility functions in one BSS since the situation is the same to single-sliced utility functions in the other BSS. Five utility functions including U_{sn}^{0} send the Football sequence which has high motion in video frames, and another four utility functions along with U_{sn}^{1} send the Crew sequence which has medium motion, and the others including U_{sn}^{2} send the Foreman sequence which has low motion characteristics. Figure 3 shows that different video sequences need different bit rates to achieve similar PSNR, for example the Foreman sequence with low motion needs a lower bit rate than the Football sequence with high motion to obtain similar PSNR. Although there are 16 utility functions within a BSS, the results of three representative utility functions U_{sn}^{0}, U_{sn}^{1} and U_{sn}^{2} are only explained, because the other utility functions operate the same as their representative utility functions.

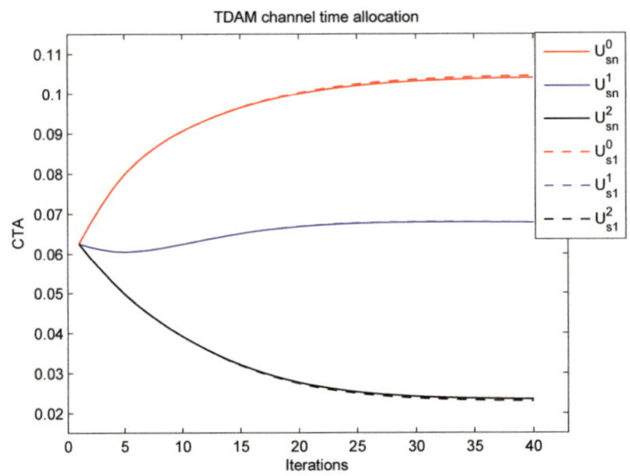

Fig. 15. Channel time allocation of three utility functions with one slice and multiple slices from An & Nguyen (2008a) (©[2008] IEEE).

From Figure 15, channel times are equally allocated to all the utility functions at the initial iteration in both BSSs. All the utility functions solve the optimization problem for given channel times, and their end-to-end distortion D_t in Figure 16 are calculated based on their optimal solutions as shown in Figure 12. From Figures 15 and 16, equal channel time allocation induces larger distortion to U_{s1}^{0} and U_{sn}^{0} which send the high-motion video streams. After several iterations, distortion of U_{s1}^{0} and U_{sn}^{0} is significantly reduced as channel times for U_{s1}^{0} and U_{sn}^{0} increase. On the contrary, distortion of U_{s1}^{2} and U_{sn}^{2} is a little bit increased due to smaller channel times. Thus, the sum of distortion of utility functions can be diminished. In Figure 15, utility functions with multiple slices induce less channel time variations from the initial iteration to the last iteration because utility functions with error resilient feature have less distortion as shown in Figure 16. However, the variations mainly depend on video contents. We can approximately allocate the same channel times without consideration of picture segmentation. In spite of similar channel time allocation, distortion of multiple-sliced utility functions U_{sn}^{s} is lower than single-sliced utility functions U_{s1}^{s} as shown in Figure 16. In addition, distortion gap among the utility functions is further reduced due to multiple slices. Figure 17 illustrates the optimal number of slices of U_{sn}^{0}, U_{sn}^{1} and U_{sn}^{2} according to the allocated channel times where the number of slice of U_{s1}^{s} is one. The more channel time is allocated to a utility function, the more number of slices is needed.

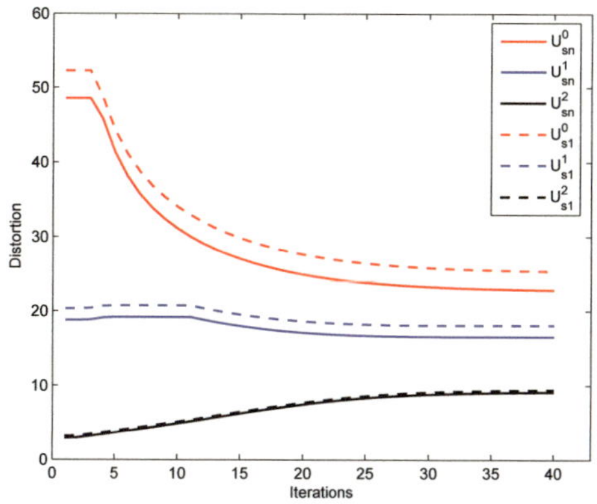

Fig. 16. End-to-end distortion D_t of three utility functions with one slice and multiple slices from An & Nguyen (2008a) (©[2008] IEEE).

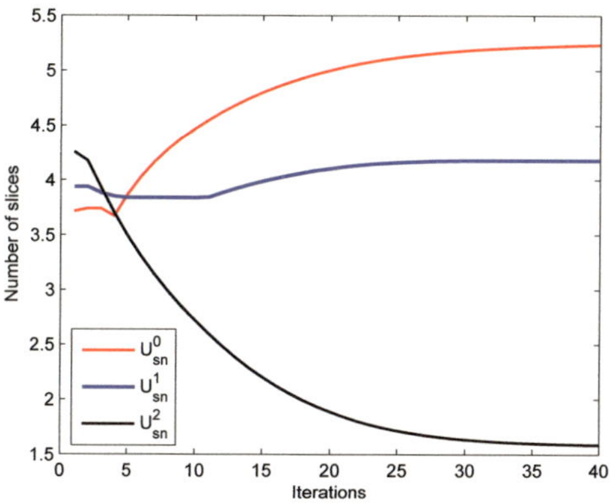

Fig. 17. Optimal number of slices of three utility functions with multiple slices from An & Nguyen (2008a) (©[2008] IEEE).

6. Conclusion

In this chapter, we show that elaborate mathematical models for resource allocation of the source code rate, channel code rate, MAC frame length and multiple slice coding with channel time allocation of TDMA can be formulated as a convex optimization problem. We also derive a mathematical model for multiple-sliced video coding to describe trade-offs between coding efficiency and error protection, and then we apply it for the joint optimization with the MAC and PHY layer constraints. The optimal sliced video coding gives larger gain at especially low SNR. Furthermore, error resilient video coding can achieve better performance along with the optimal channel time allocation. In this work, we use the distortion function as an objective method to evaluate video quality, and then we find optimal solutions to minimize the sum of end-to-end distortion.

7. References

802.11 (1999). Part 11:wireless lan medium access control (MAC) and physical layer (PHY) specifications.

802.11a (1999). Part 11: Wireless lan medium access control (MAC) and physical layer (PHY) specifications: Higher speed physical layer in the 5 ghz band.

802.11e (2005). Wireless lan medium access control (MAC) and physical layer (PHY) specifications : Medium access control (mac) quality of service enhancements.

An, C. & Nguyen, T. Q. (2007). Analysis of utility functions for video, *Proc. IEEE ICIP*.

An, C. & Nguyen, T. Q. (2008a). Resource allocation for error resilient video coding over awgn using optimization approach, *IEEE Trans. Image Processing* 17: 2347–2355.

An, C. & Nguyen, T. Q. (2008b). Resource allocation for TDMA video communication over AWGN using cross-layer optimization approach, *IEEE Trans. on Multimedia* 10: 1406–1418.

Boyd, S. & Vandenberghe, L. (2004). *Convex Optimization*, Cambridge University Press.

Bystrom, M. & Modestino, J. W. (2000). Combined source-channel coding schemes for video transmission over an additive white gaussian noise channel, *IEEE J. Select. Areas Commun.* 18: 880–890.

Cheung, G. & Zakhor, A. (2000). Bit allocation for joint source/channel coding of scalable video, *IEEE Trans. Image Processing* 9: 340 – 356.

Chiang, M., Low, S. H., Calderbank, A. R. & Doyle, J. C. (2007). Layering as optimization decomposition: A mathematical theory of network architectures, *Proc. of IEEE*. to appear.
URL: *http://www.princeton.edu/ chiangm/publications.html*

Chiang, T. & Zhang, Y.-Q. (1997). A new rate control scheme using quadratic rate distortion model, *IEEE Trans. Circuits Syst. Video Technol.* 7: 246–250.

Chiew, T.-K., Hill, P., Ferre, P., Agrafiotis, D., Chung-how, J. T., Nix, A. & Bull, D. R. (2005). Error-resilient low-delay h.264/802.11 transmission via cross-layer coding with feedback channel, *Proc. Visual Communications and Image Processing*.

Chou, P. A. & Miao, Z. (2006). Rate-distortion optimized streaming of packetized media, *IEEE Trans. Multimedia* 8: 390–404.

Cote, G., Shirani, S. & Kossentini, F. (2000). Optimal mode selection and synchronization for robust videocommunications over error-prone networks, *IEEE J. Select. Areas Commun.* 18: 952–965.

D.P.Bertsekar (2003). *Nonlinear Programming*, second edn, Athena Scientific.

H.264, I.-T. R. (2009). Advanced video coding for generic audiovisual services.

Hagenauer, J. (1988). Rate-compatible punctured convolutional codes (RCPC Codes) and their applications, *IEEE Trans. Commun.* 34: 389–400.

Haratcherev, I., Taal, J., Langendoen, K., Lagendijk, R. & Sips, H. (2005). Fast 802.11 link adaptation for real-time video streaming by cross-layer signaling, *Proc. IEEE ISCAS*.

Haratcherev, L., Taal, J., Langendoen, K., Lagendijk, R. & Sips, H. (2006). Optimized video streaming over 802.11 by cross-layer signaling, *IEEE Communications Magazine* 8: 115–121.

Harmanci, O. & Tekalp, A. (2005). Rate distortion optimized slicing over bit error channels, *Proc. SPIE*.

Hochwald, B. & Zeger, K. (1997). Tradeoff between source and channel coding, *IEEE Trans. Inform. Theory* 43: 1412–1424.

Izzat, I., Mayer, M., Rhodes, R. & Stahl, T. (2005). Real time transmission of mpeg2 video over 802.11a wireless lans, *Proc. IEEE ICCE*.

JM (2007). *H.264/AVC reference software (JM11.0)*, HHI.
URL: *http://iphome.hhi.de/suehring/tml/download/*

Johansson, B. & Johansson, M. (2005). Primal and dual approaches to distributed cross-layer optimization, *Proc. 16th IFAC World Congress*.

k. Jain, A. (1989). *Fundamentals of Digital Image Processing*, Prentice-Hall International Editions.

K, S., Farber, N., Link, M. & Girod, B. (2000). Analysis of video transmission over lossy channels, *IEEE J. Select. Areas Commun.* 18: 1012 – 1032.

Kalman, M. & Girod, B. (2005). Optimal channel-time allocation for the transmission of multiple video streams over a shared channel, *Proc. IEEE MMSP*.

Kelly, F. P., Maulloo, A. & Tan), D. (1998). Rate control for communication networks: Shadow prices, proportional fairness and stability, *J. Oper. Res. Soc.* 49: 273–252.

Kim, H. (2003). Adaptive rate control using nonlinear regression, *IEEE Trans. Circuits Syst. Video Technol.* 13: 432–439.

Lee, H., Chiang, T. & Zhang, Y. (2000). Scalalble rate control for mpeg-4 video, *IEEE Trans. Circuits Syst. Video Technol.* 10: 878–894.

Lee, J. W., Chiang, M. & Calderbank, R. A. (2006). Price-based distributed algorithm for optimal rate-reliability tradeoff in network utility maximization, *IEEE J. Select. Areas Commun."* 24: 962–976.

Li, Z., Zhu, C., Ling, N., Yang, X., Feng, G., Wu, S. & Pan, F. (2003). A unified architecture for real-time video-coding systems, *IEEE Trans. Circuits Syst. Video Technol.* 13: 472– 487.

Lin, S. & Costello, D. J. (2004). *Error Control Coding*, second edn, Prentice Hall.

Masala, E., Yang, H., Rose, K. & Marthin, J. D. (2004). Rate-distortion optimized slicing, packetization and coding for error resilient video transmission, *Proc. IEEE DCC*.

Palomar, D. (2005). Convex primal decomposition for multicarrier linear mimo transceivers, *IEEE Trans. Signal Processing* 53(12): 4661–4674.

Palomar, D. & Chiang, M. (2007). Alternative distributed algorithms for network utility maximization: Framework and applications. to be published.
URL: *http://www.princeton.edu/ chiangm/publications.html*

Qiao, D. & Choi, S. (2001). Goodput enhancement of ieee 802.11a wireless lan via link adaptation, *Proc. IEEE ICC*.

Reichel, J., Schwarz, H. & e. Wien, M. (2007). Joint scalable video model jsvm-9.

Richardson, I. E. G. (2003). *H.264 and MPEG-4 video compression: video coding for next-generation Multimedia*, John Wiley & Sons Press.

Sullivan, G. J. & Wiegand, T. (1998). Rate-Distortion Optimization for Video Compression, *IEEE Signal Processing Mag.* 15: 74–99.

Takagi, K. (2002). Lagrange Multiplier and RD-characteristics.

Taubman, D. S. & Marcellin, M. W. (2002). *JPEG2000 : Image Compression Fundamentals, Standards and Practice*, Kluwer Academic Publishers.

Wang, Y., Wu, Z. & Boyce, J. M. (2006). Modeling of transmission-loss-induced distortion in decoded video, *IEEE Trans. Circuits Syst. Video Technol.* 16: 716–732.

Weigand, T., Schwarz, H., Joch, A., Kossentini, F. & Sullivan, G. J. (2003). Rate-Constrained Coder Control and Comparison of Video coding Standards, *IEEE Trans. Circuits Syst. Video Technol.* 13: 688–703.

Wenger, S. (2003). H.264/avc over ip, *IEEE Trans. Circuits Syst. Video Technol.* 13: 645–656.

Wiegand, T. & Girod, B. (2001). Lagrange multiplier selection in hybrid video coder control, *Proc. IEEE ICIP*.

Wu, Q., Chan, S.-C. & Shum, H.-Y. (2006). A convex optimization-based frame-level rate control algorithm for motion compensated hybrid dct/dpcm video coding, *Proc. IEEE ICIP*.

Wu, Z. & Boyce, J. M. (2007). Adaptive error resilient video coding based on redundant slices of h.264/avc, *Proc. IEEE ICME*.

Z.He, j. Cai & Chen, C. W. (2002). Joint source channel rate-distortion analysis for adaptive mode selection and rate control in wireless video coding, *IEEE Trans. Circuits Syst. Video Technol.* 12: 511–523.

11

An Adaptive Error Resilient Scheme for Packet-Switched H.264 Video Transmission

Jian Feng[1], Yu Chen[2,3], Kwok-Tung Lo[2] and Xudong Zhang[3]
[1]Dept. of Computer Science, Hong Kong Baptist Uni.,
[2]Dept. of Electronic and Information Eng., Hong Kong Polytechnic Uni.,
[3]Dept. of Electronic Eng., Tsinghua Uni., Beijing,
[1,2]Hong Kong
[3]China

1. Introduction

When applying conventional standard video codecs in wireless video applications, error resilience and coding efficiency are the two main issues need to be considered. Since it is difficult to corroborate robust quality of service (QoS) in wireless networks, transmitted video packets are sometime lost or corrupted due to fading and shadowing effect of wireless channel. Providing robust video transmission in wireless packet-switched networks is therefore a challenging task as compressed video is very vulnerable to channel error.
In recent years, many error resilient tools have been proposed to enhance the robust performance of video transmission in wireless environment (Chen et al., 2008)(Stockhammer et al., 2003) (Stockhammer et al., 2005) (Vetra et al., 2005) (Wang et al., 2000) (Wiegand et al. 2003). Coding efficiency is one of the important issues to be taken into account for the limited bandwidth of wireless networks (Etoh and Yoshimura, 2005). To achieve a robust video transmission over wireless channels, the video codec on one hand should have supreme error resilient performance, on the other hand, it should also maintain a good coding efficiency by limiting the overhead information introduced by the error resilient tools. Hence, a good compromise between the error resilience performance and coding efficiency should be made.
Interactive error control is one of the effective error resilient techniques adopted in video codec. In this category, some error resilient techniques based on data hiding are proposed (Zeng, 2003) (Yilmaz and Alatan, 2003) (Kang and Leou, 2005). In such techniques, the important information for error concealment is extracted and embedded into video bitstream at the video encoder. When some packets are lost or corrupted, their corresponding embedded data at proper positions can enhance the error concealment effect at the video decoder. Although data hiding methods can obtain satisfied error resilient effect, their notable increase of bits overhead is disadvantageous for coding efficiency. Since the principle of embedding important information (Yin el al., 2001) they adopted modifies the original AC coefficients, not only video quality is degraded, but also coding overhead will be increased significantly. In wireless channels, as the transmission rate is limited, an obvious increase on coding overhead results in inevitable delay. Moreover, in wireless

packet-switched networks, when a packet arrives at receiver beyond the maximum system waiting time, the receiver will consider this as packet lost [11]. Hence, embedded information should be essential and refined.
In order to simultaneously obtain better error resilient performance and preserve original coding efficiency in the video stream, a low redundancy error resilient scheme for H.264 video transmission in packet-switched environment is proposed in this chapter. The proposed method firstly utilizes content analysis to classify macroblocks (MBs) in a P frame into four categories with different protection measures. Each MB will then be protected by inserting proper information in next frame, which is determined by its protection type. Considering limited bandwidth of wireless channel, the inserted redundancy is selected as concise as possible while it can still facilitate error concealment to obtain better reconstruction effect. Finally, with the feedback from receiver, an adaptive transmission strategy of video packet is developed to effectively mitigate the required transmission rate especially in low packet loss rate (PLR) environments. Simulation results on H.264 JM 8.2 codec in different PLRs show that the proposed method can obviously outperform some reference methods in both PSNR and subjective quality. And it just brings little increase in coding overhead.
In the following of this chapter, a review on various error resilient techniques for wireless video transmission will be reviewed in section 2. A new error resilient scheme for H.264 video will then be described in section 4. Simulation results will be presented and discussed in section 4. Finally, some concluding remarks will be given in section 5.

2. Error resilient video coding

With the rapid development of wireless communications technologies, the demand for transmission of various video contents over wireless environments has been greatly increasing in recent few years. Therefore, providing robust video transmission in wireless environments draws much people's attention from different communities. However, it is a challenging task to make video information robust in wireless transmission. First, the quality of service (QoS) of wireless channel is hardly reliable for its high bit error rate and limited transmission bandwidth. Second, as techniques like predictive coding and variable length coding are generally adopted in most of the existing video codecs, it will cause not only spatial error propagation in present frame, but also temporal error propagation in successive frames. Hence, the visual quality at the receiving end will be greatly reduced.
To achieve an optimum transmission over a noisy wireless channel, both the source coding and network should be jointly adapted. An acceptable video quality in wireless environment can be obtained by the adjustment of parameters in video codec and wireless network. For the former, people have proposed many error resilient video encoding algorithms to enhance the robust performance of the compressed video stream in wireless networks (Wang and Zhu, 1998) (Villasenor et al, 1999) (Wang et al., 2000) (Chen et al., 2008). These algorithms can be divided into three categories: 1) error detection and error concealment algorithms used at video decoder of wireless receiver; 2) error resilient video encoding algorithms located at video encoder of wireless transmitter; 3) robust error control between video encoder and decoder based on 1) and 2). Figure 1 summarizes different techniques at different parts of a wireless video transmission system.

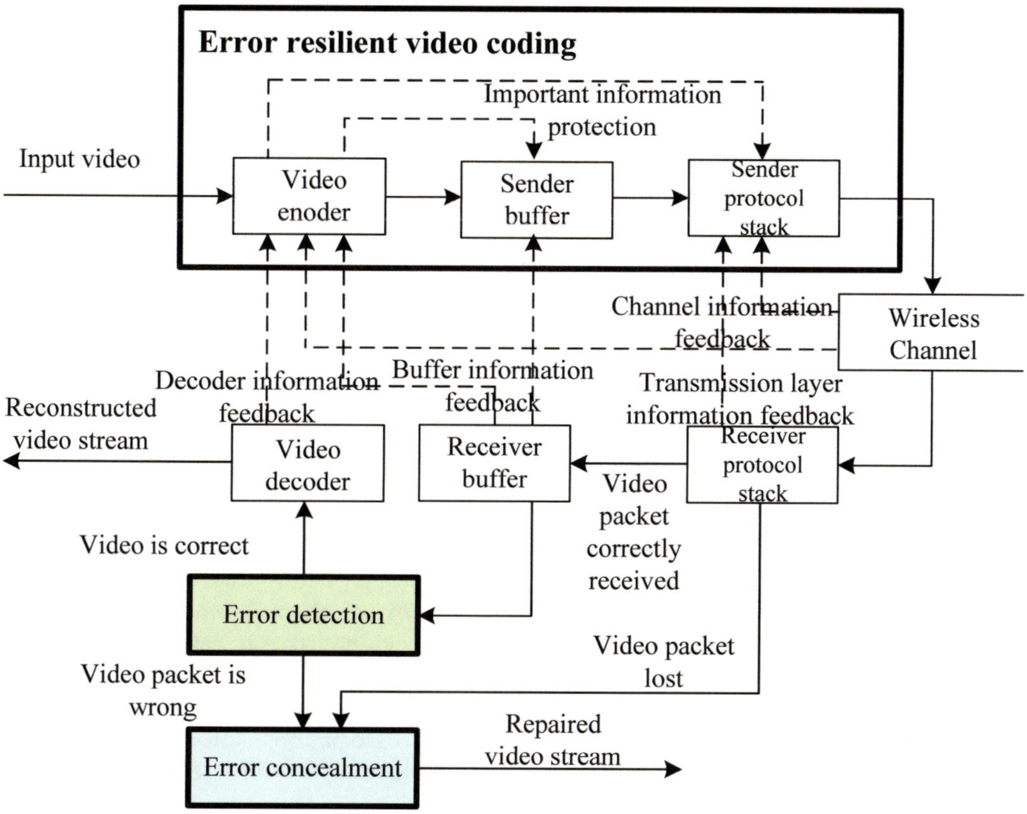

Fig. 1. Error resilient methods used in packet-switched wireless networks

Since error concealment algorithms are only used at video decoder in wireless receiver, they do not require any modification of video encoder and channel codec. Hence, there is not any increase of coding computing complexity and transmission rate. Therefore, error concealment algorithms can be easily realized in present wireless video transmission system. However, since error concealment algorithms make full use of spatial and temporal correlation in video stream to estimate the corrupted region of video frames, when the correlation between corrupted region and correctly received frames is weak, error concealment algorithms cannot achieve good effect so that there is apparent distortion in repaired reconstructed video frames. In addition, although error concealment algorithms can reduce the intensity of temporal error propagation, it cannot reduce the length of temporal error propagation. As we know, human visual system (HVS) is not very sensitive to short term obvious error propagation while long term even slight error propagation will annoy the observation of HVS impressively. Therefore, desirable error repaired effect should make the intensity and length of error propagation minimum simultaneously.

In order to compensate the defects of error concealment algorithms, a number of error resilient video encoding algorithms had been developed in the last decade to make the compressed video stream be accustomed to wireless transmission environment. These algorithms can be divided into five categories as discussed in the following.

The first category is concerned on the location of error protection information. Its main purpose is to reduce the length and intensity of spatial and temporal error propagation. In this category, four kinds of representative algorithms are developed based on resynchronization mode, adaptive intra coding, flexible reference frame and multiple reference frames.

The second category of error resilient algorithms utilizes data partition scheme to aggregate same type of syntax information, such as the aggregation of motion vector, header and texture information. When channel error appears in this type of video stream, all of information in the same region is not simultaneously wrong, and there is some correct information left for corrupted region. So with residual correct information, coarse reconstruction effect is still achieved at video decoder, which is always more satisfactory than that of error concealment.

The redundant error resilient video encoding algorithms can efficiently improve the performance of robust decoding for their inserted redundancy to mitigate the corrupted probability of video stream. Reversible Variable Length Coding (RVLC) (Takishima et al., 1995) can effectively reduce the range of spatial error propagation by reversely decoding from the position of next resynchronization mode with expense of apparent increase of encoding overhead. Multiple Description Coding (MDC) (Wang et al., 2005) divides conventional compression video stream into several pieces of sub-video stream, and each of them has same priority for transmission. When any of them is corrupted or lost in transmission, residual correctly received pieces of video stream can still be used to reconstruct coarse picture. Flexible Graphic Scalable (FGS) coding (Jens-rainer, 2005) is another type of error resilient algorithms to adopt multiple layers coding for video compression. In FGS coding, there are depending associations among base layer and enhanced layers that if only base layer is correctly decoded, the other enhancement layers can be decoded.

The fourth category is developed to compensate the defects of existing error concealment algorithms. For the spatial and temporal correlation in video stream is not always high, and the correct data used as reference by error concealment is not always enough, practical prediction effect of error concealment is not precise, whose final repaired effect is not better than direct replacement and weighted interpolation. In order to avoid this, some essential verification information are necessary to add into original video stream in order to improve the preciseness of error concealment prediction effect.

The last category is the wireless channel based error resilient video coding algorithms (Stockhammer et al. 2002). With respect to original rate distortion optimization (RDO) model in conventional video codec, these algorithms are designed to get better video quality and compression efficiency simultaneously. This type of RDO model may not be best suited to the wireless transmission environment. The distortion caused by channel error should be taken into RDO model so that the corresponding optimization parameters in the RDO model can be adjusted according to varied channel parameters, such as, packet lost rate (PLR), bit error rate (BER) and burst error average length (BEAL).

3. Content-based error resilient scheme

In a generic packet-based video transmission system (Katsaggelos et al., 2005), both the source coding and network will be jointly adapted to achieve an optimum transmission over a noisy channel.

A formulation is given in (Katsaggelos et al., 2005) to minimize the cost required to send video stream confined to a desirable level of distortion and tolerable delay. This is suitable for mobile terminal where transmission power, computational resource and wireless bandwidth are limited. The optimization for this formulation is

$$C_{tot}(S^*,N^*)=\min C_{tot}(S,N) \ \ \{S^* \in S, N^* \in N\} \tag{1}$$

$$s.t.: D_{tot}(S^*,N^*) \le D_0 \quad \text{and} \quad T_{tot}(S^*,N^*) \le T_0$$

where D_0 is the maximum allowable distortion, and T_0 is the end-to-end delay constraint. Here, S denotes the set including available error resilient source coding types, and N represents the network parameters and transmission strategy to be controlled. S^* and N^* are the best selection of S and N to obtain minimum coding overhead min C_{tot} (S^*,N^*) while their end-to-end distortion $D_{tot}(S^*,N^*)$ is not beyond D_0, and their delay $T_{tot}(S^*,N^*)$ does not exceed T_0.
In this chapter, one effort is to find an optimized error resilient tool S^* from S that can guide error concealment to get the best reconstruction effect with minimum amount of redundancy. Another effort concerns an adaptive transmission strategy N^* for video packets based on the receiver's feedback to reduce burden on channel overhead. Here, we assume that network parameters, such as channel coding and network protocols, have been optimized.

3.1 New error resilient approach

To derive an efficient error resilient scheme, we consider the following issues for embedded video coding used in error resilience: (1) how to use correct evaluation tools to find MBs with important information that is crucial to human vision system (HVS), (2) how to extract these crucial information from the video stream and represent them with minimum bits, and (3) how to add extracted important information into the video stream at proper position with little coding overhead increase and modification on original video stream. Since slice video coding is resilient to wireless channel error, in this paper, we assume that each row of MBs in a P frame is a slice transmitted by a video packet.
To locate the important information in P frames, we consider using the pre-error concealment scheme (Kang and Leou, 2005). In this scheme, a process called pre-error concealment is performed to each MB and the mean absolute error (MAE) between the error-free MB and pre-concealed MB is calculated. Those macroblocks having large MAE values are regarded as important ones since missing of them will result in larger reconstruction error. More embedded protection information will then be allocated to them. However, this result may not be consistent with human visual system. Since mobile video phone and video conference are the common applications of current wireless video communication, the main content of such services is human portrait. According to (Wang et al., 2003), the region of human face is recognized as the foveation area of HVS. In this region, even a slight variation in face between neighboring frames such as blink and smile can draw HVS more attention than other MBs that may have a larger MAE in the background. In this regard, we propose to make a refinement of the pre-error concealment scheme with the concern of HVS by taking into account whether the MB is located in the foveation area or not. The weighted pre-error concealed distortion (WPECD) f_i of the ith MB is defined as follows.

$$f_i = \begin{cases} q_i m_f : (MB_i \in \Gamma) \\ q_i m_{nf} : (MB_i \notin \Gamma) \end{cases} \quad (2)$$

where m_f (m_f >1) and m_{nf} (0< m_{nf} <1) are the weighted values assigned to the MBs in the foveation region and the background, respectively, which are determined by the network parameters and the size of the foveation region. Γ denotes the foveation region (removed), Here, we uses q_i to denote the original pre-error concealed distortion (PECD) value of the ith MB obtained by pre-concealment as follows.

$$q_i = \frac{\sum_{x=1}^{16}\sum_{y=1}^{16} \left| m_{org_i}(x,y) - m_{prc_i}(x,y) \right|}{\sum_{x=1}^{16}\sum_{y=1}^{16} m_{org_i}(x,y)} \quad (3)$$

where $m_{org_i}(x,y)$ and $m_{prc_i}(x,y)$ are the original and pre-concealed pixel value of the luminance component of the ith MB. In this paper, we adopt the error concealment method in (Tsekeridou and Pitas, 2000) to obtain those pre-concealed values.

After identifying the important information, we have to determine which information should be embedded for protecting the content. For the MB having a small PECD value based on (3), it means that the error concealment process can reconstruct the original information with little visual degradation especially in the foveation area (removed) because of the high temporal correlation between the reference MB and lost MB. But when the MB is in the moderate and high motion region, it will have a larger PECD value. If it is lost, existing error concealment methods may not accurately estimate its motion vector (MV), as well as its residual transform coefficients. To measure the deviation of the error concealment method in estimating MV and residual error, the following two parameters are defined.

$$q_{mc_i} = \frac{\sum_{x=1}^{16}\sum_{y=1}^{16} \left| m_{mc_i}(x,y) - m_{prc_i}(x,y) \right|}{\sum_{x=1}^{16}\sum_{y=1}^{16} m_{mc_i}(x,y)} \quad (4)$$

where q_{mc_i} denotes the deviation level between error concealed MB and original motion compensated MB without the residual distortion, $m_{mc_i}(x,y)$ is the original motion compensated pixel value of luminance component of ith MB.

$$q_{res_i} = \frac{\sum_{x=1}^{16}\sum_{y=1}^{16} \left| m_{mc_i}(x,y) - m_{org_i}(x,y) \right|}{\sum_{x=1}^{16}\sum_{y=1}^{16} m_{org_i}(x,y)} \quad (5)$$

where q_{res_i} is the deviation level between original MB and original motion compensated MB. These two parameters reflect to a certain extend the degree of temporal and spatial correlation of subsequent frames. Based on these two factors, we classify MBs in a P frame into four categories (two extra bits are required for MB classification) as follows.

i. *Class I MB*: The MB has a small PECD value, i.e., $q_{mc} < T_{mc}$ or $q_{res} < T_{res}$, where T_{mc} and T_{res} are two thresholds. As mentioned before, the error-concealed effects of Class I MBs are very close to the original video quality. Hence, it is not necessary to insert protection information for them. Also, in most cases, the previous frame is the best predicted frame and there are little distortion among the reconstruction effects of 16×16 block mode and other block modes. Thus, we make a compromise that these MBs can be restored desirably with 16×16 mode and previous frame. Therefore, additional bits overhead for best mode and predicted frame for important MB in (Kang and Leou, 2005) are saved.

ii. *Class II MB:* The MB has a larger PECD value and $q_{mc} >> q_{res}$. In this situation, it is necessary to insert motion vector (MV) information to compensate the defect of error concealment. As in (Kang and Leou, 2005), 16 bits for entire MV of important MB is embedded in next P frame. Based on the method in (Lee et al., 2005), only 8 bits inserted into the video stream for residual MV is enough to regenerate the original MV.

iii. *Class III MB:* The MB has a larger PECD value and $q_{mc} << q_{res}$. In this situation, these MBs are usually intra-coded, and they have stronger correlation with spatial neighboring MBs than that of temporal neighboring MBs. Hence, spatial error concealment is desirable for this category of MBs. We use Soble operator to extract the direction of edge in them as embedded information to facilitate spatial error concealment where 4 bits are used to denote potential 16 possible directions.

iv. *Class IV MB:* The MB has a larger PECD value and ($q_{mc} > T_{mc}$ and $q_{res} > T_{res}$). In this situation, both the spatial and temporal neighboring MBs have certain correlation with this category of MBs. Certainly, corresponding residual MV and edge direction information should be inserted. With respect to the characters of error concealment method in (Al-Mualla et al., 1999), we extract following temporal and spatial correlation parameters q_{t_i} and q_{s_i} of ith MB to enhance its multi-hypothesis error concealment compensation effect.

$$q_{t_i} = 1 - q_{mc_i} \tag{6}$$

$$q_{s_i} = 1 - \frac{\sum_{x=1}^{16}\sum_{y=1}^{16} \left| m_{sperc_i}(x,y) - m_{org_i}(x,y) \right|}{\sum_{x=1}^{16}\sum_{y=1}^{16} m_{org_i}(x,y)} \tag{7}$$

where $m_{sperc_i}(x,y)$ is the spatial pre-error concealed pixel value of the luminance component of ith MB.

$$s_{t_i} = \frac{q_{t_i}}{q_{s_i} + q_{t_i}} \tag{8}$$

$$s_{s_i} = 1 - s_{t_i} \tag{9}$$

where s_{t_i} and s_{s_i} represent the weighted values of temporal and spatial error concealed pixel value of luminance component of ith MB for multi-hypothesis error concealment compensation. The final reconstructed pixel value $m_{mul_i}(x,y)$ of luminance component in i^{th} MB is obtained by

$$m_{mul_i}(x,y) = s_{s_i} m_{sperc_i}(x,y) + s_{t_i} m_{tperc_i}(x,y) \tag{10}$$

where $m_{tperc_i}(x,y)$ equals to above $m_{prc_i}(x,y)$. Here, 4 bits are used for one of these two weighted values inserted into the video stream.

As a result, the total number of inserted bits for these four categories of MBs is only two bits, ten bits, six bits and eighteen bits respectively.

Because the methods in (Yilmaz and Alatan, 2003) and (Kang and Leou, 2005) use the strategy in (Yin et al., 2001) to embed extracted information, video quality and coding efficiency are greatly degraded when the original AC coefficients are modified. In this paper, we directly insert extracted information at the end of each video packet in next P frame with fixed length coding after all of MBs of this video packet have been encoded.

3.2 New adaptive transmission scheme for wireless packet video transmission

In (Yilmaz and Alatan, 2003) and (Kang and Leou, 2005), embedded important information is transmitted in wireless channel without considering whether the protected MBs are received correctly or not. With respect to the practical loss environment mentioned in (Katsaggelos et al., 2005), most of video packets in practical situation can be correctly received. Therefore, when one video packet is correctly received, it is not necessary transmit its protecting information in next frame. Based on the feedback of receiver, an adaptive transmission strategy that determines whether it is necessary to transmit embedded information for video packet is proposed here.

Using QCIF P frame as an example to describe this new transmission strategy as shown in Fig.2 (We assume that one video packet includes one row of MBs in each P frame), when k^{th} P frame arrives at receiver, receiver will find whether some video packets are lost in this frame, and give transmitter a nine bits feedback to represent the receiving situation of nine video packets of kth P frame. If j^{th} ($1 \le j \le 9$) video packet is lost, j^{th} bit in feedback is set as 1 to denote j^{th} packet is lost, and other bits are zero in feedback when their corresponding video packets are correctly received. In the buffer of wireless video transmitter, there are two types of encapsulation for same video packets of $(k+1)^{th}$ P frame to be transmitted, one is TYPE-I packet including original video stream only, the other is TYPE-II packet including both the original video stream and the extracted important information for the video packet of the same position in k^{th} P frame. Hence, when feedback from receiver is 100000000, it means that only first video packet is lost, and others arrive at receiver correctly. Therefore, in wireless video transmitter, only the first video slice is transmitted by the TYPE-II packet followed by other eight TYPE-I video packets. This strategy can effectively mitigate the volume of unnecessary transmitted redundant information in wireless channel especially in low LPR situation. Here, we consider k^{th} P frame is lost when its feedback verification information cannot arrive at transmitter in time. So we have to adopt TYPE-II packet to transmit all of video packets of $(k+1)^{th}$ P frame in this situation.

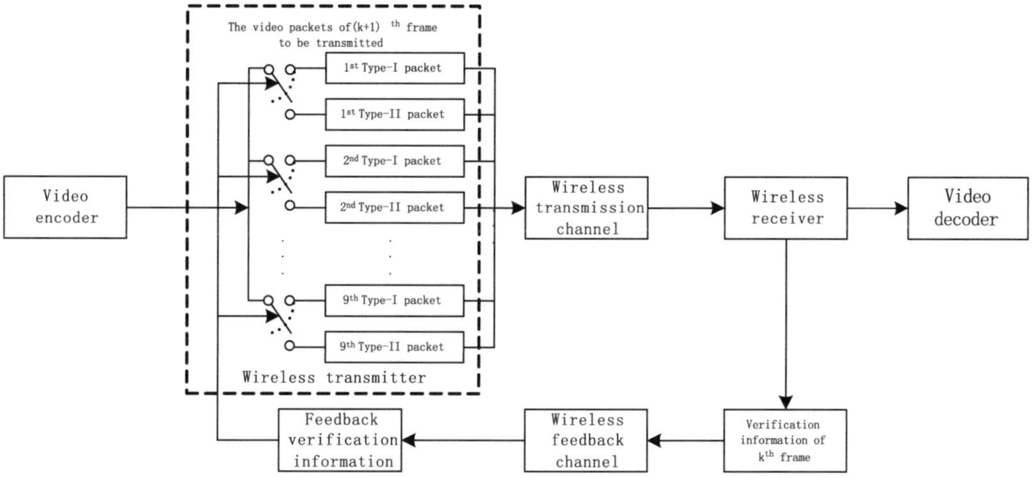

Fig. 2. Adaptive transmission strategy based on feedback information from receiver in QCIF video stream

4. Simulation results

Computer simulations are performed in this section to evaluate the performance of the proposed error resilient scheme for video transmission in noisy environment. In our experiments, the H.264 JM 8.2 baseline codec is used, where the number of reference encoding frame is five. The frames from 5th to 145th frame in QCIF sequences *"Susie"* and *"Foreman"* are used for simulation. The video are encoded as IPPP..., and their QP is set at 28. The wireless channel adopted by simulation is random packet lost channel. We assume that each P frame is transmitted by nine video packets. For q_{mc} and q_{res}, they should be tuned according to real time video content. However, with respect to computation complexity, we assumed that they have fixed value. In simulation, both of them are set as 0.1. We compare our method with the data embedding based error resilient method (Kang and Leou, 2005) with Type-I data (denoted as Ref 1) and both Type-I and Type-II data (denoted as Ref 2).

We first look at the objective performance of error concealed effects in terms of the PSNR value of reconstructed pictures with a PLR as 0.1, which is illustrated in Fig.3. The PSNR result generated by an error free H.264 codec is also plotted in the figure, which is denoted as H.264 JM 8.2. It is seen that the proposed method always has a higher PSNR value than the other methods. For sequence *"Foreman"*, which contains rather high motions, the proposed method has an obvious PSNR improvement with respect to Ref 1 and Ref 2, and its reconstruction effect is also more robust than other methods. In this scene, the average PSNR achieved by Ref 1, Ref 2, our proposed method and H.264 JM 8.2 is 34.97dB, 35.06dB, 35.37dB and 35.77dB respectively. We can find that the achieved PSNR distance between the proposed method and H.264 JM 8.2 is not very apparent. For sequence *"Susie"*, which contains mostly medium motions, the proposed method can still obtain more desirable effect in the middle of selected range of video sequence than other methods, where there is apparent motion of human portrait. While at the beginning and end of selected range of video sequence, where high temporal correlation is in neighboring video frames, there are no apparent difference in reconstruction effect between the proposed method and reference

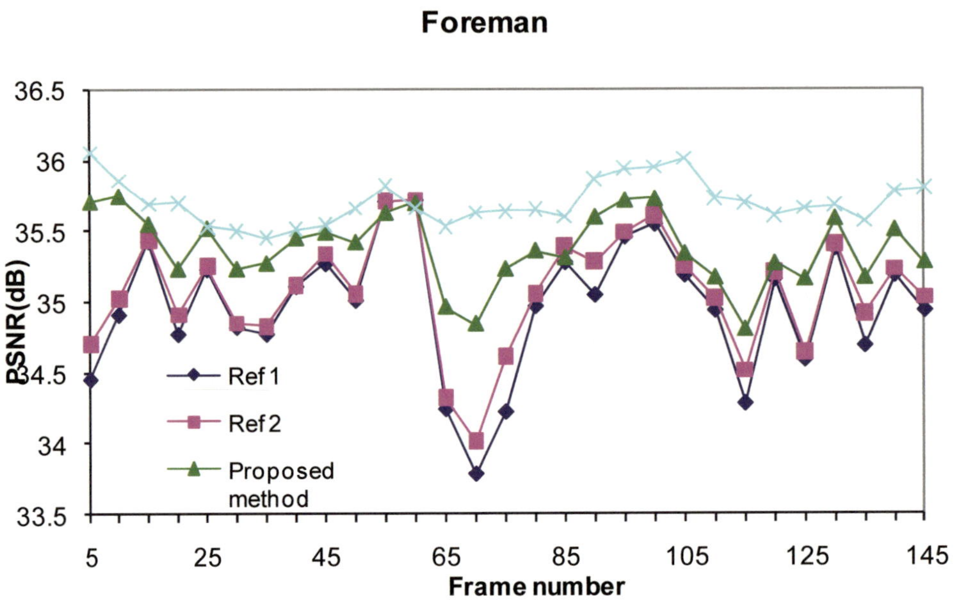

(a)

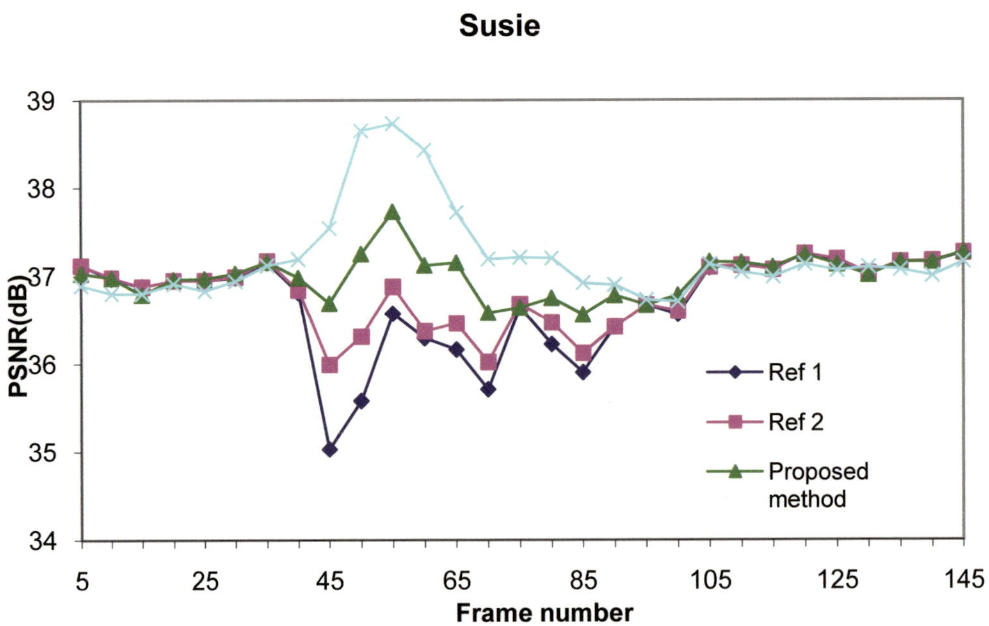

(b)

Fig. 3. Objective error concealed effect comparison between the proposed method and reference methods.

methods. Though the proposed method cannot always outperforms the reference methods in this video sequence, the average PSNR achieved by Ref 1, Ref 2, proposed method and H.264 JM 8.2 is 36.68dB, 36.79dB, 37.01dB and 37.21dB respectively. We can find that the PSNR value of the proposed is very close to that of H.264 JM 8.2. Hence, a better error concealment performance is obtained by our method as it can accurately extract visually important information to be protected.

After evaluating the error concealed effect in Fig.2, we then examine the coding rate requirement to see how many coding overhead is imposed by different error resilient schemes. The results for the two test sequences are shown in Table 1. In the table, only Ref 1 for the method in [9] is shown because it always needs fewer bits than Ref 2 (less data are embedded). It is seen that the coding rate increases for the proposed method are only 9% and 5%, while those of Ref 1 are about 23% and 16 %, for sequence "*Susie*" and "*Foreman*" respectively. It reveals that our method can obtain better coding efficiency as it directly inserts concise important data into the video stream.

Method	Susie	Foreman
H.264 JM8.2	104.73	142.32
Ref 1	128.79	164.78
Proposed method	114.24	149.98

Table 1. Coding rate (kb/s) comparison with the proposed method and comparison methods.

In the following, we apply the proposed adaptive transmission scheme in sending the video in noisy environment. We assume that both the forward channel and feedback channel are random pocket lost channels. We vary PLR in the forward channel and the feedback verification information loss probability (FVILP) in the feedback channel to see the effectiveness of the proposed scheme in saving coding overhead for the error resilient video stream. The results for the two sequences are shown in Table 2 and Table 3, for different PLR and FVILP settings. It is shown that the required transmission rate of the error resilient stream in different PLR can be significantly mitigated by the proposed video packet transmission strategy even in the loss of feedback verification information.

Method\PLR	0.05	0.1	0.15	0.2
H.264 JM8.2	104.73	104.73	104.73	104.73
Ref 1	128.79	128.79	128.79	128.79
Propose method (FVILP = 0)	106.16	106.64	107.12	107.59
Propose method (FVILP = 0.05)	106.56	107.02	107.48	107.92
Propose method (FVILP = 0.1)	106.97	107.4	107.83	108.25
Propose method (FVILP = 0.15)	107.37	107.78	108.19	108.59
Propose method (FVILP = 0.2)	107.77	108.16	108.54	108.92

Table 2. Required transmission rate (kb/s) comparison with the proposed method and comparison methods at different FVILP and PLR in Susie sequence.

Method\PLR	0.05	0.1	0.15	0.2
H.264 JM8.2	142.32	142.32	142.32	142.32
Ref 1	164.78	164.78	164.78	164.78
Propose method (FVILP = 0)	143.66	144.05	144.43	144.81
Propose method (FVILP = 0.05)	143.98	144.35	144.71	145.07
Propose method (FVILP = 0.1)	144.29	144.64	144.99	145.35
Propose method (FVILP = 0.15)	144.61	144.94	145.26	145.59
Propose method (FVILP = 0.2)	144.92	145.24	145.54	145.84

Table 3. Required transmission rate (kb/s) comparison with the proposed method and comparison methods at different FVILP and PLR in Foreman sequence.

And then, we look at the actual visual quality of the reconstructed pictures by different error resilient schemes. The reconstructed pictures of the 22nd frame of "*Foreman*" sequence for different methods are shown in Fig.4. It is seen that the fourth row MBs are lost, with respect to original picture shown by Fig.4(a), the proposed method in Fig.4(d) has more vivid subjective effect in human eyes area than Ref 1 and Ref 2 shown by Fig.4(b) and (c).
Finally, as we know, the proposed algorithm needs q_i , q_{mc} and q_{res} to classify MB. The increasing encoding time for this process is listed in Table 4 for H.264 JM 8.2 baseline profile. In our experiments, the tested hardware platform is DELL Latitude D820 Notebook PC (Intel Core2 Duo 2GHz, 1024 Memory), and the total encoding time of first 150 frames (only first frame is I frame) in *Susie* and *Foreman* video sequence is given. The additional encoding time for these three parameters is limited. The total encoding time increase for them in tested video sequences is only less than 1%.

Sequence	Original	Proposed method	Increase %
Susie	111.58	112.48	0.81%
Foreman	109.17	109.98	0.74%

Table 4. Encoding time (s) comparison between original H.264 JM8.2 and proposed method

5. Conclusions

In this chapter, a review on various error resilient video coding techniques for wireless packet video transmission is given. Then a new error resilient method based on content analysis together with an adaptive transmission scheme are proposed for compressed video transmission over noisy environments. Simulation results show that the proposed method can obtain good error concealment effect with low redundancy by carefully extracting and inserting essential information in video encoder. It is also shown that the proposed adaptive transmission scheme can help further reduce the coding overhead.

(a)

(b)

(c)

(d)

Fig. 4. The error concealment subjective effect comparison between the proposed method and comparison methods. (a) No error, (b) Ref 1, (c) Ref 2, (d) Proposed method.

6. Acknowledgements

The work of K.-T.Lo was supported by the Hong Kong Polytechnic University under Grant A/C 1-BB9G. The work of J. Feng was supported by the Hong Kong Baptist University under Grant No. FRG-06-07-II-06.

7. References

Al-Mualla, M., Canagarajah, N., and Bull, D.R. (1999). Temporal error concealment using motion field interpolation. *IEE Electronics Letters*, Vol.35, No.4, pp.215-217.

Chen, Y., Feng, J., Lo, K.T., and Zhang, X.D. (2008). Wireless Networks: Error Resilient Video Transmission. *Encyclopedia of Wireless and Mobile Communications*, pp.1434-1441, edited by B.Furht, CRC Press, ISBN 9781420043266, USA.

Etoh, M., and Yoshimura, T. (2005). Advances in wireless video delivery. *Proceeding of the IEEE.*, Vol.93, No.1, pp.111-122.

Jens-rainer, O. (2005). Advances in scalable video coding. *Proceedings of the IEEE*, Vol.93, No.1, pp.42-56.

Kang, L.W., and Leou, J.J. (2005). An error resilient coding scheme for H.264 video transmission based on data embedding. *Journal of Visual Communication and Inage Representation*, Vol.16, No.1, pp.93-114.

Katsaggelos, A.K., Eisenberg, Y., Zhai, F., Berry, R., and Pappas, T.N. (2005). Advances in efficient resource allocation for packet-based real-time video transmission. *Proceedings of the IEEE*, Vol.93, No.1, p.135-147.

Lee, J.S., Lim, J.W., Lee, K.H., and Ko, S.J. (2005). Residual motion coding method supporting error concealment in low bitrate video coding. *IEE Electronics* Letters, Vol.41, No.7, pp.406-408.

Stockhammer, T., Kontopodis, D., and Wiegand, T. (2002). Rate-distortion optimization for JVT/H.26L coding in packet loss environment. Proceedings of 2002 Packet Video Workshop, Pittsburgh, USA.

Stockhammer, T., Hannuksela, M.M., and Wiegand, T. (2003). H.264/AVC in wireless environments. *IEEE Trans. Circuits and Systems for Video Technol.*, Vol.13, No.7, pp. 657-673.

Stockhammer, T., and Hannuksela, M.M. (2005). H.264/AVC video for wireless transmission. *IEEE Wireless Communications*, Vol.12, No.4, pp.6-13.

Takishima, Y., Wada, M., and Murakami, H. (1995). Reversible variable length codes. *IEEE Transaction on Communications*, Vol.43, No.2, pp.158-162.

Tsekeridou, S., and Pitas, I. (2000). MPEG-2 error concealment based on block matching principles. *IEEE Trans. Circuits and Systems for Video Technol.*, Vol.10, No.6, pp.874-879.

Vetro, A., Xin, J. and Sun, H.F. (2005). Error resilience video transcoding for wireless communication. *IEEE Wireless Communications*, Vol.12, No.4, pp.14-21.

Villasenor, J., Zhang, Y.Q., and Wen, J. (1999). Robust video coding algorithms and systems. *Proceedings of the IEEE*, Vol.87, No.10, pp. 1724-1733.

Wang, Y., and Zhu, Q.F. (1998). Error control and concealment for video communication: a review. *Proceedings of the IEEE*, Vol. 86, No.5, pp.974-997.

Wang, Y., Wenger, S., Wen, J., and Katsaggelos, A.K (2000). Error resilient video coding techniques. *IEEE Signal Processing Magazine*, Vol.17, No.4, pp.61-82.

Wang, Y., Reibman, A.R., and Lin, S.N. (2005). Multiple descriptions coding for video delivery. Proceedings of the IEEE, Vol.93, No.1, pp.57-70.

Wang, Z., Lu, L., and Bovik, A.C. (2003). Foveation scalable video coding with automatic fixation selection. *IEEE Trans. Image Processing,* Vol. 12, No.2, pp.243-254.

Wiegand, T., Sullivan, G.J., Bjontegaard, G., and Luthra, A. (2003). Overview of the H.264/AVC video coding standard. *IEEE Trans. Circuits and Systems for Video Technol.*, Vol.13, No.7, pp.560-576.

Yilmaz, A., and Alatan, A.A. (2003). Error concealment of video sequence by data hiding. *Proceedings of IEEE ICIP'2003,* Vol.3, pp.679-682, Barcelona, Spain.

Yin, P., Wu, M., and Liu, B. (2001). Error concealment using data hiding. *Proceedings of IEEE ICASSP'2001,* pp.1453-1456, Salt Lake City, Utah, USA.

Zeng, W. (2003). Spatial-temporal error concealment with side information for standard video codecs. *Procedings of ICME2003,* Vol.2, pp.113-116, Baltimore, Maryland, USA.

Part 5

Hardware Implementation of Video Coder

12

An FPGA Implementation of HW/SW Codesign Architecture for H.263 Video Coding

A. Ben Atitallah[1,2], P. Kadionik[2], F. Ghozzi[1], P.Nouel[2],
N. Masmoudi[1] and H. Levi[2]
[1]*Laboratory of Electronics and Information Technology National Engineers School of Sfax (E.N.I.S.), BP W 3038 Sfax*
[2]*IXL laboratory –ENSEIRB - University Bordeaux 1 - CNRS UMR 5818, 351 Cours de la Libération, 33 405 Talence Cedex,*
[1]*Tunisia*
[2]*France*

1. Introduction

Video is fundamental component of a wide spectrum of the multimedia embedded systems. The great interest for digital as opposed to analog video is because it is easier to transmit access, store and manipulate visual information in a digital format. The key obstacle to using digital video is the enormous amount of data required to represent video in digital format. Compression of the digital video, therefore, is an inevitable solution to overcome this obstacle. Consequently, academia and industry have worked toward developing video compression algorithms [1]-[3], which like ITU-T H.261, H.263, ISO/IEC MPEG-1, MPEG-2 and MPEG-4 emerged with a view to reduce the data rate to a manageable level by taking advantage of the redundancies present both spatial and temporal domains of the digital video.

The ITU-T H.263 standard is an important standard for low bit rate video coding, enabling compression of video sequences to a bit rate below 64 kbps [4]. H.263 coding algorithm can be found in different application such as videoconferencing, videophone and video emailing. Due to the different profiles and levels of the H.263 standard, every application can have specific ratio between performance and quality. Since modern digital video communication applications increase both aspects of the H.263 compression, it is therefore necessary to achieve best performance in terms of real-time operation.

The H.263 standard includes several blocks such as Motion Estimation (ME), Discrete Cosine Transform (DCT), quantization (Q) and variable length coding (VLC). It was shown that some of these parts can be optimized with parallel structures and efficiently implemented in hardware/software (HW/SW) partitioned system. However, there exists a trade-off between hardware and software implementation. Various factors such as flexibility, development cost, power consumption and processing speed requirement should be taken into account. Hardware implementation is generally better than software implementation in processing speed and power consumption. In contrast, software can give a more flexible design solution and also be more suitable for various video applications [5].

Recently, several H.263 encoders have been developed either as software based applications [6]-[7] or hardware based VLSI custom chips [8].
In [6], the H.263 implementation based on general purpose microprocessors, including PCs or workstations. All the efforts are focused on the optimization of the code that implements the encoder for the target microprocessor. In [7], an architecture based on a Digital Signal Processor (DSP) is described to implement a real-time H.263 encoder using fast algorithms to reduce the encoder computational complexity. Architecture based on a dedicated sequencer and a specialized processor is detailed in [8]. It is implemented on Xilinx FPGA and carrying out the basic core of H.263 without motion estimation. The depicted architectures lack flexibility because of their dedicated controller.
In literature, we haven't found any description of combined HW/SW implementation of the H.263 encoder on a single chip. The reason is probably the lack of technology that provides efficient HW/SW implementation. With the recent advantages in technology from leading manufacturers of the programmable devices, such as Xilinx [9] and Altera [10], the proposed approach gains importance. In order to take advantages of both software and hardware implementation, each functional module of the H.263 video encoder is studied to determine a proper way for HW/SW partitioning. Based on this study, DCT and inverse DCT (IDCT) algorithm are implemented with fast parallel architectures directly in hardware. Also, the quantization and inverse quantization (IQ) are implemented in hardware using NIOS II custom instruction logic. These parts are described in VHDL (*VHSIC Hardware Description language*) language and implemented with the NIOS II softcore processor in a single Stratix II EP2S60 FPGA (*Field Programmable Gate Array*) device and the remaining parts are performed in software on NIOS II softcore processor and using μClinux , an embedded Linux flavour, as operating system. This partitioning has been chosen in order to achieve better timing results.
This paper is organized as follows: section 2 describes the baseline H.263 video encoder. Section 3 presents the HW/SW codesign platform. Timing optimization of the H.263 encoder using the HW/SW codesign is described in section 4. The design environment and FPFA implementation of the encoder is presented in section 5. The experiment results are shown in section 6. Finally, section 7 concludes the paper.

2. Baseline H.263 video coding

The coding structure of H.263 is based on H.261 [11]. In these standards, motion estimation and compensated are used to reduce temporal redundancies. DCT based algorithms are then used for encoding the motion compensated prediction difference frames. The quantized DCT coefficients, motion vector and side information are entropy coded using variable length codes. In this section, one describes first the picture formats used by H.263 encoders and the organization of pictures into smaller structures. It then reviews the general coding principles used by this encoder and describes their different blocks.

A. Picture format and organization

H.263 supports five standardized picture formats: CIF (Common Intermediate Format), 4CIF, 16CIF, QCIF (quarte-CIF) and sub-QCIF. Custom picture formats can also be negotiated by the encoder. However only the QCIF and sub-QCIF are mandatory for an H.263 decoder and the encoder only needs to support one of them.

The luminance component of the picture is sampled at these resolutions, while the chrominance components, Cb and Cr, are downsampled by two in both the horizontal and vertical directions. The picture structure is shown in Fig.1 for the QCIF resolution. Each picture in the input video sequence is divided into macroblocks (MB), consisting of four luminance blocks of 8 pixels x 8 lines followed by one Cb block and one Cr block, each consisting of 8 pixels x 8 lines. A group of blocks (GOB) is defined as an integer number of MB rows, a number that is dependent on picture resolution. For example, a GOB consists of a single MB row at QCIF resolution.

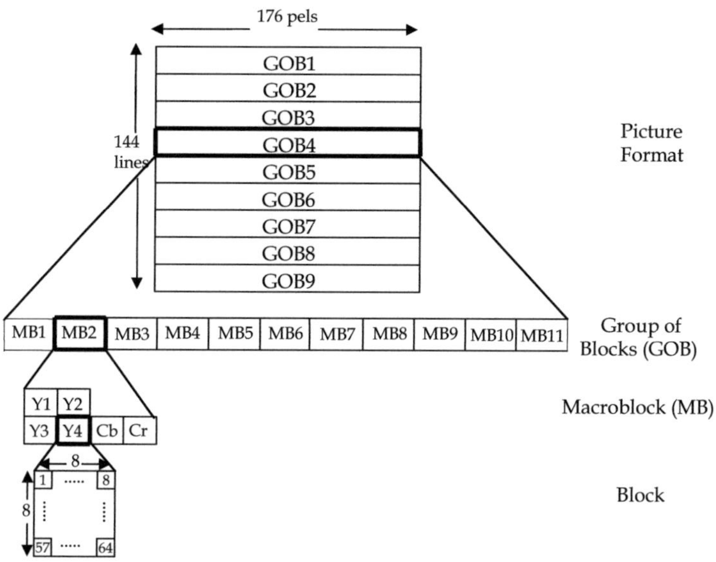

Fig. 1. H.263 picture structure for QCIF resolution

B. Overview of the H.263 video coding standard

The block diagram of an H.263 baseline video encoder is shown in Fig.2. The encoder operation is based on hybrid differential/transform coding, and is a combination of lossy and lossless coding. There are two fundamental modes which are jointly used for maximum compression efficiency: the intra and inter modes. Different types of frames correspond to these modes.

In the intra mode, the contents of a video frame are first processed by a DCT. The resulting coefficients are quantized with a chosen quantizer step size, thus leading to a loss of information. The quantized DCT coefficients are entropy coded using VLC, scanned across the picture (often using a zig-zag strategy), and delivered to an encoder buffer. The intra mode produces intra frames (I-frames). This kind of frame is needed for the decoder to have a reference for prediction. However, I-frames use a large amount of bits, so that they should be used sparingly in low bit rate applications. In the inter mode, the same operations are applied to the motion-predicted difference between the current frame and the previous (or earlier) frame, instead of the frame itself. To this end a motion estimation algorithm is applied to the input frame, and the extracted motion information (in the form of motion vectors, MV) is used in predicting the following frames, through a motion-compensation bloc. In order to avoid a drift between the encoder and decoder due to motion prediction,

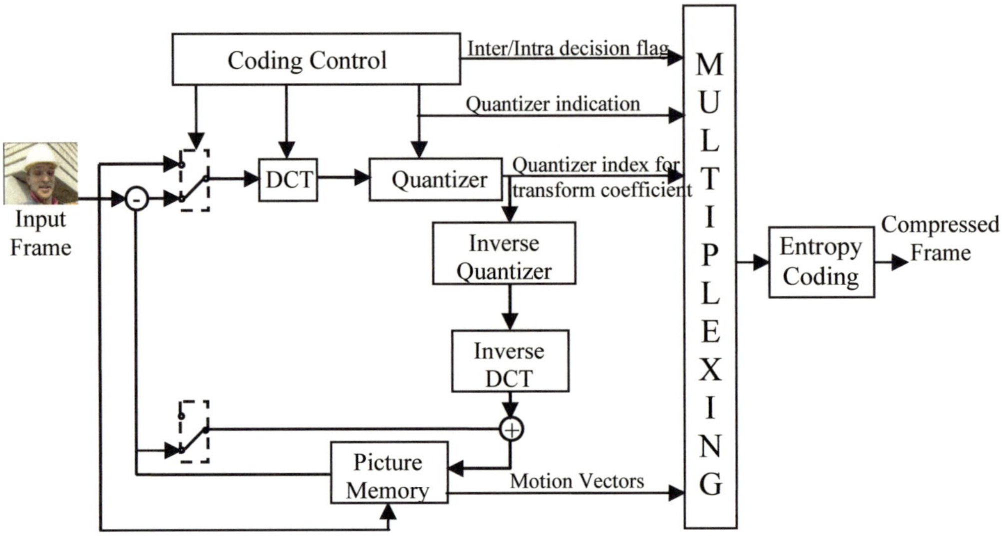

Fig. 2. Baseline H.263 video encoder block diagram

the motion compensation bloc needs to use a locally reconstructed version of the compressed frame being sent: this explains the presence of an inverse quantizer and an inverse discrete cosine transform in the feedback loop. The MV is differentially coded in order to realize bit rate savings. The inter mode produces prediction frames (P-frames) which can be predicted from I-frames or others P-frames. These in general use considerably less bits than I-frames, and are responsible for the large compression gain.

1) Motion estimation and compensation: It is often the case that video frames that are close in time are also similar. Therefore, when coding a video frame, it would be judicious to make as much use as possible of the information presented in a previously coded frame. One approach to achieve this goal is to simply consider the difference between the current frame and a previous reference frame, as shown in Fig. 3, and code the difference or residual. When the two frames are very similar, the difference will be much more efficient to code than coding the original frame. In this case, the previous frame is used as an estimate of the current frame.

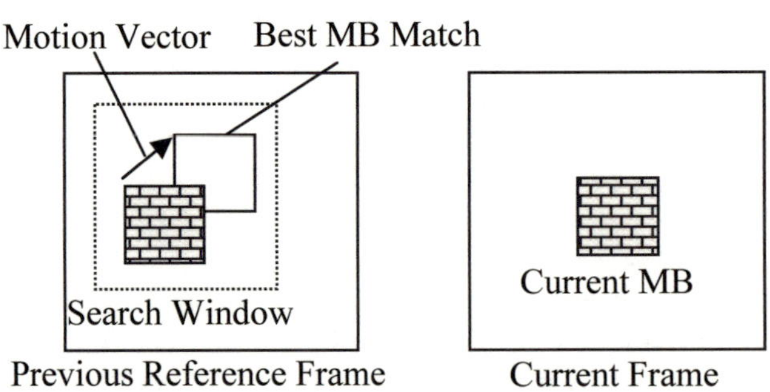

Fig. 3. Block-matching algorithm

A more sophisticated approach to increase coding efficiency is to work at the macroblock level in the current frame, instead of processing the whole frame all at once as described above. The process is called motion compensated prediction, and is based on the assumption that most of the motion that the macroblocks undergo between frames is a translational motion. This approach attempts to find, for each 16x16 luminance block of a macroblock in the current frame, the best matching block in the previous frame. A search window is usually defined and bounds the area within which the encoder can perform the search for the best matching block. The motion of a macroblock is represented by a motion vector that has two components; the first indicating horizontal displacement, and the second indicating vertical displacement. Different criteria could be used to measure the closeness of two blocks [12]. The most popular measure is the Sum of Absolute Differences (SAD) defined by

$$SAD = \sum_{i=0}^{15}\sum_{j=0}^{15}\left|Y_{k,l}(i,j) - Y_{k-u,l-v}(i,j)\right| \tag{1}$$

Where $Y_{k,l}(i,j)$ represents the $(i,j)th$ pixel of a 16 x 16 MB from the current picture at the spatial location (i,j) and $Y_{k-u,l-v}(i,j)$ represents the $(i,j)th$ pixel of a candidate MB from a reference picture at the spatial location (k,l) displaced by the vector (i,j). To find the macroblock producing the minimum mismatch error, we need to compute SAD at several locations within a search window. This approach is called full search or exhaustive search, and is usually computationally expensive, but on the other hand yields good matching results.

2) *DCT Transform*: The basic computation element in a DCT-based system is the transformation of an NxN image block from the spatial domain to the DCT domain. For the video compression standards, N is usually 8. The 8 x 8 DCT is simple, efficient and well suited for hardware and software implementations. The 8 x 8 DCT is used to decorrelate the 8 x 8 blocks of original pixels or motion compensated difference pixels and to compact their energy into few coefficient as possible. The mathematical formulation for the (two-dimensional) 2-D DCT is shown in equation (2) [13].

$$\begin{aligned} y_{k,l} &= \frac{c(k)c(l)}{4}\sum_{i=0}^{7}\sum_{j=0}^{7} x_{i,j}\cos\left(\frac{(2i+1)k\pi}{16}\right)\cos\left(\frac{(2j+1)l\pi}{16}\right) \\ with\quad & c(k),c(l) = \frac{1}{\sqrt{2}}(k,l=0)...otherwise\ 1 \end{aligned} \tag{2}$$

The 2-D DCT in (2) transforms an 8 x 8 block of pictures samples $x_{i,j}$ into spatial frequency components $y_{k,l}$ for $0 \le k,\ j \le l$. The 2-D IDCT in (3) performs the inverse transform for $0 \le i, j \le 7$.

$$x_{i,j} = \frac{1}{4}\sum_{k=0}^{7}\sum_{l=0}^{7} y_{k,l}c(k)c(l)\cos\left(\frac{(2k+1)i\pi}{16}\right)\cos\left(\frac{(2l+1)j\pi}{16}\right) \tag{3}$$

Although exact reconstruction can be theoretically achieved, it is often not possible using finite-precision arithmetic. While forward DCT errors can be tolerated, IDCT errors must meet the H.263 standard if compliance is to be achieved.

3) *Quantization*: The quantization is a significant source of compression in the encoder bit stream. Quantization takes advantage of the low sensitivity of the eye to reconstruction

errors related to high spatial frequencies as opposed to those related to low frequencies [14]. Quick high frequency changes can often not be seen, and may be discarded. Slow linear changes in intensity or color are important to the eye. Therefore, the basic idea of the quantization is to eliminate as many of the nonzero DCT coefficients corresponding to high frequency components.
Every element in the DCT output matrix is quantized using a corresponding quantization value in a quantization matrix. The quantizers consist of equally spaced reconstruction levels with a dead zone centered at zero. In baseline H.263, quantization is performed using the same step size within a macroblock by working with a uniform quantization matrix. Except for the first coefficient of INTRA blocks is nominally the transform DC value uniformly quantized with a step size of eight, even quantization levels in the range from 2 to 62 are allowed. The quantized coefficients are then rounded to the nearest integer value. The net effect of the quantization is usually a reduced variance between the original DCT coefficients as compared to the variance between the original DCT coefficients. Another important effect is a reduction in the number of nonzero coefficients.
4) Entropy coding: Entropy coding is performed by means of VLC, and is used to efficiently represent the estimated motion vectors and the quantized DCT coefficients. Motion vectors are first predicted by setting their component values to median values of those of neighboring motion vectors already transmitted: the motion vectors of the macroblocks to the left, above, and above right of the current macroblock. The difference motion vectors are then VLC coded.

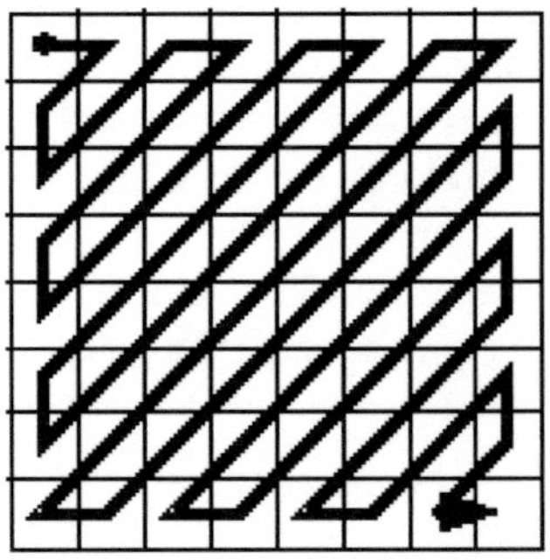

Fig. 4. Zig-zag positioning of quantized transform coefficients

As for the quantized DCT coefficients, they are first converted into a one-dimensional array for entropy coding by an ordered zigzag scanning operation. The resulting array contains a number of nonzero entries and probably many zero entries. This rearrangement places the DC coefficient first in the array, and the remaining AC coefficients are ordered from low to high frequency. This scan pattern is illustrated in Fig. 4. The rearrangement array is coded using three parameters (LAST, RUN, LEVEL). The symbol RUN is defined as the distance between two nonzero coefficients in the array (i.e., the number of zeros in a segment). The symbol LEVEL is the nonzero value immediately following a sequence of zeros. The symbol LAST, when set to 1, is used to indicate the last segment in the array. This coding method produces a compact representation of the 8x8 DCT coefficients, as a large number of the coefficients are normally quantized to zero and the reordering results (ideally) in the grouping of long runs of consecutive zero values. Other information such as prediction types and quantizer indication is also entropy coded by means of VLC.

3. The HW/SW codesign platform

A. FPGA platform

Field Programmable Devices are becoming increasingly popular for implementation of digital circuits. The case of FPGA is the most spectacular and is due to several advantages, such as their fast manufacturing turnaround time, low start-up costs and particularly ease of design. With increasing device densities, audacious challenges become feasible and the integration of embedded SoPC (System on Programmable Chip) systems is significantly improved [15].

Furthermore, reconfigurable systems on a chip became a reality with softcore processor, which are a microprocessor fully described in software, usually in a VHDL, and capable to be synthesized in programmable hardware, such as FPGA. Softcore processors can be easily customized to the needs of a specific target application (e.g. multimedia embedded systems). The two major FPGA manufacturers provide commercial softcore processors. Xilinx offers its MicroBlaze processor [16], while Altera has Nios and Nios II processors [17]. The benefit of a softcore processor is to add a micro-programmed logic that introduces more flexibility. A HW/SW codesign approach is then possible and a particular functionality can be developed in software for flexibility and upgrading completed with hardware IP blocks (Intellectual Property) for cost reduction and performances.

Fig. 5. Stratix II Development Board

B. The NIOS II development board - the HW/SW platform

For SW implementation of image and video algorithms, the use of a microprocessor is required. The use of additional HW for optimization contributes to the overall performance of the algorithm. For the highest degree of HW/SW integration, customization and configurability, a softcore processor was used.

For the main processing stage, the Altera NIOS II development board was chosen (Fig. 5) [18]. The core of the board is the Altera Stratix II EP2S60F672C3 FPGA. Several peripheral devices and connectors (UART, LCD, VGA, Ethernet etc) serve as interfaces between the Stratix II FPGA and the external environment. 8MByte FLASH, 16MByte SRAM and 1MByte SRAM allow implementation of complex FPGA video applications. For the video embedded systems, we are using flash memory, SRAM, SDRAM, UART, timer, Ethernet and Camera for frame acquisition.

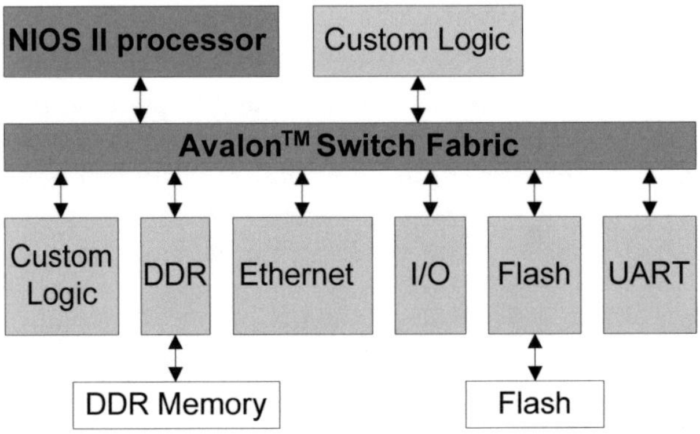

Fig. 6. NIOS II embedded system

Altera introduces the SOPC builder tool [19], for the quick creation and easy evaluation of embedded systems. The integration off-the-shelf intellectual property (IP) as well as reusable custom components is realized in a friendly way, reducing the required time to set up a SoPC and enabling to construct and designs in hours instead of weeks. Fig. 6 presents the Stratix II FPGA with some of the customizable peripherals and external memories, as an example of their applicability.

1) NIOS II CPU: The Altera NIOS II softcore processor (*FAST version*) is a 32-bits scalar RISC with Harvard architecture, 6 stages pipeline, 1-way direct-mapped 64KB data cache, 1-way direct-mapped 64KB instruction cache and can execute up to 150 MIPS [17].

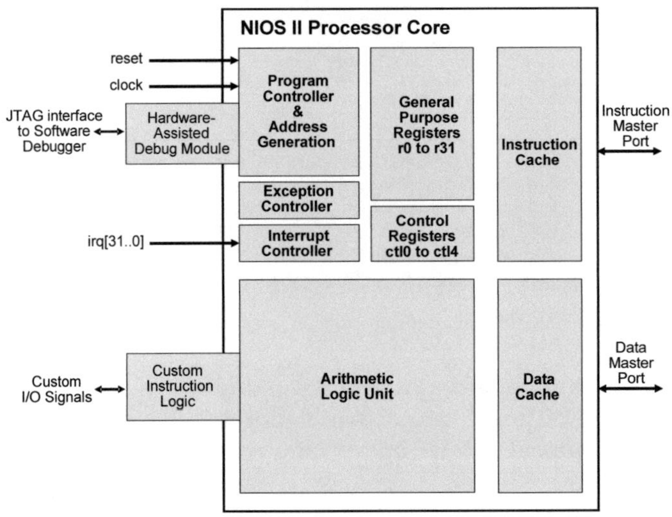

Fig. 7. NIOS II processor core block diagram

The main interest of this softcore processor is its extensibility and adaptability. Indeed, users can incorporate custom logic directly into the NIOS II Arithmetic Logic Unit (ALU) [20]. Furthermore, users can connect into the FPGA the on-chip processor and custom peripherals to a dedicated bus (Avalon Bus). Thus, users can define their instructions and processor peripherals to optimize the system for a specific application. Fig.7 show the block diagram of the NIOS II softcore processor core which defines the following user-visible functional units: register file, arithmetic logic unit, interface to custom instruction logic, interrupt controller, instruction and data bus, instruction and data cache memories and JTAG debug module.

2) *NIOS II custom instruction logic:* With Nios II custom instructions [21], system designers are able to take full advantage of the flexibility of FPGA to meet system performance requirements. Custom instructions allow system designers to add up to 256 custom functionalities to the Nios II processor ALU. As shown in Fig.8, the custom instruction logic connects directly to the Nios II ALU (Arithmetic Logic Unit). There are different custom instruction architectures available to suit the application requirements. The architectures range from simple, single-cycle combinatorial architectures to extended variable-length, multi-cycle custom instruction architectures. The most common type of implementation is the single-cycle combinatorial architecture that allows for custom logic realizations with one or two inputs and one output operand.

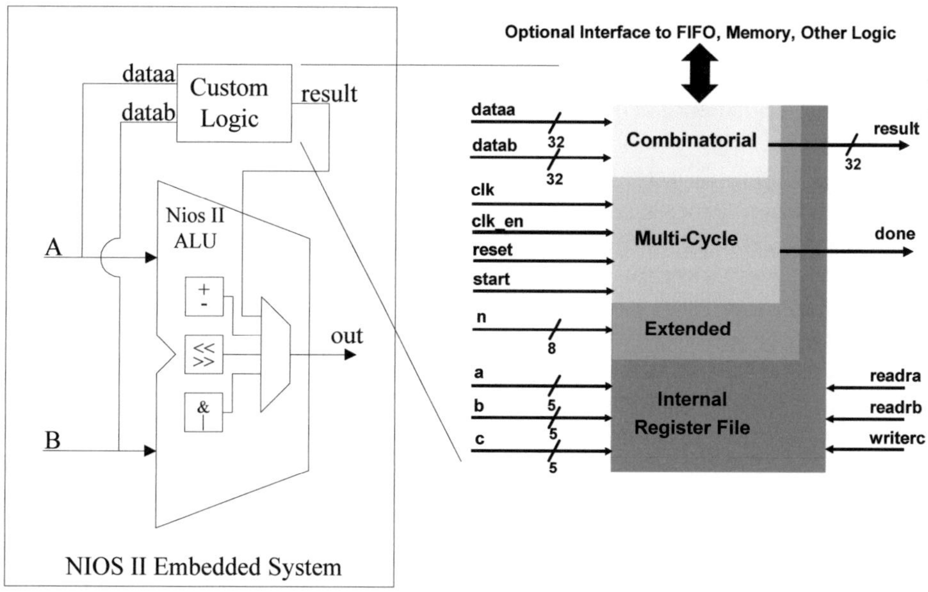

Fig. 8. Custom Instruction Logic Connects to the Nios II ALU

Using the custom instruction in an ANSI C program is straightforward. Two kinds of define macros are used as the instructions can have one or two input operands:

- #define INSTR1(X) __builtin_custom_ini(Code_INSTR1,X)
- #define INSTR2(X,Y) __builtin_custom_ini(Code_INSTR2,X,Y)

C) The HW/SW codesign process

The HW/SW codesign process for the implementation into the platform can be summarized in three main steps:

- Algorithm implementation in SW.
- Detecting critical software parts.
- HW/SW optimization of the algorithm.

The first step is implementing algorithm in SW. The ANSI C language and the assembly programming language are supported. Generally, the preferable choice is the

implementation of the SW code using ANSI C. In this way, instead of rewriting the code from scratch, the use of an already existing code for the algorithm shortens the design cycle. The portability of ANSI C allows also the code to be created and tested for functionality on other platforms.
Once the SW code has been tested for functionality and implemented into the target platform, the performance analysis has to be applied. In order to reach the required constraints, critical software parts has to be detected and optimized. To have precision on the time processing, a CPU timer can be used for the cycle-accurate time-frame estimation of a focused part of the SW code execution.
The final step is the SW code refinement and optimization of critical SW parts using HW description. The general idea is to implement parallel structures in HW for fastest data processing. The SW and HW parts are dependent and, regarding the interface between them, can be incorporated into the algorithm as separate HW component (access register) or custom instruction (the custom instruction is integrated directly into CPU as an additional instruction).
In the HW/SW codesign process, the designer iterates through the last two design steps until the desired performance is obtained.

D) Using embedded linux with codesign

The HW/SW codesign process uses different kinds of peripherals and memories. The basic idea is to use Linux in an embedded system context. Linux for embedded systems or embedded Linux gives us several benefits:

- Linux is ported to most of processors with or without Memory Management Unit (MMU). A Linux port is for example available for the NIOS II softcore.
- Most of classical peripherals are ported to Linux.
- A file system is available for data storage.
- A network connectivity based on Internet protocols is well suited for data recovering.
- Open source Linux projects may be used.

The embedded Linux environment is also a real advantage for the software development during the HW/SW codesign process.

4. Timing optimisation of the H.263 encoder

A) Timing optimisation

In order to optimize and achieve best performance in terms of real-time operation of the H.263 video encoder, we have used the HW/SW codesign process. At first, the algorithms were coded in ANSI C programming language on a PC platform. The tested SW code was then rebuilt and transferred into the Nios II system. The execution times have been measured with the high_res_timer that provides the number of processor clock cycles for the execution time. Afterwards, the SW critical parts were implemented in HW in VHDL language.
In our experiments of coding a general video clip in QCIF (Quarter Common Intermediate Format: Spatial resolution of 176x144 and temporal resolution 10 frames/s (fps)) format. The average frame rate achieved on a NIOS II system is only about 0.7 fps. For this reason, we investigated the resource distribution of the H.263 video encoder which uses full search motion estimation, search window size +/-7 and fixed quantization parameters QP=16. Fig.9 shows the distribution of the execution time of Miss America and Carphone sequences.

In this figure ME, DCT/IDCT and Q/IQ which utilize 23.1%-27.7%, 67.3-71.9% and 2%-2.2% of the total execution time respectively are the three primary computationally intensive components. Thus, main purpose is to improve these three components using HW/SW codesign

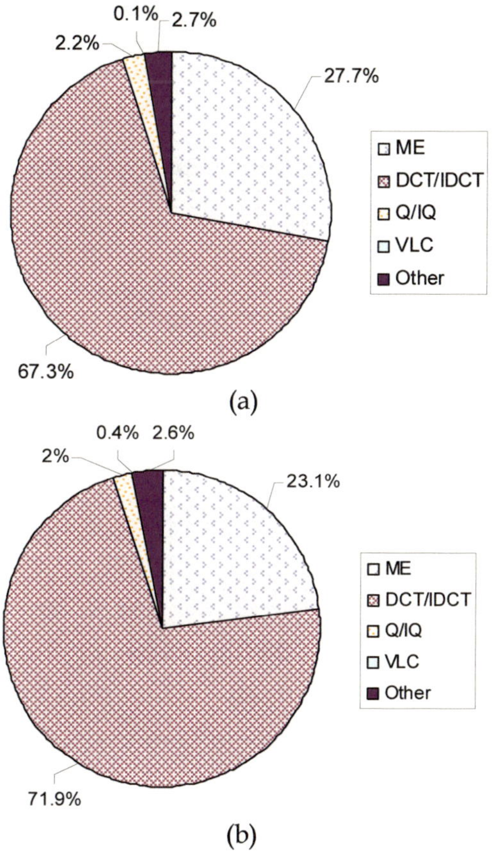

Fig. 9. Execution time distribution of (a) Miss America and (b) Carphone sequences at QCIF resolution

B) Hardware/Software partitioning

The main idea of our encoder is to exploit advantages of the parallel structures which can be efficiently implemented in hardware. Hardware implementation of 2-D DCT/IDCT and Q/IQ promise better results compared to software based algorithms. The key point of a parallel hardware structure is a reduced number of operation and ability to function parallel. However, there is still a good chance to reduce the complexity of the ME in software using fast motion estimation algorithms.

1) Optimization in Motion estimation: Motion estimation (ME) removes temporal redundancy between successive frames in digital video. The most popular technique for motion estimation is the block-matching algorithm [11]. Among the block-matching algorithms, the full search or exhaustive search algorithm examines all search points inside the search area. Therefore, the amount of its computation is proportion to the size of the search window.

Although it finds the best possible match, it requires a very large computational complexity (600 MOPS "million operations per second" for QCIF@10 Hz and +/-15 search window). Hence, many fast algorithms are proposed in literature such as the hexagon-based search [22], the diamond search [23]-[24], the block-based gradient descent search [25] and the cross-diamond search [26], which allow to reduce the computational complexity at the price of slightly performance loss. The basic principle of these fast algorithms is dividing the search process into a few sequential steps and choosing the next search direction according to the current search result.

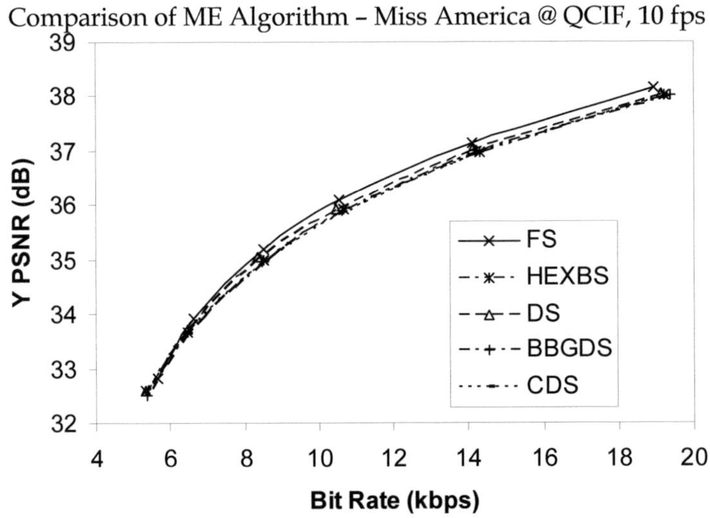

(a)

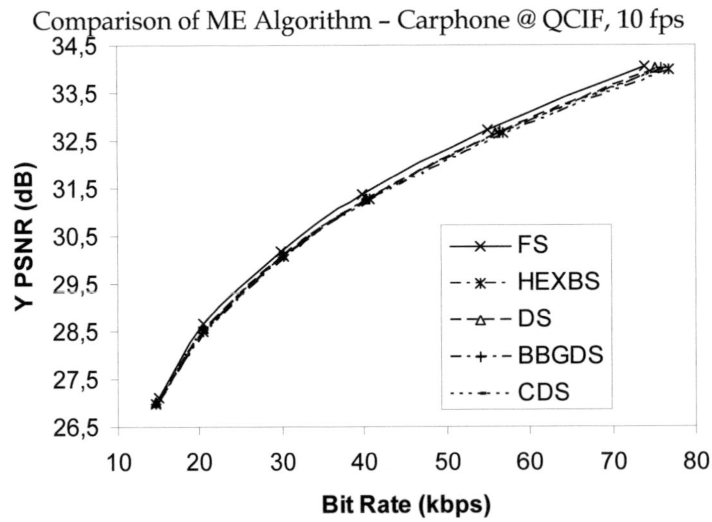

(b)

Fig. 10. Comparison of motion estimation algorithms of: (a) Miss America and (b) Carphone at QCIF resolution and 10fps

In order to reduce the encoder computational complexity, we analyze the performance and speed of the different fast algorithms. The average peak signal-to-noise ratio (PSNR) is used as a distortion measure, and is given by

$$PSNR = 10\log\frac{1}{M}\sum_{n=1}^{M}\frac{255^2}{(o_n - r_n)} \tag{4}$$

Where M is the number of samples and o_n and r_n are the amplitudes of the original and reconstructed pictures, respectively. The average PSNR of all encoded pictures is here used as a measure of objective quality.

Fig.10 illustrates the rate-distortion performance of several popular block-matching algorithms namely full search (FS), hexagon-based search (HEXBS), diamond search (DS), block-based gradient descent search (BBGDS) and cross-diamond search (CDS) algorithms. Fig.11 presents the clock number necessary to perform these fast motion estimation algorithms (HEXBS, DS, BBGDS and CDS). For Miss America and Carphone sequences, we can conclude, using the HEXBS method, a 12.5 to 13 fold speed increase on motion estimation is achieved compared to the FS method whilst the PSNR degradation is marginal.

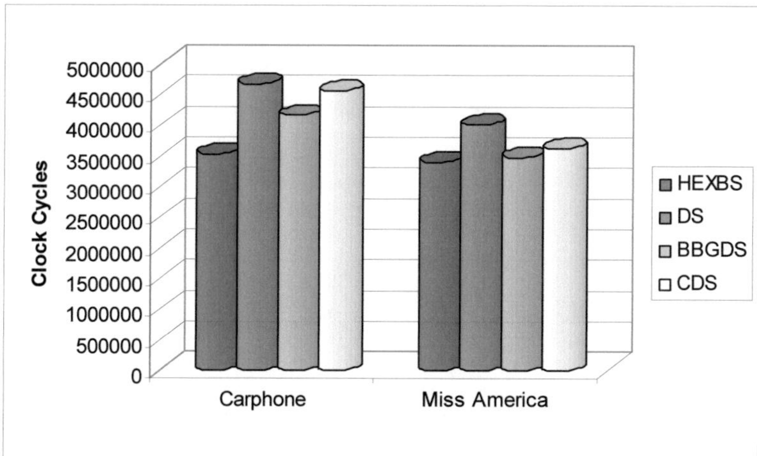

Fig. 11. Cycles required to perform the fast motion estimation algorithms

The HEXBS is the popular fast block-matching algorithms and it can reduce computational complexity. The HEXBS algorithm employs two search patterns as illustrated in Fig. 12. The first pattern, called *large hexagon search pattern* (LHSP), comprises seven checking points from which six points surround the center one to compose a hexagon shape. The second pattern consisting of five checking points forms a smaller hexagon shape, called *small hexagon search pattern* (SHSP).

In the searching procedure of the HEXBS algorithm, LHSP is repeatedly used until the step in which the minimum block distortion (MBD) occurs at the center point. The search pattern is then switched from LHSP to SHSP as reaching to the final search stage. Among the five checking points in SHSP, the position yielding the MBD provides the motion vector of the best matching block. Fig. 13 shows an example of the search path strategy leading to the motion vector (-3, -1), where 20 (7+3+3+4) search points are evaluated in 4 steps sequentially.

(a) Large hexagonal search pattern (LHSP) (b) Small hexagonal search pattern (SHSP)

Fig. 12. Two search patterns derieved are employed in the HS algorithm

The procedure of the HEXBS is described below:

Step 1. The initial LHSP is centered at the origin of the search window, and the 7 checking points of LHSP are tested. If the MBD point calculated is located at the center position, go to Step 3; otherwise, go to Step 2.

Step 2. The MBD point found in the previous search step is repositioned as the center point to form a new LHSP. If the new MBD point obtained is located at the center position, go to Step 3; otherwise, recursively repeat this step.

Step 3. Switch the search pattern from LHSP to SHSP. The MBD point found in this step is the final solution of the motion vector which points to the best matching-block.

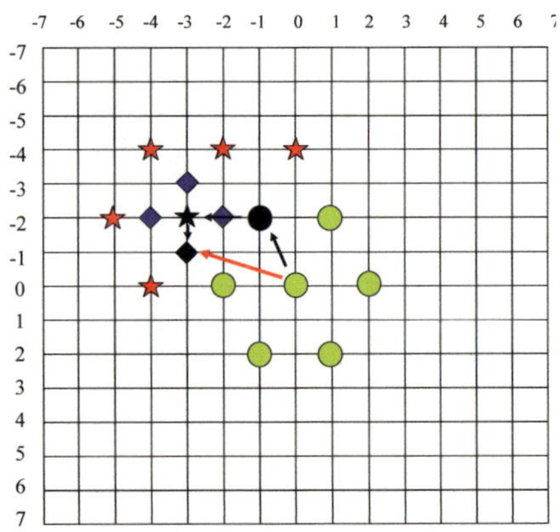

Fig. 13. Search path example which leads to the motion vector (-3, -1) in four search steps

2) Optimization in DCT and IDCT: Since the straightforward implementation of (2) and (3) are computationally expensive (with 4096 multiplications), many researches have been done to optimize the DCT/IDCT computational effort using the fast algorithms such as Lee [27], Chen [28] and Loeffler [29]. Most of the efforts have been devoted to reduce the number of operations, mainly multiplications and additions. In our DCT/IDCT hardware implementation, we use an 8-point one-dimensional (1-D) DCT/IDCT algorithm, proposed by van Eijdhoven and Sijstermans [30]. It was selected due the minimum required number of additions and multiplications (11 Multiplications and 29 additions). This algorithm is obtained by a slight modification of the original Loeffler algorithm [29], which provides one of the most computationally efficient 1-D DCT/IDCT calculation, as compared with other known algorithms [31]-[33]. The modified Loeffler algorithm for calculating 8-point 1-D DCT is illustrated in Fig.14.

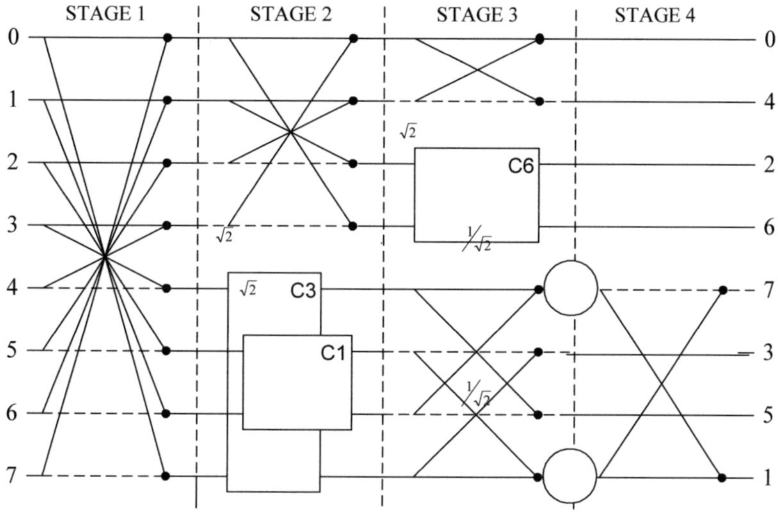

Fig. 14. The 8-point DCT modified Loeffler algorithm

The stages of the algorithm numbered 1 to 4 are parts that have to be executed in serial mode due to the data dependency. However, computation within the first stage can be parallelized. In stage 2, the algorithm splits in two parts: one for the even coefficients, the other for the odd ones. The even part is nothing else than a 4 points DCT, again separated in even and odd parts in stage3. The round block in figure 14 signifies a multiplication by $1/\sqrt{2}$. In Fig.15, we present the butterfly block and the equations associated.

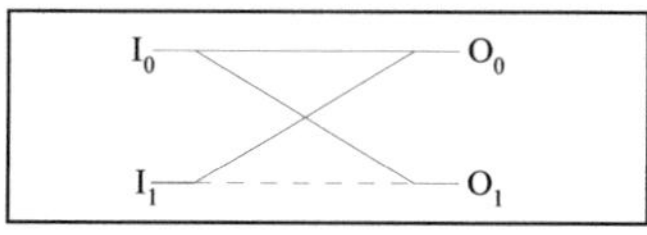

$$O_0 = I_0 + I_1$$
$$O_1 = I_0 - I_1$$

Fig. 15. The Butterfly block and its associated equations

The rectangular block depicts a rotation, which transforms a pair of inputs $[I_0,I_1]$ into outputs $[O_0,O_1]$. The symbol and associated equations are depicted in Fig. 16.

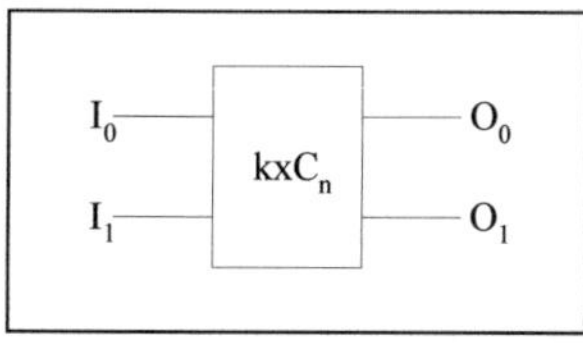

$$O_0 = I_0 k \cos\left[\frac{n\pi}{16}\right] - I_1 k \sin\left[\frac{n\pi}{16}\right]$$
$$O_1 = -I_0 k \sin\left[\frac{n\pi}{16}\right] + I_1 k \cos\left[\frac{n\pi}{16}\right]$$

Fig. 16. The rotator block and its associated equations

The rotator block operation can be calculated using only 3 multiplications and 3 additions instead of 4 multiplications and 2 additions. This can be done by using the equivalence showed in the following equations.

$$\begin{aligned} O_0 &= a.I_0 + b.I_1 = (b-a).I_1 + a.(I_0 + I_1) \\ O_1 &= -b.I_0 + a.I_1 = -(b+a).I_0 + a.(I_0 + I_1) \end{aligned} \quad (5)$$

For the fast computation of two-dimensional (2-D) DCT/IDCT, there are two categories: row/column approach from 1-D DCT/IDCT [34]-[36] and direct 2-D DCT/IDCT [37]-[39]. However, the implementation of the direct 2-D DCT/IDCT requires much more effort and large area than that of the row/column approach [40]-[41] which is used to implement 2-D DCT/IDCT algorithms.

For the row/column approach, the 1-D DCT/IDCT of each row of input data is taken, and these intermediate values are transposed. Then, the 1-D DCT/IDCT of each row of the transposed values results in the 2-D DCT/IDCT. The modified Loeffler algorithm requires only 11 multiplications for the 8-point 1-D DCT/IDCT and 176 multiplications for the row/column 2-D DCT/IDCT.

3) Optimization in Quantization and Inverse Quantization: the quantization equations are not standardized in H.263 the ITU has suggested two quantizers in their Test model 8 (TMN8) [42] corresponding to INTRA and INTER modes and are given in (6)

$$LEVEL = \begin{cases} \dfrac{|COF|}{2.QP}, & INTRA \\ \dfrac{|COF| - \dfrac{QP}{2}}{2.QP}, & INTER \end{cases} \tag{6}$$

The INTRA DC coefficient is uniformly quantized with a quantized step of 8. The quantization parameter *QP* may take integer value from 1 to 31. *COF* stands for a transform coefficient to be quantized. *LEVEL* stands for the absolute value of the quantized version of the transform coefficient.

These equations are useful as a reference not only because they are commonly used as a reference model, but also because studies performed by the ITU during the standardization process [43] indicated that the quantization equations in (6) were nearly optimal subject to the constraints of uniform scalar quantization with a dead zone.

The basic inverse quantization reconstruction rule for all non-zero quantized coefficients is defined in equation 7 which give the relationship between coefficient levels (LEVEL), quantization parameter (QP) and reconstructed coefficients (REC)

$$|REC| = \begin{cases} QP.(2.|LEVEL|+1), & if \;\; QP = "odd" \\ QP.(2.|LEVEL|+1)-1, & if \;\; QP = "even" \end{cases} \tag{7}$$

After calculation of $|REC|$, the sign is added to obtain REC:

$$REC = sign(LEVEL).|REC| \tag{8}$$

The quantization and inverse quantization equations (6 and 7 respectively) are a regular formula and use multi-cycle to code data with NIOS II processor. To improve performance of our encoder, we can use single-cycle combinatorial NIOS II custom instruction logic to implement these equations. The custom instruction interface for quantization should be presented as in Fig. 17. As the processor need a 32-bit data interface. The defined interface are 32-bit input data (COF and QP which is fixed at 16 in our cas) and the output data (LEVEL).

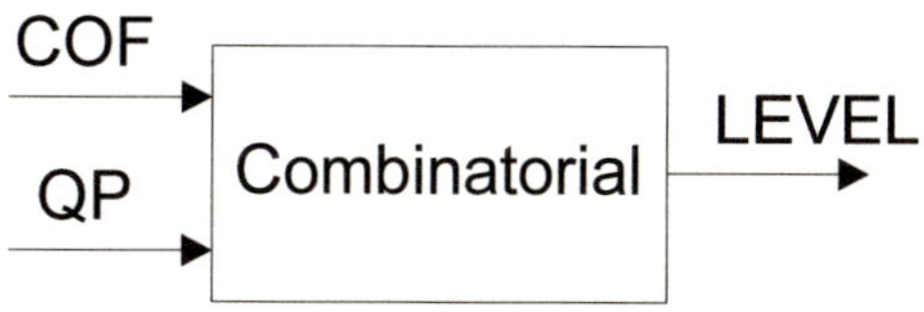

Fig. 17. Custom instruction interface for quantization

5. Design environment and FPGA implementation of H.263 encoder

A. Overview of the STRATIX II FPGA architecture

The Altera Stratix II EP2S60 FPGA is based on 1.2V, 90 nm technologies with a density that reaches 48352 Adaptive look-up tables (ALUTs), 310 KB of Embedded System Blocs (ESBs), 288 DSP blocks and 493 Input/Output Blocks (IOBs) [44]-[45].

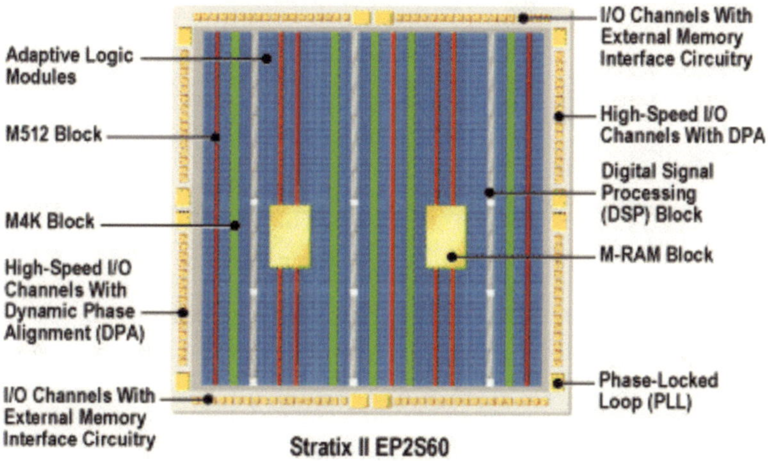

Fig. 18. Overview of Stratix II Die

An overview of the resources available in a Stratix II die is shown in Fig. 18. Three main advantages of this component led us to this choice. Firstly, Stratix II is optimized to maximize the performance benefits of SoPC integration based on NIOS II embedded processor. Secondly, Stratix II introduces DSP cores for signal processing applications. These embedded DSP Blocks have been optimized to implement several DSP functions with maximum performance and minimum logic resource utilization. The DSP blocks comprise a number of multipliers and adders. These can be configured in various widths to support multiply-add operations ranging from 9x9-bit to 36x36-bit, and including a wide range of operations from multiplication only, to sum of products, and complex arithmetic multiplication. Lastly, the Stratix II device incorporates a configurable internal memory called *TriMatrix* memory which is composed of three sizes of embedded RAM blocks. The Stratix II EP2S60 *TriMatrix* memory includes 329 M512 blocks (32x18-bit), 255 M4K blocks (128x36-bit) and 2 M-RAM (4Kx144-bit). Each of these blocks can be configured to support a wide range of features and to synthesize a wide variety of RAM (FIFO, double ports). With up to 310 KB of fast RAM, the *TriMatrix* memory structure is therefore appropriate for handling the bottlenecks arising in video embedded system.

B. FPGA Implementation of H.263 Video Encoder

The block diagram of the implemented H.263 encoder is shown in Fig.19. It is composed of three parts: a NIOS II softcore processor and 2-D DCT and 2-D IDCT hardware core. The main processing core of our system is the NIOS II CPU which is connected to hardware peripherals via a custom Altera's Avalon bus. The bus is a configurable bus architecture that is auto generated to fit the interconnection needs of the designer peripherals. The Avalon bus consists of the control, data and address signals and arbitration logic that are connected to the peripheral components.

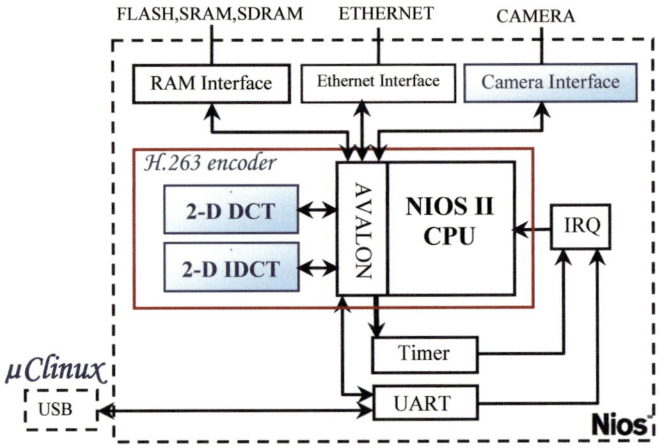

Fig. 19. Block diagram of the implemented H.263 encoder

Our system can receive frames from camera. For this purpose, we have developed a Camera interface for video acquisition [46]. The H.263 generated bit-stream has been downloaded through Ethernet Interface (FTP server) to PC platform in order to visualize the coded frames. Every hardware core is described in VHDL. Using Altera SOPC builder, the system was designed according to the block schematic diagram. The VHDL files were generated and the system was routed, compiled and downloaded into the FPGA using Altera Quartus II software. We have used the Modelsim™ simulator from Model Technology for circuit simulation.

1) System Environment: When the hardware is designed and fitted into a FPGA, there are two options how to port software applications on the board. The first is to use Linux operating system. μClinux is a port of the Linux operating system for embedded processors lacking a Memory Management Units (MMUs) [47]. Originally targeting the Motorola's 68K processor series, it now supports several architectures including NIOS II. The port of μClinux on the NIOS II core is licensed under the terms of the GNU General Public License (GPL) [48]. The second option is to use the monitor program which is loaded into the RAM of the NIOS II controller. This method is used during the development cycle. When the application meets the requirements, it is compiled for the Linux operating system.

2) 2-D DCT/IDCT coprocessor core: The 2-D DCT/IDCT transformation is implemented using the row/column approach which requires three steps: 8-point 1-D DCT/IDCT along the rows, a memory transposition and another 8-point DCT/IDCT along the transposed columns. Fig. 20 is a block diagram of the 2-D DCT/IDCT coprocessor core, showing the main interfaces and functional blocks.

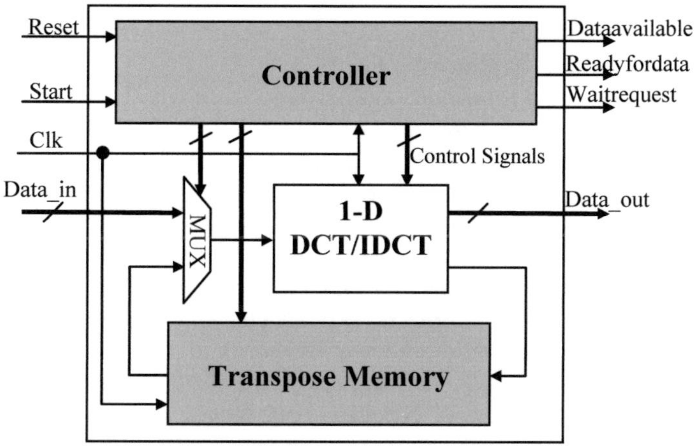

Fig. 20. 2-D DCT/IDCT coprocessor core

The controller is the control unit for the DCT/IDCT transformation. It receives input control signals (Reset, Start) and generates all the internal control signals for each stage and the output control signals for Avalon Bus communication (Dataavailable, Readyfordata, Waitrequest). When the Start signal is activated, the controller enables input of the first data row through Data_in signal. It then activates the 1-D DCT/IDCT unit for row data treatment. The first row of the transpose memory stores the results in an intermediate memory. This process repeats for the remaining seven rows of the input block. Next, the 1-D DCT/IDCT unit receives input data from the columns of the transpose memory under the MUX. The results of the column-wise 1-D DCT/IDCT are available through the Data_out signal.

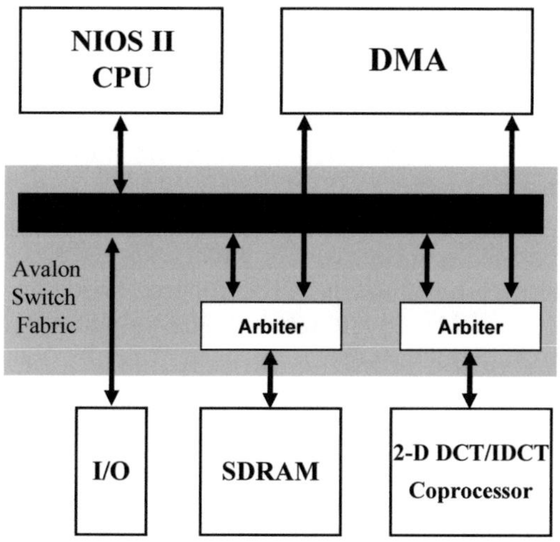

Fig. 21. Overview of the data path of a DMA with 2-D DCT/IDCT coprocessor and SDRAM

Data_in and Data_out signals are connected to the Avalon Bus. The 2-D DCT/IDCT coprocessor read/store the data from/to SDRAM through this Bus. Using processor to move data between SDRAM and 2-D DCT/IDCT coprocessor is less efficient. The system performance is greatly improved when the data are passed to the coprocessor with hardware. This is based on the concept of minimizing the interaction between the NIOS II

processor and the 2-D DCT/IDCT coprocessor. For better performance, data is handled by Direct Memory Access (DMA) as shown in Fig.21.
The 1-D DCT/IDCT unit based modified Loeffler algorithm which use 11 multipliers and 29 adders. In order to optimize speed and area of the 1-D DCT/IDCT implementation, we use Altera embedded DSP blocks to implement multipliers [49]. To conform to IEEE 1180-1990 accuracy specifications [50], the multiplier constants in Loeffler algorithm require a 12-bit representation. The DCT/IDCT use 24 internal registers to store intermediate values. The arithmetic units and registers use multiplexers to select inputs from internal and external registers. With these resources, a 1-D DCT/IDCT operation completes in 12 clock cycles and overall 2-D DCT/IDCT process concludes in 97 clock cycles.
The transpose memory is an internal memory of 64 words that holds the intermediate values from the first eight 1-D DCT/IDCT. The transpose memory receives input in a row-wise fashion and provides outputs in a column-wise fashion, thus performing a matrix transposition. Each row of the transposition memory is enabled for input from the 1-D DCT/IDCT unit after the first eight 1-D DCT/IDCT. For the next eight 1-D DCT/IDCT the column of the transposition memory output their data to the 1-D DCT/IDCT unit.

C. Implementation results

In table 1, implementation results of the H.263 encoder in Stratix II EP2S60 FPGA are shown.

	NIOS II (FAST)	2-D DCT coprocessor	2-D IDCT coprocessor
ALUTs	11%	3%	3%
ESBs	44%	1%	1%
DSPs	3%	8%	8%
IOBs	41%	15%	15%
Fmax (MHz)	227	133	139

Table 1. The implementation results in Stratix II FPGA

Results in the Table 1 have been obtained with separate implementation of the particular modules (NIOS II softcore processor, 2-D DCT and 2-D IDCT coprocessor core). The HW custom instruction for quantization and inverse quantization use only 1% of the ALUTs. The entire H.263 encoder utilizes 23% of the ALUTs, 44% of the ESBs, 18% of the DSP blocks and 41% of the IOBs. We can see that there is sufficient free space for other applications. The whole design works with a 120 MHz system clock. The implementation of H.263 encoder on the FPGA allows us to obtain a SoPC system.

6. Experimental results

The results discussed in this section are based on our HW/SW implementation of the H.263 which is tested on the Altera NIOS II development board. The results illustrate the tradeoffs among compression performance and coding speed. For all experiments the QCIF test sequences coded at 10frames/s with fixed quantization parameter QP=16. We focus on the following video test sequences: "Carphone", "News", "Claire", and "Miss America". These test sequences have different movement and camera operations. Carphone has frequent motion and camera movement. News has a combination of fast and slow motion which includes rotation movement and slow motion. Claire and Miss America have little motion with a stable camera.

	Software	Hardware	Speed up
2-D DCT	159881	720	222
2-D IDCT	159881	720	222
Q	4736	64	74
IQ	2560	64	40

Table 2. Clock cycles to code 8x8 block

Once the whole design are described in VHDL at the RTL level and fitted into the FPGA, we have determined coding time of H.263 encoder before and after timing optimization. The processor core clock and system clock are set to 120 MHz, thus 8.33 ns delay for each coded data is required. Table 2 shows a comparison of the clock cycles necessary to code an 8x8 block by software and hardware using the 2-D DCT, 2-D IDCT, Q and IQ.

Fig.22 presents a breakdown of the execution time before and after optimization of the H.263 encoder. The percentage distribution was very similar for all four sequences, so only the results for the Carphone and Miss America sequences are shown here. However, we can note that The HW/SW implementation of the H.263 provides a 15.8-16.5 times improvement in coding speed compared to software based solution.

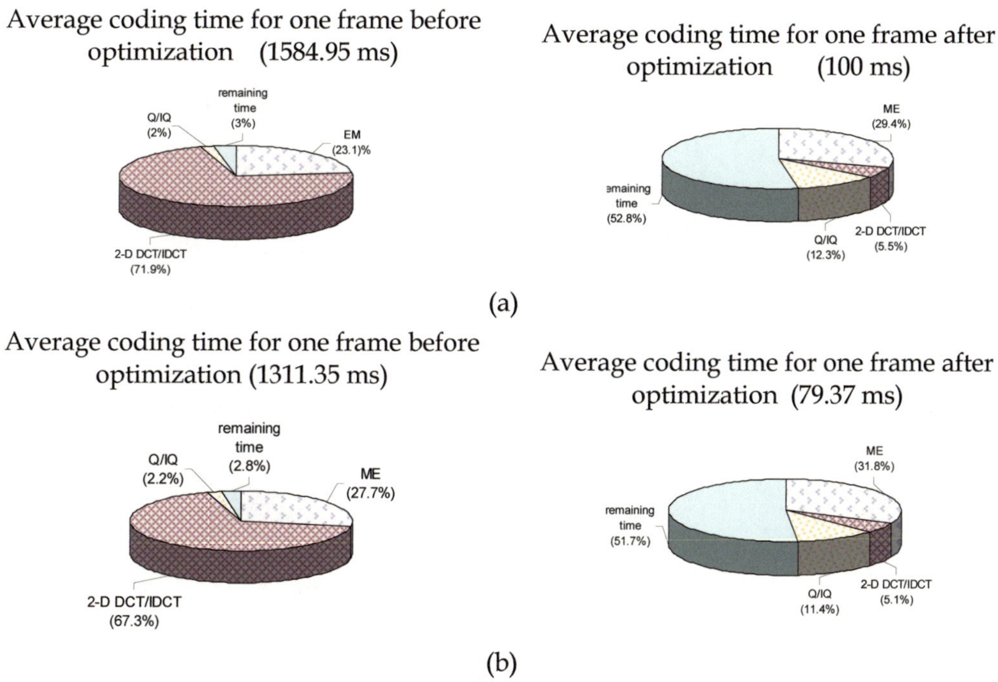

Fig. 22. CPU time percentage according to the processing before and after optimization of (a) Carphone and (b) Miss America sequences

The whole project was made under µClinux and performed on the NIOS II softcore processor. The H.263 generated bit-stream is send to the PC through Ethernet to analyse the results. The Fig.23 presents the original and the two reconstructed (one from SW, the other from HW/SW) of the 12th frame of the test video sequences. Also, Table 3 shows measurements of the PSNR of the luminance signal, Bit rate and coding speed.

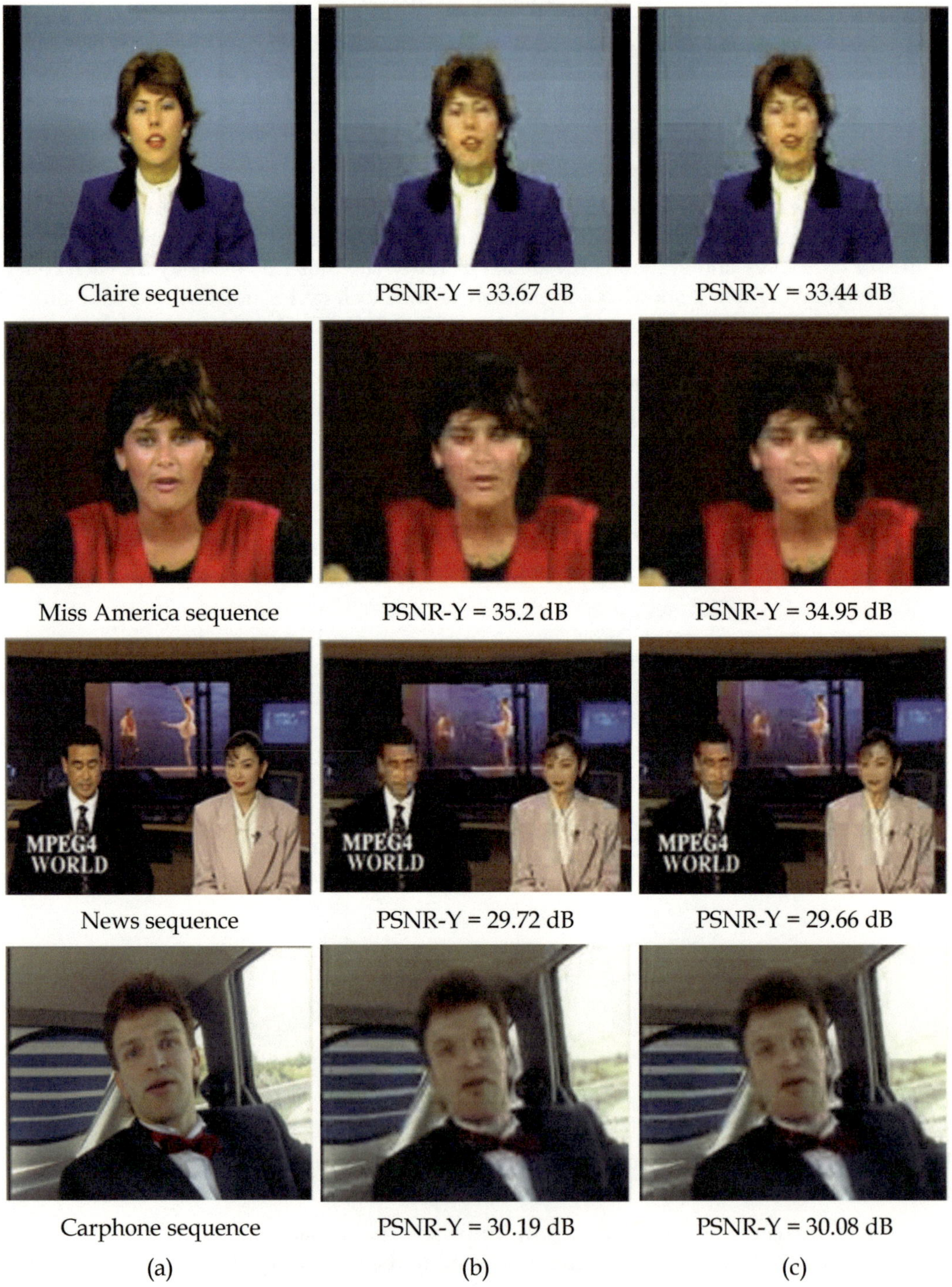

Fig. 23. (a) Original, (b) Reconstructed from SW and (c) Reconstructed from HW/SW of the 12th frame of the test video sequences

Sequence	PSNR-Y (dB)	Bit Rate (Kbps)	Coding speed (fps)
Software Encoder			
Claire	33.67	8.22	0.78
Miss America	35.2	8.5	0.76
News	29.72	21.13	0.7
Carphone	30.19	29.82	0.63
HW/SW Encoder			
Claire	33.44	8.1	11.47
Miss America	34.95	8.44	12.6
News	29.66	21.35	10.94
Carphone	30.08	30.25	10

Table 3. Experimental results for HW/SW implementation of the H.263 video encoder

The quantities in Table 3 show the subjective visual impression that the image quality of the decompressed bit stream of the HW/SW encoder is nearly as good as it is with the output of the software encoder.

These results prove that after optimization our H.263 encoder can process 10-12.6 frames QCIF/sec which depend on the CPU clock frequency.

7. Conclusions

In this paper, we have described an efficient HW/SW codesign architecture of the H.263 video encoder into an embedded Linux environment. We have proposed timing optimization of the encoder. We have shown that a 15.8-16.5 times improvement in coding speed compared to software based solution can be obtained using the HW/SW implementation. We have presented a modern implementation method where the complex embedded system (H.263 encoder) can be efficiently HW/SW partitioned and optimized. Our architecture codes QCIF at 10-12.6 frames/sec with a 120 MHz system clock and can be improved with another FPGA platform having higher operating frequency.

8. References

[1] H. Li, A. Lundmark, and R. Forchheimer, "Image sequence coding at very low bitrates: A review," IEEE Trans. Image Processing, vol. 3, pp. 568–609, Sept. 1994.

[2] B. Girod, K. B. Younes, R. Bernstein, P. Eisert, N. Farber, F. Hartung, U. Horn, E. Steinbach, T. Wiegand, and K. Stuhlmuller, "Recent advances in video compression," in IEEE Int. Symp. Circuits Syst., Feb. 1996.

[3] B. Girod, "Advances in digital image communication," in Proc. 2nd Erlangen Symp., Erlangen, Germany, Apr. 1997.

[4] ITU-T Rec. H.263, Video Coding for Low Bit Rate communication. 1998.

[5] Y. li and Al "Hardware-Software Co-Design of Embedded Reconfigurable Architectures," Design Automation Conference 2000, Los Angeles, California.

[6] S. M. Akramullah, I. Ahmad and M. L. Liou. "Optimization of H.263 Video Encoding Using a Single Processor Computer: Performance Tradeoffs and Benchmarking," IEEE Trans. on Circuits and Syst. for Video Technology, vol. 11, pp. 901-915, Aug. 2001.

[7] K. -T. Shih, C.-Y. Tsai, H.-M. Hang, " Real-Time Implementation of H.263+ Using TMS320C6201 Digital Signal Processor," in Proc. IEEE ISCAS '03, vol. 2, pp. 900-903, May 2003.

[8] G. Lienhart, R. Lay, K. H. Noffz, R. Manner. "An FPGA-based video compressor for H.263 compatible bitstreams," in Proc. IEEE ICCE, pp. 320-321, June 2000.

[9] http://www.xilinx.com

[10] http://www.altera.com

[11] G. Côté, B. Erol, M. Gallant and F. Kossentini, "H.263+: Video Coding at Low Bit Rates," IEEE Trans. On Circuits And Systems. For Video Technology, vol. 8, pp. 849-866 , Nov. 1998.

[12] J. R. Jain and A. K. Jain "Displacement measurement and its applications in interframe image coding," IEEE Trans. on Communications, vol. 29, pp. 1799-1808, Dec. 1981.

[13] N. Ahmed, T. Natarajan and K. R. Rao, "On image processing and a discrete cosine transform," IEEE Trans, On Computers, vol. C-23,pp. 90-93, 1974.

[14] J. Johnston, N. Jayant, and R. Safranek, "Signal compression based on models of human perception," Proc. IEEE, vol. 81, pp. 1385-1422, Oct. 1993.

[15] R. Tessier and W. Burleson, "reconfigurable computing for digital signal processing: a survey," Journal of VLSI Signal Processing 28, 7-27, 2001

[16]Microblaze Integrated Development Environment http://www.xilinx.com/xlnx/xebiz/designResources/ip_product_details.jsp?key=micro_blaze

[17] Nios II Integrated Development Environment http://www.altera.com/literature/lit-index.html

[18] Nios II Development Kit, Stratix II Edition, ALTERA 2006, http://www.altera.com/products/devkits/altera/kit-niosii-2S30.html

[19] SOPC Builder Applications ALTERA 2006, http://www.altera.com/products/software/products/sopc/sop-index.html

[20] J. Cong, Y. Fan, G. Han, A. Jagannathan, G. Reinman, Z. Zhang, "Instruction Set Extension with Shadow Registers for Configurable Processors," FPGA'05, February 20–22, 2005, Monterey, California, USA.

[21] Altera "NIOS Custom Instructions Tutorial", June 2002, http://www.altera.com/literature/tt/tt_nios_ci.pdf

[22] C. Zhu, X. Lin, and L. P. Chau, "Hexagon-Based Search Pattern for Fast Block Motion Estimation", IEEE Trans. On Circuits And Systs. For Video Technology, vol. 12, pp. 349-355, May 2002

[23] J. Y. Tham, S. Ranganath, M. Ranganath, and A. A. Kassim, "A novel unrestricted center-biased diamond search algorithm for block motion estimation," IEEE Trans. Circuits Syst. Video Technol., vol. 8, pp. 369–377, Aug. 1998.

[24] S. Zhu and K. K. Ma, "A new diamond search algorithm for fast blockmatching motion estimation," IEEE Trans. Image Process., vol. 9, no. 2, pp. 287–290, Feb. 2000.

[25] L. K. Liu and E. Feig, "A block-based gradient descent search algorithm for block motion estimation in video coding," IEEE Trans. Circuits Syst. Video Technol., vol. 6, no. 4, pp. 419–423, Aug. 1996.

[26] C. H. Cheung and L. M. Po, "A novel cross-diamond search algorithm for fast block motion estimation," IEEE Trans. Circuits Syst. Video Technol., vol. 12, no. 12, pp. 1168–1177, Dec. 2002.

[27] Y.P Lee and all "A cost effective architecture for 8x8 two-dimensional DCT/IDCT using direct method," IEEE Trans. On Circuit and System for video technology, VOL 7, NO.3, 1997
[28] W.c Chen, C.h Smith and S.C. Fralick, "A fast Computational Algorithm for thr Discrete Cosine Transform," IEEE Trans. On Communications, Vol. COM-25, No. 9, pp.1004-1009, Sept.1997
[29] C. Loeffler and A. Lightenberg, "Practical fast 1-D DCT algorithms with 11 Multiplications," in Proceedings IEEE ICASSP '89, vol. 2, pp. 988-991, May 1989.
[30] T.J. van Eijndhven and F.W. Sijstermans, "Data Processing Device and method of Computing the Cosine Transform of a Mtrix", PCT Patent WO 99948025, to Koninklijke Philips Electronics, World Intellectual Property Organization, International Bureau, 1999.
[31] P. Duhamel and H. H'Mida, "New 2^n DCT algorithms suitable for VLSI implementation," in Proc. ICASSP'87, vol. 12, pp. 1805–1808, Apr. 1978.
[32] M. T. Heidemann, "Multiplicative Complexity, Convolution, and the DFT," New York: Springer-Verlag, 1988.
[33] E. Feig and S. Winograd, "On the multiplicative complexity of discrete cosine transforms," IEEE Trans. Inform. Theory, vol. 38, pp. 1387–1391, July 1992.
[34] M. D. Wagh and H. Ganesh, "A new algorithm for the discrete cosine transform of arbitrary number of points," IEEE Trans. Comput., vol. C-29, pp. 269–277, Apr. 1980.
[35] B. G. Lee, "A new algorithm to compute the discrete cosine transform," IEEE Trans. Acoust., Speech, Signal Processing, vol. ASSP-35, pp. 1243–1245, Dec. 1984.
[36] Y. Chan and W. Siu, "A cyclic correlated structure for the realization of discrete cosine transform," IEEE Trans. Circuits Syst.-II, vol. 39, pp. 109–113, Feb. 1992.
[37] M. Vetterli, "Fast 2-D discrete cosine transform," in Proc. IEEE ICASSP'85, vol. 10, pp. 1538–1541, Mar. 1985.
[38] N. I. Cho and S. U. Lee, "DCT algorithms for VLSI parallel implementation," IEEE Trans. Acoust., Speech, Signal Processing, vol. 38, pp. 121–127, Jan. 1990.
[39] N.I. Cho, S.U. Lee, "A fast 4 _ 4 DCT algorithm for the recursive 2-D DCT," IEEE Trans. Signal Processing, vol. 40, pp. 2166–2173, Sept. 1992.
[40] C. Y. Lu, K. A. Wen, "On the design of selective coefficient DCT module", IEEE Trans. Circuits Syst. Video Technol., vol. 8, pp. 143–146, Dec. 2002.
[41] J. Liang, "Fast multiplierless approximations of the DCT with the lifting scheme", IEEE Trans. Signal Process., vol. 49, pp. 3032–3044, Dec. 2001.
[42] ITU Telecom. Standardization Sector of ITU, "Video codec test model near-term, Version 8 (TMN8), Release 0," H.263 Ad Hoc Group, June 1997.
[43] Proposal for Test Model Quantization Description, ITU-T doc. Q15-D-30, Apr. 1998.
[44] D.Lewis and Al, "The Stratix II Logic and Routing Architecture," FPGA'05, February 20–22, 2005, Monterey, California, USA.
[45] Altera Startix II Architecture http://www.altera.com/products/devices/stratix2/st2-index.jsp
[46] A. Ben Atitallah, P. Kadionik, F. Ghozzi, P.Nouel, N. Masmoudi, Ph.Marchegay "Hardware Platform Design for Real-Time Video Applications," in Proc. IEEE ICM'04, pp. 722-725, Dec. 2004.
[47] The μClinux project http://www.uClinux.org.

[48] The NIOS Forum http://www.niosforum.com/forum.
[49] A. Ben Atitallah, P. Kadionik, F. Ghozzi, P. Nouel, "Optimization and implementation on FPGA of the DCT/IDCT algorithm", in Proc. IEEE ICASSP'06, vol. 3, pp. 928-931, May 2006.
[50] IEEE Std 1180-1990, "IEEE standard specification for the implementation of 8x8 inverse cosine transform," Institute of Electrical and Electronics Engineers, New York, USA, International Standard, Dec. 1990